BRIDGES
NOT
WALLS

FOURTH EDITION

BRIDGES NOT WALLS

A Book About Interpersonal Communication

Edited by

John Stewart

UNIVERSITY OF WASHINGTON

*RANDOM
HOUSE*

NEW YORK

Fourth Edition

9 8 7 6 5 4 3 2

Copyright © 1973, 1977, 1982, 1986 by Newbery Award Records, Inc.
All rights reserved under International and Pan-American Copyright Conventions. No part of this book may be reproduced in any form or by any means,
electronic or mechanical, including photocopying, without permission in
writing from the publisher. All inquiries should be addressed to Newbery
Award Records, Inc., 201 East 50th Street, New York, N.Y. 10022. Published
in the United States by Newbery Award Records, Inc., a subsidiary of Random
House, Inc., New York and simultaneously in Canada by Random House of
Canada Limited, Toronto. Distributed by Random House, Inc.

Library of Congress Cataloging in Publication Data

Bridges not walls.

   Includes bibliographical references and index.
   1. Interpersonal communication.   I. Stewart,
John Robert.
BF637.C45B74   1986   158'.2   86-73
ISBN 0-394-35403-6

Manufactured in the United States of America

Cover photo:
Milton Avery, "Conversation," 1956 Museo de Arte de Ponce, Puerto Rico;
The Luis A. Ferre Foundation, Inc.; Donated by the Chase Manhattan Bank.

Chapter Opening Photo Credits
Chapter 1 John Stewart;   Chapter 2 Jean-Claude Lejeune/Stock, Boston;
Chapter 3 John Stewart;   Chapter 4 Joel Gordon;   Chapter 5 Rod Kahaian/The
Picture Cube;   Chapter 6 Frank Siteman/The Picture Cube: Chapter 7 David
Barnes/Photo Researchers;   Chapter 8 John Stewart;   Chapter 9 David S. Strickler/
The Picture Cube;   Chapter 10 Mark Antman/The Image Works;   Chapter 11 Joel
Gordon;   Chapter 12 Michal Heron/Woodfin Camp & Associates;
Chapter 13 Photo by C. Steven Short, Courtesy of Fawcett;   Chapter 14 John T.
Wood;   Chapter 15 UPI/Bettmann Newsphotos;   Chapter 16 UPI/Bettman
Newsphotos.

Cover design: Robert Sugar
Book design: Dorothy Sparacino

BOOKS AND MEN

Imagine yourself in a situation where you are alone, wholly alone on earth, and you are offered one of the two, books or men. I often hear men prizing their solitude, but that is only because there are still men somewhere on earth, even though in the far distance. I knew nothing of books when I came forth from the womb of my mother, and I shall die without books, with another human hand in my own. I do, indeed, close my door at times and surrender myself to a book, but only because I can open the door again and see a human being looking at me.

MARTIN BUBER

Preface

This edition of *Bridges Not Walls* continues, updates, and expands the approach of the previous three editions. It is written primarily for college students enrolled in interpersonal communication classes. Its perspective is focused by my commitment to humanistic approaches and to relational or transactional theories of human communication. Yet its coverage is broad; readings address all the topics included in most interpersonal communication courses and are drawn from a wide range of disciplines, including communication, philosophy, social science, and psychology.

This is a book for persons who want to communicate more effectively with their spouses, family, co-workers, and friends. It resists, however, the tendency to popularize interpersonal effectiveness and to reduce it to techniques or formulas. One way it does this is to emphasize the conceptual foundations of its subject matter. There are substantive discussions of important issues and questions by distinguished scholars. Students will be challenged, for example, by some of the philosophy in Part One, the readings on perception and confirmation, and especially the "Approaches" of Erich Fromm and Martin Buber. Comments on earlier editions demonstrate, though, that students can grow from, and even enjoy, these challenges.

The book also makes the point that, despite the claims of popular self-help materials, there is no successful "technology" of interpersonal communication. *Bridges Not Walls* includes systematic treatments of nonverbal cues, self-awareness, listening, disclosure, intercultural communication, and conflict. It also emphasizes that the unique situation, idiosyncratic expectations, and the constancy of change make it impossible to design and execute a purely technical approach to *human* relationships.

That point is rooted in the book's definition of its subject matter. Interpersonal communication is not limited to face-to-face settings, discussions of weighty topics, or long-term intimate relationships. The term "interpersonal" designates a quality, type, or kind of communication that emerges whenever communicators are able to highlight in their speaking and listening aspects of their own and the other's "personness." The editor's introduction and several other readings discuss those aspects of personness and emphasize that different levels of interpersonal contact are possible or appropriate in different situations. Throughout the book the point is made that while "peak communication" is rare, many more of our contacts could be interpersonal in quality, and if they were, our personal, educational, and professional lives would be the better for it.

Another way to discuss this book's approach is to underscore my fundamental conviction that communication is more than just a way to get things done. Who we are as persons emerges in our contacts with others. I think of that as the "ontological" dimension or function of communication; it supplements the "instrumental" dimension or function, and I introduce and discuss it in Chapters 1 and 2. While Martin Buber continues to be the most important single expositor of this approach, my continued reading of and recent contact with Hans-Georg Gadamer have convinced me that he also offers a fundamentally dialogic philosophy. I'm excited about the way the "Sculpting Mutual Meanings" essay in Chapter 7 integrates Buber and Gadamer in a student-focused discussion of listening.

The "student-focused" part is important. In each edition of *Bridges Not Walls* I have attempted to include readings that consistently develop this substantive, humanistic, and relational perspective and that speak directly to the student. In fact, a primary selection criterion is readability. Whenever possible I have included materials by authors who "write with their ears," that is, who talk with their readers. Hugh Prather, Neil Postman, Virginia Satir, Carl Rogers, Paul Tournier, and Leo Buscaglia are some of the authors in this edition whose work has that quality.

What's new in this edition? First, several chapters have been significantly updated. Russell A. Jones's treatment of person perception integrates material through the early eighties, as does Judy Pearson's discussion of the language usage of women and men, and Mark Knapp's revision of his "Nonverbal Communication: Basic Perspectives." There is also a new introductory essay and new treatments of listening, self-awareness, assertiveness, and intercultural communication.

I have also added a chapter on Confirmation. This interpersonal construct is receiving increased attention from communication scholars and teachers. Moreover, the discussions in Chapter 9 illustrate how philosophy and social science can be blended into an informative and practical synthesis.

Leo Buscaglia has been added to the "Approaches" section. His essay balances the "heavier" readings in that section and offers several worthwhile ideas. Finally, although I've kept the basic structure of the book, I've revised section and chapter headings to better reflect the relational, transactional characteristics of this approach.

Plan of the Book

Users of *Bridges Not Walls* tell us that it makes sense to them to begin with "Basic Ingredients," then to treat the "output," or speaking, dimensions separately from the "input," or listening, dimensions, to address conflict or "Bridging Differences" in a separate section, and to include several synthesizing "Approaches" at the end. This structure also makes the materials easy to adapt to each instructor's approach to the course. When I use the book, I assign the readings in the order they are presented, but both the sections and the chapters within each section are self-contained enough to be read in whatever sequence fits the individual course emphases and teaching methods.

Part One lays the foundation for what follows. The first chapter introduces the editor and the primary assumptions behind the book. I include this material in the text rather than as front matter in order to emphasize the potential for, and the limits of, interpersonal-quality communication between writer and reader. I hope that readers will respond to everything in this book not as "true because it's down here in black and white" but as the thoughtful speech of a person addressing them.

Chapter 2 includes three readings that introduce the book's humanistic and relational, or transactional, approach. My essay outlines how I think about interpersonal communicating and why the book approaches the topic as it does. Neil Postman clarifies and brings alive what it means to have a relational perspective, and Dean Barnlund's classic essay applies this perspective to a meaning-centered view of communication.

Chapters 3 and 4 treat verbal codes and nonverbal cues, respectively. The discussions of language attempt to go beyond the typical rehash of general semantics principles and yet be practical, useful, and focused on interpersonal contexts. Both Virginia Satir and David Johnson offer readable, helpful advice.

Mark Knapp's clear and comprehensive overview of nonverbal communication begins Chapter 4, and essays on silence and touch exemplify the operation of nonverbal communication in face-to-face situations. Space limitations force this chapter to be selective — teachers may well want to supplement what's here with their own favorite treatments of other sets of nonverbal cues, such as posture, voice, and movement, for example.

Part Two is called "Openness as Inhaling," and focuses on the "input," or receiving, dimensions of interpersonal communication. In the Introduction I discuss my struggle with the labels for Parts Two and Three. On the one hand, we can only treat one topic at a time, and on the other hand, "sending" and "receiving" sound like vestiges of a linear view of communication, not a relational one. My compromise is to use the profitably ambiguous term "openness" in both Part Two and Part Three and to highlight its "inhaling" meaning in Part Two and its "exhaling" meaning in Part Three. The allusions to breathing also emphasize the indivisibility of the two parts of the whole.

Chapter 5 includes two discussions of self-awareness, one a classic by Carl Rogers and the other a section from William S. Howell's book, *The Empathic Communicator*. Chapter 6 shifts the focus to perceiving others or person perception. A thorough, substantive, and challenging overview by Russell A. Jones begins the chapter, and readings by Paul Tournier and R. D. Laing round it out. As I have noted, users of earlier editions will notice that the Jones essay significantly updates the Hastorf, Schneider, and Polefka reading that formerly began this chapter, and Tournier's "The World of Things and the World of Persons" has been retrieved from the second edition — by request.

In Chapter 7 there are three treatments of listening. Robert Bolton's introductory overview is clear and helpful. Next, Milt Thomas and I describe a new approach to listening that is creating all kinds of sparks in our interpersonal classes. Then naturalist Malcom Brenner describes his experience listening to — and being listened to by — a dolphin.

Part Three is called "Openness as Exhaling," and I hope the rationale for that title is now obvious. In Chapter 8 Fritz Steele discusses disclosure in the organizational context. David Augsburger suggests how we can productively disclose anger, and Neil Postman offers a crisp and spicy counterpoint. Postman argues persuasively against treating openness as a panacea, and his words should promote some lively class discussion.

As was also noted, Chapter 9, "Confirmation," is new in this edition. For more than forty years confirmation has been a useful construct for Buber, Laing, Watzlawick, and others, and now it is becoming increasingly important to speech communication teachers and scholars. In this chapter's first reading, Ken Cissna and Evelyn Sieburg review the construct and its applications. Then Maurice Friedman discusses relationships between interpersonal confirmation and "intrapersonal" awareness, and in the final essay anthropologist Paul Rabinow tells a story about how confirmation and its opposite can materially affect the quality of one's contact with others.

Part Four, "Bridging Differences," includes discussions of conflict, male–female communication, and communicating across cultures. Jack Gibb's classic essay on defensiveness begins chapter 10. Then an excerpt from Susan Campbell's assertiveness book contrasts aggressive, non-assertive, and assertive approaches to conflict. In the third essay, Ron Arnett outlines a realistic and practical approach to conflict, grounded in Martin Buber's philosophy of dialogue.

An excerpt from Judy Pearson's new book on male–female communication begins Chapter 11. Pearson's overview is followed by a brief discussion by Maurice Friedman of "Personal Calling and Social Role."

The final chapter in Part Four treats intercultural communication. Here the overview is by L. E. Sarbaugh, and then Don Cushman and Dudley A. Cahn, Jr. discuss specific applications to interpersonal relationships, especially those between the Japanese and westerners.

As in previous editions, Part Five collects four "Approaches to Interpersonal Communication," statements by noted writers that summarize their views of and ways of being-in-relation. Leo Buscaglia's irrepressible humor and conversational style make his essay at least as much fun as it is informative. The section also includes essays that have been a part of *Bridges Not Walls* since the beginning — by Carl Rogers, Erich Fromm, and Martin Buber. Buber's piece is the one that continues to draw the most complaints, both from students and from some teachers. But I respect his ideas and this book's readers too much to delete "Elements of the Interhuman." Some additions in my introduction to the book, references to Buber in the essays by Tournier, Friedman and Arnett, and the continued explication of Buber's ideas in other works should help to make his concepts increasingly accessible.* Most impor-

---

* See, e.g., Maurice Friedman's three-volume *Margin Buber's Life and Work* (New York: E. P. Dutton, 1981, 1983) and *Martin Buber: A Centenary Volume,* ed. Haim Gordon and Jochanan Bloch (Beersheba, Israel: KTAV Publishing House, 1984).

tantly, though, my own professional and personal life continues to tell me that his ideas are too important to omit.

Other Features

Hugh Prather's brief but insightful comments have been a highlight of each edition of *Bridges Not Walls*. In this edition his thoughts continue to preview and summarize chapters and readings with economy and wit.

Discussion questions called "Probes" follow each reading. Some help students to focus on highlights of the reading. Others encourage the reader to reflect critically on or to challenge points the author has made. Still other probes emphasize relationships between authors and their ideas. For example, some questions encourage readers to contrast Rogers with Buber, Tournier with Jones, and Stewart-Thomas with Bolton.

Many essays also include extensive references that can function as additional readings. There are lengthy bibliographies, for example, of verbal and nonverbal communication, person perception, listening, confirmation, male–female communication, and Japanese–U.S. cultural differences. Finally, a detailed index locates and provides cross references to authors and key ideas.

As before, I want to emphasize that this book *about* interpersonal communicating cannot substitute for the real thing — for direct contact between vital human beings in the concrete, everyday world. That's why I've again begun the book with Buber's comment about "Books and Men" and ended with Prather's words about the world of ideas and the world of persons. (Some readers will rankle at the manifest sexism of Buber's language. Please read what I've written in Chapters 1, 2, 3, 7, and 11 before drawing conclusions about my awareness of and position on problems of sexist language, and please read Buber's remarks in Chapter 16 before drawing the same conclusions about him.)

Acknowledgments

The authors and publishers of material reprinted here have been very cooperative. I'm especially pleased that Hugh Prather agreed again to let me use materials from two of his books, *Notes to Myself* (Lafayette, CA: Real People Press, 1970), and *I Touch the Earth The Earth Touches Me* (New York: Doubleday, 1972).

I am also grateful to faculty and student reviewers. Five persons wrote insightful and helpful reviews that guided the entire revision process. They were Rebecca J. Cline, University of Maryland; G. Dawn Cramer, Boise State University; Roger L. Garrett, Central Washington University; Joseph A. Munshaw, Southern Illinois University at Edwardsville; and Susan M. Sorensen, University of Nevada–Reno. In addition, I appreciate the direct and indirect contributions of the persons I'm lucky enough to contact regularly: students and former students who are continually helping me grow, like Donal Carbaugh, Milt Thomas, Michele Cawley, Tamar Katriel, and Mara Adelman; colleagues like John Campbell, Mac Parks, Teri Albrecht, Gerry Philipsen, Jody Nyquist, and Bob Gaines, who both support and challenge my ideas; and important friends like Michael Held, Chip Hughes, and Greg Welch.

Michael's been especially supportive. My most important living relationships — with Kris, Marcia and Mark, Lisa and Corey, Mom and Bob, "Mother Bear," my sister Barbara and her husband Michael — are still the central reasons for and the ultimate tests of this perspective.

In other words, I continue to be convinced of the difficulty and necessity of interpersonal communicating and excited by the challenge of working toward achieving it. I hope that some of that excitement will rub off on you.

J.R.S.
Seattle, Washington

Contents

BRIDGES NOT WALLS

PART 1

The Basic
Ingredients

CHAPTER 1

INTRODUCTION TO THE EDITOR AND TO THE ASSUMPTIONS BEHIND THIS BOOK

"Writing about interpersonal communication, especially in a context like this one, is extremely difficult, primarily because it's almost impossible to practice what you preach." In 1972, I began the introduction to the first edition of *Bridges Not Walls* with that sentence, and it is as true for me now—in 1985—as it was thirteen years ago. Now, as then, the problem is that I could simply think of you as "reader" or "student" and of myself as "author," "editor," or "teacher" and then proceed to "tell you what I want you to know." But the result of that kind of thinking would be a lot closer to superficial role-relating than to interpersonal communication.

The reason that such an approach doesn't work is that, although I am obviously writing this, I am *not* simply "author," "editor," or "teacher," and you are not just "reader" or "student." Each of us is a unique person. My name is John Stewart, I have been teaching college for about nineteen years, and I like almost everything about my job—the constant contact with young, growing persons; the excitement of keeping up with changes in my field; the satisfaction that comes from experiencing a good class session or finishing a good paragraph; and the freedom to work at my own pace. I also like to sail on saltwater, to watch what sunsets do to mountains, to smell the wet freshness of Pacific Northwest winters, to feel the exhilaration of making it up a steep hill on my bike or down a moguled hill on my skis, to celebrate Christmas with a crowd of family, and to hug friends. I don't like phony smiles, smog, pretentious academicians, rules that are vaguely stated but rigidly enforced, unfulfilled commitments, or clam chowder. I was raised in a small town in Washington state and live with Kris, the woman I'm married to, in a house in Seattle that overlooks the Cascade Mountains and Lake Washington. Kris and I are in the ninth year of our marriage, and we are managing to iron out most of our relational rough spots. My daughters, Marcia and Lisa, who were 11 and 12 when I edited the first edition of this book, are now both married, and their husbands, Mark and Corey, are both special additions to our family. I continue to feel challenged as I teach courses I've never taught before and research aspects of interpersonal communication that are new to me. This year—1984–1985—a sabbatical leave has given me the opportunity to return to graduate school for a term in Boston, and Kris and I are about to leave on a six-week study and exploring trip to Israel and western Europe. For the past five years I've also enjoyed balancing a part-time interpersonal communication consulting practice for engineers and architects with my academic and family life. My days and years are filled and productive, and I am grateful to be able to say, as I have before, that I like where I am.

The longer I work with the subject matter of interpersonal communication, the more I'm struck by the extent to which who I am today is a function of the experiences of genuine contact I've had with others. Some of those persons are no longer alive—my first real "boss," Mark Burdick; my closest friend, Allen Clark, who died while I was finishing the second edition of this book; and my dad and father-in-law, who died six and four years ago. I also recall especially important teachers, Alice Atkinson, Robert Harris, Peter Ristuben, and Walter Fisher; close colleagues like Frank Bussone, Gary D'Angelo, Helen Felton, and John Campbell; and several important authors who have made themselves available for contact in their writing—I'm thinking especially of Martin Buber, Carl Rogers, Gregory Bateson, and Hans-Georg Gadamer. Contacts with all those persons have helped shape me. At the same time, I sense the presence of an unchanging, central me, a core self that's never static but that's firmly anchored in values, understandings, goals, and blind spots that make me who I am.

If I were just "writer" or "author" I could also conceal the fact that I am still excited about doing this fourth edition of *Bridges* and that I'm pleased and a little amazed that the book continues to speak to so many different people. I am also still grateful that I get to share some ideas and feelings about interpersonal communication that have helped me grow. As with the second and third editions, I'm no longer worried about readers allowing me to talk with them directly and personally instead of in the safe, sterile, distant style of most "educational materials." Most readers still seem to accept and even to appreciate this direct address, and I'm pleased by that.

The role-restricted attitudes I mentioned will also get in the way of our communicating, because *you* are not simply "reader" or "student." Where were you born and raised, and what effects has it had on you? Are you reading this book because you want to or because somebody told you to? If you're reading this as part of a college course, how do you expect the course to turn out? Challenging? Boring? Threatening? Useful? Exciting? Inhibiting? How do you generally feel about required texts? About administrative regulations? About going to school? What groups have you chosen to join? A sorority or fraternity? Student government? An honor society? Alateen? Young Life? What other important choices have you made recently? To move? Change majors? End a relationship? Quit work? Make a new commitment?

I'm not trying to say that you have to pry into the intimate details of somebody's life before you can communicate with him or her, but I am trying to say that interpersonal communication happens between *persons,* not between roles or masks or stereotypes. Interpersonal communication can happen between you and me only when each of us makes available some of what makes us a person *and* when each is aware of some of what makes the other a person too.

One way to conceptualize what I'm saying is to think about what I call your Contact Quotient, or CQ. Your CQ is a measure of how well you *connect* with another person or persons. It's the quotient that expresses the ratio between the quality of contact you accomplish and the quality of contact that's possible. In other words:

$$CQ = \frac{\text{Richness or quality of contact achieved}}{\text{Richness or quality of contact possible}}$$

A husband and wife who've been married for forty years have a huge CQ denominator. When one is giving the other the silent treatment, his or her numerator is painfully small, as is the CQ. When they're making languorous love, their numerator is very high and their CQ approaches unity. You and I, on the other hand, have a pretty small denominator. The quality of contact we can achieve is relatively low. But we can still strive toward a CQ of 1/1, and that's my primary goal in this introduction.

It's going to be difficult, however, to maximize the CQ between you and me. I can continue to share with you some of who I am, but I don't know whether what

I write is what you need to know me as me. In addition, I know almost nothing about what makes you a person—nothing about your choices, your feelings, your individuality. That's why *writing* about interpersonal communication is sometimes frustrating for me; interpersonal communication can be discussed in print, but not much of it can happen here.

More can happen, though, than usually happens with a "textbook." The relationship can be closer to interpersonal-quality communication than it often is. I will work toward that by continuing to share some of what I'm actually thinking and feeling in my introductions to the readings, the probes at the end of each selection, and the three essays I've authored or coauthored. I hope you'll be willing to share yourself by becoming honestly involved enough in this book to see clearly which of the ideas are worthwhile for you and which are not. I also hope you'll be able to make yourself available to other persons reading this book, so they can benefit from your insights and you can benefit from theirs.

TWO BASIC ASSUMPTIONS

Before we begin breaking human communication down into some manageable parts, I want to discuss a couple of assumptions that guided my selection and organization of the materials in this book. I believe that when you know something of this book's rationale, it'll be easier for you to understand what's being said about each topic, and you'll be in a better position to accept or adopt what works for you while leaving aside the rest.

One of my basic assumptions is that the *quality of each person's life is directly linked to the quality of the communication he or she experiences.* One way to clarify and explain this assumption is to talk about "quality of life" from a medical point of view. In two recent books, James J. Lynch, who is codirector of the Psychophysiological Clinic and Laboratories at the University of Maryland School of Medicine, discusses the connection between physical health and interpersonal communication. He previews his 1985 book with these words:

> As we shall see, study after study reveals that human dialogue not only affects our hearts significantly but can even alter the biochemistry of individual tissues at the farthest extremities of the body. Since blood flows through every human tissue, the entire body is influenced by human dialogue.[1]

One of Lynch's important discoveries is that blood pressure changes much more rapidly and consistently than we used to believe, and that some of the most radical blood pressure changes occur when we speak and listen. Lynch was led to this discovery by his interest in hypertension, or sustained high blood pressure, a disease that afflicts an estimated 40 million people in the United States and that killed over a million of us in 1980.[2] Computerized instruments permit Lynch and other medical researchers to monitor blood pressure constantly and to map the effects of a person entering the room, nonverbal contact, reading aloud, and conversation. Speech appears to directly affect blood pressure; in one study the mean arterial pressure of healthy nurses went from 92 when they were quiet to 100 when they "talked calmly."[3] In another study using graduate students, vocalization raised their mean arterial pressure from 87 to 94, and as Lynch emphasizes, "Surprisingly, talking about feelings did not increase a student's pressure more than simply reading a book aloud: that is, all verbal activities elicited statistically equal rises in blood pressure and heart rate, while all quiet periods were accompanied by significantly lower blood-pressure readings."[4]

Listening has the opposite effect. Rather than just returning to baseline when a person stops speaking, blood pressure actually drops below baseline when we concentrate on the other person.[5] And this only happens when we talk with people; "conversation" with pets does not produce the same result.[6]

Lynch's 1977 book discusses some of the more global effects of essentially the same phenomenon. There he reports the results of literally hundreds of studies that correlate loneliness and poor health. For example, people with few interpersonal relationships tend to die before their counterparts who enjoy a network of family and friends.[7] And a 1970 study by two Swedish doctors of identical twins found that smoking habits, obesity, and cholesterol levels of the twins who had heart attacks were *not* significantly different from the twins with healthier hearts. But there were some other important differences, one of which was what the doctors called "poor childhood and adult interpersonal relationships." The twins with heart disease were the ones who had experienced more unresolved conflict, more arguments at work and home, and less emotional support.[8] After thirty years of work with heart disease patients in this country, two other doctors reached some similar conclusions. They found that although there are some relationships between heart problems and such factors as heredity, weight, and smoking, there is a much stronger link with one's pattern of interpersonal behavior. The person who is most likely to suffer a heart attack is the one who is "aggressively involved in a *chronic, incessant* struggle to achieve more and more in less and less time . . . against the opposing efforts of other things or other persons."[9] These doctors believe that continuous competitve and aggressive communication can increase your chances of heart disease.

What conclusions can we draw from evidence like this? In 1977 Lynch put it this way:

> Human companionship does affect our hearts, and . . . there is reflected in our hearts a biological basis for our need for loving human relationships, which we fail to fulfill at our peril. . . . The ultimate decision is simple: we must either learn to live together or increase our chances of prematurely dying alone.[10]

In other words, quality of life is not just a matter of ample food, warm clothing, education, and modern conveniences. *The quality of your life is directly linked to the quality of your communication.* I believe that learning to communicate can not only help you to develop trust, clarify an idea, obtain a job, make a sale, get an 'A,' or make the right group decision. Communication *can* help with these things, but even more fundamentally, it affects your growth, your health, and your development as a person.

Interestingly, philosophers make this point as strongly as medical researchers do. For example, Reuel Howe writes,

> To say that communication is important to human life is to be trite, but that bit of triteness witnesses to an invariable truth: communication means life or death to persons. . . . Both the individual and society derive their basic meaning from the relations that exist between [persons]. It is through dialogue that man accomplishes the miracle of personhood and community.[11]

Martin Buber's entire philosophy of communication is based on the idea that you and I discover and build our humanness in relationships with other persons. To paraphrase Buber,

> The fundamental fact of human existence is person with person. The unique thing about the human world is that something is continually happening between one person and another, something that never happens in the animal or plant world.... *Humans are made human by that happening.*... That special event begins by one human turning to another, seeing him or her as this particular other being, and offering to communicate with the other in a mutual way, building from the individual world each person experiences to a world they share together.[12]

Jesuit psychologist John Powell puts the same idea in simpler terms: "What I am, at any given moment in the process of my becoming a person, will be determined by my relationships with those who love me or refuse to love me, with those I love or refuse to love."[13]

I am not saying that the quality of your communication is the be-all and end-all of your life, but I do believe that it is very important. I am not saying that if you fail to experience what I call interpersonal-quality communication *all* the time, you will become impoverished, inhumane, or antisocial. But I am saying that communicating is not just one of the many trivial and mundane things you do—along with combing your hair, washing the dishes, and earning a living. My basic belief is this: The quality of your life is directly related to the quality of your communication.

My other basic assumption is that *there is a basic movement in the human world, and it is toward relation not toward division.* This may also sound a little vague, but I think it'll get clearer if you bear with me for a couple of paragraphs. First, I believe that human life is a process or activity and that the general kind of process we humans are engaged in is the activity of becoming who we are, growing into fully developed persons. So far, no big deal, right?

Second, persons are relational, not solitary, beings. To be a person is to experience relationships with other persons. If you could create a human organism in a completely impersonal environment—an artificial uterus, machine-assisted birth, mechanical feeding and changing, and so on—what you'd end up with would *not* be a person. That's because in order to become a person you have to experience relationships with other persons. That's one point made by various accounts of "feral," or "wild," children. For example, in *The Forbidden Experiment: The Story of the Wild Boy of Aveyron,* Roger Shattuck tells about a "remarkable creature" who came out of the woods near a small village in southern France on January 9, 1800, and was captured while digging for vegetables in a village garden. The "creature"

> was human in bodily form and walked erect. Everything else about him suggested an animal. He was naked except for the tatters of a shirt and showed no modesty, no awareness of himself as a human person related in any way to the people who had captured him. He could not speak and made only weird, meaningless cries. Though very short, he appeared to be a boy of about eleven or twelve....[14]

The creature was taken for treatment to a distinguished physician named Dr. Pinel. Dr. Pinel, one of the founders of psychiatry, was unable to help him, partly because, as Shattuck puts it, "the boy had no human sense of being in the world. He had no sense of himself as a person related to other persons."[15] The "savage of

Aveyron" made progress toward becoming human only after he was taken on as a project by another medical doctor named Jean-Marc Gaspard Itard. Itard's first move was to give the boy a foster family and to put him in the care of a mature, loving mother, Madame Guérin. In that context they were able to teach the boy to "use his own chamberpot," dress himself, come when he was called, and even associate some letters of the alphabet with some pictures.

Itard's first report about his year of efforts to train and socialize the wild boy emphasizes the importance of human contact in becoming a person. Itard describes in detail events that demonstrate the significance of "the feeling of friendship" between the boy and Itard and especially between the boy and Mme. Guérin: "Perhaps I shall be understood if people remember the major influence on a child of those endless cooings and caresses, those kindly nothings which come naturally from a mother's heart and which bring forth the first smiles and joys in a human life."[16] Without that contact, this young human organism was a "creature," a "savage"; with them, he began to develop into a person.

If it's true that what we're doing as persons is becoming who we are, and that we are relational beings, then you can say that the basic movement in the human world is toward relating, not away from it. Another way to put it is to say that the underlying, fundamental force in the human world is centripetal, not centrifugal. (Remember that when you whirl a weight on a string, centrifugal force is what forces the weight *out,* away from the center, and centripetal force is what holds it *in.*)

So what about all this? Well, to say that humans are fundamentally "relaters" is to say that we are fundamentally "communicators," since relating happens by means of communication. That's another way of saying what I said already—that communication is not just one of the mundane things we do as we trip through life; it is the defining thing; communication is what makes us who we are. But it also means something else. If humans are *fundamentally* communicators, then whenever we are freed from ignorance and fear, we *will* move toward others, not away from them. So my approach as an interpersonal communication teacher is not to say, "You *should* establish person-to-person relations," or, "You had *better* communicate more effectively or you'll be a bad person," but to recognize that if we can work together to increase your knowledge and diminish your fear, you *will* establish more person-to-person relations. So will I. *Naturally.* That will happen not because we're "being good" or buying into a certain value system but because we're being who we are: persons.

Again I'm not saying that if everybody just relaxes, holds hands, smiles, and stares at the sunset, all conflict will disappear and the world will be a happy place. Sometimes the fear that prohibits interpersonal communication is legitimate; we are often acutely vulnerable to another person's gossip, lies, or manipulation. Our ignorance can also be devastating. If I don't know how to listen, how to tell you my feelings, or how to clarify an abstract idea, that fact alone can inhibit our contact.

But the point is, the kind of communicating outlined in this book is not just a trendy, pop psychology exercise in narcissism. It's grounded in some basic beliefs about who we are and what communication means in human life. In the first selection of Chapter 2 I say more about this point by distinguishing between the instrumental and the ontological functions of communication (pp. 23–24). When you read that, you might want to refer back to these two assumptions.

So far I 've tried to say that for me, interpersonal communication differs from noninterpersonal communication in that it consists of *contact between* (inter) *persons*. That means that for interpersonal communication to happen, each participant has to be willing and able to make available some of what makes him or her a person and to be aware of some of what makes the other a person. That willingness and ability will happen only when the people involved (1) are familiar with the basic ingredients of the human communication process, (2) are willing and able accurately to perceive and listen to others, (3) are willing and able to make themselves and their ideas available to others, (4) have some resources to deal with differences, and (5) can put the whole complex of attitudes and skills together into a human synthesis that works for them.

That's why I've organized this book into five sections. This chapter introduces me and a couple of my basic assumptions. The second chapter explores some of what it means to say that interpersonal communication means contact between persons. I feel strongly that it's vital to understand both concepts—"contact between" and "persons"—so I've discussed them in some detail in Chapter 2, and I've included two additional articles that speak to some of the same ideas in different ways. The third and fourth chapters complete the outline of the basic ingredients of human communication. Chapter 3 discusses verbal codes—how words can help people understand you and help bring people together. In Chapter 4, several authors talk about how nonverbal codes work in human communication, and specifically how silence and touch affect our relationships with others.

In Part Two the focus shifts to one aspect or dimension of communication that I label Openness as Inhaling. I explain why I chose that label at the end of my article in Chapter 2. In the first chapters of Part Two, two essays explore self-perception, and in Chapter 6 there are three treatments of how we perceive others. Chapter 7 concentrates on effective listening and includes two "theoretical" articles and one "applied" one.

Part Three looks at the other dimension of communicating, which you might think of as "sending" or "output." I call it Openness as Exhaling. In Part Three, Chapter 8 deals with self-disclosure, the process of making yourself available. Chapter 9 includes three articles that discuss confirmation, which I think is the most important kind or function of Exhaling.

Part Four focuses on bridging differences. More and more communication scholars and teachers are studying conflict, and we now have some understanding of defensiveness, and the potential values of conflict. These are the topics of Chapter 10. Communicating across differences between women and men and communicating across cultures are the topics of Chapters 11 and 12. You've probably experienced some or all of those potentially difficult phenomena in your daily living, and each reading in these three chapters offers insights and practical suggestions for improving.

In the final part of the book I've collected four statements, each of which integrates, synthesizes, and pulls together the ideas in the other readings. Most of the authors in Part Five are important in the development of the ideas in this book; you will find their names scattered throughout the writings in other chapters. Leo Buscaglia has been famous for several years for his university courses on love and his insightful and inspirational speeches and books about improving communication. Carl Rogers is a well-known humanistic psychotherapist who is an important figure in the human potential movement. Erich Fromm has been called a social prophet; he brings a sociological perspective to some of the same ideas as he talks about love as an important part of society and culture. Finally, Martin Buber is a philosopher and the person who is most responsible for originally explaining the basic ideas everyone else in this book developed.

Before each essay or article there are some introductory comments that pinpoint what I think are the key ideas that appear there. At the end of each reading I've included some "probes," questions intended to provoke your thinking, especially your thinking about how the ideas in that reading relate (1) to your own life experience and (2) to ideas in the other readings. I've also included twenty of Hugh Prather's comments as connecting thoughts. As you may have discovered already by reading his books *Notes to Myself* and *I Touch the Earth the Earth Touches Me,* Hugh is uniquely able to capture in a few lines insights that it takes most of us pages to explain.

So that's what's coming. I hope it will be helpful *and* fun.

References

1. James J. Lynch, *The Language of the Heart: The Body's Response to Human Dialogue* (New York: Basic Books, 1985), p. 3.
2. Lynch, p. 33, citing *Cardiovascular Primer for the Workplace,* Health Education Branch, Office of Prevention, Education, and Control. National Heart, Lung, and Blood Institute. U.S. Department of Health and Human Services. Public Health Service. National Institutes of Health. NIH Publication no. 81–2210 (January 1981).
3. Lynch, pp. 123–124.
4. Lynch, p. 127.
5. Lynch, pp. 160ff.
6. Lynch, pp. 150–155.
7. James J. Lynch, *The Broken Heart: The Medical Consequences of Loneliness* (New York: Basic Books, 1977), pp. 42–51.
8. E. A. Liljefors and R. H. Rahe, "Psychosocial Characteristics of Subjects with Myocardial Infarction in Stockholm," in *Life Stress Illness.* ed. E. K. Gunderson and Richard H. Rahe (Springfield, Ill.: Charles C Thomas, 1974), pp. 90–104.
9. Myer Friedman and Ray H. Rosenman, *Type A Behavior and Your Heart* (New York: Knopf, 1974), p. 67.
10. Lynch, *The Broken Heart,* p. 14.
11. From *The Miracle of Dialogue* by Reuel L. Howe, copyright 1963 by the Seabury Press, Inc. Used by permission of the publisher. Cited in *The Human Dialogue,* ed. F. W. Matson and A. Montagu (New York: The Free Press, 1968), pp. 148–149.
12. This is a paraphrase of what Buber says in *Between Man and Man* (New York: Macmillan, 1965), p. 203. Italics added.
13. John Powell, *Why Am I Afraid to Tell You Who I Am?* (Chicago: Argus Communications, 1969), p. 43.
14. Roger Shattuck, *The Forbidden Experiment: The Story of the Wild Boy of Aveyron* (New York: Farrar Straus Giroux, 1980), p. 5.
15. Shattuck, p. 37.
16. Shattuck, p. 119.

CHAPTER 2

INTRODUCTION TO INTERPERSONAL COMMUNICATION

> *Perceptions are not of things but of relationships. Nothing, including me, exists by itself—this is an illusion of words. I am a relationship, ever-changing.*
>
> HUGH PRATHER

One of the best courses I took during my first year of college was Introduction to Philosophy. Part of the appeal was the teacher; he knew his stuff, and he loved to teach it. But as I discovered a few years later, I also enjoyed the course because the kind of thinking that was going on in the materials we read and the discussions we had were comfortable for me. It seemed as though I usually thought that way myself. As I continued through college, I supplemented my speech communication courses with other work in philosophy. The topics I talk about in this essay reflect that dual interest.

Originally, the Greek words for "philosophy" meant the love of wisdom, where "wisdom" was contrasted with the kind of knowledge it takes to do art, politics, or science. That meant that *"philo-sophia"* was concerned with "eternal truths" and such general questions as "What does it mean to be a 'good' person?" or, "How do you know that you really *know* something?" Later, philosophy was defined as the "systematic critique of presuppositions," which is another way of saying that it's concerned with first principles, basic understandings, underlying assumptions. If you've read much philosophy you may have the impression that it can be stuffy or even nit-picking to the point of irrelevance. But frequently it's exciting and important, because the philosopher says, "Hold it! Before you go off to spin a complicated web of explanations about human communication, or an economic system, or the history of culture, or the operation of a political system, or whatever, try to get clear about some *basic* things: When you're talking about human communication, what are you assuming, for example, about what actually gets passed between people when they communicate or about whether part of being a person is *wanting* to get in contact with others?" "If each human perceives the world in his or her own way," the philosopher might say, "then I can only communicate with *my perception* of you; I can *never* really get in touch with you. All I can do, when it comes right down to it, is communicate with myself!"

Such basic issues intrigue me. I know that many potentially exciting conversations have been squelched by someone's dogmatic insistence that everybody "define the terms." But I also know that a great deal of fuzziness can be cleared up when a conversation starts with some shared understandings about what's being discussed.

In the following essay I describe my understanding of the topic of this book—interpersonal communication. I talk mostly about what's meant by the two halves of the word "interpersonal," *contact between* (inter) and *person*. My main goal is to clarify how the approach to interpersonal communication taken in this book is a little different from what you might be expecting. Basically, it's different because it acknowledges and emphasizes the fact that communication is not only important for getting things done; it also affects *who we are as persons.*

Interpersonal Communication: Contact Between Persons

John Stewart

You've decided, maybe under some duress, and maybe not, to read, think, and hopefully to discuss the topic of interpersonal communication. You could have made many different choices. You could have decided to study public speaking, television production, or organizational communication. You could also have decided to read, think, and talk about geology, mathematics, English literature, or religion—in fact, you may be doing some of that now too. But what is this "interpersonal communication"? What does it mean to study *this* topic?

Does it just mean "two-person" communication? Or perhaps two- to five-person communication (but after five people it becomes "group discussion" or "small group decision making")? Or does the term mean informal, face-to-face communication? Or warm, supportive communication? Or therapeutic communication? What *are* you using this book to study?

I don't want to make too big a deal out of "defining our terms," but I believe that interpersonal communication is more than any of the things I've mentioned so far. For me, when the term "interpersonal" is used to modify the word "communication," it means something more than just "two-person," "face-to-face," "informal," or "warm and supportive." The term "interpersonal" designates a type or quality of human contact that can characterize many different communication events, including a telephone conversation (which obviously isn't face to face), an intense argument (which is hardly ever warm and supportive), a ten-person committee meeting, or even a public speech. This definition or approach grows out of the two assumptions I discussed in this book's introduction, and it expands the study of interpersonal communication from just an instrumental enterprise to one with ontological implications. For me *interpersonal communication is the type or quality or kind of contact that occurs when each person involved talks and listens in ways that maximize their own and the other person's humanness.*

So what does all *that* mean? "Ontological not instrumental"? "Type or quality or kind"? "Contact"? "Maximize humanness"? Well, I mean all those terms to do more than just confuse or to generate jargon. My purpose in this first reading is to unpack that definition and to explain how this approach to interpersonal communication underlies everything that's in this book.

PERSONS

Let's start with "maximize humanness." It seems to me that as you and I move through our daily family, work, social, and school lives, we tend to relate with others in two different ways: We treat others and are treated by them as objects or as humans. I don't mean that there is a sharp dichotomy; sometimes we treat others and are treated by them more as persons than as objects, and sometimes it's the other way around. But "personifying" (or "humanifying") and "objectifying" seem to be two ends of a continuum that describes how we relate with others. Communication with bank tellers, receptionists, registration clerks, and most other institutional representatives tends to be objectifying, and much of the time that's completely expected and legitimate; in fact, it's almost impossible to do anything else. Communication with family members, lovers, and spouses tends at least part of the time to be personifying. One central theme of this book is that although all our communicating cannot maximize humanness or personness (i.e., it cannot be all interpersonal-quality communication), *more of it could be.* If it were, things would be greatly improved both for us and for the people we contact.

In order to move in that direction, it's important to come to see what that object–person communication continuum or relationship scale looks like. Early in this century a man named Martin Buber described that sliding scale in a little book that became a classic. The name of the book is *I and Thou,* and since its publication in 1922, it's been translated into more than twenty languages, sold millions of copies all over the world, and continues to be read, discussed, and cited by communication scholars and teachers, philosophers, psychologists, educators, sociologists, anthropologists, and theologians. You might think from its title that Buber's book is a religious work, but it's not just that. The "Thou" in the title is the English translation of the German word for the familiar form of the pronoun "you." Buber originally wrote the book in German and called it *Ich und Du,* which became *Je et Tu* in French, and since English used to include "thee" and "thou," it was translated into English as *I and Thou.* The most recent translation, as you will see in a minute, keeps that title but renders *Du* as "You" in the text of the book itself.

In his book and in virtually all the writings he did between 1922 and his death in 1965, Buber focused in one way or another on the relationship scale or communication continuum between objects and persons. In a three-paragraph section near the end of the first part of *I and Thou,* Buber summarized the distinctions between objects and persons that were the foundation of his entire approach to interpersonal communication. Here's my paraphrase of what he says with some marginal notes I'll explain in a minute:

> The world is twofold for humans in accordance with their twofold perspective. [This, by the way, is the same sentence as the first one in his book. Buber's signaling that these paragraphs are a summary of his main point.]
>
> On the one hand, a human perceives the surrounding world, plain things and beings as things; he or she perceives what happens in the world, plain processes and actions as processes, things that consist of qualities and processes that consist of moments, things recorded in terms of spatial coordinates and processes recorded in terms of temporal coordinates, things and processes that are bounded by other things and processes and capable of being measured against and compared with those others—an ordered world, a detached world. This world is somewhat reliable; it has density and duration, its structure can be surveyed; one can get it out again and again: one recounts it with one's eyes closed and then checks with one's eyes open. There it stands—right next to your skin if you think of it that way, or nestled in your soul if you prefer that: it is your object and remains that, according to your pleasure—and remains primally alien both outside and inside you. You perceive it and take it for your "truth"; it permits itself to be taken by you, but it does not give itself to you. It is only *about* it that you can come to an understanding with others: although it takes a somewhat different form for everybody, it is prepared to be a common object for you; but you cannot encounter others in it. Without it you cannot remain alive; its reliability preserves you; but if you were to die into it, then you would be buried in nothingness.
>
> Or the human encounters being and becoming as what confronts him or her—always only *one* being and everything only as a being. What

⟨space–time⟩
⟨measurable⟩

⟨reliable⟩

⟨talk *about* not *to*⟩

⟨unique⟩

is there reveals itself in occurrence, and what occurs there happens to one as being. Nothing else is present but this one. . . . Measure and comparison have fled. It is up to you how much of the immeasurable becomes reality for you. . . . The world that appears to you in this way is unreliable, for it appears always new to you, and you cannot take it by its word. It lacks density, for everything in it permeates everything else. It lacks duration, for it comes even when not called and vanishes even when you cling to it. It cannot be surveyed: if you try to make it surveyable, you lose it. It comes—comes to fetch you—and if it does not reach you or encounter you it vanishes—but it comes again, transformed. It does not stand outside you, it touches your ground. . . . Between you and it there is a reciprocity of giving: you say You to it and give yourself to it; it says You to you and gives itself to you. You cannot come to an understanding *about* it with others; you are lonely with it; but it teaches you to encounter others and to stand your ground in such encounters. . . .

⟨**unmeasurable**⟩

⟨**unreliable**⟩

⟨**not space–time**⟩
⟨**addressable**⟩

⟨**talk *to* not just *about***⟩

The It-world hangs together in space and time.

The You-world does not hang together in space and time.[1]

As you can see, Buber's words for objects and persons are "It" and "You." His point is that as humans we have the twofold ability to relate to what's around us as either an "it" or as a "you." And the difference between these two modes of relating is very significant.

Unique

Consider for a minute the characteristics of Its and Yous (objects and persons) that I've highlighted in the margins of the preceding quotation. Perhaps most important, persons are unique, and objects aren't. Although a microscopic examination of the pencil I'm writing with right now might reveal some nicks, coloration, or erasure contours that are different from any other pencil, for all practical purposes, this pencil is the same as any other no. 2 pencil. The same can be said for all the other objects around me now—my typewriter, chair, lamp, paperweight, coffee cup, pocket calculator, and so on. There might be some minute distinctions, but for all practical purposes this typewriter is interchangeable with others of the same model, and so are the other objects here.

Persons aren't that way. We can be treated as if we're interchangeable parts, but for *many* practical purposes it's important to remember that we are not; each of us is unique. I remember hearing of a geneticist who said that given the complexity of each individual's makeup of genes and chromosomes, the probability of two persons other than identical twins having the same genetic materials was one in ten to the ten-thousandth power. That's less than one chance in a billion trillion! In other words, each of us is virtually a genetic one of a kind. But even if we weren't—even when identical twins have the same biological raw material—each is still unique because each experiences the world differently. If you doubt it, recall the differences between any twins you've known. Or you might check the uniqueness of others with a little experiment. After you finish this chapter, ask a friend who's also read it how he or she is experiencing this book, or this paragraph, or this sentence. Superficially, your experiences may be similar, but if you probe them even a little, it will be clear that they're unique. There's only one you.

Unmeasurable

A second difference that Buber notes is that the object world is completely measurable, it's a space-and-time (spatiotemporal) world, and the human world is not.

17

Part of what he means is that even extremely complex objects, such as giant computers, well-equipped automobiles, and fifty-story buildings, can be described completely in terms of space and time. That's what blueprints do; they record all the measurements necessary to re-create the object—length, width, height, velocity, amperage, voltage, specific gravity, circumference, hardness, and so on. Although it's difficult to measure some things directly—the velocity of a photon, the temperature of a kiss, the duration of an explosion—the parts of all objects are measurable, at least in theory.

The same can't be said for persons. Even if I accurately identify your height, weight, temperature, specific gravity, velocity, and electric potential, I will not have exhaustively accounted for the person who's you. Some psychologists acknowledge this point by including in their model of the person the notion of a "black box," an unmeasurable, uniquely human something that is continuously affecting human behavior and that escapes all the rigorously scientific measurement that can be applied to it. Less scientifically inclined people call this unmeasurable part the human "spirit," "soul," "psyche," or "personality." But whatever you call it, it's there.

The clearest manifestations of this unmeasurable part of us are those phenomena we call "emotions" or "feelings." Although we can measure things related to feelings—brainwaves, sweaty palms, heart rate, paper-and pencil responses—what the measurements record is a long way from the feelings themselves. "Pulse 110, respiration 72, Likert rating 5.39, palmar conductivity .036 ohms" might be accurate, but it doesn't quite capture all of what's going on in me when I greet somebody I love.

Another thing, these unmeasurable emotions or feelings can't be turned off or on at will; they're always part of what we are experiencing. Contemporary educators pretty much agree now that it's unrealistic to try to focus a class exclusively on the "intellectual," "objective" aspect of some subject matter, because people are always thinking *and* feeling. As one writer put it, "it should be apparent that there is no intellectual learning without some sort of feeling, and there are no feelings without the mind's being somehow involved."[2] Sometimes what we are experiencing is more thinking than feeling and sometimes vice-versa, but neither function is ever entirely missing. We're always feeling something, or perhaps more accurately "feeling somehow."

In short, there is more to persons than just what's observable and measurable. Although the human "spirit" and human "feelings" are concretely *real* in the sense that we are experiencing them all the time, those elements of us cannot be exhaustively accounted for in space-and-time terms. Commmunication that is responsive to those unmeasurable, uniquely human parts is more interpersonal than communication that isn't.

Choice

A third distinction Buber identifies is that the It world is "reliable" and the You world is unreliable. That means that things and processes occur in predictable patterns. If I leave my hammer on the dock next to the boat, it will rust, because unprotected metal with a given iron content always oxidizes in a saltwater environment. *Always.* It can't choose not to. The difference between the reliability of the object world and the unreliability of the human world is choice. My typewriter can't choose to start typing, this pencil can't choose to start writing, and my pocket calculator can't choose to start balancing my checkbook. Automatic pilots, photoelectric switches, and thermostats sometimes seem to "operate on their own" or "turn themselves off and on," but they too are dependent on actions initiated outside them. The pilot has to be programmed; the thermostat reacts to the temperature, which reacts to the sun rays, which react to the earth's rotation, and so on. Similarly, a ball can only react to the force of a foot that kicks it, and if you're good enough at physics calculations, you can pretty much pinpoint how far and where it will go, based on weight, velocity, the shape of your shoe, atmospheric conditions, and so on.

But you can't predict what will happen very accurately if you kick your roommate, your teacher, or the grocery clerk. The reason you can't is that when persons are involved, human choice intervenes between cause and effect, stimulus and response. If you tap my knee, you may cause a reflex jerk, but the behavior that accompanies my reflex might be anything from giggles to a lawsuit, and there is no way that you can predict for sure which it will be. Like objects, persons sometimes react, but we can also *choose, decide, act.*

The importance of choice is a key point of several approaches to studying persons that go under the general heading "existential." You've probably heard that term before in reference to plays, novels, philosophy, or psychology. One of the existentialists' main insights is that persons are subjects, not objects. Part of what they mean is that human subjects, like grammatical subjects, "define themselves through their own activities while objects are defined by the activities of subjects; subjects modify [choose]; objects are modified [get chosen upon]."[3] Nobody argues that humans are *completely* free to choose to do anything they want to. I can't fly, return to my childhood, or run faster than a speeding bullet. But my future is not determined by my past or present, and neither is yours. We can choose to respond to conditions that confront us.

The more we're aware of our ability to choose, the more human we are. When I feel like, "I *had* to shout back; he was making me look silly!" or "I just *couldn't* say anything!" or "Sure I *withdrew,* but she made me—she was always on my back about something!" I'm out of touch with part of what it means to be a person. Persons can act, not just react; persons can choose. And interpersonal communication is in part communication that maximizes our ability to do those uniquely personlike things.

Addressable

The fourth distinction Buber identifies is that persons are addressable and objects aren't; you can only talk *about* objects but you can talk *to* persons, or better yet, *with* them. Notice how he makes that point. An It, he says, "permits itself to be taken by you, but it does not give itself to you." A You, on the other hand, "comes to fetch you. . . . Between you and it there is a reciprocity of giving: you say You to it and give yourself to it; it says You to you and gives itself to you."

Addressability is the clearest difference between the kind of contact you can have with a person and the kind you can have with the "almost human" pet cat, dog, or horse. For example, you may have looked into the eyes of a pet animal and noticed what seemed to be a real glance of reciprocity—almost as if you were being addressed. Buber describes an experience like that which he often had with a house cat.

> Undeniably, this cat began its glance by asking me with a glance that was ignited by the breath of my glance: Can it be that you mean me? Do you actually want that I should not merely do tricks for you? Do I concern you? Am I there for you? Am I there? What

is coming from you? What is that around me? What is that?!'' . . . There the glance of the animal, the language of anxiety, had risen hugely—and set almost at once.[4]

Later he explains that animals are not "twofold," like humans; they cannot perceive both the it-world and the you-world. Especially tame animals can step up to the threshold of mutuality, but they cannot cross it. All the unasked "cat" questions that Buber paraphrases dissolved in a twitch of feline ears and tail, and the cat stayed an "it." Experiments with chimpanzees, dolphins, and whales are raising new questions about this phenomenon. (See, for example, the "Say Roo-bee!" reading in Chapter 7.) But so far the evidence supports the point that animals are not addressable in the sense that persons are.

In short, addressability also characterizes the human world. We certainly treat each other as objects and as animals—for example, in crowds, bureaucracies, and wars. But we also engage in fully mutual address-and-response. As you sit in an audience of several hundred, the speaker can say your name and single you out for immediate contact: "Jeff Peterson? Are you here? Your question is about apartheid, and I want to try to answer it now." Or even more commonly and more directly, you may sit across from a friend and know from the touch of the friend's eyes, her hand, and her voice that she means *you;* she "comes to fetch you" and "touches your ground."

In summary, when I say that interpersonal communication maximizes the humanness of the persons involved, the word "persons" means more than just "thinking quadriped" or the "animal who laughs." Persons are different from objects or Its in four special ways, and it's impossible to communicate with them as persons unless you keep those differences in mind.

1. Each person is a unique, noninterchangeable part of the communication situation.
2. A person is more than just an amalgamation of observable, measurable elements; he or she is always experiencing feelings or emotions.
3. Persons are "unreliable" because they are choosers who are free to act, not just react to the condition therein.
4. Persons are addressable; they can be talked *to* not just *about* and they can respond in kind with mutuality.

The first step toward communicating interpersonally, then, is to contact others in ways that affirm your and their "personness." That means doing several things, and each chapter that follows is about one or more of those things. For example, it means looking for the uniqueness in each person (Chapter 6) instead of being satisfied with what makes this person "just like every other _____ (jock, company man, sorority Sally, farm kid, etc.)." It also means remembering that even in a conflict situation, both you and the other person are *choosing* to feel as you do, so you both need to own your feelings, to be responsible for them (Chapter 10). Sharing some of your feelings (Chapter 8) and listening to the feelings of the other (Chapter 7) are also important, as is the process of using addressability to sculpt mutual meanings (Chapter 7). The key is to be aware of your own and the other's personness and to communicate in ways that manifest, that demonstrate your awareness.

CONTACT

When I say that interpersonal communication is a type or quality or kind of contact, I mean to emphasize that it's something that happens *between* people, not something one person does to someone else. Just as your ability to communicate interpersonally is affected by your recognition of what it is to be a *person,* it will also be affected by your recognition of what it means to say that communication occurs *between* persons. There are several practical reasons why it's important to develop your ability to see the betweenness, or relational nature, of human communication. For one thing, until you do, it's hard to keep from getting mad at the person who criticizes you or to keep from feeling defensive whenever you're being evaluated or controlled. Until you see the betweenness, it's also hard to keep track of the complex, continually changing myriad of things that affect your communication with a person you are close to. Without a relational perspective that focuses on the contact, it's also difficult to stay in the here and now and not to let the past determine what's going on in the present. In fact, all the communication behaviors discussed in later chapters—touch, tone of voice, self-disclosure, confirmation, interpretive listening, and so on—make real sense only when you see them relationally, as part of what's going on *between* persons.

The problem is, most people don't actually see communicating that way. If you were to ask the person on the street what communication means, he or she would probably say something like "getting your ideas across" or "making yourself understood." That's a common view of the communication process, a view that's operating every time someone says, "How did you screw that up? I *told* you what to do!" or "I'm sure they understood; I *explained* it three times." In those cases the conception that is operating is that communication is something *I do.* From this point of view, communication doesn't occur "between," but rather "in" the communicator. When things don't work out, it's because I didn't communicate well or because you didn't, the company didn't, the supervisor didn't, or whatever. From this point of view, in other words, communication is an *action,* something determined entirely by the communicator's choices. As the diagram below indicates, this point of view says that communication is like giving or getting an inoculation; ideas and feelings are prepackaged in a mental and physical syringe and then forced under pressure in a straight line into the receiver.

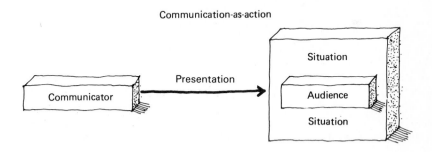

Communication-as-action

If you think about it for a minute, it becomes pretty clear why that view is inaccurate. When you see communication as just an action, you're ignoring feedback, something that's present whenever people communicate. Even on the phone, we make noises to indicate we're listening to a long comment or story. If you doubt the importance of that feedback, try being completely silent and see how soon the person on the other end asks, "Are you still there?"

The model of communication as action is also oversimplifed in another way. It suggests that when you speak, there can be "an audience"; that is, a group of persons who are homogeneous—whose backgrounds, thoughts, feelings, and attitudes toward the topic and communicator are more similar than different. It also implies that the communicator's identity is not greatly affected by what goes into, or goes on during, the communication experience. In other words, it implies that regardless of any changes in the situation, the communicator is, for example, always "teacher" and never "learner," always "boss" and never "friend."

The point is, the common view that communication is an *action,* something one person *does* to somebody else, is drastically oversimplifed. All of our communication behavior is affected by not only our own expectations, needs, attitudes, and goals, but also the responses we are getting from the other person involved. So it's more accurate to view communication as an *interaction,* as a process of *reciprocal* influence.

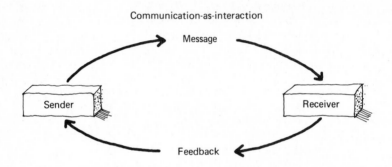

Communication-as-interaction

Message

Sender

Receiver

Feedback

The interactional point of view can account for quite a bit of complexity. Communicologist David Berlo, for example, includes in an interaction the expectations, hypotheses, or guesses that you sometimes make about how the person will respond.[5] This point of view emphasizes that communication involves not just action, but rather action and reaction; not just stimulus, but also stimulus and response. According to this perspective, a "good" communicator not only skillfully prepares and delivers messages, but also watches for significant reactions to his or her communication. The study of human communication becomes a study of how people "talk" and how they "respond."

Although the interactional viewpoint is an improvement over communication-as-action, it still has some weaknesses. The most serious one, it seems to me, is that although it's not as oversimplified as the action view, the interactional view still distorts human communication by treating it as a series of causes and effects, stimuli and responses. For example, think about the last time you had a conversation with someone you know. What was the stimulus that caused you to greet the other person? His or her greeting? His or her look? Your expectations about the other's eagerness to talk with you? Was your greeting a response, or was it a stimulus to his or her next utterance? Or was it both? What caused you to say what you said? What the other person said? What you thought the other's words *meant?* What you *felt* because of those words? What you felt because of *how* the other person said what she or he said? What you felt because of how the other *looked* when speaking? Are you able to distinguish clearly between the stimuli and responses in that conversation or between the actions, the hypotheses about the reactions, and the reactions?

George Kelly, a fairly well-known psychologist, reports that he has "pretty well given up trying to figure out" the relationship between stimuli and responses. He writes, "some of my friends have tried to explain to me that the world is filled with 'S's' and 'R's' and it is unrealistic of me to refuse to recognize them. But before they have talked themselves out they become pretty vague about which is which."[6]

What I'm saying is that it's more accurate to see communication as an interaction than to see it as just an action one person performs. But if you stick to an interactional view, you will still miss an important part of what it means to focus on the *contact* or the "between," and the part you will miss is the one part that makes the most difference, the part that can make interpersonal-quality communication happen.

Over the last ten years I've found that helping students see this "part," helping them to see communication from this relational point of view, is one of the most important and most difficult things I do as a teacher. In my own life I am also continually reminded of how important it is to see communication relationally or to focus on the contact—every time I try to explain a concept in class, discuss a disagreement over a grade, pursue an idea with a colleague or student, or divide housekeeping responsibilities or plan a weekend with Kris. Every time my communication is really important, in other words, I rediscover how necessary it is to view what's happening relationally, to see that it's occurring *between* persons. Since this perspective is so vital, I want to talk about it in different ways using three different terms: "transaction," "relationship," and "spiritual child."

Transaction

One way to say what I mean is to use the term "transaction" and to contrast it with the *action* and *interaction* points of view.* As I said, if you see communication as an *action,* you're likely to be most concerned with each individual's performance. But human communication is much more than just independent message-sending. If you view communication as an interaction, you'll begin to see *some* of this "much more." The most obvious additional element you will see is feedback—how one's communication behavior is in part a response to the other person's, how human communication continually involves mutual and reciprocal influences.

It is important to see beyond performance to feedback, but there is another element that you will still miss if you stick within the interactional perspective. That element is this: *Every time persons communicate, they are continually offering definitions of themselves and responding to definitions of the other(s) which they perceive.* That process goes on all the time. Your clothes are part of your "this is how I define myself" message, just as mine are. Your tone of voice also reveals how you define yourself in relation to the situation and the person you're talking with. Recall in your mind's ear the sound of your voice when you're talking with a young person whom you define yourself as superior to. Contrast that with your tone of voice when you see yourself as an inferior talking with your supervisor or your parent. Touch, distance, eye contact, and choice of words all contribute to self-definition too. Look at the ways I've defined myself in relation to you in this book—the words I have chosen, the examples I have used, and so on. I have also assumed how you're defining yourself, and part of what I'm doing is responding to what I think is your self-definition. *And I could not not do these things.* This pro-

---

*John Dewey and Arthur Bentley originally made this three-part distinction in their book *Knowing and the Known* (Boston: Beacon Press, 1949).

cess of self-definition and response to the definition of the other is going on whenever people communicate.

Recently the term "transaction" has been introduced to talk about this process. When it's used this way, it means more than it does in the phrase "business transaction." A dictionary of psychological terms defines a transaction as "a psychological event in which all parts or aspects of the concrete event derive their existence and nature from active participation in the event."[7] In other words, a transaction is an event in which *who we are* (our "existence and nature") emerges out of the event itself. Human communication is that kind of event. Human communication is transactional. Whenever humans communicate, part of what's going on is that each is defining himself or herself in relation to the other persons involved.

Here's where the "instrumental" and "ontological" terms become important. "Ontology" is the philosopher's word for the study of being, especially human being. What is it to be a person? How is a human being different from other kinds of being? These are some of the questions of ontology. "Instrumental" means used as an instrument to accomplish a goal, to produce a product or effect. If you think about it, when you recognize that all communication is transactional, because it's where the "existence and nature" of the persons happens, you've noticed something ontological about communication. As I said in this book's introduction, communication is more than just instrumental. We do use communication to "do" things, but it's also the way we become who we are. The quality of each person's life is directly linked to the quality of communication he or she experiences. Our human being happens or comes-to-be in the contacts we experience. Whenever humans communicate, part of what's going on is that each is defining himself or herself in relation to the other persons involved.

Obviously, this defining process has some limits. I am male, forty-four, and brown-eyed; I can't define myself as female, ten, and blue-eyed. But I *can* offer a definition of myself that says I see myself as more masculine—or more feminine—than you and as in some sense younger or older than you. Then it's up to you to respond to the definition of self I offer. You may accept, partly accept, or reject it altogether. The point is, at a given moment, neither of us can change our identity absolutely, but we do change in relation to each other.

The only even nearly adequate "model" of this transactional perspective that I've ever seen is the "Bond of Union" print shown here by M. C. Escher. It graphically illustrates two persons whose "existence and nature" are intertwined. Each one is a "function," in the mathematical sense, of the other, so much so that not only are the bands that constitute each head joined at the top and bottom, but they also intersect at one additional point. This image does not highlight how communication accomplishes our relational be-ing, but it does clearly illustrate much of the "transactional" and "ontological" points I've been making.

To review, then, you can see human communication as an action if you want to, but if you do you will miss a lot of what's happening. You can look at human communication as an interaction too, but you will still miss an important part of what's going on. The part you will miss is the ongoing process of self-definition-and-response-to-definition-of-the-other—the ontological part—and you won't see that clearly until you recognize that communication is a transaction, an event defined by that very process. All human communication is transactional. We're always engaged in the definition-and-response-to-definition process. Sometimes we see our communication as transactional and sometimes we don't. I'm convinced

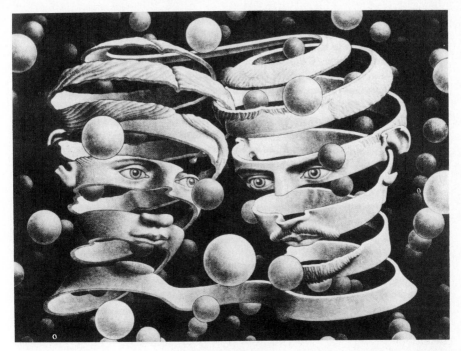

From M. C. Escher: His Life and Work *by F. H. Boul, J. R. Kist, J. C. Loder, and F. Wjerda, ed. J. L. Loder (New York: Abrams, 1981). The print is #409, "Bond of Union," April 1956, Lithograph, 253 × 339 (10 × 13 3/8″).*

that when we don't, it's a lot harder to help interpersonal-quality communication happen.

The main reason is that when you see communication as an action you aren't focusing on the *contact between* the persons involved. All you're seeing is one person's choices, one person's behavior. When you see communication as an inter-action, you still aren't seeing the contact between person A and person B. You see each person functioning something like a sophisticated billiard ball—reacting to forces from the other billiard balls, the table surface, cue stick, pads, and so on. From an interactional point of view, one's actions are affected by the others, but *who one is* doesn't change.

When you adopt a transactional point of view, though, you can't help but look at the contact *between* the persons involved. If you focus your attention on just person A, for example, you realize that since person A is who he or she is only in relation to person B, you have to look immediately at what's happening *between* them. The same goes for person B. Since *who the persons are*—their "existence and nature"—emerges out of their meeting with each other, you can't help but focus on the meeting itself rather than on the individual meeters.

Relationship

I want to shift vocabularies now and make the same point in slightly different terms. The authors of one of the two or three most influential communication books writ-ten in the last twenty years earned their well-justified fame in part by distinguishing between the *content* aspect of communication and the *relationship* aspect.[8] As these authors, whose names are Paul Watzlawick, Janet Beavin, and Don Jackson, describe it, the content aspect of communication is the information, the "facts," the data in the message. The difference between "I'll meet you here in twenty minutes" and "I'll meet you at the post office in an hour" is a difference in communication *content*. Up to the publication of their book, most communication studies focused on content. People concentrated on creating and researching ideas, organizing information systematically, and building persuasive arguments. If attention was paid to style or delivery, it was mainly to insure that the message had vitality, smoothness, or the right amount of ornamentation.

Watzlawick, Beavin, and Jackson argued persuasively that there's also another aspect of communication that most communication scholars and teachers have overlooked, the *relationship* aspect. They called it that because it has to do with the way the people communicating are relating with each other. The difference between "I'll meet you here in twenty minutes" and "Why the hell didn't you call before now? Get over here in twenty minutes or you're in deep trouble!" is a difference in *relationship* communication: How I perceive myself, how I see you, how I see you seeing me, and vice versa—how you perceive yourself, your perception of me, and how you see me seeing you. So whereas the information makes up the content aspect, the relationship aspect refers to the quality of type or kind of *contact* that's occurring *between* the communicators.

Watzlawick, Beavin, and Jackson point out that the relationship aspect is a part of *all* human communicating. You cannot write or say or respond to anything without at least implicitly offering a definition of the relationship between yourself and the other(s) involved. In addition, any response from the other will include his or her own definition-and-response-to-yours. For example, if you begin a letter with "Dear Professor Nichols:" the "Professor" title and the colon help define the relationship as more formal than a letter to the same person which begins, "Dear Marie,". You decide which to use by noticing how the other person defines herself in relation to you. I've already mentioned in my discussion of basic assumptions how, in face-to-face contacts, the communicators' tone of voice, touch, distance, and eye contact also contribute to this process of relationship defining.

Another way we define the relationships we're in is by organizing—or what Watzlawick, Beavin, and Jackson call "punctuating"—the sequence of communication events we experience. For example, let's assume that a couple you are friends with has heard that you're studying interpersonal communication, so they ask you to help them out. Jill tells you that Jack withdraws all the time; he won't talk with her and it's driving her nuts. Jack tells you that Jill consistently nags him. "Sure I withdraw," he says, "You would too if she nagged you like she does me."

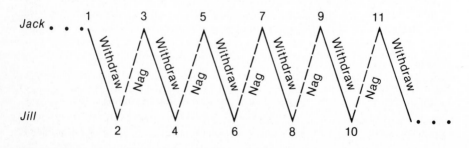

If you were going to apply this insight about relationship communication, you might diagram the couple's relationship as has been done on page 26.[9]
The diagram allows you to see that, for Jill, the sequence goes 1–2–3, 3–4–5, 5–6–7, and so on. She believes that Jack "starts" the pattern; it's his fault because he won't talk to her. As Jill says to you, "I'm just responding to him—like any normal person would."

Jacks sees it differently; for him the sequence goes 2–3–4, 4–5–6, 6–7–8, and so on. He thinks it starts with Jill's nagging, and he's just reponding the way any normal person would—by withdrawing. For our purposes, the point is that Jack and Jill each define the relationship differently, depending on how they organize, or "punctuate," it—specifically, where each believes it "starts." The ellipses at the left and right of the diagram indicate that both Jack and Jill are "right" *and* "wrong." Things actually started before this nag–withdraw sequence got going, and they will continue beyond it. The definition of the *between,* the quality of the *contact,* or the *relationship* depends on how each person punctuates the ongoing flow of events.

I want to emphasize that both the relationship aspect of communication and the "punctuation" notion focus your attention not on the individual communicators but on their *contact,* what's *between* them, the *transaction* in which they're involved. It's like the "bridges" in the title of this book. The metaphor of *Bridges Not Walls* is meant to highlight not only the difference between separation and connection but also the importance of the *between.* Think of a bridge that spans a deep canyon. The structure of the bridge is that-which-connects the two sides. When you're focusing on the bridge itself, your attention is not on the forest on one side or the rocks on the other, but on the contact, the relationship, the between.

That's exactly where your attention needs to be if you're going to promote and enhance what this book means by interpersonal-quality communication. As I've already indicated, our inability—or unwillingness—to see communication relationally has the most impact when we're in the middle of a conflict. When you're really arguing with someone, it *seems* obvious that he or she is "making you mad," that the argument is the other person's "fault," because he or she "started" it, that you're "right" about important points and that the other person is "wrong." But all those conclusions that *seem* so obvious come from seeing what's happening not as a relationship, but as a cause–effect, stimulus–response thing. For example, as Chapter 8 points out, nobody *makes* you feel angry; your anger emerges in the relationship, and it's partly *your* choice to feel angry. Similarly, you won't get anywhere trying to figure out whose "fault" an argument is. You will probably get something like this: "I clam up because you keep nagging me; it's your fault!" "But I only nag you because you won't say anything; it's your fault!" In a sense, neither person is "right" or "wrong," and both are. The conflict emerges in the relationship. As long as you're looking at just one side, you'll stay stuck in the blaming game and communication won't improve much.

Spiritual Child

Let me briefly put this point one more way, then we'll go on to something else. I was discussing this transactional, relational idea with John Keltner several years ago. John is an interpersonal communication teacher at Oregon State University who wrote the first widely used interpersonal speech communication textbook. He said that the idea reminded him of an interesting concept that he and Loraine Halfen Zephyr had talked about. John and Zephyr suggested that it's easier to see human communication transactionally or relationally if you think in terms of a "spiritual child" that is the inevitable offspring of every human meeting.

In other words, whenever you encounter someone, the two of you together create a spiritual child—your *relationship*. Unlike the creation of physical children, there are no contraceptives available for spiritual children; when two people meet, they always create a relationship of some sort. Also unlike physical children, the spiritual child lives as long as at least one person lives. If two persons once have a relationship, their relationship endures, even though years and continents may separate them. The spiritual child can change drastically, but it can't be killed. That's one of the reasons why it's so hard to deal with the breakup of a long-term, intimate relationship. Since the spiritual child won't die, the relationship won't cease to exist, and each person has to learn to live with a radically, maybe even tragically different "child."

Zephyr describes the creation of this "third being" in these words:

> In human interaction, a natural spiritual child is conceived, and there is no available contraceptive. . . . When you and I interact, something new is present, a new organism, we. Yet you or I are not lost. The bits and pieces of the relating come together in a holographic process, and an entity emerges which embodies all the qualities of the actors and the process of the interacting. . . . If we come together in care, authenticity, honesty, and positive regard, our child will be healthy, vibrant, winsome, and beautiful. We will love it. We will receive much joy in the nurturing of it and we will be nourished in return.

> If our child is created in dishonesty, exploitation, contempt, disregard, our child will be sickly, crippled, distorted, toxic, frustrated. It will be ugly. We will fly from it, abandon it, but its influence will linger.[10]

At first it probably feels a little strange to think of your relationship with someone as a "spiritual child." But try letting the metaphor work for you. Many people today are rediscovering the power of "right brain" or metaphoric thinking.[11] They emphasize that metaphors are one of the best ways to "make the strange familiar." Metaphors do that by linking something unknown with something we know very well. So a complex ethical idea gets labeled "moral bankruptcy" and it immediately becomes clearer. Or we can say, "My love is a red rose," "That's just part of the game of life," "They want to rape the earth," or "This office is a zoo." Each metaphor economically illuminates a complex idea by linking something strange with something familiar.

The spiritual child metaphor can work that way too. Here are two examples of how it helped Zephyr respond to communication problems she experienced:

> I had not "seen" a spiritual child for some time. A situation developed in which a friend, with whom I had a very strong and healthy, delightful, nurturing child, became angry and afraid and felt invaded when a third person began living in our apartment. I found myself becoming more and more disgusted with the whole scene; I was very anxious and didn't know what to do to change what was happening.

> One day, I thought of the spiritual child concept. I realized I had never consciously attempted to evoke an image. I had never asked or told my subconscious mind to produce one for me. I decided to do it, but I really didn't know how.

> I sat in a rocking chair alone and said aloud, "I am experiencing our child as stubborn, balky, angry, afraid." Then I realized I was talking about the way I was experiencing my friend. So I closed my eyes, cleared my mind, and became very still and calm. Bingo! There it was, so clear—the child was about a year old, perfectly formed, but very very delicate. It was in a crawling position with a long white garment on. As soon as it rec-

ognized that it had my attention, it put its thumb in its mouth and turned over in a fetal position. In my mind was the question, "What are you telling me?" The answer came back in a plaintive tone, "What's going to happen to me?"

Immediately I recognized how close I was to walking out of that relationship. I was fed up, but I had not been aware of it. As soon as I got that understanding, the image left.

Now, I had a choice. Did I really want to end our interaction? No, I valued this relationship. Yet, it was also clear that it wasn't only my decision. We had often spoken of our "child" and how healthy it was and how its influence was such a comfort to us.

When my friend came home from work, I told her of my experience. Out of the discussion that followed came two conclusions. We both wanted that child, but what we had to nourish it with right now was poisonous. So we decided to withdraw all nourishment for a time. I was moving into a house for the summer. We had no contact for two months. At the end of that time, I invited her to dinner, and we very tentatively, carefully, and gently resumed interaction. Today, five years later, our child is robust, stable, mature and truly a delight.

Another incident made it clear to me that the child can be represented in the mind's eye in the form of a symbol. I had had a wounding experience with my secretary at the end of a long hard day. We were both very weary and irritable. I was rather ruthlessly pressing her for information, and she was responding to that pressure with a lot of expressed anger. I didn't know how to approach her to heal that wound, and again decided to evoke an image of the child.

I put myself in a quiet place and cleared my mind. What I got was an onion! I couldn't believe it, and tried to make it go away so I could get the "real" image. It wouldn't go, so I said to myself, "How is this onion like our relationship? What are the qualities of an onion?" I thought of how an onion is layered and the core is very deep inside. One has to probe very deeply to get to (understand) the core. "Ah, that's it. Our child is very deep; we have to take off a lot of layers to understand it." Although there was some relief, it was not complete, and the image remained. I knew I hadn't gotten it yet, so I just watched. As I did, I noticed the golden brown skin of the onion began to separate like it was peeling itself away from the top of the onion. As I watched I noticed how very thin that skin was—thin skin. We had a very thin-skinned child! Immediately the image vanished. What does one do with a very thin-skinned child? Treat it very very carefully and gently.

I was very consciously careful and gentle in all my interactions. At the end of the second day, my secretary told me she was embarrassed about her outburst. Now that she had selected the time, I told her of my evoking our child and what had happened. As we discussed it, we learned a lot about our relationship and came to a new level of trust. The visualization of the onion was a holographic process in which the activities of the left brain were sufficiently quieted so that material from the unconscious could emerge through the right brain activity of imaging. When the left brain began to dominate, to "figure it out," the insight was momentarily blocked. So, when we need some information, we contact the storehouse. In the beginning, relaxation of the body and attending to the breathing will help to "clear the mind." When you feel sufficiently relaxed and quiet, ask for a picture and calmly and patiently and confidently wait. Make no effort. Efforting delays or completely frustrates the process. It is important to accept whatever comes. What you see will always be appropriate to that point in time. And of course as with all children, it changes, so at another time you may see something different. The visualization techniques used above successfully quieted or cleared my mind so the contents of the unconscious mind could be shown in images. It is similar to a meditative state, and one way of beginning to experience this method of "seeing" is to block the left brain messages by concentration on the breath. Once the picture appears, an interpersonal dialogue can take place. Sometimes just watching tells everything.[12]

I hope that the spiritual child metaphor is useful for you. It gives me another way to look at the contact, the relationship, the transaction, what's between the persons. As a child, you are neither of your parents, but the result of their meeting, their contact. Similarly, the spiritual child who is born whenever two persons communicate is an entity that emerges *between* them.

I also hope that you will keep this "contact," "transaction," "relationship" point in mind when you read the titles of Part Two and Part Three of this book. On the one hand, I want those parts of the book's organization to acknowledge that communication contact is made up of two parts or "moves": "input and output," "receiving and sending." On the other hand, those labels won't work because they're not relational; they highlight the sides of the canyon rather than the bridge. So I've chosen two other language strategies.

The first is to use the word "openness," because it has both meanings. "Being open" can mean being both receptive to others' ideas and feelings *and* willing to disclose. A person can be open in the sense that he or she is tolerant, broadminded, and willing to listen (open to "input") and open in the sense that he or she does not hesitate to share ideas and feelings with others (open with "output"). So I used "open" in the titles of both Part Two and Part Three.

My second language move is to use "exhaling" and "inhaling" to identify which sense of "openness" each part deals with. I chose those words because each of us has firsthand experience with how inseparable they are. Try inhaling without exhaling or vice versa. I'd like you to think of "output and input" or "sending and receiving" that way too—as inseparable, *always* occurring together. The one disadvantage is that inhaling and exhaling can't happen simultaneously, but both senses of openness can and do. So my choice of labels is a bit of a compromise. But I hope that the titles for Parts Two and Three help reinforce the transactional, relational point I've been making.

The communicative challenge here is to use terms that clarify without distorting. Milt Thomas, a friend who's contributed a great deal to this book, suggests the metaphor of velcro. That fabric fastener or zipper substitute is made up of the hook side and the loop side, but neither is worth anything without the other. Velcro works because of the *between,* the *contact.*

SUMMARY

All of this can be summarized by saying that when I use the term *interpersonal communication* I mean "contact between persons." Both key concepts—*contact between* and *persons*—carry a lot of meaning in that statement. But if you keep in mind what it is to be a person and what's meant by contact, you can come up with a fairly straightforward definition of interpersonal communication:

> Interpersonal communication is the kind, type, or quality of transaction, relationship, or spiritual child that happens when two or more humans are willing and able to meet as persons by making available some of their personness—their uniqueness, unmeasurable aspects, active choosing, and addressability—and by being sensitive to or aware of some of the other's personness. Or more briefly, interpersonal communication is the quality of contact that occurs when each person involved talks and listens in ways that maximize their own and the other person's humanness.

As I've already said, this book is organized around that definition, and each chapter further explains and gives examples of one aspect of interpersonal-quality communication. Part One (Chapters 1–4) explores the basic ingredients—the assumptions, the transactional perspective, the function of words, and the working of nonverbal cues. Part Two (Chapters 5–7) deals with the "inhaling" dimensions—self-awareness, awareness of others, and listening. In Part Three (Chapters 8–9) the readings explore the "exhaling" dimensions of communication—self-disclosure and confirmation. The readings in Part Four (Chapters 10–12) suggest how the approach to interpersonal communication outlined in the rest of the book can apply to communication across differences—in conflict, in male–female contacts, and across cultures. Part Five (Chapters 13–16) includes essays by four people who have been able to put all of these ideas together.

I hope the ideas and suggestions here work for you. They make a real difference to me!

References

1. Paraphrased from Martin Buber, *I and Thou,* trans. Walter Kaufmann (New York: Scribner, 1970), pp. 82–84.
2. George Isaac Brown, *Human Teaching for Human Learning: An Introduction to Confluent Education* (New York: Viking, 1971), p. 4.
3. Ervin Singer, *Key Concepts in Psychotherapy,* 2nd ed. (New York: Basic, 1970), p. 17.
4. Buber, *I and Thou,* p. 145.
5. David Berlo, "Interaction: The Goal of Interpersonal Communication," in *The Process of Communication* (New York: Holt, Rinehart and Winston, 1960), pp. 106–131.
6. George A. Kelly, "The Autobiography of a Theory," *Clinical Psychology and Personality: The Selected Papers of George Kelly,* ed. Brendan Maher (New York: Wiley, 1969), p. 47.
7. Horace B. English and Ava Champney English, *A Comprehensive Dictionary of Psychological and Psychoanalytical Terms* (New York: Longmans, Green, 1958), p. 561.
8. Paul Watzlawick, Janet Helmick Beavin, and Don D. Jackson, *Pragmatics of Human Communication* (New York: Norton, 1968), see especially Chapter 2.
9. Watzlawick, Beavin, and Jackson, pp. 54–59.
10. Loraine Halfen Zephyr, "Creating Your Spiritual Child," in *Bridges Not Walls: A Book About Interpersonal Communication,* 3rd ed., ed. John Stewart (Reading, Mass.: Addison-Wesley, 1982), p. 34.
11. See, e.g., Paul Watzlawick, *The Language of Change: Elements of Therapeutic Communication* (New York: Basic Books, 1978); and Roger von Oech, *A Whack on the Side of the Head: How to Unlock Your Mind for Innovation* (Menlo Park, Calif.: Creative Think, 1982).
12. Zephyr, pp. 37–38.

The transactional, relational perspective that I discussed is crucial to your communication improvement—and to mine. Very often misunderstandings and conflicts occur in the first place because the persons involved are not viewing their communication relationally. This same lack or absence of a relational perspective also contributes to the growth and perpetuation of hostility and disagreement. In this chapter from his book *Crazy Talk, Stupid Talk,* Neil Postman further clarifies what it means to view situations relationally.

Postman's terms are different from mine. He talks about putting ourselves "outside the context of any semantic environment so that we may see it in its entirety," and he calls that move "metasemantics." The point he is making is the same one I tried to make: As long as we "frame" or "label" a *human* situation in simple cause-and-effect terms, we distort what's going on. Only when we have a broader (relational) perspective do we begin to perceive more accurately.

Postman's first example is an experiment a Stanford professor did to see how "sane" people were distinguished from the "insane." Postman shows how the experiment demonstrates the importance of seeing the whole context and the operation of what he calls "the principle of nonadditiveness" and self-fulfilling prophecies.

Postman explains that what I call taking a relational perspective means, in part, "declining the temptation to attend solely to *what* people are saying" and focusing our attention "on the relationships of the *what* to the *whys* and *hows*." As a result, "Talking or listening to talk changes its character—from a limited reflexive [knee jerk] response to a wide-ranging act of inquiry. And inquiry is, and always has been the most desirable and effective antagonist of unwise speech."

He also notes that the shift in perception isn't easy for most of us, because we've consistently been taught otherwise. As children we're taught to focus on the "whats," and as he puts it, "to think fast, not reflectively."

Postman concludes that the point of metasemantic (or relational) perception is that it increases our choices. This perspective can help free us from precipitous, reactive thinking and can encourage a broad range of responses (as contrasted with reactions), including "reverence, indifference, and skepticism." In other words, it can help maximize our humaneness.

Minding Your Minding

Neil Postman

Sometime in 1970, a man had himself admitted to a mental hospital. He assumed a false name and told the doctor who interviewed him a false story—that he heard strange voices that said "empty," "hollow," and "thud." Upon being admitted to the hospital, he proceeded to tell the truth about himself (as best he could and for as long as he was there) to everyone he came in contact with. Seven other people did the same thing in hospitals on the East and West coasts. All of this was part of a three-year "experiment" led by Dr. David L. Rosenhan, a professor of psychology and law at Stanford University.

Dr. Rosenhan claims he was trying to find out if the "sane" can be distinguished from the "insane" in psychiatric hospitals. In an article which appeared in *Science* magazine, he revealed that the "pseudopatients" were not detected at any of the hospitals used in the experiment. Each pseudopatient was discharged with a diagnosis of schizophrenia "in remission," the length of hospital confinement ranging from seven to fifty-two days, with an average of nineteen days. Dr. Rosenhan concluded from all this that the methods of diagnosing "insanity" are not very reliable, and he put forth what appears to him the melancholy view that diagnoses are almost always influenced by the environment and context in which the psychiatrist examines the patient; i.e., the hospital setting predisposes the doctor to assume that a patient is mentally ill.

Naturally. That is the equivalent of saying that if you enter a restaurant, sit down, and call for the menu, the waiter will be predisposed to assume you want to eat. Nonetheless, research is research, and what Dr. Rosenhan seems to have redis-covered are two intertwined principles of human communication which have long been known and which are the basis of much of this book. The first is that the meanings of sentences are not in *sentences* but in *situations*—in the relationship between *what* is said and to whom, by whom, for what purposes, and in what set of circumstances. A psychiatrist sitting at the admissions desk of a "mental hospi-tal" is told by a person who wishes to be admitted that he hears strange voices. What is the psychiatrist supposed to assume? And what are the doctors and nurses in the wards supposed to assume when they speak to the man the next day, or the next week? They will assume that there is "something wrong with him," and that any statement he makes must be viewed in a different light from statements made by a man at a cocktail party or a basketball game. Which leads to the second idea Dr. Rosenhan has stumbled upon. It is the ecological principle of nonadditiveness. If you put a small drop of red ink into a beaker of clear water, you do not end up with a beaker of clear water plus a small drop of red ink. *All* of the water becomes colored. Telling a psychiatrist at a mental hospital that you hear strange voices works in exactly the same way. It changes the coloration of all subsequent state-ments you are likely to make.

To take another example, a witness who has been caught in one lie to a jury will find it difficult to persuade them that any of his testimony is truthful. Com-munication, in other words, is not a matter of simple addition—one statement plus another plus another. Every statement we make is limited and controlled by the context established by previous statements. If, on Monday, you insist that you hear strange voices, your denial of this on Tuesday will merely have the effect of con-firming that there is "something wrong" with you. All things considered, the "pseu-dopatients" in Dr. Rosenhan's experiment did pretty well to be released after an average confinement of nineteen days.

But there is still another principle of human communication in this "exper-iment" which, to this day, Dr. Rosenhan has perhaps failed to uncover. It is the idea that whatever you think is going on in any situation depends on how you "frame" or "label" the event, that is, where you stand in relation to it. For exam-ple, Dr. Rosenhan believes that his pseudopatients are "sane" because (1) they did not, in fact, hear any strange voices and (2) they claimed they did only as part of an "experiment." But from another and wider angle, the pseudopatients can be judged to be, if not insane, then at least very curious people. Why, for example, would a "normal" person deliberately have himself committed to a mental hospi-tal? How many people do you know who would even contemplate such an act? And if you knew someone who actually went through with it, you might think that a mental hospital is exactly where he belongs—with or without strange voices. But Dr. Rosenhan and his co-conspirators have legitimized the act—have "sanified" it, if you will—by calling it "an experiment." To them, an experiment is a semantic environment of unimpeachable legitimacy—which is to say, experimenters do not need to explain *their* behavior. Not only that, but Dr. Rosenhan wrote an article about his "experiment" which got published in a prestigious scientific journal. And so, Dr. Rosenhan, his pseudopatients, and the editors of *Science* magazine think they are all quite sane, that patients who *do* hear voices are insane, and that the doctors who labeled the experimenters "schizophrenic" are unreliable. I do not say that they are wrong. But it is just as reasonable to suppose that Dr. Rosenhan and his pseudopatients are strange and unreliable people themselves, and that the doctors in the mental hospitals were entirely competent and judicious. What *Sci-*

ence magazine should have done was publish two articles—one by Dr. Rosenhan about his experiment and another, from a broader perspective, about people who do such experiments and the various labels which might be used to evaluate their behavior. The first article would probably come under the heading of "psychology" (which Dr. Rosenhan is a professor of). The second would come under the heading of "meta-semantics." And it is to "meta-semantics" that I would like to call your attention. . . .

Meta-semantics is the discipline through which we may make our minds behave themselves. It is the best way I know to regulate and minimize the flow of our own stupid and crazy talk, and to make ourselves less accessible to the stupid and crazy talk of others.

The fundamental strategy of meta-semantics is to put ourselves, psychologically, outside the context of any semantic environment so that we may see it in its entirety, or at least from multiple perspectives. From this position—or variety of positions—it is possible to assess the meaning and quality of talk in relation to the totality of the environment in which it occurs, and with a relatively high degree of detachment. We become less interested in *participating* in semantic environments, more interested in *observing* them.

The move from a participant to a participant-observer position is almost always accompanied by a lessening of fervor, a suspicion of ideology, a willing suspension of belief, and a heightening of interest in the process of communication. For by declining the temptation to attend solely to *what* people are saying, we may focus our attention on the relationships of the *what* to the *whys* and *hows*. Every remark we hear or make is then transformed into a question or a series of questions about its purpose, its tone, its assumptions, its metaphorical structure, its grammatical biases, its conformity to the rules of discourse. Talking or listening to talk changes its character—from a limited reflexive response to a wide-ranging act of inquiry. And inquiry is, and always has been, the most durable and effective antagonist of unwise speech.

But one's will to conduct such inquiries is not summoned easily. Few of us have ever received much encouragement to reflect on the character of the semantic environments we are in. As children, we are educated to respond to *what* is being said to us, not to why and how. Any questions we might be tempted to ask about tone or role-structure or the purposes of a situation are usually disdained—in the home, in school, in church, in the army, in most places. Whatever natural inclinations we might have toward trying to understand "communication as a whole" are dealt with as impertinences, even as threats. We learn soon enough to think fast, not reflectively. The best metaphor I know for this state of affairs is the school examination. Can you imagine a student, upon being handed a test, expressing a desire to discuss the purposes of the test, the assumptions (about people and learning) on which it is based, the metaphors of the mind which are implicit in the form of the test, or the silent questions to which the idea of a test is the answer? The scene is close to unimaginable, but surely the teacher would insist that the student "Get on with it—and fast!" We want people to do what they are supposed to do, say what they are supposed to say, and think, if at all, strictly in the channels assigned to the matter. The rush to do and say, as well as fixed-channel thinking, are the essentials, the catalysts of almost all stupid and crazy talk. Yet the pressures toward them are very good indeed.

I suspect that behind it all is the fear that an excess of awareness will jeopardize the stability and continuity of a situation and thereby destroy it. But this fear, in my opinion, is not well-founded. Consider the case of two people attending a church service. The first knows what she is supposed to do and say but has little awareness of how her behavior is being managed. The second also knows what she is supposed to do and say but, at the same time, knows about how the environment has been designed and is fully aware of its multileveled purposes. She knows about identification reactions and reification and role-structures and fanaticism and all the rest. Will the meaning of the event be the same for both of them? I doubt it. But this does not mean that the second woman will refuse to participate in the event. Knowing that the semantic environment of religion may provide her with a sense of transcendence and her community with a sense of social cohesion, she may be quite willing to do and say exactly what is required of her. But her actions would rest on a foundation of awareness which permits her to be in control of her responses in a way that is not available to the other.

The key idea, then, in meta-semantics, is awareness, not cynicism or rejection. To be aware of what is going on in church, in school, in the army, in a sports arena, in a courtroom, in an office, in a laboratory does not imply that you will refuse to do and say what you are supposed to. In fact, the greater one's awareness of the purposes and structures of different semantic environments, the greater is one's sensitivity to the precariousness of all social order, that is, of all communication. To discover that what keeps us together is nothing more substantial than a curious set of symbols and a delicate system of rules is more likely to lead one to humility and conservatism than to iconoclasm and rebelliousness. Shaw's widely known observation that those who worship symbols and those who desecrate them are both idolators captures the sense of what I am trying to say. The man who genuflects without knowing why and the man who spits on the altar both suffer from a lack of control. They are *victims* of a mode of discourse. What we want are not victims but critics, and criticism can be done inside the church as well as out.

However, I am not prepared to argue that awareness of how semantic environments do their work will lead in one direction or another. Among those who have such knowledge, we will find a wide range of attitudes, including reverence, indifference, and skepticism. The point of a meta-sematic view of situations is that it frees us from both ritualistic compliance and reflexive rejection. Once free, we may reenter the situation (or refuse to reenter it) from an entirely different point of view and with a heightened degree of control. Although Dr. Skinner denies it, there can be important differences in levels of consciousness between two people who are doing exactly the same thing. One of them may have the potential to offer reasoned criticism, to modify his own behavior, to resist frivolous change or encourage judicious change, or even to retreat from the environment altogether, in an orderly fashion. The other may be completely dominated by the environment and have no options. And in that difference lies all the difference. For what distinguishes us from other species is not that we can say yes or no (which a dog or a crocodile can do as well), but that we can say yes while reserving the *option* to say no (or vice versa). The distinctively human capability is the provisional response, the critical response, the rational response, the delayed response, the self-conscious response. The meta-semantic response.

PROBES

Compare what Postman says about the meanings of sentences being not in sentences but in *situations* with Dean Barnlund's discussion of a "meaning-centered philosophy of communication" at the end of this chapter.

Give an example of your own experience of the operation of what Postman calls the "ecological principle of nonadditiveness."

Notice what happens when Postman "reframes" Dr. Rosenhan's experiment so that the doctor and the editors of *Science* magazine are the objects of inquiry rather than the mental hospital staff. What meaning shifts occur for you when he does that?

What does it mean to move from participant to participant-observer?

Does Postman's sketch of our typical childhood experience ring true for you? How so?

What point does Postman make in his description of the two churchgoers? How does his point relate to interpersonal communication?

In this essay Dean Barnlund, a speech communication teacher in San Francisco, outlines an approach to communication based on the transactional, or relational, perspective introduced and explained by Postman and me. Barnlund uses still another set of terms for the same basic idea. He calls the communication-as-action point of view "message-centered" and the relational, transactional view "meaning-centered."

Barnlund shows how theories that are not meaning-centered can't adequately explain human communication, a process he describes as being complex, circular, irreversible, unrepeatable, and involving the total personality of all the participants. He also explains that a meaning-centered philosophy focuses on "the state of mind, the assumptive world and the needs of the listener or observer." At the end of this piece, Barnlund talks about some of the ethical implications of this viewpoint.

Persons in my classes have often been able to use this message-centered/ meaning-centered distinction to summarize and clarify the whole action–interaction–transaction analysis I talked about before. If you view human communication as a process of message-creating, message-sending, and message-receiving, you're looking at it as an action or interaction. Only when you see how our communicating is a process of *meaning*-sharing do you begin to view it transactionally, or relationally.

Toward a Meaning-Centered Philosophy of Communication

Dean C. Barnlund

. . . To be acceptable, a philosophy of communication should fulfill the following criteria: (1) It should provide a satisfactory explanation of the aim of communi-

This is an abridgment of an article originally appearing in the *Journal of Communication* 12 (1962): 197–211. Reprinted by permission of the *Journal of Communication* and the author.

cation. (2) It should provide a technically adequate description of the process of communication. (3) It should provide a moral standard that will protect and promote that healthiest communicative behavior. Once this process is defined and its nature exposed, the way should be clear for facing the practical decisions involved in giving effective instruction.

AIM OF COMMUNICATION

We begin by asking why men communicate? What human need does it, or should it, satisfy? While there is almost universal agreement that communication is tied to the manipulation of symbols, there is widespread disagreement as to what constitutes effectiveness in this endeavor. A brief review of some abortive explanations of communication is essential because, in spite of repeated criticism, these conceptions continue to influence current training in speech.

One of these theories is that the aim of communication is to transmit information. Success hinges on mastery of the facts, effective arrangement of materials, and strength of expression. It is a message-centered philosophy of communication. And it is largely amoral. Critical standards for determining the effectiveness of communication, as in the critical evaluation of literature, are internal; they are found within the message itself. When a writer or speaker or critic asks, "Was it well said?" he is usually viewing communication as a mode of expression. The training in communication that follows from this premise and perspective is destined to be truncated and unrealistic. Talk is not a guarantee of communication. Facts and ideas are not shared because they are articulated loudly or even well. Messages do not influence automatically because of being broadcast on the mass media. The inadequacy of this approach lies in its neglect of the listener as terminus of the communicative act, in its failure to provide an explanation of how meaning arises through communication, and in its disregard for all but public and continuous discourse.

A second theory is that the aim of communication is to transfer ideas from one person to another. Here the listener is admitted as part of the communicative situation. The focus, however, in research and training, is upon the message formulator. Effectiveness in communication is thought to turn not only on the content and phrasing of the message, but on the intelligence and credibility of the source. Relatively little attention is paid to the listener other than to note that messages should be adapted to his interests. It ends by becoming a speaker-centered philosophy. Communicative events are explained largely in terms of the experiential milieu that shaped the mind of the speaker and find expression in his messages.

As an explanation of communication it, too, fails in several important respects. First, the listener tends to be regarded as a passive object, rather than an active force in communication. Unfortunately, it is not that simple to deposit ideas in another mind. Teachers of great intelligence and high purpose often find their lessons disregarded or misapplied. Messages flowing through an industrial complex are not received undistorted like images in a hall of mirrors. Second, this approach also fails to provide a satisfactory theory of meaning, and of how messages from highly credible sources can provoke so many and such contradictory meanings. Finally, it is too parochial. It neglects man's communication with himself—an area that is fast becoming one of the most vital in communication research—and it fails to account for the fact that communication is as often a matter of hiding or protecting what is in men's minds as it is a matter of revealing their thoughts and intentions.

Neither of these schools of thought, of course, omits the constituent elements in communication altogether. It is, rather, a question of emphasis. Questions of emphasis, however, are not irrelevant or inconsequential in establishing a productive orientation for a discipline. The pedagogical consequences of both of these approaches is to place a disproportionate emphasis on the source and message elements in communication. Both schools of thought tend, also, to minimize or overlook completely, the interactive and dynamic nature of the communicative process.

Communication, as I conceive it, is a word that describes the process of creating a meaning. Two words in this sentence are critical. They are "create" and "meaning." Messages may be generated from the outside—by a speaker, a television screen, a scolding parent—but meanings are generated from within. This position parallels that of Berlo when he writes, "Communication does not consist of the transmission of meaning. Meanings are not transmitted, nor transferable. Only messages are transmittable, and meanings are not in the message, they are in the message-user."[1] Communication is man's attempt to cope with his experience, his current mood, his emerging needs. For every person it is a unique act of creation involving dissimilar materials. But it is, within broad limits, assumed to be predictable or there could be no theory of communication.

The second, and more troublesome, word is "meaning." Meaning is not apparent in the ordinary flow of sensation. We are born into, and inhabit a world without "meaning." That life becomes intelligible to us—full of beauty or ugliness, hope or dispair—is because it is assigned that significance by the experiencing being. As Karl Britton put it, "A world without minds is a world without structure, without relations, without facts."[2] Sensations do not come to us, sorted and labeled, as if we were visitors in a vast, but ordered, museum. Each of us, instead, is his own curator. We learn to look with a selective eye, to classify, to assign significance.

Communication arises out of the need to reduce uncertainty, to act effectively, to defend or strengthen the ego. On some occasions words are used to ward off anxiety. On other occasions they are means of evolving more deeply satisfying ways of expressing ourselves. *The aim of communication is to increase the number and consistency of our meanings within the limits set by patterns of evaluation that have proven successful in the past, our emerging needs and drives, and the demands of the physical and social setting of the moment.* Communication ceases when meanings are adequate; it is initiated as soon as new meanings are required. However, since man is a homeostatic, rather than static, organism, it is impossible for him to discover any permanently satisfying way of relating all his needs; each temporary adjustment is both relieving and disturbing, leading to successively novel ways of relating himself to his environment.

. . . Communication, in this sense, may occur while a man waits alone outside a hospital operating room, or watches the New York skyline disappear at dusk. It can take place in the privacy of his study as he introspects about some internal doubt, or contemplates the fading images of a frightening dream. When man discovers meaning in nature, or in insight in his own reflections, he is a communication system unto himself. Festinger refers to this as "consummatory communication." The creation of meanings, however, also goes on in countless social situations where men talk with those who share or dispute their purposes. Messages are exchanged in the hope of altering the attitudes or actions of those around us.

This can be characterized as "instrumental communication," as long as we remember that these two purposes are not mutually exclusive.

What I am describing is a meaning-centered philosophy of communication. It admits that meaning in the sender, and the words of the messages, are important, but regards as most critical the state of mind, the assumptive world and the needs of the listener or observer. The impact of any message from "See me after class" to "What's good for General Motors is good for the country" is determined by the physical, personal, and social context, the most critical ingredient of which is the mind of the interpreter. Communication, so defined, does not require a speaker, a message, or a listener in the restricted sense in which these terms are used in the field of speech. All may be combined in a single person, and often are.

A theory that leaves out man's communication with himself, his communication with the world about him and a large proportion of his interactions with his fellow man, is not a theory of communication at all, but a theory of speechmaking. Indeed, it seems applicable to speechmaking only in the most formal and restricted sense of that word. There is little in the traditional view of speech that is helpful in the analysis of conversation, interviewing, conflict negotiations, or in the diagnosis of the whole span of communicative disorders and breakdowns that are receiving so much attention currently. Upon so limited a view of communication it is unlikely that there can develop theories of sufficient scope and stature to command the respect of other disciplines or of the larger public that ultimately decides our role in the solution of man's problems. The field of speech seems to be fast approaching what the airlines call a "checkpoint" where one loses the freedom to choose between alternative flight plans, between a limited interest in speechmaking, and a broad concern with the total communicative behavior of man. By defining communication operationally, by examining a wider range of communicative acts, the way might be prepared for making the startling theoretical advances that have, so far, not characterized our field.

THE COMMUNICATION PROCESS

A satisfactory philosophy should also provide a starting point for the technical analysis of communication. One way of accomplishing this is to ask what characteristics would have to be built into a scientific model that would represent, at the same time and equally well, the entire spectrum from intrapersonal to mass communication. It should not be a model that is mechanically or structurally faithful, but one that is symbolically and functionally similar. Space is too limited here to more than suggest a few of the principles that would have to be reflected in such a model.

1. Communication is not a thing, it is a process. Sender, message, and receiver do not remain constant throughout an act of communication. To treat these as static entities, as they often are in our research, is questionable when applied to the most extreme form of continuous discourse, is misleading when used to analyze the episodic verbal exchanges that characterize face-to-face communication, and is totally useless in probing man's communication with himself. Changes in any of these forces, and few forces remain constant very long, reverberate throughout the entire system. Students of communication are not dissecting a cadaver, but are probing the pulsing evolution of meaning in a living organism.
2. Communication is not linear, it is circular. There are many situations in

life where a simple, linear, causal analysis is useful. One thing leads to another. A, then B, then C. I push over the first domino and the rest, in turn, topple over. But this sort of thinking is not very helpful, though quite appealing in its simplicity, in studying communication. There is not first a sender, then a message, and finally an interpreter. There is, instead, what Henderson calls "mutual dependence" or what I have termed "interdependent functionalism." The words "sender" and "receiver" no longer name the elements in a communicative act, but indicate the point of view of the critic at the moment.

3. Communication is complex. Someone once said that whenever there is communication there are at least six "people" involved: The person you think yourself to be; the man your partner thinks you are; the person you believe your partner thinks you are; plus the three equivalent "persons" at the other end of the circuit. If, with as few as four constants, mathematicians must cope with approximately fifty possible relations, then we, in studying communication, where an even greater number of variables is concerned, ought to expound with considerable humility. In this age of Freudian and non-Freudian analysts, of information theory specialists, of structural linguists, and so on, we are just beginning to unravel the mysteries of this terribly involved, and therefore fascinating, puzzle.

4. Communication is irreversible and unrepeatable. The distinction being suggested here is between systems that are deterministic and mechanical, and those that are spontaneous and evolutionary. One can start a motor, beat a rug, or return a book. But you cannot start a man thinking, beat your son, or return a compliment with the same consequences. The words of a teacher, even when faithfully repeated, do not produce the same effect, but may lead to new insight, increased tension, or complete boredom. A moment of indifference or interest, a disarming or tangential remark, leave indelible traces.

5. Communication involves the total personality. Despite all efforts to divide body and mind, reason and emotion, thought and action, meanings continue to be generated by the whole organism. This is not to say that some messages do not produce greater or lesser dissonance, or shallower or deeper effects on the personality; it is only to hold that eventually every fact, conclusion, guilt, or enthusiasm must somehow be accommodated by the entire personality. The deeper the involvement produced by any communication, the sooner and more pervasive its effects upon behavior.

Research or instruction that disregards these characteristics of the communicative act would appear both unsound and of dubious value.

THE MORAL DIMENSION

The perennial and legitimate concern with ethics in the field of speech arises out of the inherent moral aspect of every interpersonal communication. As was noted earlier, the aim of communication is to transform chaotic sense impressions into some sort of coherent, intelligible, and useful relationship. When men do this privately, either in confronting nature or in assessing their own impulses, they are free to invent whatever meaning they can. But when men encounter each other, a moral issue invades every exchange because the manipulation of symbols always involves a purpose that is external to, and in some degree manipulative of, the interpreter of the message. The complexity of communication makes it difficult to know in advance, and with certainty, the impact of any bundle of words upon the receiver of them. The irreversibility of communication means that whatever means is provoked by a message cannot be annulled. A teacher may erase a blackboard, a colleague apologize, or an employer change his mind, but there is no way of erasing the effect of a threatening ultimatum, a bitter remark, or a crushing personal evaluation.

Meaning, in my opinion, is a private preserve and trespassers always run a risk. To speak of personal integrity at all is to acknowledge this. Any exchange of words is an invasion of the privacy of the listener which is aimed at preventing, restricting, or stimulating the cultivation of meaning. Briefly, three types of interference may be distinguished. First, there are messages whose intent is to coerce. Meaning is controlled by choosing symbols that so threaten the interpreter that he becomes capable of, and blind to, alternative meanings; second, there are messages of an exploitative sort in which words are arranged to filter the information, narrow the choices, obscure the consequences, so that only one meaning becomes attractive or appropriate; third, there is facilitative communication in which words are used to inform, to enlarge perspective, to deepen sensitivity, to remove external threat, to encourage independence of meaning. The values of the listener are, in the first case, ignored, in the second, subverted, in the third respected. While some qualification of this principle is needed, it appears that only facilitative communication is entirely consistent with the protection and improvement of man's symbolic experience. Unless a teacher is aware of these possibilities and appreciates the differences in these kinds of communication, it is unlikely that he will communicate responsibly in the classroom. . . .

Alfred North Whitehead once said that any discipline deserving a place in the curriculum must have a philosophy, a method, and a technique. The statement is undoubtedly true, but somewhat incomplete if philosophy, method, and technique exist as isolated units of instruction. Too often what results is that the technical and moral aspects remain separate, lacking any vital connection in the classroom, and more importantly, in the personality of the student. The result is schizophrenic communication. Men learn to blot out all but technical considerations when communicating in a coercive or prejudicial way, but turn around and attack someone else's communication on moral grounds when it proves technically superior to their own. It is this sort of inconsistency that fosters pathological communication and pathological personalities.

Integrative instruction in communication encourages the student to work out better meanings concerning his own communication with himself and his fellowmen. By "better" I refer to meanings that permit more consistency in his personality between what he assumes, what he sees, and what he does. By "better" I refer to meanings that will increase his openness, curiosity, and flexibility. By "better' I refer to meanings that will make him more independent, and more confident of his own judgment. . . .

References

1. David Berlo, *The Process of Communication* (New York: Holt, Rinehart and Winston, 1960), p. 175.
2. Karl Britton, *Communication: A Philosophical Study of Language* (New York: Harcourt, Brace, 1939), p. 206.

PROBES

How do you respond when Barnlund defines communication as the "process of creating a meaning"? Does that describe what you're doing when you communicate?

What are some examples from your own experience of the irreversibility and unrepeatability of communication?

Do you agree with Barnlund that communication has a "moral dimension"? How so?

Barnlund says that communication is "meaning-centered" and that meanings are "within" persons. How are these ideas similar to, and different from, what I say at the beginning of this chapter about communication happening *between* persons? Are meanings "inside" or "between"?

> *The difference between talking "at" and talking "with" is the difference between touching, and touching and being touched.*
>
> HUGH PRATHER

CHAPTER 3

VERBAL CODES

He wished to be crowned
robed in language
and seated on a verb
                    JOHN ANGUS CAMPBELL

▏▌

The basic ingredients, or raw materials, of human communication are usually divided into two large categories—verbal cues and nonverbal cues. As Knapp mentions in the next chapter, there are some problems with that division; it's sort of a "words" and "other" categorization. But the division is made because those two ingredients tend to work differently; they perform somewhat different communicative functions.

I say "tend to" and "somewhat" because the differences between words and nonwords are often differences of degree. Words generally carry most of the information load in human communication. You use words to describe, explain, outline, detail, compare and contrast, and so on. Nonverbal cues, on the other hand, generally indicate a lot about how each person defines himself or herself, what the feeling or emotional content is, and so on.

It's important, though, to develop an awareness of both codes. Consequently, the purpose of the next two selections is to introduce how words work in communication; the three articles in Chapter 4 will do the same for nonverbal codes.

Gary D'Angelo and I wrote this next selection to make several points. The first point is that the study of verbal language is complex and has been going on for a long time. The second is that words don't do just one thing; in fact, they work in at least seven different ways; to refer to or stand for something else, to perform an action, to evoke emotion, to affect the way you perceive things and people, to reduce uncertainty, to express abstract ideas, and to bring people together. We also mention how the English language makes it difficult to talk about ongoing processes, a phenomenon you might have noticed as you read the attempts in Chapter 2 to talk about the ongoing processes of communicative transactions and relationships. We also note the subtle sexism that's present in much of our language. But the final function of language is the one that relates most clearly to our interest in *interpersonal* communication. Words, as we suggest there, can bring people together.

How Words Work in Communication

John Stewart and Gary D'Angelo

All communication situations include nonverbal cues, and most of them consist of *both* verbal and nonverbal cues. Occasionally, verbal and nonverbal cues "work" in similar ways.

For example, the traffic sign serves the same purpose as the words NO LEFT TURN. But it's important to remember that in most human communication situations, these two kinds of cues "work" in significantly different ways. In other words,

John Stewart and Gary D'Angelo, *Together: Communicating Interpersonally,* 2nd ed. © 1980, Addison-Wesley Publishing Co., Inc., Chapter 1, pp. 23–33. Reprinted with permission.

when humans are communicating, a word just doesn't do the same thing as a sign; vocabulary choice doesn't affect the situation or the persons involved in the same way that tone of voice or facial expression does. Words are good for some things and almost worthless for others. Nonverbal cues are sometimes the most important part of human communication, and sometimes they're almost irrelevant. . . .

As we said, verbal cues are words. That seems easy enough; everybody knows what a word is, right? Well, yes and no. Scholars have been studying language since about 400 B.C., when an ancient named Panini wrote a lengthy commentary on the *Vedas,* the sacred books of India. In the nineteenth century, such researchers as Wilhelm von Humboldt and Ferdinand de Saussure made important advances in linguistics, and the twentieth century's leading linguist, MIT's Noam Chomsky, became almost as famous as Andrew Young. But these scholars have not yet agreed on the defining characteristics of the basic unit of their study, the *word*.

There are several problems involved. For example, if you define language as what people write, then you can define a word as a group of letters set off by space. But linguists generally agree that written language is only a reflection of what people say, that the spoken word is primary. And that creates difficulties. Would you say that your "Howareya?" to somebody you meet on the street is one *spoken* word or three? Is "loves" a different word from "love," or are they two forms of the same word? How about "lover " and "loving"? Is "bazoo" a word? The letters fit together, and some English-speaking people use it when they talk, but it doesn't seem to be in any English dictionary. What about the "words" Don Martin creates? Is "shklork" a word? "Thak"? "Shtonk"? How about "Gish Goosh"?

Obviously, we aren't going to be able to answer a question that's stumped linguists for more than 2,000 years. For our purposes it'll be good enough to avoid the problem by agreeing that things like "cat," "mainsail," and "empathy" are words and that things like

#*?%&,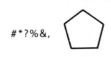

are not. That approach won't handle the borderline cases, but they're fairly uncommon, anyway. The main point we want to make is that studying words is not as simple as it might at first appear to be.

© 1971, 1978 by Don Martin and E. C. Publications, Inc.

WORDS REFER TO OR STAND FOR

Not only is it next to impossible to define exactly what you're studying; it's also difficult to identify all the ways in which words function in human communication. It's often assumed that all words are names for things, that they always *refer to* or *stand for,* in one way or another, the things they name. You've probably heard that before—the word "dog" refers to a certain kind of four-legged animal, "tree" to a certain kind of botanical life, and "rock" to a hard, stony object *or* to a type of music, or . . .

There are obviously some problems with the generalization that words function by referring to things. But it's a popular, even if inaccurate, belief. Many basic English and speech communication texts will reprint C. K. Ogden and I. A. Richards's famous triangle of meaning to explain how words work. The triangle looks roughly like this:

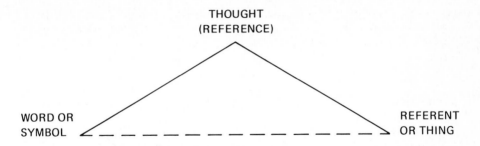

Ogden and Richards first used that diagram in 1923 to make a number of points, one of which was that words do refer to things but that there is no direct link between a word or symbol and the thing it refers to or stands for. That's why the bottom line of the triangle is dotted.[1]

The problem with their view is that it is oversimplified. Sometimes some words function in communication by referring to some "referent," but other times they don't. Consider the last sentence, for example. The word "they" in that sentence does refer—to "some words." But what referent does the word "some" stand for in that sentence? What does "by" or "sometimes" refer to? In order to answer those questions, you have to invent all sorts of strange entities, like "a conditional expectation" (the referent for "sometimes") or "a conjunctive function" (the referent for "by"). It's simpler and a whole lot more accurate to recognize that the generalization just doesn't work. Sometimes some words function by referring to "things in the world" but not always. Words work in several other important ways, too.

WORDS PERFORM ACTIONS

Sometimes you use words not to talk about things but to *perform an action*. The words "I do" or "I will" in a marriage ceremony do not refer to a thing; they make up part of the act of getting married. "I christen thee" at a ship launching works the same way, as does "I promise" or "I'll bet you. . . ." When you make a serious bet or an important bargain with somebody, the words you use to seal the agreement don't refer to objects or events or even states of mind. They constitute, for example, the act of betting itself. When you sing in the shower or curse your smashed finger, these words are also functioning as actions; they don't "stand for" or "refer to" actions. Cursing *is* a part of being angry; singing is part of being happy, romantic, melancholy, or whatever. In short, *performing actions* is one of the things we often use words for without realizing that we're doing it.

Sometimes people try to sharply divide words and actions, as with "Let's stop talking and start *doing* something!" But that kind of thinking can both cheapen your view of the language you use and distort what's happening as you communicate. Saying "I love you" is a significant action; it's more significant to some people than to others, but it is always part of some kind of commitment. If you remember that many words do perform actions, you'll be less likely to contribute to misunderstandings that are revealed by comments like "I *do* feel that way; didn't you hear what I said?" or "Look, when I said I'd do it, I meant it. Don't you trust me?"

WORDS EVOKE EMOTIONS

Have you ever had the experience of being so caught up in a book, short story, or magazine article that you began to get angry, nervous, or excited? Ever since his daughters Marcia and Lisa were born, John has been a "sucker" for stories about families with children and especially about a family crisis with a happy ending. This Sunday's paper included a story about the reunion of an Italian family whose eldest son had come to the United States nine years ago. The son, along with his new wife and in-laws, was just now returning to the village he grew up in. The story described the first meeting between the son, his widowed mother, and his brothers and sisters, and it was a great human-interest story—happy, poignant, and memory-evoking. John was so much into the story at one point that his eyes were watering and he felt like crying. And all from words! No pictures, even!

You've probably had a similar experience while reading an exciting adventure, science fiction, or love story. Many people respond that way to J. R. R. Tolkien's stories about the Magic Ring and the inhabitants of Middle Earth—Bilbo, Frodo, Gandalf the wizard, the Orcs, Nazguls, Balrogs, and Elves. Others really get into sports stories or accounts of handicapped people who succeed. You might even feel a little silly when you realize how emotional you've gotten over nothing more than a bunch of black marks on a page. But words have that power. They can evoke strong emotions.

Spoken words can, too. There are certain terms that are applied to people of your race or religion that can trigger immediate emotional responses. "Boy," for example, "Jap," "Jew," "round eye," or "Greaser." If you're black, being called "nigger" can also be a really *positive* thing—if it is said by the right person and in the right context. In one sense those words are nothing more than sounds—just as written words are nothing more than marks on a page. But we know that they have power. Language can and often does evoke all kinds of emotions.

WORDS AFFECT WHAT YOU PERCEIVE

Later we'll be talking about how your perception affects your communicating. When you get there, you might keep in mind the idea that you perceive what you do partly because of the words you know how to use. Linguists disagree on how words affect perception—and how *much*—but most language scholars agree that the existence of many words for "horse" in Arabic, for "snow" in Eskimo, and for "yam" in the language of the Trobriand Islanders is tied to how these people perceive horses, snow, and yams. This point of view, often called "linguistic determinism" or "the Sapir–Whorf hypothesis," has been summarized by the anthropologist Benjamin Lee Whorf.

> The background linguistic system [in other words the grammar] of each language is not merely a reproducing instrument for voicing ideas but rather is itself the shaper of ideas, the program and guide for the individual's mental activity, for his analysis of impressions. . . . We dissect nature along lines laid down by our native language.[2]

In other words, if you've spent enough time on boats and around the water to learn a dozen different words for water conditions, you will perceive more differences in the water than will the person who was born and raised in Cheyenne, Oklahoma City, or Calgary. That person might distinguish between "waves" and "smooth water," but you will see and feel differences between ripples, chop, and swells that he or she won't even notice.

As we wrote this book, we discovered that our native language sometimes limits our perception, too. Unlike some other languages, English maintains clear distinctions between subjects and predicates, causes and effects, beginnings and ends. The word system of the Navaho doesn't do that. According to Harry Hoijer, Navaho speakers characteristically talk in terms of processes—uncaused, ongoing, incomplete, dynamic movings. The word Navahos use for "wagon," for example, translates roughly as "wood rolls about hooplike."[3] As Hoijer explains, the Navaho words that we would translate "He begins to carry a stone" mean not that the actor produces an action, but that the person is simply linked with a given round object and with an already existing, continuous movement of all round objects in the universe.[4] The English language is significantly different from that. It requires you to talk in terms of present, past, future, cause and effect, beginning and end. But some things English speakers would like to discuss just can't be expressed in these terms. We would like to be able to talk more clearly about the ever-changing, processlike, ongoing nature of communication and about the betweenness of the quality of communication we're calling "interpersonal." But the English language makes it difficult to do that, as you'll probably notice when you read through parts of this book.

You may also notice that we've had some trouble with the male orientation of standard American English. Many people have made the point that our language includes an incredible number of terms that subtly but effectively limit our perception of women, and in our culture we often use the male pronoun "he," "his," or "him" to make a general or universal reference to people.[5] For example, we speak of "mankind"; we tend to say that a person goes "his" way; and professional limitations are suggested by such job titles as "salesman," "foreman." "fireman," "policeman," "chairman of the board," and "metermaid." As Aileen Hernandez, past president of the National Organization for Women, has noted:

> There's a "housewife" but no "househusband"; there's a "housemother" but no "housefather"; there's a "kitchenmaid" but no "kitchenman"; unmarried women cross the threshold from "bachelor girl" to "spinster" to "old maid," but unmarried men are "bachelors" forever.[6]

Much of the sexism of American English may seem trivial and unimportant. But when all the subtle terms and uses are put together, they significantly affect the way we perceive female persons.

The same thing happens to other groups. Ozzie Davis's essay, "The English Language Is My Enemy,"[7] details the way our meanings for the words "black" and "white" affect our perceptions of black and white persons. Similarly, language terms and uses also severely limit the ways in which people perceive Asians, Chicanos, native Americans, and other racial and ethnic minorities.

We don't pretend to offer a simple solution to this potential problem, although this entire book suggests one set of ways to respond. But if you see your language as just something that *represents* your thinking, something that enables you to make public what you've been privately perceiving, you are missing one of its important functions. *Your language does not just represent your reality; it helps to shape it.* And the same thing is true for each person you communicate with.

WORDS CAN REDUCE UNCERTAINTY

When you see a large, retangular, green and white freeway sign in the distance, you know that it could possibly indicate many different things including an approaching exit, a lane change, or the mileage to the next large town. When you get close enough to read the first word, the number of possibilities is reduced significantly, and when you can read all the words, your original uncertainty about the sign is reduced even more. The goal of sign writers is to use words that reduce your uncertainty to nearly zero. They try to avoid ambiguously worded signs

> SAN FRANCISCO TRUCKS PROCEED
>
> RIGHT LANE MERGE LEFT
>
> ONE MILE

in favor of those whose meaning is unmistakable.

> LAST EXIT BEFORE
>
> TOLL BRIDGE

Words can also reduce your uncertainty about people. When a friend you're used to seeing every day suddenly disappears for several days, you know that the absence could indicate many different things. Your friend might be ill, in trouble, angry at something you've done, tired of being around you, upset about something, cramming for an exam, moving, or a dozen other things. Your uncertainty about why your friend is absent can be reduced only when the person explains verbally—in speaking or in writing—that "I took a few days off to go home and collect my thoughts."

The guessing game "Twenty Questions" is based on the ability of language to reduce uncertainty. The point of the game is for one person to guess the identity of an object that another person is thinking about. The questioner can ask no more than twenty questions, the "yes" and "no" answers to which should enable her or him to narrow the range of possible objects to the one the other person has in mind. It's often fun to see how eighteen or nineteen well-chosen questions can lead to something as unlikely as "the left front wheel of that bus" or "the statue on top of the bank building."

Not all words *do* function to reduce uncertainty, but they *can*. They can categorize, point, specify, distinguish, and clarify much more efficiently than can nonverbal cues, and that's one reason they're so important for interpersonal communication.

WORDS CAN EXPRESS ABSTRACT IDEAS

If you're standing in the kitchen and you want to tell your spouse where the coffee is, you can point. If you just want to express your anger or delight, you can shriek or chuckle. But if you want to find out why the person who interviewed you didn't think your four years on the job was "relevant work experience," if you want to analyze the effects of the Vietnam War on American foreign policy, or if you want to clarify the reasons behind your position on the abortion issue, you will need to use words. Language is the only means we have of developing ideas, solving problems, exploring complex interrelationships, or expressing anything beyond the simplest logical functions. You can express "Yes" or "No" without words, but try "Maybe," "It all depends," or "Give me a chance to talk with Allen and the people in London, and then either I'll write you or my secretary will call by next Friday." Those ideas cannot be communicated clearly without using written or spoken words.

Even the most primitive languages enable the people who speak them to develop and express abstract ideas. Since, as the Ogden and Richards triangle illustrates, words are not tied directly to the things we use them to talk about, we can discuss oil shipments, religious beliefs, time schedules, bank balances, and weather conditions even when those elements are actually not physically present. Language allows us to feel with the most complex and even the not directly observable parts of our environments. Without words our communicative transactions would be drastically limited.

Although you may well understand, at some level of awareness, that only words have this power to express abstract ideas, you may still sometimes communicate as if you didn't know it. Have you ever said or felt, "If you really cared about me, you'd *know* how I feel"? Often what that means is something like this: "I'm *nonverbally* expressing my disappointment over the canceled date, my eagerness to try again in spite of my fears, or whatever, and you should understand those complex and abstract thoughts and feelings just from my tone of voice, facial expression, and posture." When we talk about the situation that way, you can see how unreasonable a position that is. Complexities and abstractions require *verbal* expression—words. Nonverbal cues are powerful ways to express emotions, but they are inherently ambiguous, imprecise. If you want to clarify not only feelings but also judgments, opinions, or positions on an issue, you have to use words.

WORDS CAN PROMOTE HUMAN CONTACT

The final function of words that we want to mention here is rather difficult to explain. Words, especially spoken words, can work to promote human contact, to bring people together. Martin Buber describes the unifying function of words this way:

> The importance of the spoken word, I think, is grounded in the fact that it does not want to remain with the speaker. It reaches out toward a hearer, it lays hold of him, it even makes the hearer into a speaker, if perhaps only a soundless one.[8]

Buber's point is that your words are both intensely private, personal, individual things *and* public, available to someone else. Consequently, thoughtful speaking can make some parts of *you* present to others. Gerard Egan calls this kind of speaking *Logos* or "language filled with the person who is speaking. . . . Logos here means translating oneself or handing oneself over to others, through the medium of speech."[9]

If Francisco was really angry at Richard, for example, he could punch him out, avoid him, or shout him down with obscenities and verbal abuse. None of those responses would promote much contact, though. If Francisco wanted to do something *with* Richard about his anger, he might also *say* something like this: "Look, Richard, I'm really mad at you. I could try to swallow my anger, or I could blow up, but I don't think that either of those would solve anything, because I think that in a way my anger is really *our* problem, yours and mine, and I'd like to talk it through with you. How about it?"[10] If you can overlook the artificial sound that comes from those words in print, perhaps you can see that this language could work to help Francisco and Richard meet each other. It would be risky and difficult, but it might also be very satisfying and productive.

What we're talking about here is the sense in which words are truly *symbolic*. In Greek the word "symbolic" is made up of "bolos," which means "to throw," and "sym," which means "with" or "together." One meaning of "symbolic," then, is "throwing together," or *"unifying."* And words can work that way. Think of the times you've found a friend just by listening to somebody talk—in person, on the radio or television, or in a book. His or her words helped bring you together. The words we use on these pages can bring us closer together with you, too. They can help bridge the gap between us. Again, we know that they *don't* always work that way, but they *can,* just as your words can help you move closer to others.

Words, in short, are a flexible and richly varied part of many communication contexts. They can *refer* the persons involved to nonverbal things or events. Sometimes we use words to *perform actions.* Words can also *evoke emotion,* and the language you're able to use even *affects the way you perceive.* Words can *reduce uncertainty,* and they are necessary whenever you want to *express abstract ideas.* Finally, and perhaps most important for us, words can *unify* persons, can bring humans together.

References

1. C. K. Ogden and I. A. Richards, *The Meaning of Meaning* (New York: Harcourt, Brace, and World, 1923), pp. 8–12.
2. John B. Carroll, ed., *Language Thought and Reality: Selected Writings of Benjamin Lee Whorf* (New York: Wiley, 1956), pp. 212–213.
3. Harry Hoijer, "Cultural Implications of Some Navaho Linguistic Categories," *Language* **23** (1951): 117.
4. Hoijer, p. 119.
5. "One Small Step for Genkind," *New York Times Magazine,* April 16, 1972.
6. Aileen Hernandez, "The Preening of America," *Star News,* Pasadena, California, 1971 New Year's edition, cited in Haig A. Bosmajian, "The Language of Sexism," *ETC: A Review of General Semantics* 29 (September 1972): 307.
7. Ozzie Davis, "The English Language Is My Enemy," *Language in America,* ed. Neil Postman, Charles Weingartner, and Terence P. Moran (New York: Pegasus, 1969), pp. 73–82.
8. Martin Buber, "The Word That Is Spoken," *The Knowledge of Man,* ed. Maurice Friedman, trans. Maurice Friedman and Ronald Gregor Smith (New York: Harper & Row, 1965), p. 112.
9. Gerard Egan, "The Elements of Human Dialogue: Pathos, Logos, Poiesis," *Encounter: Group Process for Interpersonal Growth* (Monterey, Calif.: Brooks/Cole, 1970), p. 236.
10. Egan uses this example on p. 240.

PROBES

How do words function most often in your communication experience? To refer or stand for? To perform an action? Evoke emotion? Affect perception? Reduce uncertainty? Express abstract ideas? Bring people together?

Without jumping forward to the next chapter, can you identify some ways that the *nonverbal* parts of communication affect how the *verbal* parts function?

Do you agree that the English language promotes sexism? Why or why not?

What's your most recent experience when *words* (not touch, tone of voice, or other nonverbal cues) made it possible for you to make contact with another person?

> *If I want to talk to someone and I am stuck for something to say, one of the simplest ways for me to get started is to state honestly what I am experiencing: "I want very much to talk to you but no words are coming."*
>
> HUGH PRATHER

Virginia Satir is a family counselor who has spent over forty years helping parents and children communicate. Her small book *Making Contact* is her response to the many persons who asked her to write down the ideas and suggestions that she's been sharing in workshops and seminars. As she says in the introduction, "The framework of this book is the BARE BONES of the possible, which I believe applies to *all* human beings. You, the reader, can flesh out the framework to fit you."

I like the simple, straightforward, no-nonsense way she talks about words, and I think she's pinpointed several insights that can help all of us communicate better. If we did, as she suggests, pay more attention to the ways we use the ten key words she discusses, I'm convinced that we'd experience considerably less conflict, misunderstanding, and frustration. See if you don't agree.

Paying Attention to Words

Virginia Satir

Words are important tools for contact. They are used more consciously than any other form of contact. I think it is important to learn how to use words well in the service of our communication.

Words cannot be separated from sights, sounds, movements, and touch of the person using them. They are one package.

However, for the moment, let's consider only words. Using words is literally the outcome of a whole lot of processes that go on in the body. All the senses, the nervous system, brain, vocal chords, throat, lungs, and all parts of the mouth are involved. This means that, physiologically, talking is a very complicated process. . . .

Virginia Satir, *Making Contact* (Millbrae, Calif.: Celestial Arts, 1976). The excerpt covers twelve pages in the text of Satir's book. Courtesy of Celestial Arts Pub. Co., 231 Adrian Rd., Millbrae, Calif. 94030.

If you think of your brain as a computer, storing all your experiences on tapes, then the words you pick will have to come from those tapes. Those tapes represent all our past experiences, accumulated knowledge, rules, and guides. There is nothing else there until new tapes are added. I hope that what you are reading will help you to add new tapes out of getting new experiences.

The words we use have an effect on our health. They definitely influence emotional relationships between people and how people can work together.

WORDS HAVE POWER

Listen to what you say and see if you are really saying what you mean. Nine people out of ten can't remember what they said sixty seconds ago, others remember.

There are ten English words that it is well to pay close attention to, to use with caution and with loving care: *I, You, They, It, But, Yes, No, Always, Never, Should.*

If you were able to use these special words carefully it would already solve many contact problems created by misunderstanding.

I

Many people avoid the use of the word *I* because they feel they are trying to bring attention to themselves. They think they are being selfish. Shades of childhood, when you shouldn't show off, and who wants to be selfish? The most important thing is that using "I" clearly means that you are taking responsibility for what you say. Many people mix this up by starting off with saying "you." I have heard people say "You can't do that." This is often heard as a "put-down," whereas "I think you can't do that" makes a more equal relationship between the two. It gives the same information without the put-down.

"I" is the pronoun that clearly states "me" when I am talking so it is important to say it. If you want to be clear when you are talking, no matter what you say, it is important to state clearly your ownership of *your* statement.

"I am saying that the moon is made of red cheese."

(This is clearly your picture)

instead of saying . . .

"The moon is made of red cheese."

(This is a new law)

Being aware of your clear use of "I" is particularly crucial when people are already in crisis. It is more clear to say "It is my picture that . . ." (which is an ownership statement). Whoever has the presence of mind to do this can begin to alter an escalating situation. When "I" is not clear, it is easy for the hearer to get a "you" message, which very often is interpreted as a "put-down."

You

The use of the word *you* is also tricky. It can be felt as an accusation when only reporting or sharing is intended.

"You are making things worse" can sound quite different if the words "I think" are added. "I think you are making things worse. . . ."

When used in clear commands or directions, it is not so easily misunderstood. For example, "I want you to . . ." or "You are the one I wanted to speak to."

They

The use of *they* is often an indirect way of talking about "you." It is also often a loose way of spreading gossip.

"They say . . ."

"They" can also be some kind of smorgasbord that refers to our negative fantasies. This is especially true in a situation where people are assessing blame. If we know who "they" are we can say so.

How many times do we hear "They won't let me." "They will be upset." "They don't like what I am doing." "They say . . ."

If someone else uses it, we can ask "Who is your *they?*"

The important part of this is to have clear who "they" are so that inaccurate information is not passed on and it is clear exactly who is being referred to. Being clear in this way seems to add to everyone's security. Information becomes concrete which one can get hold of, instead of being nebulous and perhaps posing some kind of threat.

It

It is a word that can easily be misunderstood because it often isn't clear what "it" refers to. "It" is a word that has to be used with care.

The more clear your "it" is, the less the hearer fills it in with his own meaning. Sometimes "it" is related to a hidden "I" message. One way to better understand your "it" is to substitute "I" and see what happens. "It isn't clear" changed to "I am not clear" could make things more accurate and therefore easier to respond to.

"It often happens to people" is a statement that when said straight could be a comfort message that says, "The thing you are talking about has happened to me. I know how feeling humiliated feels."

To be more sure that we are understood, it might be wiser to fill in the details.

But

Next is the word *but*.

"But" is often a way of saying "yes" and "no" in the same sentence.

"I love you *but* I wish you would change your underwear more often."

This kind of use can easily end up with the other person feeling very uncomfortable, uneasy, and frequently confused.

Try substituting the word "and" for "but," which will clarify the situation. Your body will even feel different.

By using "but" the speaker is often linking two different thoughts together, which is what causes the difficulty.

Thus "I love you, but I wish you would change your underwear more often" could be two expressions.

"I love you" and "I wish you would change your underwear more often."

It could also represent someone's best, although fearful, attempt to make an uncomfortable demand by couching the demand in a love context, hoping the other person would not feel hurt.

If this is the case, what would happen if the person were to say "I want to ask something of you that I feel very uncomfortable about. I would like you to change your underwear more often.''

Yes, No

A clear "yes" and "no" are important. Too many people say "yes, but" or "yes, maybe" or "no" just to be on the safe side, especially if they are in a position of power.

When "yes" or "no" are said clearly, and they mean NOW and not forever, and it is further clear "yes" and "no" relate to an issue rather than a person's value, then "yes" and "no" are very helpful words in making contact.

People can get away with much misuse of words when trust and good feeling have been established and when the freedom to comment is around. However, so often people feel so unsure about themselves that the lack of clarity leaves a lot of room for misunderstanding and consequent bad feelings. It is easy to build up these bad feelings once they are started.

"No" is a word that we all need and need to be able to use when it fits. So often when people feel "no," they say "maybe" or "yes" to avoid meeting the issue. This is justified on the basis of sparing the other's feelings. It is a form of lying and usually invites distrust, which, of course, is death to making contact.

When the "no" isn't clear, the "yes" can also be mistrusted. Have you ever heard "He said yes, but he doesn't really mean it."

Always, Never

Always is the positive form of a global word. *Never* is the negative form. For example:

Always clean up your plate.

Never leave anything on your plate.

The literal meaning of these words is seldom accurate and the directions seldom applicable to life situations. There are few cases in life where something is always *or* never. Therefore to try to follow these demands in all situations will surely end up in failure like the rules I described earlier.

Often the use of these words is a way to make emotional emphasis, like . . .

"You *always* make me mad."

meaning really . . .

"I am NOW very mad at you."

If the situation were as the speaker states, the adrenals would wear out.

Sometimes the words *always* and *never* hide ignorance. For example, someone has spent just five minutes with a person and announces,

"He is always bright."

In most cases the literal use of these two words could not be followed in all times, places and situations. Furthermore, they are frequently untrue. For the most part they become emotionally laden words that harm rather than nurture or enlighten the situation.

I find that these words are often used without any meaning in any literal sense.

These words are related to the inhuman rules I talked about earlier, so they have the potential for the same unnecessary guilt and inadequacy feelings because they are almost impossible to apply.

Should

"Ought" and "should" are other trap words from which it is easy to imply that there is something wrong with you—you have failed somehow to measure up.

Often the use of these words implies stupidity on someone's part . . .

"You should have known better."

This is frequently heard as an accusation. Sometimes it merely represents some friendly advice. When people use the words "ought" and "should," often they are trying to indicate a dilemma in which they have more than one direction to go at a time—one may be pulling harder than the rest although the others are equally important . . .

"I like this, but I should get that."

When your words are these, your body often feels tight. There are no easy answers to the pulls which "ought" and "should" represent. Biologically we really can go in only one direction at a time.

When your body feels tight your brain often freezes right along with your tight body, and so your thinking becomes limited as well.

Hearing yourself use the words *ought* and *should* can be a tip-off to you that you are engaged in a struggle. Perhaps instead of trying to deal with these opposing parts as one, you can separate them and make two parts.

"I like this . . ." (one part)

"But I should get that"

translated into . . .

"I also need that . . ." (a second part).

Such a separation may be helpful in considering each piece separately and then considering them together.

When you do this your body has a chance to become a little looser, thus freeing some energy to negotiate a bit better.

When I am in this spot, I can help myself by asking whether I will literally die in either situation. If the answer is *no,* then I have a different perspective, and I can more easily play around with alternatives, since I am now out of a win-loss feeling in myself. I won't die. I may be only a little deprived or inconvenienced at most.

Start paying attention to the words you use.

Who is your *they?*

What is your *it?*

What does your *no* mean?

What does your *yes* mean?

Is your *I* clear?

Are you saying *never* and *always* when you mean sometimes and when you want to make emotional emphasis?

How are you using *ought* and *should?*

PROBES

When you're in a conversation, can you recall what you said sixty seconds earlier? Try it. What do you notice?

How does Virginia's point about using "I" relate to Pemberton's distinctions among absolutistic, relativistic, and transactional assumptions?

Notice how, as she says, "it" and "they" both often work to hide the fact that some *I* is actually talking. When do you hear yourself using "it" and "they" that way?

What happens when you substitute "and" for "but"?

Do you experience your body responding as Virginia describes to the words "ought" and "should"?

||||||||||||||||||||||||||||||||||||||||||||||||||||||||||||||||||||||||||||||||||||||||||||||||||||||||||||||||||||||||||||||||||||||||||||||||

This discussion comes from a widely used, practical book about interpersonal effectiveness and self-actualization. David Johnson is a researcher and teacher who has written a great deal about how interpersonal communication can enhance personal health and well-being. Although this selection is brief, it includes some very helpful advice.

Johnson makes the point, as does Robert Bolton in Chapter 7, that as we are growing up, most of us are not taught many of the attitudes and skills that could make us more effective communicators. Johnson's target is our lack of training in how to use words to express feelings so that others can understand us. As he says, "Years and years of our education focus on communicating ideas clearly and unambiguously, yet relatively little education is given in communicating feelings clearly and unambiguously."

Johnson echoes one of the points I made in Chapter 2 about objects and persons when he writes, "A person without feelings is not a person at all; he or she is a machine." He lists almost forty words you can use to label feelings and emphasizes the importance of thinking about feelings in order to express them appropriately.

You might want to discuss with others Johnson's list of six difficulties that can arise when people don't recognize, accept, and constructively express feelings. It seems to me that he's making several important points here, including number 2 about the fallacy of "being rational, logical, and objective," and number 5 about "implying a demand while expressing your feelings."

After acknowledging the point that expressions of feeling can be both verbal and nonverbal, Johnson focuses on the former. His primary point is that we can profit greatly from learning to express feelings directly in words. He outlines the four elements of a full verbal feeling-description and highlights its two most essential features: a first-person pronoun and a "feeling name, simile, action urge, or figure of speech."

Try not to assume from the brevity and clarity of what Johnson says here that the skill he's discussing is simple. It takes thought, discussion with others, commitment, and practice to translate Johnson's suggestions into effective action. But it is well worth the effort.

Expressing Your Feelings Verbally

David W. Johnson

SAYING WHAT YOU FEEL

Feeling the warmth, support, acceptance, and caring of close friendships is one of the most exciting aspects of being alive. And feelings are especially wonderful when they are shared with other people. One of the most rewarding aspects of relationships is sharing personal feelings. The more you share your feelings with other people, the happier and more meaningful your life will be. Yet one of the characteristics of our society is that we are not given much training in how to express feelings in such a way that there will be little chance of misunderstanding. Years and years of our education focus on communicating ideas clearly and unambiguously, yet relatively little education is given in communicating feelings clearly and unambiguously. And although the words that describe aspects of friendships, such as "like," "love," "dislike," and "hate," are among the most frequently used in the English language, our language has relatively few words that label feeling states. Sanskrit, for example, is reputed to have over nine hundred words describing various feeling states, but English has fewer than fifty, if one excludes slang and figures of speech.

To experience emotions and express them to another person is not only a major source of joy, it is also necessary for your psychological well-being. It is natural to have feelings. The capacity to feel is as much a part of being a person as is the capacity to think and reason. A person without feelings is not a person at all; he or she is a machine. The quest of individuals who really enjoy life is to feel a greater range of emotions and to build relationships in which emotions are aroused and allowed positive expression. Feeling and expressing caring for another person, feeling and expressing love for another person, even feeling and expressing anger toward another person are all potentially highly rewarding and beautiful experiences. And it is through experiencing and sharing feelings that close friendships are built and maintained.

There is a wide variety of feelings you may have while relating to other people. Here is a partial list of the feelings you may experience:

happy	confused	cautious	proud
pleased	surprised	confident	anxious
daring	silly	glad	grieving
bored	lonely	excited	confused
satisfied	elated	delighted	overjoyed
uncomfortable	apathetic	fearful	frightened
ecstatic	hopeful	embarrassed	humiliated
angry	weary	supported	accepted
shy	scared	discontented	
loved	appreciated	sad	

Feelings are internal physiological reactions to your experiences. You may begin to tremble, sweat, or have a surge of energy. Your heart may beat faster. Tears may come. Although feelings are internal reactions, they do have outward signs.

Excerpted from *Reaching Out: Interpersonal Effectiveness and Self-Actualization,* 2nd ed., by David W. Johnson. Reprinted by permission of the author.

Sadness is inside you, but you cry or frown on the outside. Anger is inside you. But you may stare and shout at the person you are angry with. Feelings are always internal states, but you use overt behaviors to communicate your feelings to other people.

It is often difficult to express feelings. Whenever there is a risk of being rejected or laughed at, expressing feelings becomes very difficult. The more personal the feelings, the greater the risk you may feel. It is also sometimes difficult to control your expression of your feelings. You may cry when you don't want to, get angry when it is best not to, or even laugh at a time it disturbs others. Expressing feelings appropriately often means thinking before you communicate them.

Having feelings is a natural and joyful part of being alive and being human. Feelings provide the cement holding relations together as well as the means for deepening the relationships and making them more personal. The accurate and constructive expression of feelings, furthermore, is one of the most difficult aspects of building and managing your relations with other people. The purpose of this chapter is to provide the material and experiences necessary for becoming more skillful in appropriately saying how you feel. . . .

WHEN FEELINGS ARE NOT EXPRESSED

One of the most frequent sources of difficulty in building and maintaining good relationships is communicating feelings. We all have feelings about the people we interact with and the experiences we share, but many times we do not communicate these feelings effectively. Problems arise in relationships not because we have feelings but because we are not effective in communicating our feelings in ways that strengthen our relationships. When we repress, deny, distort, or disguise our feelings, or when we communicate them in an ineffective way, we are asking for trouble in our relationships.

There are several difficulties that arise when feelings are not recognized, accepted, and expressed constructively.

1. Suppressing and denying your feelings can create relationship problems. If you suppress your feelings, it can result in increased conflicts and barriers that cause deterioration in the relationship. A friend's actions may be irritating, and as the irritation is suppressed, anger and withdrawal from the relationship may result.

2. Suppressing and denying your feelings can interfere with the constructive diagnosis and resolution of relationship problems. Maintaining a relationship requires an open expression of feelings so that difficulties or conflicts can be dealt with constructively. There is a common but mistaken belief that being rational, logical, and objective requires you to suppress and ignore your feelings. Nothing is further from the truth! If you want to be effective in solving interpersonal problems, you need all the relevant information (including feelings) you can get. This means that your feelings need to be conscious, discussable, and controllable.

3. Denying your feelings can result in selective perception. When feelings are unresolved, your perceptions of events and information may be affected. If you are denying your anger, you may perceive all hostile actions but be completely blind to friendly overtures. Threatening and unpleasant facts are often distorted or not perceived. Unresolved feelings tend to increase blind spots and selective perception.

4. Suppressing your feelings can bias your judgments. It is common for people to refuse to accept a good idea because someone they dislike sug-

gested it, or to accept a poor idea because someone they like is for it. If you are aware of your feelings and manage them constructively, you will be far more unbiased and objective in your judgments.

5. Implying a demand while expressing your feelings can create a power struggle. Many times feelings are expressed in ways that demand changes in the receiver's behavior. If someone says to you, "You make me angry when you do that," she is indirectly saying, "Stop doing it." Or if a friend says, "I like you, you are a good friend," he may be indirectly demanding that you like him. When feelings imply demands, a power struggle may result over whether or not the demands are going to be met.

6. Other people often ask you to suppress or deny your feelings. A person may say, "Don't feel that way" whenever you express a feeling. If you say, "I feel depressed," he will say, "Cheer up!" If you say, "I'm angry," she will say, "Simmer down." If you say, "I feel great," she will say, "The roof will cave in any moment now." All these replies communicate: "Don't feel that way. Quick, change your feeling!"

EXPRESSING YOUR FEELINGS VERBALLY

There are two ways of communicating feelings: verbally and nonverbally. If you want to communicate clearly, your verbal and your nonverbal expression of feelings must agree or be congruent. Many of the communication difficulties experienced in relationships spring from giving contradictory messages to others by indicating one kind of feeling with words, another with actions, and still another with nonverbal expressions. This chapter focuses on the verbal expression of feelings. The next chapter focuses on the nonverbal expression of feelings. The congruence between the verbal and nonverbal expression of feelings is emphasized in both chapters.

Communicating your feelings depends on your being aware of your feelings, accepting them, and being skillful in expressing them constructively. When you are unaware or unaccepting of your feelings, or when you lack skills in expressing them, your feelings may be communicated indirectly through:

1. *Labels:* "You are rude, hostile, and self-centered" versus "When you interrupt me I get angry."
2. *Commands:* "Shut up!" versus "I'm annoyed at what you just said."
3. *Questions:* "Are you always this crazy?" versus "You are acting strangely, and I feel worried."
4. *Accusations:* "You do not care about me!" versus "When you do not pay attention to me I feel left out."
5. *Sarcasm:* "I'm glad you are early!" versus "You are late; it has delayed our work, and that irritates me."
6. *Approval:* "You are wonderful!" versus "I like you."
7. *Disapproval:* "You are terrible!" versus "I do not like you."
8. *Name Calling:* "You are a creep!" versus "You are embarrassing me."

Such indirect ways of expressing feelings are common. But they are ineffective because they do not give a clear message to the receiver. And the receiver often will feel rejected and "put down" by the remarks. We are taught how to describe our *ideas* clearly and correctly. But we are rarely taught how to describe our *feelings* clearly and correctly. We express our feelings, but we do not usually name and describe them. Here are four ways you can describe a feeling.

1. Identify or name it: "I feel angry." "I feel embarrassed." "I like you."
2. Use sensory descriptions that capture how you feel: "I feel stepped on."

"I feel like I'm on cloud nine." "I feel like I've just been run over by a truck." Because we do not have enough names or labels to describe all our feelings, we make up ways to describe them.

3. Report what kind of action the feeling urges you to do: "I feel like hugging you." "I feel like slapping your face." "I feel like walking on your face."

4. Use figures of speech as descriptions of feelings: "I feel like a stepped-on toad." "I feel like a pebble on the beach."

You describe your feelings by identifying them. A description of a feeling must include:

1. A personal statement—refer to "I," "me," "my," or "mine."
2. A feeling name, simile, action urge, or figure of speech.

Anything you say can convey feelings. Even the comment, "It's a warm day," can be said so that it expresses resentment or irritation. To build and maintain a friendship or any relationship, you must be concerned with communicating your feelings clearly and accurately, especially the feelings of warmth, affection, and caring. If you convey your feelings by commands, questions, accusations, or judgments, you will tend to confuse the person with whom you are interacting. When you want to express your feelings, your ability to describe them is essential for effective communication.

When you describe your feelings, expect at least two results. First, describing your feelings to another person often helps you to become more aware of what it is you actually do feel. Many times we have feelings that seem ambiguous or unclear to us. Explaining them to another person often clarifies our feelings to ourselves as well as to the other person. Second, describing your feelings often begins a dialogue that will improve your relationship. If other people are to respond appropriately to your feelings, they must know what the feelings are. Even if the feelings are negative, it is often worthwhile to express them. Negative feelings are signals that something may be going wrong in the relationship, and you and the other person need to examine what is going on in the relationship and figure out how it may be improved. By reporting your feelings, you provide information that is necessary if you and the other person are to understand and improve your relationship. When discussing your relationship with another person, describing your feelings conveys maximum information about what you feel in a more constructive way than giving commands, asking questions, making accusations, or offering judgments.

PROBES

Johnson claims that, "The more you share your feelings with other people, the happier and more meaningful your life will be." Do you agree? Give an example from your own experience that reinforces Johnson's point and an example that suggests that he may be overgeneralizing.

Do you agree that "even feeling and expressing anger toward another person" can be a "highly rewarding and beautiful" experience? How so?

Johnson lists six difficulties that arise when feelings are not recognized, accepted, and expressed constructively. Which one of the six have you noticed most in your family communicating? Which one surfaces most often in your dating relationships or your relationship with your lover or spouse? Which occurs most frequently on the job?

What does it mean for your verbal and nonverbal expressions of feeling to be "congruent"?

Explain whether each of the following is or is not an effective verbal feeling expression:

"You hurt my feelings when you talk about my work that way."

"Do you always get this bitchy before a big meeting?"

"I'm mad because we're going to be late and I'll feel embarrassed if we're the last ones there."

"You've done an outstanding job with that client. Good going!"

"I feel that you are ignoring what we want and only thinking of yourself."

"I like it when you rub my neck like that. I feel loved."

CHAPTER 4

NONVERBAL CUES

It is not necessary to always think words. Words often keep me from acting in a fully intuitive way. Fears, indecision, and frustration feed on words. Without words they usually stop. When I am trying to figure out how I should relate to someone, especially a stranger, if I will stop thinking words, and listen to the situation, and just be open, I find I act in a more appropriate, more spontaneous, often original, sometimes even courageous way. Words are at times good for looking back, but they are confining when I need to act in the present.

HUGH PRATHER

|||||||||||||||||||||||||||||||||||||||||||||||||||||||||||||||||||||||||||||||||||||||||||||||||||||||||||||||||||||||||||||||||||||||||

Did you ever stop to think how your communication is affected by breath and body odors? Furniture placement and window location? Dilation of the pupils of your and other people's eyes? Angle of pelvic tilt or thrust? Visible cigarette butts? Audibility of breathing? It's not always obvious, but we are affected by the meanings we give these and a multitude of other nonverbal cues. Some nonverbal cues are more obvious—tone of voice, rate of speaking, amount and type of gesture, proximity, facial expression, touch, and so on. But whether they're obvious or subtle, nonverbal cues strongly affect communication. In fact, Knapp indicates that some researchers believe that about 65 percent of social meaning of most human communication events is carried by nonverbal cues. Sixty-five percent! If you want to promote interpersonal quality communication, it is obviously crucially important to become aware of what nonverbal cues are and how they work.

This chapter moves toward that end by presenting an overview of nonverbal cues, and a discussion of two important and frequently overlooked cues, silence and touch. The purpose of this first article is, frankly, to increase your awareness of how many types of nonverbal cues there are and how many different ways they function in our day-to-day contact. If you count both main and subcategories, Knapp identifies thirteen types of nonverbal cues, each of which can operate in six different ways. That adds up to a mind-boggling set of possible combinations, more than anybody could keep absolute track of.

The point, though, is not to overwhelm you with categories, but to emphasize that what we do nonverbally and how we do it makes a difference in our communicating. People sensitive to nonverbal cues are much more able to listen effectively and empathically, to distinguish appropriate from inappropriate self-disclosure, to reduce others' defensiveness, to provide meaningful support, and to handle conflict interpersonally. So the sensitivity you can pick up from this article and the information and skills available in the next three selections can help you apply much of what is in the rest of the book.

Nonverbal Communication: Basic Perspectives

MARK L. KNAPP

> *Those of us who keep our eyes open can read volumes into what we see going on around us.*—E. T. HALL

Herr von Osten purchased a horse in Berlin, Germany, in 1900. When von Osten began training his horse, Hans, to count by tapping his front hoof, he had no idea that Hans was soon to become one of the most celebrated horses in history. Hans was a rapid learner and soon progressed from counting to addition, multiplication, division, subtraction, and eventually the solution of problems involving factors and fractions. As if this were not enough, von Osten exhibited Hans to public audiences, where the horse counted the number of people in the audience or simply the number who were wearing eyeglasses. Still responding only with taps, Hans could tell time, use a calendar, display an ability to recall musical pitch, and perform numerous other seemingly fantastic feats. After von Osten taught Hans an alphabet that could be coded into hoofbeats, the horse could answer virtually any question—oral or written. It seemed that Hans, a common horse, had a complete comprehension of the German language, the ability to produce the equivalent of words and numerals, and an intelligence beyond that of many human beings.

Even without the promotion of Madison Avenue, the word spread quickly, and soon Hans was known throughout the world. He was soon dubbed Clever Hans. Because of the obviously profound implications for several scientific fields and because some skeptics thought there was a gimmick involved, an investigating committee was established to decide, once and for all, whether there was any deceit involved in Hans' performances. A professor of psychology and physiology, the director of the Berlin Zoological Garden, a director of a circus, veterinarians, and cavalry officers were appointed to this commission of horse experts. An experiment with Hans from which von Osten was excluded demonstrated no change in the apparent intelligence of Hans. This was sufficient proof for the commission to announce that there was no trickery involved.

The appointment of a second commission was the beginning of the end for Clever Hans. Von Osten was asked to whisper a number into the horse's left ear while another experimenter whispered a number into the horse's right ear. Hans was told to add the two numbers—an answer none of the onlookers, von Osten, or the experimenter knew. Hans failed, and with further tests he continued to fail. The experimenter, Pfungst, discovered on further experimentation that Hans could only answer a question if someone in his visual field knew the answer.[1] When Hans was given the question, the onlookers assumed an expectant posture and increased their body tension. When Hans reached the correct number of taps, the onlookers would relax and make a slight movement of the head—which was Hans' cue to stop tapping.

The story of Clever Hans is frequently used in discussions concerning the capacity of an animal to learn verbal language. It also seems well suited to an introduction to the field of nonverbal communication. Hans's cleverness was not in his ability to verbalize or understand verbal commands, but in his ability to respond to almost imperceptible and unconscious movements on the part of those surrounding him. It is not unlike that perceptiveness or sensitivity to nonverbal cues exhibited by a Clever Carl, Chris, Frank, or Harriet when they are closing a business deal, giving an intelligent and industrious image to a professor, impressing a date, knowing when to leave a party, and in a multitude of other common situations . . .

PERSPECTIVES ON DEFINING NONVERBAL COMMUNICATION

Conceptually, the term *nonverbal* is subject to a variety of interpretations—just like the term *communication*. The basic issue seems to be whether the events that are traditionally studied under the heading *nonverbal* are literally nonverbal. Ray Birdwhistell, a pioneer in nonverbal research, is reported to have said that studying *nonverbal* communication is like studying *noncardiac* physiology. His point is well taken. It is not easy to dissect human interaction and make one diagnosis that concerns only verbal behavior and another that concerns only nonverbal behavior.

The verbal dimension is so intimately woven and so subtly represented in so much of what we have previously labeled nonverbal that the term does not always adequately describe the behavior under study. Some of the most noteworthy scholars associated with nonverbal study refuse to segregate words from gestures and hence work under the broader terms *communication* or *face-to-face interaction*.

Another possible source of confusion in defining nonverbal communication is whether we are talking about the signal *produced* (nonverbal) or the internal code for *interpreting* the signal (frequently verbal). Generally, when people refer to nonverbal behavior they are talking about the signal(s) to which meaning will be attributed—not the process of attributing meaning.

The fuzzy line between verbal and nonverbal communication is augmented by an equally difficult distinction between vocal and nonvocal phenomena. Consider the following: (1) Not all acoustic phenomena are vocal—for example, knuckle-cracking; a gurgling stomach; farting; slapping one's thigh, another's back, or a desk top; snapping one's fingers; and clapping. (2) Not all nonacoustic phenomena are nonverbal—for example, some of the gestures used in American Sign Language used by many deaf people. (3) Not all vocal phenomena are the same—some are respiratory and some are not. A sigh or prespeaking inspiration of breath may be considered vocal and respiratory; a click or "tch, tch!" might be classified as vocal but nonrespiratory. (4) Not all words or "apparent" word strings are clearly or singularly verbal—for example, onomatopoetic words such as *buzz* or *murmur* and nonpropositional speech used by auctioneers and some aphasics. Neat categorization for each behavior under consideration is often difficult. Realistically, we should expect that there will be points of overlap—behaviors that fit some aspects of one category and some aspects of another.

Instead of trying to classify behavior as either nonverbal or verbal, Mehrabian chose instead to use an "explicit-implicit" dichotomy.[2] In other words, Mehrabian believed that it was the subtlety of a signal that brought it into the nonverbal realm—and subtlety seemed to be directly linked to a lack of explicit rules for coding. Mehrabian's work has focused primarily on the referents people have for various configurations of nonverbal and/or implicit behavior—that is, the meaning you attach to these behaviors. The results of extensive testing reveal a threefold perspective.[3] (1) Immediacy. Sometimes we react to things by evaluating them—positive or negative, good or bad, like or dislike. (2) Status. Sometimes we enact or perceive behaviors that indicate various aspects of status to us—strong or weak, superior or subordinate. (3) Responsiveness. This third category refers to our perceptions of activity—slow or fast, active or passive.

PERSPECTIVES ON CLASSIFYING NONVERBAL BEHAVIOR

The following classification schema was derived from an examination of writing and research currently being conducted in which the authors either explicitly or implicitly categorized their own work as being subsumable under the label *nonverbal*.

Body Motion or Kinesic Behavior

Body motion, or kinesic behavior, typically includes gestures, movements of the body, limbs, hands, head, feet and legs, facial expressions (smiles), eye behavior (blinking, direction and length of gaze, and pupil dilation), and posture. The furrow of the brow, the slump of a shoulder, and the tilt of a head—all are within the purview of kinesics. Obviously, there are different types of nonverbal behavior just as there are different types of verbal behavior. Some nonverbal cues are very specific, and some are more general. Some are intended to communicate, and some are expressive only. Some provide information about emotions, and others carry information about personality traits or attitudes. In an effort to sort through the relatively unknown world of nonverbal behavior, Ekman and Friesen[4] developed a system for classifying nonverbal behavior acts. These categories include:

Emblems These are nonverbal acts that have a direct verbal translation or dictionary definition, usually consisting of a word or two or a phrase.[5] There is high agreement among members of a culture or subculture on the verbal "translation" of these signals. The gestures used to represent "A-OK" or "Peace" (also known as the victory sign) are examples of emblems for a large part of our culture. Mostly, these emblems are culture specific. For example, Fig. 1 shows variations in suicide emblems depending on the popularity of a method (hanging, shooting, or stabbing) for a particular culture. However, some emblems portray actions that are common to the human species and seem to transcend a given culture. Eating (bringing hand up to mouth) and sleeping (tilting head in lateral position, almost

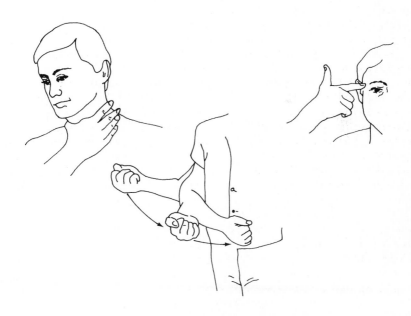

FIGURE 1

Emblems for suicide. Top left, the South Fore, Papua, New Guinea; Top right: the United States; Bottom: Japan.

perpendicular to the body, accompanied sometimes with eye closing and/or a hand or hands below the head like a pillow) are two examples of emblems that Ekman and his colleagues have observed in several cultures. Ekman also found that different cultures also seem to have emblems for similar classes of messages, regardless of the gesture used to portray it, for example, insults, directions (come, go, stop), greetings, departures, certain types of responses (yes, no, I don't know), physical, state, and emotion. The number of emblems used within a given culture may vary considerably, from less than 100 (United States) to more than 250 (Israeli) students.

Emblems are often produced with the hands—but not exclusively. A nose wrinkle may say "I'm disgusted!" or "Phew! It stinks!" To say "I don't know" or "I'm helpless" or "I'm uncertain" one might turn both palms up, shrug shoulders, or do both simultaneously. Ekman believes that facial emblems probably differ from other facial expressions by being more stylized and being presented for longer or shorter durations. Facial emblems may also emphasize particular parts of the face; for example, the smile may be used to indicate happiness or surprise by mechanically dropping the jaw or dramatically raising the eyebrows.

Emblems are frequently used when verbal channels are blocked (or fail) and are usually used to communicate. Some of the sign language of the deaf, nonverbal gestures used by television production personnel, signs used by two underwater swimmers, or motions made by two people who are too far apart to make audible signals practical are all situations ripe for emblem production.

Our own awareness of emblem usage is about the same as our awareness of word choice. Also, like verbal behavior, context can sometimes change the interpretation of the signal; that is, giving someone "the finger" can be either humorous or insulting, depending on the other cues accompanying it. Ekman has also observed "emblematic slips," analogous to slips of the tongue. He gives an example of a woman who was subjected to a stress interview by a person whose status forbade free expressions of dislike. The woman, unknown to herself or the interviewer, displayed "the finger" on the arm of her chair for several minutes during the interview.

Unlike verbal behavior, emblems are not generally strung together like words, although there are exceptions. You may be talking on the phone when a visitor enters and you have to indicate "wait a minute," "come in," and "sit down" in succession. Finally, some emblems seem to be specifically adapted to particular subgroups within a given culture. For instance, Fig. 2 shows two gestures, one which seems to be used primarily when adults are talking to children ("no-no") and one which seems primarily limited to usage by children ("shame on you").

Illustrators These are nonverbal acts that are directly tied to, or accompany, speech and serve to illustrate what is being said verbally. These may be movements that accent or emphasize a word or phrase, sketch a path of thought, point to present objects, depict a spatial relationship, depict the rhythm or pacing of an event, draw a picture of the referent, or depict a bodily action. They may also be emblems used to illustrate verbal statements, either repeating or substituting for a word or phrase. Illustrators seem to be within our awareness, but not as explicitly as emblems. They are used intentionally to help communication, but not as deliberately as emblems. Many factors can alter the frequency with which illustrators are displayed. We would expect to find more illustrators in face-to-face communica-

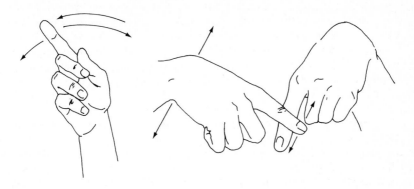

FIGURE 2

Finger emblems. (United States) for "No" (left) and "Shame on you" (right).

tion than when communicating over an intercom;[6] we would expect people who are excited and enthusiastic to display more illustrators than those who are not; and we would expect more illustrators during "difficult" communication situations; for example, not being able to find the right words to express a thought or being confronted by a receiver who either isn't paying attention or isn't comprehending what you're trying to say. Illustrators are probably learned by watching others.

Affect Displays These are primarily facial configurations that display affective states. Although the face is the primary source of affect, the body can also be read for global judgments of affect; for example, a drooping, sad body. Affect displays can repeat, augment, contradict, or be unrelated to, verbal affective statements. Once the display has occurred, there is usually a high degree of awareness, but it can occur without any awareness. Affect displays are often not intended to communicate, but they can be intentional.

Regulators These are nonverbal acts that maintain and regulate the back and forth nature of speaking and listening between two or more interactants. They tell the speaker to continue, repeat, elaborate, hurry up, become more interesting, give the other a chance to talk, and so forth. Some of the behavior associated with greetings and good-byes may be regulators to the extent that they indicate the initiation or termination of face-to-face communication.

In recent years the various nonverbal behaviors associated with turn-taking are the regulators that have been given the most attention.[7] Turn-taking refers to the cues we use: to tell another person we want to talk, to keep another person from getting the floor away from us, to give up a speaking turn and ask the other person to continue, and to show we are finished speaking and the other person can take a turn. Generally we don't say these things verbally; they are communicated by many nonverbal behaviors. Probably the most familiar regulators are head nods and eye behavior. If head nods occur frequently in rapid succession, the message may be "hurry up and finish," but if the nods follow points made by the speaker and appear slow, deliberate, and thoughtful they may signal "keep talking" or "I like what you're saying." We found people who were trying to terminate a conversation severely decreased the amount of eye contact with the other person.[8]

Regulators seem to be on the periphery of our awareness and are generally difficult to inhibit. They are like overlearned habits and are almost involuntary, but we are very much aware of these signals when they are sent by others.

Adaptors   These nonverbal behaviors are perhaps the most difficult to define and involve the most speculation. They are labeled adaptors because they are thought to develop in childhood as adaptive efforts to satisfy needs, perform actions, manage emotions, develop social contacts, or perform a host of other functions. Ekman and Friesen have identified three types of adaptors: self-, object-, and alter-directed.

Self-adaptors, as the term implies, refer to manipulations of one's own body, such as holding, rubbing, squeezing, scratching, pinching, or picking oneself. These self-adaptors will often increase as a person's anxiety level increases. Picking one's nose can be a self-adaptor; an adult who wipes the corner of his or her eye during times of sadness (as if to brush away tears) may be showing a response that reflects that person's early experiences with sadness. Ekman and his colleagues have found the "eye cover act" to be associated with shame and guilt, and the "scratch-pick act" to be associated with hostility—aggression toward oneself or toward another displaced onto oneself.

Alter-adaptors are learned in conjunction with our early experiences with interpersonal relations—giving and taking from another, attacking or protecting, establishing closeness or withdrawing, and the like. Leg movements may be adaptors, showing residues of kicking aggression, sexual invitation, or flight. Ekman believes that many of the restless movements of the hands and feet, which have typically been considered indicators of anxiety, may be residues of adaptors necessary for flight from the interaction. An example from the interaction behavior of baboons will help illustrate the nature of these alter-adaptors. When a young baboon is learning the fundamentals of attack and aggression, the mother baboon will watch from close by. The young baboon will enact aggressive behavior, but will also turn the head laterally to check whether the mother is still there. As an adult, the baboon may still perform this lateral head movement during threatening conditions even though the mother is no longer there and no functional purpose seems to be served by this movement.

Object-adaptors involve the manipulation of objects and may be derived from the performance of some instrumental task—such as smoking, writing with a pencil, and so on. Although we are typically unaware of performing these adaptor behaviors, we are probably most aware of the object-adaptors. These behaviors are often learned later in life, and there seem to be fewer social taboos associated with them.

Since there seem to be social constraints on displaying these adaptive behaviors, they are more often seen when a person is alone. At least, we would expect that we would see the full act rather than just a fragment of it. Alone you might pick your nose without inhibition; when other people are around you may just touch your nose or rub it "casually." Adaptors are not intended for use in communication, but they may be triggered by verbal behavior in a given situation associated with conditions occurring when the adaptive habit was first learned.

Physical Characteristics

Whereas the previous section was concerned with movement and motion, this category covers things that remain relatively unchanged during the period of interaction. They are influential nonverbal cues that are not movement bound. Included are such things as physique or body shape, general attractiveness, body or breath odors, height, weight, hair, and skin color or tone.

Touching Behavior

For some, kinesic study includes touch behavior; for others, however, actual physical contact constitutes a separate class of events. Some researchers are concerned with touching behavior as an important factor in the child's early development, and others are concerned with adult touching behavior. Subcategories of touch behavior may include stroking, hitting, holding, guiding another's movements, and other, more specific instances.

Paralanguage

Simply put, paralanguage deals with how something is said and not what is said. It deals with the range of nonverbal vocal cues surrounding common speech behavior. Trager believed that paralanguage had the following components.[9]

Voice Qualities   This includes such things as pitch range, pitch control, rhythm control, tempo, articulation control, resonance, glottis control, and vocal lip control.

Vocalizations   (1) *Vocal characterizers.* This includes such things as laughing, crying, sighing, yawning, belching, swallowing, heavily marked inhaling or exhaling, coughing, clearing of the throat, hiccuping, moaning, groaning, whining, yelling, whispering, sneezing, snoring, stretching, and the like. (2) *Vocal qualifiers.* This includes intensity (overloud to oversoft), pitch height (overhigh to overlow), and extent (extreme drawl to extreme clipping). (3) *Vocal segregates.* These are such things as "uh-huh," "um," "ah," and variants thereof.

Related work on such topics as silent pauses (beyond junctures), intruding sounds, speech errors, and latency would probably be included in this category.

Proxemics

Proxemics is generally considered to be the study of our use and perception of social and personal space. Under this heading, we find a body of work called small group ecology, which is concerned with how people use and respond to spatial relationships in formal and informal group settings. Such studies deal with seating arrangements and spatial arrangements as related to leadership, communication flow, and the task at hand. The influence of architectural features on residential living units and even on communities is also of concern to those who study human proxemic behavior. On an even broader level, some attention has been given to spatial relationships in crowds and densely populated situations. Our personal space orientation is sometimes studied in the context of conversational distance, and how it varies according to sex, status, roles, cultural orientation, and so forth. The term *territoriality* is also frequently used in the study of proxemics to denote the human tendency to stake out personal territory—or untouchable space—much as wild animals and birds do.

Artifacts
Artifacts include the manipulation of objects with the interacting persons that may act as nonverbal stimuli. These artifacts include perfume, clothes, lipstick, eyeglasses, wigs and other hairpieces, false eyelashes, eyeliners, and the whole repertoire of falsies and "beauty" aids.

Environmental Factors
Thus far we have been concerned with the appearance and behavior of the persons involved in communicating. This category concerns those elements that impinge on the human relationship, but are not directly a part of it. Environmental factors include the furniture, architectural style, interior decorating, lighting conditions, smells, colors, temperature, additional noises or music, and the like, within which the interaction occurs. Variations in arrangements, materials, shapes, or surfaces of objects in the interacting environment can be extremely influential on the outcome of an interpersonal relationship. This category also includes what might be called traces of action. For instance, as you observe cigarette butts, orange peels, and wastepaper left by the person with whom you will soon interact, you are forming an impression that will eventually influence your meeting.

PERSPECTIVES ON NONVERBAL COMMUNICATION IN THE TOTAL COMMUNICATION PROCESS
There is a danger that the reader may forget that nonverbal communication cannot be studied in isolation from the total communication process. Verbal and nonverbal communication should be treated as a total and inseparable unit. Argyle states, "Some of the most important findings in the field of social interaction are about the ways that verbal interaction needs the support of nonverbal communications."[10] What are some of the ways in which verbal and nonverbal systems interrelate?

Before outlining some of the verbal/nonverbal interrelationships, we should recall that there may be nonverbal interrelationships as well—that is, nonverbal channels interacting others. An example of a nonverbal interrelationship is a loud "Well!" preceding a handshake, which makes you anticipate a firm handshake. Odors can shorten or lengthen distance, interaction distance can affect vocal loudness, and so on. Argyle has identified the primary uses of nonverbal behavior in human communication as: (1) expressing emotion, (2) conveying interpersonal attitudes (like/dislike, dominance/submission, and the like), (3) presenting one's personality to others, and (4) accompanying speech for the purposes of managing turn-taking, feedback, attention, and the like.[11] None of these functions of nonverbal behavior is limited to nonverbal behavior alone—that is, emotions and attitudes can be expressed and interaction can be managed verbally, as well. In some cases, however, we rely more heavily on verbal behavior for some purposes and on nonverbal behavior for others. Like words and phrases, nonverbal signals can have multiple meanings and multiple uses—for example, a smile can be part of an emotional expression, an attitudinal message, part of a self-presentation, or a listener response to manage the interaction. Nonverbal behavior can repeat, contradict, substitute for, complement, accent, or regulate verbal behavior.[12]

Repeating Nonverbal communication can simply repeat what was said verbally. For instance, if you told someone that he or she had to go north to find a newspaper stand and then pointed in the proper direction, this would be considered repetition.

Contradicting   Nonverbal behavior can contradict verbal behavior.[13] A classic example is the parent who yells to his or her child in an angry voice, "Of course I love you!" Or the not-so-confident person about to make a public speech who, despite trembling hands and knees and beads of perspiration on the brow, says, "I'm not nervous." If there is no reason to suspect that conflicting cues might be present, we probably rely mainly on verbal messages. It has been said that when we receive contradictory messages on the verbal and nonverbal levels, we are more likely to trust and believe in the nonverbal message.[14] It is assumed that nonverbal signals are more spontaneous, harder to fake, and less apt to be manipulated. It is probably more accurate to say, however, that some nonverbal behaviors are more spontaneous and harder to fake than others, and that some people are more proficient than others at nonverbal deception.[15] With two contradictory cues, both of which are nonverbal, we predictably place our reliance on the cues we consider harder to fake. Sometimes we choose to be more direct with nonverbal cues because we know that they will be perceived as being less direct.

Young children seem to give less credence to certain nonverbal cues than do adults when they are confronted with conflicting verbal and nonverbal messages.[16] Conflicting messages in which the speaker smiled while making a critical statement were interpreted more negatively by children than by adults. This was particularly true when the speaker was a woman. Other work casts a further shadow on the "reliance on nonverbal cues in contradictory situations" theory.[17] Shapiro found student judges to be extremely consistent in their reliance on either linguistic or facial cues when they were asked to select the affect being communicated from a list of incongruent faces (sketched) and written messages. Vande Creek and Watkins extended Shapiro's work by using real voices and moving pictures. The stimulus persons were portraying inconsistencies in the degree of stress in verbal and nonverbal channels. Again they found that some respondents tended to rely primarily on verbal cues, some on nonverbal cues, and some responded to the degree of stress in general—regardless of the channels manifesting it. The cross-cultural research of Solomon and Ali suggests that familiarity with the verbal language may affect the reliance that one has on verbal or nonverbal cues. They found, for instance, that persons who were not as familiar with the language used to construct the contradictory message would rely on the content for judgments of affective meaning. Those who knew the language well were more apt to rely on the vocal intonation for the affective meaning. It thus appears that some people will rely more on the verbal message whereas others will rely on the nonverbal. We do not know all the conditions that would affect these preferences. Although one source of our preferences for verbal or nonverbal cues may be learned experiences, others believe that there may also be an even more basic genesis—such as right-left brain dominance.

Although there are times when inconsistent messages are produced to achieve a particular effect, such as sarcasm, there are some who believe that a constant barrage of inconsistent messages can contribute to a psychopathology for the receiver. This may be particularly true when people have a close relationship and the receiver has no other people to whom he or she can turn for discussion and possible clarification of the confusion. Some research finds that parents of disturbed children produce more messages with conflicting cues,[18] whereas other work suggests that the differences are not in conflicting cues, but in negative messages; that is, parents with disturbed children sent more negative messages.[19] Either situation is undesirable and the combination of negativity, confusion, and punishment can be very harmful.

Substituting Nonverbal behavior can substitute for verbal messages. When a dejected and downtrodden executive (or janitor) walks into his or her house after work, a facial expression substitutes for the statement, "I've had a rotten day." With a little practice, people soon learn to identify a wide range of these substitute nonverbal displays—all the way from "It's been a fantastic, great day!" to "Oh God, am I miserable!" We do not need to ask for verbal confirmation of our perception. Sometimes, when substitute nonverbal behavior fails, the communicator resorts back to the verbal level. Consider the woman who wants her date to stop "making out" with her. She may stiffen, stare straight ahead, or act unresponsive and cool. If the suitor persists, she is apt to say something like, "Look Larry, please don't ruin a nice friendship," and so on.

Complementing Nonverbal behavior can modify, or elaborate on, verbal messages. An employee may nonverbally reflect an attitude of embarrassment when talking to his or her supervisor about a poor performance. Further, nonverbal behavior may reflect changes in the relationship between the employee and the supervisor. When the employee's slow, quiet verbalizations and relaxed posture change—when posture stiffens and the emotional level of the verbalized statement increases—this may signal changes in the overall relationship between the interactants. Complementary functions of nonverbal communication serve to signal one's attitudes and intentions toward another person.

Accenting Nonverbal behavior may accent parts of the verbal message much as underlining written words or *italicizing* them serves to emphasize them. Movements of the head and hands are frequently used to accent the verbal message. When a father scolds his son about staying out too late at night, he may accent a particular phrase with a firm grip on the son's shoulder and an accompanying frown on his face. In some instances, one set of nonverbal cues can accent other nonverbal cues. Ekman found that emotions are primarily exhibited by facial expressions, but that the body carries the most accurate indicators regarding the level of arousal.[20]

Regulating Nonverbal behaviors are also used to regulate the communicative flow between the interactants. The way one person stops talking and another starts in a smooth, synchronized manner may be as important to a satisfactory interaction as the verbal content that is exchanged. After all, we do make judgments about people based on their regulatory skills—for example, "talking to him is like talking to a wall" or "you can't get a word in edgewise with her." When another person frequently interrupts or is inattentive we may feel that this is a statement about the relationship—perhaps one of disrespect. There are rules for regulating conversations, but they are generally implicit. It isn't written down, but we seem to "know" that two people shouldn't talk at the same time, that each person should get an equal number of turns at talking if he or she desires it, that a question should be answered, and so forth. Wiemann's research found that relatively minute changes in these regulatory behaviors (interruptions, pauses longer than three seconds, unilateral topic changes, and the like) resulted in sizable variations in how competent a communicator was perceived.[21] As listeners, we are apparently attending to, and evaluating a host of, fleeting, subtle, and habitual features of another's conversational behavior. There are probably differences in the actual behaviors used to manage conversational flow across cultures or with certain subcultural groups. We know that as children are first learning these rules they use less subtle cues—for example, tugging on clothing, raising a hand, and the like. Some of the behaviors used to facilitate this conversational regulation follow.[22]

When we want to indicate that we are finished speaking and the other person can start, we may increase our eye contact with the other person. This is often accompanied by the vocal cues associated with ending declarative or interrogative statements. If the other person still doesn't pick up the conversational "ball," we might extend silence or interject a "trailer," for example, "you know . . ." or "so, ah . . . ." Keeping another from getting in the conversation requires us to keep long pauses from occurring, decrease eye contact, and perhaps raise our volume if the other person tries to "get in." When we do not want to take a speaking turn we might give the other person some reinforcing head nods and maintain attentive eye contact, and, of course, keep from speaking when the other begins to yield. When we do want the floor we might raise our index finger or enact an audible inspiration of breath with a straightening of the posture as if we were "ready" to take over. Rapid nodding may also signal the other person to hurry up and finish, but if we have trouble getting in we may have to talk simultaneously for a few words or engage in "stutter starts" that, hopefully, will be more easily observed cues to exemplify our desire to speak.

Conversational beginnings and endings also act as regulatory points. When greeting others, our eye contact signals that the channels of conversation are open. A slight head movement and an "eyebrow flash" (a barely detectable but distinct up-and-down movement of the eyebrows) may be present. The hands are also used in greetings for salutes, waves, handshakes, hand slaps, emblematic signals like the peace or victory sign, a raised fist, or thumbs up. Hands may also perform grooming activities (putting fingers through one's hair) or be involved in various touching activities like kissing, embracing, or hitting another on the arm. The mouth may form a smile or an oval shape as if one were ready to start talking.[23]

Saying good-bye in semiformal interviews brought forth many nonverbal behaviors, but the most common included the frequent breaking of eye contact and for increasingly longer periods of time, positioning one's body toward an exit, leaning forward, and rapidly nodding. Less frequent, but also very noticeable were accenting behaviors; for example, "This is the termination of our conversation and I don't want you to miss it!" These accenters included what we called *explosive* hand and foot movements—raising the hands and/or feet and bringing them down with enough force to make an audible slap while simultaneously using the hands and feet as leverage to catapult out of the seat. A less direct manifestation of this is to place your hands on your thighs or knees in a "leveraging" position (as if you were soon to catapult) and hope that the other person picks up the good-bye cue.[24]

It should be clear from the preceding that verbal and nonverbal behavior work together in many ways. In order to fully understand a communicative transaction we must analyze both types of behavior as an inseparable unit.

PERSPECTIVES ON NONVERBAL COMMUNICATION IN AMERICAN SOCIETY

The importance of nonverbal communication would be undeniable if sheer quantity were the only measure. Birdwhistell, who is generally considered as a noted authority on nonverbal behavior, makes some rather astounding estimates of the amount of nonverbal communication that takes place. He estimates that the average person actually speaks words for a total of only 10 to 11 minutes daily—the standard spoken sentence taking only about 2.5 seconds. He goes on to say that in a normal two-person conversation, the verbal components carry less than 35 percent of the social meaning of the situation; more than 65 percent of the social meaning is carried on the nonverbal band.

Another way of looking at the quantity of nonverbal messages is to note the various systems that humans use to communicate. Hall outlines ten separate kinds of human activity that he calls "primary message systems."[25] He suggests that only one involves language. Ruesch and Kees discuss at least seven different systems— personal appearance and dress, gestures or deliberate movements, random action, traces of action, vocal sounds, spoken words, and written words. Only two of the seven systems involve the overt use of words.[26]

It is not my purpose here to argue the importance of the various human message systems, but to put the nonverbal world in perspective. It is safe to say that the study of human communication has for too long ignored a significant part of the process.

Further testimony to the prevalence and importance of nonverbal communication is available if we scrutinize specific facets of our society. For example, consider the role of nonverbal signals in therapeutic situations; an understanding of "disturbed" nonverbal behavior would certainly help in diagnosis and treatment. Nonverbal cues are also important in certain situations in which verbal communication is constrained—for example, doctor-nurse interaction during an operation. The significance of nonverbal cues in the arts is obvious—dancing, theatrical performances, music, pictures, and so on. It is the nonverbal symbolism of various ceremonies and rituals that creates important and necessary responses in the participants—for example, the trappings of the marriage ceremony, the Christmas decorations, religious rituals, funerals, and the like. We can also see how an understanding of nonverbal cues would better prepare us for communicating across cultures, classes, or age groups—and with different ethnic groups within our culture. Teaching and understanding the blind and deaf is largely a matter of developing a sophistication with nonverbal signals. Everyday matters like forming impressions of people you meet, getting through a job interview, understanding advertising or the audience/speaker relationship in a public speech are all heavily laden with nonverbal behavior. Nonverbal cues are also being analyzed in the hope of predicting future behavior of people.[27] One expert claims to have analyzed hand gestures of prospective jurors in eleven major trials in 1975, hoping to predict how they would vote on the defendant. . . .

Classroom Behavior   The classroom is a veritable gold mine of nonverbal behavior, which has been nearly untapped by scientific probes. Acceptance and understanding of ideas and feelings on the part of both teacher and student, encouraging and criticizing, silence, questioning, and the like—all involve nonverbal elements. Consider the following instances as representative of the variety of classroom nonverbal cues: (1) the frantic hand waver who is sure that he or she had the correct answer; (2) the student who is sure that he or she does not know the answer and tries to avoid any eye contact with the teacher; (3) the effects of student dress and hair length on teacher-student interaction; (4) facial expressions—threatening gestures, and tone of voice are frequently used for discipline in elementary schools; (5) the teacher who requests student questioning and criticism, but whose nonverbal actions make it clear that he or she will not be receptive; (6) a student's absence from class communicates; (7) a teacher's trust of students is sometimes indicated by the arrangement of seating and monitoring behavior during examinations; (8) the variety of techniques used by students to make sleeping appear to be studying or listening; (9) the professor who announces that he or she has plenty of time for student conferences, but whose fidgeting and glancing at a watch suggest otherwise; (10) teachers who try to assess visual feedback to determine student comprehension;[28] (11) even classroom design (wall colors, space between seats, windows) has an influence on student participation in the classroom.

> To summarize our speculations, we may say that by what she said, by how and when she said it, by her facial expressions, postures, and perhaps by her touch, the teacher may have communicated to the children of the experimental group that she expected improved intellectual performance. Such communications together with possible changes in teaching techniques may have helped the child learn by changing his self-concept, his expectations of his own behavior, and his motivation, as well as his cognitive style and skills.[29]

Courtship Behavior   We know there is "something" that is highly influential in our nonverbal courtship behavior. Like other areas of nonverbal study, however, we are still at a very early stage in quantifying these patterns of behavior. On a purely intuitive level, we know that there are some men and some women who can exude such messages as "I'm available," "I'm knowledgeable," or "I want you" without saying a word. For the male, it may be such things as his clothes, sideburns, length of hair, an arrogant grace, a thrust of his hips, touch gestures, extra long eye contact, carefully looking at the woman's figure, open gestures and movements to offset closed ones exhibited by the woman, gaining close proximity, a subtleness that will allow both parties to deny that either had committed themselves to a courtship ritual, making the woman feel secure and wanted, "like a woman," or showing excitement and desire in fleeting facial expressions. For the woman, it may be such things as sitting with her legs symbolically open, crossing her legs to expose a thigh, engaging in flirtatious glances, stroking her thighs, protruding her breasts, using an appealing perfume, showing the "pouting mouth" in her facial expressions, opening her palm to the male, using a tone of voice that has an "invitation behind the words," or any of a multitude of other cues and rituals—some of which vary with status, subculture, region of the country, and the like. A study by some students in Milwaukee of a number of singles' bars suggested that smoking a cigar was taboo for any male who wished to pick up a female in these places. Other particularly important behaviors for males operating in this context seemed to be looking the female in the eyes often; dressing slightly on the "mod" side, but generally avoiding extremes in dress; and staying with one woman for the entire evening.

Another group of Milwaukee undergraduate students focused on the nonverbal courtship behavior of homosexuals and found many similarities to heterosexual courtship rituals. Homosexuals were found to lavishly decorate their living quarters to impress their partners, to use clothing for attraction and identification, and to use eye behavior to communicate their intentions. Scheflen has outlined four categories of heterosexual nonverbal courtship behavior—courtship readiness, preening behavior, positional cues, and actions of appeal or invitation.[30] The Milwaukee students found these to be useful categories in analyzing homosexual nonverbal courtship behavior, as well. Contrary to a popular stereotype, most homosexuals do not have effeminate and lisping characteristics. This raises the question of what nonverbal cues are used for identification purposes between two homosexuals. Certainly the environmental context may be influential (gay bars), but other cues are also used. For instance, brief bodily contact (leg to leg) and other body movements, such as certain tilts of the head or hands, have been reported. In public places, however, the most common and effective signals used by homosexuals are extended eye glances. Uninterested males will most likely avoid these long, lingering glances whereas those males who maintain such eye contact suggest that they are open for further interaction.

Nielsen, citing Birdwhistell, described the "courtship dance" of the North American adolescent.[31] He claims to have identified twenty-four steps between the "initial contact between the young male and female and the coitional act." He explains that these steps have an order to them. By this he means that when a male begins holding a female's hand, he must wait until she presses his hand (signaling a go-ahead) before he can take the next step of allowing his fingers to intertwine with hers. Females and males are labeled "fast" or "slow" according to whether they follow the order of the steps. If a step is skipped or reversed in the order, the person who does so is labeled "fast." If a person ignores the signal to move on to the next step, or takes actions to prevent the next step, he or she is considered "slow." This ordering would suggest that only after the initial kiss may the male attempt to approach the female's breasts. She will probably block his approach with her upper arm against her side since protocol forbids approaching the breast from the front. The male really does not expect to reach the breast until after a considerable amount of additional kissing.

We have thus far concentrated on nonverbal courtship behavior of unmarried men and women. Certainly additional volumes can be written on marital nonverbal courtship behavior patterns, as the whole repertoire of messages for inviting or avoiding sexual intercourse is largely nonverbal. For example, some observers have noted that "staying up to watch the late show" is a common method of saying "not tonight."

SUMMARY

The term *nonverbal* is commonly used to describe all human communication events that transcend spoken or written words. At the same time we should realize that these nonverbal events and behaviors can be interpreted through verbal symbols. When we consider a classification schema of vocal/nonvocal, verbal/nonverbal, acoustic/nonacoustic, respiratory/nonrespiratory we learn to expect something less than discrete category placement. Instead we might more appropriately put these behaviors on continua with some behaviors overlapping two continua.

The theoretical writings and research on nonverbal communication can be broken down into the following seven areas: (a) body motion or kinesics (emblems, illustrators, affect displays, regulators, and adaptors), (2) physical characteristics, (3) touching behavior, (4) paralanguage (vocal qualities and vocalizations), (5) proxemics, (6) artifacts, (7) environment. Nonverbal communication should not be studied as an isolated unit, but as an inseparable part of the total communication process. Nonverbal communication may serve to repeat, contradict, substitute, complement, accent, or regulate verbal communication. Nonverbal communication is important because of the role it plays in the total communication system, the tremendous quantity of informational cues it gives in any particular situation, and because of its use in fundamental areas of our daily life.

References

1. O. Pfungst, *Clever Hans, The Horse of Mr. Von Osten* (New York: Holt. Rinehart and Winston, 1911).
2. A. Mehrabian, *Nonverbal Communication* (Chicago: Aldine-Atherton, 1972), p.2.
3. In various verbal and nonverbal studies over the last three decades, dimensions similar to Mehrabian's have been consistently reported by investigators from diverse fields studying diverse phenomena. It is reasonable to conclude, therefore, that these three dimensions seem to be basic responses to our environment and are reflected in the way we assign meaning to both verbal and nonverbal behavior. Cf. A. Mehrabian, "A Semantic Space for Nonverbal Behavior," *Journal of Consulting and Clinical Psychology* 35 (1970): 248–257; and A. Mehrabian, *Silent Messages* (Belmont, Calif.: Wadsworth, 1971).
4. P. Ekman and W. V. Friesen, "The Repertoire of Nonverbal Behavior: Categories, Origins, Usage and Coding," *Semiotica* 1 (1969): 49–98. Also see the following for updated reports with specific research foci: P. Ekman and W. V. Friesen, "Hand Movements," *Journal of Communication* 22 (1972): 353–374 and P. Ekman and W. V. Friesen, "Nonverbal Behavior and Psychopathology," in *The Psychology of Depression: Contemporary Theory and Research* ed. R. J. Friedman and M. M. Katz (Washington, D. C.: Winston, 1974).
5. One treatment of emblems per se can be found in P. Ekman, "Movements with Precise Meanings,"*Journal of Communication* 26 (1976): 14–26. Figures 1.1, 1.2, and the research reported in this section are drawn primarily from this work. Additional information on American emblems can be found in Chapter 6.
6. A. A. Cohen and R. Harrison, "Intentionality in the Use of Hand Illustrators in Face-to-Face Communication Situations," *Journal of Personality and Social Psychology* 28 (1973): 276–279. See also A. A. Cohen, "The Communicative Functions of Hand Illustrators," *Journal of Communication* 27 (1977): 54–63.
7. For a summary of these efforts, see J. M. Wiemann and M. L. Knapp, "Turn-Taking in Conversations," *Journal of Communication* 25 (1975): 75–92.
8. M. L. Knapp, R. P. Hart, G. W. Friedrich, and G. M. Shulman, "The Rhetoric of Goodbye: Verbal and Nonverbal Correlates of Human Leave-Taking," *Speech Monographs* 40 (1973): 182–198.
9. G. L. Trager, "Paralanguage: A First Approximation," *Studies in Linguistics* 13 (1958):1–12.
10. M. Argyle, *Social Interaction* (New York: Atherton Press, 1969), pp. 70–71.
11. M. Argyle, *Bodily Communication* (New York: International Universities Press, 1975).
12. See P. Ekman, "Communication Through Nonverbal Behavior: A Source of Information About an Interpersonal Relationship," in *Affect, Cognition and Personality,* ed. S.S. Tomkins and C. E. Izard (New York: Springer, 1965).
13. A sometimes subtle inconsistency can also be perceived within verbal communications. When you are trying to express an idea with which you basically disagree, the linguistic choices may reflect differences in directness—for example, "John has done good work" is less direct than "John does good work." See M. Wiener and A. Mehrabian, *Language Within Language* (New York: Appleton-Century-Crofts, 1968).
14. Some evidence to support this notion is found in the following two sources: E. Tabor, "Decoding of Consistent and Inconsistent Attitudes in Communication" (Ph.D. diss., Illinois Institute of Technology, 1970); and A. Mehrabian, "Inconsistent Messages and Sarcasm," in A. Mehrabian, *Nonverbal Communication* (Chicago: Aldine-Atherton, 1972),

pp. 104–132. For an understanding of the cognitive processes used in interpreting inconsistent messages, see: D. E. Bugental, "Interpretations of Naturally Occurring Discrepancies Between Words and Intonation: Modes of Inconsistency Resolution," *Journal of Personality and Social Psychology* 30 (1974): 125–133.

15. See pages 70–76 for a discussion of our level of awareness of various nonverbal behaviors.

16. D. E. Bugental, J. W. Kaswan, L. R. Love, and M. N. Fox, "Child Versus Adult Perception of Evaluative Messages in Verbal, Vocal and Visual Channels," *Developmental Psychology* 2 (1970): 367–375. Also see D. E. Bugental, L. R. Love, and R. M. Gianette, "Perfidious Feminine Faces," *Journal of Personality and Social Pscyhology* 17 (1971): 314–318.

17. J. G. Shapiro, "Responsivity to Facial and Linguistic Cues," *Journal of Communication* 18 (1968): 11–17; L. Vande Creek and J. T. Watkins, "Responses to Incongruent Verbal and Nonverbal Emotional Cues," *Journal of Communication* 22 (1972): 311–316; and D. Solomon and F. A. Ali, "Influence of Verbal Content and Intonation on Meaning Attributions of First-And-Second-Language Speakers," *Journal of Social Psychology* 95 (1975): 3–8.

18. D. E. Bugental, L. R. Love, J. W. Kaswan, and C. April, "Verbal-Nonverbal Conflict in Parental Messages to Normal and Disturbed Children," *Journal of Abnormal Psychology* 77 (1971): 6–10.

19. N. G. Beakel and A. Mehrabian, "Inconsistent Communications and Psychopathology," *Journal of Abnormal Psychology* 74 (1969): 126–130.

20. P. Ekman, "Body Position, Facial Expression and Verbal Behavior During Interviews," *Journal of Abnormal and Social Psychology* 68 (1964): 194–301. Also P. Ekman and W. V. Friesen, "Head and Body Cues in the Judgment of Emotion: A Reformulation," *Perceptual and Motor Skills* 24 (1967): 711–724.

21. J. M. Wiemann, "An Exploration of Communicative Competence in Initial Interactions: An Experimental Study" (Ph.D. diss., Purdue University, 1975).

22. Vocal cues involved in the turn-taking mechanism are treated in Chapter 10 and kinesic signals are listed in Chapter 6. For further reading in this area, see S. Duncan, "Some Signals and Rules for Taking Turns in Conversations," *Journal of Personality and Social Psychology* 23 (1972): 283–292; S. Duncan, "Toward a Grammar for Dyadic Conversation," *Semiotica* 9 (1973): 29–46; and J. M. Wiemann, "An Exploratory Study of Turn-Taking in Conversations: Verbal and Nonverbal Behavior," (M.S. thesis, Purdue University, 1973).

23. P. D. Krivonos and M. L. Knapp, "Initiating Communication: What Do You Say When You Say Hello?" *Central States Speech Journal* 26 (1975): 115–125.

24. Knapp, Hart, Friedrich, and Shulman, "The Rhetoric of Goodbye: Verbal and Nonverbal Correlates of Human Leave-Taking."

25. E. T. Hall, *The Silent Language* (Garden City, N.Y.: Doubleday, 1959).

26. J. Ruesch and W. Kees, *Nonverbal Communication: Notes on the Visual Perception of Human Relations* (Berkeley and Los Angeles, Calif.: University of California Press, 1956).

27. M. J. Saks, "Social Scientists Can't Rig Juries," *Psychology Today* 9 (1976): 48–50, 55–57. Also see R. T. Stein, "Identifying Emergent Leaders from Verbal and Nonverbal Communications," *Journal of Personality and Social Psychology* 32 (1975): 125–135; and P. Ekman, R. M. Liebert, W. V. Friesen, R. Harrison, C. Zlatchin, E. J. Malmstrom, and R. A. Baron, "Facial Expressions of Emotion While Watching Televised Violence as Predictors of Subsequent Aggression" (report to the Surgeon General's Scientific Advisory Committee on Television and Social Behavior, June, 1971).

28. At least one study suggests that even experienced teachers are not very successful at this. Cf. J. Jecker, N. Maccoby, M. Breitrose, and E. Rose, "Teacher Accuracy in Assessing Cognitive Visual Feedback from Students," *Journal of Applied Psychology* 48 (1964): 393–397.

29. R. Rosenthal and L. Jacobson, *Pygmalion in the Classroom* (New York: Holt, Rinehart and Winston, 1968).

30. A. E. Scheflen, "Quasi-Courtship Behavior in Psychotherapy," *Psychiatry* 28 (1965): 245–257.

31. G. Nielsen, *Studies in Self-Confrontation* (Copenhagen: Munksgaard; Cleveland: Howard Allen, 1962), pp. 70–71.

PROBES

How are Knapp's points about defining nonverbal cues related to what Gary and I said at the beginning of Chapter 3 about defining *verbal* cues?

What is an example from your own experience of the cultural differences among what Knapp calls "emblems"? What other cultural differences in nonverbal communication have you noticed?

Pay attention during your next conversation to your own use of *regulators*. How do you indicate that it's your conversation partner's turn to talk? When you're in a group, how do you nonverbally "ask" to speak?

What messages about "territory" do you get from the furniture placement in your employer's office? If you were in the position your boss is in, would you change the furniture placement? Why?

Give an example from your own communication experience of verbal and nonverbal cues contradicting each other. Which did you believe?

In addition to waving, how do you "say" goodbye nonverbally?

As I mentioned in Chapter 1, we frequently think of communicating as something we do "to" someone else. In this essay Rollo May reminds us of the communicative importance of *not*-doing, of pausing. May is a well-known counselor who has written several influential and insightful books about communication and human growth. I've found a great deal of wisdom in his books, and if you hear some of that here, I'd encourage you to read *Freedom and Destiny*—the book this comes from—or *Love and Will* or *Power and Innocence,* two of his other works.

This essay is in this chapter to underscore the importance of silence as a kind of nonverbal communication. Knapp mentioned silence in his first essay in this chapter, but we don't usually recognize how significant it can be. If you doubt its importance, remember how it can actually reverse your meaning, as in the old joke punchline, "Don't . . . stop!" versus "Don't stop!

May points toward some parts of Eastern cultures as helpful reminders to those of us in the West about the significance of the pause. His quotations from Lao Tzu illustrate how negation can become affirmation, "the void can be where most happens." He also illustrates how aspects of the native North American culture affirmed this same insight—that silence can be rich and full.

May's discussion connects with a theme that's important to me when he notes that, "there seems to be no pause in technology. Or when there is it is called a 'depression' and is denied and feared," and that, "The significance of the pause is that the rigid chain of cause and effect is broken." My way of making this point is to say that we often "technologize" much of what's human out of our human communicating, and we do that in part by failing to realize that linear causality simply doesn't apply to *human* systems and processes.

May also makes the point that even infinitesimally small pauses can be packed with significance. Again, if you doubt this, reflect on your own experience.

How important is a pause of even a few milliseconds when you ask someone, "Do you really mean that?" "How good *are* my chances?" or "Are you sure that's everything?"

May argues that the pause, even for only a moment, is the "locus of the speaker's freedom." By that he means that pauses help shape the unique dimensions of each individual speaker's comments. When it is the pause before a response to a thoughtful question, it can also be the locus of the speaker's creativity.

You may or may not agree with everything May says here, but I hope that his words will provoke you to think about silence as part of your nonverbal communication. May is clearly not a social scientist; he's not quantifying silence or subjecting it to a rigorously causal analysis. But there's wisdom of a different kind here, if you'll pause and listen for it.

The Significance of the Pause
Rollo May

I don't think I handle the notes much differently from other pianists. But the pauses between the notes—ah, there is where the artistry lies!
—Artur Schnabel's answer to reporters who inquired about the secret of his genius.

The goal of fasting is inner unity. This means hearing but not with the ear; hearing, but not with the understanding; it is hearing with the spirit, with your whole being. The hearing that is only in the ears is one thing. The hearing of the understanding is another. But the hearing of the spirit is not limited to any one faculty, to the ear, or to the mind. Hence, it demands the emptiness of all the faculties. And when the faculties are empty, then the whole being listens. There is then a direct grasp of what is right before you that can never be heard with the ear or understood with the mind. Fasting of the heart empties the faculties, frees you from limitations and from preoccupations.
—Thomas Merton, *The Living Bread*

In a previous chapter we defined freedom as the capacity to pause in the midst of stimuli from all directions, and in this pause to throw our weight toward this response rather than that one. The crucial term, and in some ways the most interesting, is that little word *pause*. It may seem strange that this word is the important one rather than terms like *liberty, independence, spontaneity*. And it seems especially strange that a word merely signifying a lack of something, an absence, a hiatus, a vacancy, should carry so much weight. In America especially, the word pause refers to a gap, a space yet unfilled, a nothing—or, better yet, a "no thing."

The pause is especially important for the freedom of being, what I have called essential freedom. For it is in the pause that we experience the context out of which freedom comes. In the pause we wonder, reflect, sense awe, and conceive of eternity. The pause is when we open ourselves for the moment to the concepts of both freedom and destiny.

The word *pause,* like the word *freedom,* seems essentially to signify what something is *not* rather than what it is. We have seen that freedom is defined almost universally by what it is not—or, in a sentence definition, "Freedom is when you are anchored to nobody or nothing." Similarly, the pause is a time when no thing is happening. Can the word *pause* give us an answer not only as to why *freedom* is a negative word, but is also loved as the most affirmative term in our language? It was, notes the anthropologist Dorothy Lee, "this conception of *nothingness* as *somethingness* that enabled the philosophers of India to perceive the integrity of non-being, to name the free space and give us the zero."

One version of a famous question is "How many Zen Buddhists does it take to screw in a light bulb?" The answer is two: one to screw it in and one *not* to screw it in. And the latter is as important as the former, for emptiness is something in Eastern thought.

It should not surprise us that this contribution to our thinking and experience comes mainly from the East, especially from India, China, and Japan. In our crisis of thought and religion in the West, the wisdom of the East emerges as a corrective. This wisdom recalls us to truths in our own mystic tradition that we had forgotten, such as contemplation, meditation, and especially the significance of the pause.

Freedom is experienced in our world in an infinite number of pauses, which turn out not to be negative but to be the most affirmative condition possible. *The ultimate paradox is that negation becomes affirmation.* Thus, *freedom* remains the most loved word, the word that thrills us most readily, the condition most desired because it calls forth continuous, unrealized possibilities. And it is so with the "pause." The "no thing" turns out to bespeak a reality that is most clearly something. It is paradoxical that in our lives empty can be full, negative can be affirmative, the void can be where most happens. In the *Tao Teh Ching,* for example, Lao Tzu says,

We put thirty spokes to make a wheel:
But it is on the hole in the center that the use of the cart hinges.

We make a vessel from a lump of clay;
But it is the empty space within the vessel that makes it useful

We make doors and windows for a room;
But it is the empty spaces that make the room livable.

Thus, while existence has advantages,
It is the emptiness that makes it useful.

THE LANGUAGE OF SILENCE

This conception of the pause gives us a whole new world. It is in the pause that people learn to *listen to silence.* We can hear an infinite number of sounds that we normally never hear at all—the unending hum and buzz of insects in a quiet summer field, a breeze blowing lightly through the golden hay, a thrush singing in the low bushes beyond the meadow. And we suddenly realize that this is *something*—the world of "silence" is populated by a myriad of creatures and a myriad of sounds.

Luther Standing Bear, describing his childhood as an Oglala Dakotan in the 1870s, wrote that children "were taught to sit still and enjoy [the silence]. They were taught to use their organs of smell, to look when apparently there was nothing to see, and to listen intently when all seemingly was quiet." And Modupe, writing of his so-so childhood in French Guinea, says, "We learned that silences as well as sounds are significant in the forest, and [we learned] how to listen to the silences. . . . Deeply felt silences might be said to be the core of our Kofon religion. During these times, *the nature within ourselves found unity with the nature of the earth.*"

In Japan, free time and space—what we call pauses—are perceived as *ma*, the valid interval or meaningful pause. Such perception is basic to all experience and specifically to what constitutes creativity and freedom. This perception persists in spite of the adoption of Western culture and science. Even in 1958, Misako Miyamoto wrote of the Nō plays, "The audience watches the play and catches the feeling through not only the action and words but also the *intervals of the period of pauses.* . . . There is a free creation in each person's mind . . . ; and the audience relates to this situation with free thinking." Of silent intervals in speech, she says, "Especially [in] the pauses in a tone of voice, I can feel the person's unique personality and his joy, sorrow or other complicated feelings." On listening to a robin in early spring, "It sang with pauses, . . . I could have time to think about the bird [in] the silent moment between one voice and others, . . . The pauses produced the effect of the relation between the bird and me."

Lest these examples seduce us into assuming that this valuing of the pause is chiefly in Oriental and esoteric cultures, let me point out that the phenomenon is just as clear, though not as frequent, in our own modern culture. John Cage, a composer noted for his originality, gave a concert in New York which consisted of his coming out on the stage, sitting down at the keyboard for a period of time, and not playing a note. His aim, as he explained to a less-than-pleased audience, was to give them an opportunity to listen to the silence. His recorded music shows precisely this—many pauses are interspersed with heterogeneous notes. Cage sharpens our awareness, makes our senses keener, and renders us alive to ourselves and our surroundings. Listening is our most neglected sense.

The very essence of jazz is in the space between notes, called the afterbeat. The leader of a band in which I once played used to sing out "um-BAH," the "Bah"—or the note—coming always between the beats. This syncopation is a basis of jazz. Duke Ellington, for example, keeps the audience tantalized, on edge, expectant—we *have* to dance to work out the emotion building up within us. On an immediate level this expectancy has a similarity to the exquisite levels of feeling before orgasm. Hence, some musicians can simulate the process of sexual intercourse in the tantalizing beat of their songs. In the ever-changing jazz group at Preservation Hall in New Orleans, this infinite variety, with each person improvising, produces each time a piece of music never before played and never to be played again. This is freedom *par excellence.*

There seems to be no pause in technology. Or when there is, it is called a "depression" and is denied and feared. But pure science is a different matter. We find Einstein remarking that "the intervals between the events are more significant than the events themselves."

The significance of the pause is that the rigid chain of cause and effect is broken. The pause momentarily suspends the billiard-ball system of Pavlov. In the person's life response no longer blindly follows stimulus. There intervenes between the two our human imaginings, reflections, considerations, ponderings. Pause is the prerequisite for wonder. When we don't pause, when we are perpetually hurrying from one appointment to another, from one "planned activity" to another, we sacrifice the richness of wonder. And we lose communication with our destiny.

TIME AND THE PAUSE

The length of time of the pause is, in principle, irrelevant. When we look at what actually happens in people's experience, we note that some pauses can be infinitesimally small. When I am giving a lecture, for example, I select one word rather than another in a pause that lasts for only a millisecond. In this pause a number of possible terms flash before my mind's eye. If I want to say the noise was "loud," I may consider in this fraction of second such words as "deafening," "startling," or "overwhelming." Out of these I select one. All this happens so rapidly—strictly speaking, on the preconscious level—that I am aware of it only when I stop to think about it afterward.

Note in this last sentence I say "stop to think." This habitual phrase is another proof of the importance of the pause. Hannah Arendt remarks in *Thinking* (volume 2 of *The Life of the Mind*) on the necessity of "stopping" to think—i.e., pausing as essential to the process of reflection.

But something else, even more interesting, occurs in those small, multitudinous pauses as one speaks. This is the time when I "listen" to the audience, when the audience influences me, when I "hear" its reaction and ask silently, What connotations are they taking from my words? For any experienced lecturer the blank spaces that constitute the pauses between the words and sentences is the time of openness to the audience. At such times I find myself noting: There someone seems puzzled; here someone listens by tipping his head to one side so as not to miss any word; there in the back row—what every speaker dreads to see—is someone nodding in sleep. Every experienced speaker that I know is greatly helped by the cultivation of his awareness of facial expressions and other subtle aspects of unspoken communication from the audience.

Walt Whitman once remarked that "the audience writes the poetry," and in an even clearer sense the audience gives the lecture. Hence, a lecture delivered from the same notes, say once to a social club and then again to graduate students at a large university, will often seem to be two entirely different speeches.

The pause for milliseconds while one speaks is *the locus of the speaker's freedom*. The speaker may mold his speech this way or that, he may tell a joke to relax the audience, or—in a thrilling moment of which there cannot be too many in a lecturer's career—he may even be aware of a brand new idea coming to him from heaven knows where in the audience.

Cassandra, we are told in Aeschylus' drama, foretold the doom of Mycenae. A prophetess, she was sensitive to communications on many different levels of which the average person is unaware. This sensitivity caused her much pain, and she would gladly have given up her role if she could have. She was "doomed," or destined to listen on these different levels; she could not escape hearing the messages coming in her pauses. Quite apart from the roles of prophetess or mystic—which we see also in Tiresias and Jeremiah and Isaiah—it would seem that multitudes of us have such capacities, but we train ourselves (a process abetted by much contemporary education) to suppress this sensitivity to the pauses. And we may do this in the hope of avoiding the pain. The difference between the charlatan and the genuine prophet may well be the sense of pain the latter experiences in his or her prophecies.

The pauses may be longer, for instance, when one is answering questions after a lecture. In response to a question, I may silently hem and haw for a moment while different possible answers flash through my mind. At that time I do not usually think of Kierkegaard's proclamation "Freedom is possibility," but that is what I am living out in those moments of pause. The thrilling thing is that at such a time a new answer that I have never thought of may suddenly emerge. It is often said that intellectually creative people—like John Dewey, for example—are a strain to listen to and are not good public speakers, because the time they pause to consider different possibilities requires a capacity to wait that most people find tedious.

One's freedom may involve still larger pauses. "Let me sleep on it" is a not infrequent remark when one is making an important decision like buying a house. These are the situations in which a longer interval between stimuli is desired; there may be many different houses available, or one can decide not to buy any at all. The decision then requires complex consideration, pondering, setting up possibilities for choice, and playing "as if" games with oneself to assess various factors like view and design and so on. My point is simply that freedom consists of these possibilities. The pauses are the exercise of one's freedom to choose among them.

We recall that Jesus and Buddha, each following his own inner guidance, went off into his separate wilderness to engage in his quest. Both "paused" for forty days, if the records are to be believed. These were assumedly times for each of intense concentration, times of considering possibilities, of listening to whatever voices were available on deeper levels within themselves, voices from nature, voices from what we now term archetypal experiences, voices from what Jesus called God and Buddha called Atman and I would call Being. These assumedly were periods in which they experienced their visions and integrated themselves around their messages.

But students tell me that they have professors who *pause permanently*. These teachers make a career out of pausing. The pause is then not a preparation for action but an excuse for never acting at all. It has been remarked that the academic profession is the only one in which you can make your living by questioning things. How much it is still true in academia that persons substitute talking for decision or rationalize lack of commitment by calling it "judicious pausing" I do not know. Nevertheless this is a tendency that confronts us all: to use pausing as a substitute for committed action. In our action-oriented life in America this misuse of pausing is a not infrequently found neurotic reaction. But this dilemma is not overcome by acting blindly, without consciousness and without reason. To be free obviously requires the courage to act when it is necessary to act if one's freedom is to be actualized at all.

A person may ponder for months and years or all life long, never finding satisfactory answers. This occurs particularly with the question of death. Hamlet spoke for many of us when he stated his concern with what might happen beyond death,

When we have shuffled off this mortal coil,
[It] must give us pause.

But our personal freedom can be actualized regardless of whether we find satisfactory answers or not, or even if there are no answers at all. We can exercise our freedom even against destiny. Indeed, in the long run to "know that he dies," as Pascal said, is the most essential and triumphant experience of freedom possible for a human being.

PROBES

The introductory quotation by Thomas Merton includes the idea that "the hearing of the spirit . . . demands the emptiness of all the faculties." What does Merton mean? How does this point relate to silence as nonverbal communication? How does his idea relate to what Robert Bolton says about hearing and listening in Chapter 7?

Do you agree with May that both the pause and freedom are "positive negatives," that is, phenomena defined by absence instead of the presence of something?

Briefly describe an event in your own experience that makes the same point Lao Tzu makes with his examples of the cartwheel, the vase, and the room.

What is the most vivid example you can recall of a pause or silence being signifi-cant? What's the most meaningful pause or silence you can remember?

Can May's point about the significance of the pause in jazz be made about any other kind of music? Explain.

How much of your personal schedule of this week's activities seems to reinforce May's point that in a technological society pauses are rare and often viewed as neg-ative? In other words, how technologically frenetic is your schedule this week?

Give an example from your own experience of a significant pause of just a few milliseconds.

As Mark Knapp's first essay in this chapter indicates, there are many forms or types of nonverbal communication, including appearance and dress, tone of voice, facial expression, gestures, posture and movement, distance and space relationships, and even architecture and decoration. All have potential message value; each can con-tribute to or detract from interpersonal-quality communication. So why do I omit them all and include one essay on silence and another on touch? Because, as I've mentioned in reference to May's piece, these are two modes of nonverbal com-munication that are both powerful and often overlooked.

This is especially true of touch. Partly because of the views toward sex and sexuality that are prevalent in the United States and some other Western cultures, touch and talk about it have become almost taboo. We know that touch is important in greeting, giving support, and conflict, but its sexual meanings all but over-shadow everything else. Young persons learn very clearly where and when they can legitimately touch their parents, their friends, and themselves without being branded as "effiminate" or "aggressive" if they are male or as "masculine" or "easy" if they are female. When you read Leo Buscaglia's remarks about hugging in Chapter 13 some of you will smile or grimace with disbelief or discomfort. Touch, in brief, is the one mode of nonverbal communication with which most of us are the least comfortable.

James Hardison tries to remedy that in this next reading. He notes that our genuine desires to express warmth and caring are often frustrated by our awkwardness and inability to use touch to communicate. His goal is to suggest how we can, in small ways, use touch to build more gestures of caring into our day-to-day relationships.

Hardison emphasizes how touch can build trust, even in a completely nonsexual context. Doctors, dentists, and beauty operators, for example, can enhance or reduce trust by the ways they touch their patients or clients. Trust is also obviously important in intimate relationships, and a great deal of it—or its opposite—is communicated by touch.

Touch is also an important part of our contact with strangers and with persons from other cultures. In both contexts we can profit from the recognition of (1) the reality of legitimate differences, (2) the desirability of adding appropriate touch to our repertoire of communication skills, and (3) the effectiveness of a "progressive, slowly developing, step-by-step pattern of touching behavior for specific purposes. . . ."

Hardison suggests that we begin our efforts to change with those closest to us. It's easiest to control the level of risk in these relationships and to make progress toward more effectively communicating the genuine feelings of warmth, support, and caring that we experience.

I hope this essay will at least prompt you to consider your touching attitudes and behaviors. There is no need for all of us to turn into exuberant huggers, especially if that kind of behavior violates cultural norms we've been taught. But even a little more touch could humanize our communication contacts substantially.

Touching for Improving Interpersonal Relationships

James Hardison

Interpersonal relationships form the bases of what we perceive as our state of being. Yet a common complaint today is the alienation workers feel for management, students express about teachers, youth experience with parents, and spouses sense with each other. It seems that despite our efforts to the contrary, our interactions often result in conflict and misunderstanding. On the other hand, our good intentions abound. We wish to give and receive warmth through physical affection. We desire to aid one another in emotional development and self-actualization. We try to maintain an atmosphere in which one individual cares about another's needs and welfare. In short, we care about one another and wish to convey the warmth we feel.

Warmth is a measurable physical quality; however, the type of warmth we are talking about has an internal dimension. How do we derive the concept of "warmth"? In our earliest years, particularly in that period before we developed verbal skills, we depended on tactual senses for a large portion of our learning, coping, and experiencing. We were touched by our parents for consolation, companionship, and protection. Their warm bodies provided us with a feeling of security allowing us to move about with less fear and more emotional strength. Our behavior and adjustment in later life were fundamentally influenced by the degree of emotional warmth we received through our parents' touching. In feeding, bathing, clothing, comforting, and entertaining us, our parents gave us our first concept of love and affection—warmth.

Each of us has the potential for giving physical affection and communicating warmth as we truly seek to improve our interpersonal relations. Our associates, colleagues, and friends also have the need to be touched. They subconsciously have the desire to make human contact, but they may be held back because many of them feel that "it's not nice to touch," or that touching will imply or lead to "something sexual." As individuals in search of a better way to relate to others, we must take the initiative, be slightly daring, and transcend the taboos and unreasonable social restrictions placed on us. We must turn to one of our most natural instincts, the tendency to touch in a caringly human way.

TOUCHING IN TIMES OF CRISIS

Have you ever noticed how interpersonal relationships take on more importance in times of crisis? Little children might feel independent as they play outside with their buddies, but an injury will quickly bring them to their parents in search of reassurance and care. Even the momentary crisis experienced by young lovers descending the steepest drop on a roller coaster is enough to trigger the need (or at least the pretext of it) to hold each other securely until the danger passes. Other minor crises include fender-bender auto accidents, final exams, and major business transactions. In any one of these crises, significant persons frequently give us verbal consolation as well as tactual reassurances.

Accordingly, interpersonal relationships are intensified in times of severe crisis, as in interactions between survivors after a death or even between distraught individuals who are separated by long-term physical barriers or divorce. Our friends seek us out more readily when they know we have experienced a crisis. They want us to know that they are close by to help, and they often signal this through touch. Through loving and supportive touches, a person can help to heal a friend's deepest wounds. Touching in such circumstances is something most of us do naturally. Why should we reserve our capability to use touch effectively only for times of crisis? Why not try, in small ways, to build such caring gestures into our day-to-day relationships?

TOUCH IN EVERYDAY RELATIONSHIPS

If we consider everyday activities in interpersonal relationships, we may see that we have friends and associates with whom we feel more comfortable in communication and touching exchanges. We may not even be aware of the exchanges we engage in; moreover, we may be unconscious of the messages we send out through touch. A case of unconscious touching occurred in the lounge outside a board of trustees' meeting room in a community college in Southern California. Two large lounge chairs were situated side by side, with high armrests close together. A close personal colleague and I sat in the adjoining chairs, placing our hands, parallel and palms down, on the front of each armrest. An active observer, I counted twenty-two contacts from my colleague as we conversed. He would emphasize a point in conversation or assure himself that he had my full attention by reaching over and patting the back of my hand, my forearm, or wrist. During a brief recess in our conversation, I asked him if he had been aware of any touching exchanges while we had been talking. He was surprised to learn that he, a forceful and very masculine character, had been touching the hand of another male. When I explained that I had accepted his touching as a catalyst to communication, he became aware that he could touch another male's hand to improve communication and interpersonal relationships. He later admitted that he had heretofore locked himself (as most Americans do) into the stereotyped role in which touching is generally taboo—especially between males—because of the "sexual overtones" or "sexual connotations." I have a high regard for my colleague because of his ability to accept his natural tendency to touch as a wholesome and useful behavior pattern.

Many of us have similar unconscious habits. If we become more aware of our touching practice, we can learn to use our natural inclinations in a deliberate way to improve interpersonal relationships.

TOUCH CAN BUILD TRUST

Touching can facilitate a sense of trust and empathy. From early childhood, we begin learning how much we can trust people by the way they touch us. We affix a supreme trust to our parents as we feel their tender and caring touch in feeding, bathing, clothing, and rocking us. Our trust in them stabilizes in proportion to how often they touch us and how often their contact satisfies our needs. Basically, the same commitment to touch is carried forward throughout life; we tend to trust those people whose touching either satisfies our needs or brings us pleasure. The greater the satisfaction received, the greater interest we have in maintaining the touching.

The same dynamics of trust come into play in adult touching experiences. This is particularly true in the helping professions. If we examine very closely why we go to a certain doctor, dentist, or chiropractor, we may find that we are highly influenced by the way these people have touched us and by how much trust they inspired.

Consider your dentist. When you are in the office, seated in the dental chair, you must at least be able to trust that the hands about to treat you will be clean and gentle.

I believe that dentists are acutely aware of the need to communicate trust through touch. They know that patients don't return to dentists who squeeze the inside of their lips to their teeth. Nor do they return to dentists whose novocaine needle hurts more than they imagine the treatment would.

I experienced two contrasting examples of dentists' touching activities. One dentist entered the examinination room, shook hands with me warmly, and proceeded to wash his hands in front of me before touching my mouth. Both tactually and visually, his behavior inspired trust. Another dentist neglected both these steps and cleaned my teeth so brusquely that he cut my gum tissues unnecessarily; they bled considerably. Touch and the trust it fosters accounted for the distinctly different impressions these dentists made.

Making a similar point, a woman told me of her experience at a beauty salon over a period of three years. The owner combed and set her hair each week with great care. While the owner washed the woman's hair, she took special interest to see that the strands did not become entangled; she made sure that the roots were not being pulled, nor the ends split, as she combed her hair, and she used a light touch in setting her hair. Mainly in response to the owner's touch, the patron had complete trust in her abilities. Then the owner sold the salon and moved away. The new owner, less cautious, showed little regard for the patron's comfort as she handled her hair. She failed to communicate trustworthiness to her customer and soon lost her.

The effective use of touch to improve relationships requires sensitivity and discretion. As we have seen, though touch has the potential to convey warmth and build trust, it can just as easily produce a tremendous "turn-off."

TRUST IN OPPOSITE-SEX FRIENDSHIPS

Clearly, the trustworthiness we communicate can alter our relationships. Our trust in ourselves with regard to touch can also alter relationships. When establishing a new friendship, can you trust yourself to be just friendly and not to expect sexual intimacy with a member of the opposite sex? That's a difficult task for a lot of us. We are so bound by cultural mores that many of us are locked into believing that persons of the opposite sex are not capable of being just good friends; we assume they must eventually become intimate if they maintain a close relationship. In actuality, many people form relationships with members of the opposite sex that do not lead to sexual relations.

A woman account executive of my acquaintance in San Francisco had an experience of this type. She and her friend did not follow the "expected" pattern between men and women. She had attended a business cocktail party where she met a charming man with a lot to say; he startled her with his witty comments, unusual thoughts, and sensitivity. The two later found themselves in her apartment. It was six-thirty in the morning, the sun rising, before they both realized that they had spent the whole night talking, occasionally touching and hugging, experiencing a profound interchange of conversation. They also realized and reflected on the fact that they had not performed the standard antics of a brief conversation followed by a jump into bed, not an uncommon routine for either of them. They agreed to maintain a relationship characterized by the meaningful combination of talking and touching they had enjoyed on their first meeting. Such a relationship requires a high degree of mutual trust and respect. Seven years later, these two people are still enjoying what they consider a most rewarding friendship. . . .

TOUCH IN OTHER CULTURES

Tactual expressions are a component of interpersonal relations in all cultures. Every group exhibits some form of touching to express feelings of friendship and love. North and South Americans kiss on the lips, touch cheek to cheek, kiss each other on the cheek, and round it off with hugs. Eskimos, on the other hand, hug rarely and touch noses to express their love. They lightly tap nose to nose, or one partner moves his or her nose in a circular motion around that of the mate, touching it lightly.

Samoans express their most profound love, not by prolonged kissing or touching noses, but by one partner pressing his or her flattened cheek to the cheek of the other party and taking impassioned staccato breaths that cause airjet sounds to emanate from the nose. The staccato pattern also characterizes their sexual relations. Samoans copulate in an abrupt, rapid manner, involving direct contact only between the genitals and almost never including a hug. . . .

Some African tribes use an arm grasp in greetings. Participant A extends both forearms, with the hands in a palm-up position and the elbows slightly bent. Meanwhile, participant B places an arm over each of the forearms of A. B's hands then grasp A's forearms at the inside elbow joint. This African arm clasp might well be considered as an alternative to the standard Western handshake to avoid some of its disadvantages. The standard handshake appears to have little meaning other than a cursory recognition of the individual. We might bring about a benevolent revolution by examining the various ways of revealing warmth, determining the effects of passivity in the exchange, measuring the relationship between the pressure applied and the meanings given (or received), and determining the significance of varying types of grasps and embraces. Such a study could give us some new insights and a refreshing perspective on how to use touch to express friendship and love. . . .

DIFFICULTIES IN TOUCHING STRANGERS

Touching to improve interpersonal relations cannot occur so easily between strangers. Most of us are not very open to touch as part of our communicating, a limitation that is even more pronounced among strangers. Basically, we are not a touching society, and we tend to feel discomfort in most touching interactions. Factors that contribute to this are (1) our basic lack of trust in strangers and (2) our resistance to being observed in touching interactions. We frequently have unverified suspicions about strangers, so we tend to proceed very cautiously with them, especially when it comes to touching. Although the handshake is generally an acceptable opening gesture in meeting a stranger, some people are reluctant to extend a hand to someone they do not know. This reluctance can be seen in churches where a handshake is part of the ritual; resistance is sometimes expressed as an actual refusal. Whatever the reasons for this resistance, it is clear that interpersonal relating must be entered into willingly; moreover, the imposition of a touching exchange can have an adverse effect. In some areas, congregational resistance to shaking hands has brought about a compromise from the pulpit. Religious leaders are asking their congregations to recognize their fellow church members by alternate modes: smiling or simply verbalizing a greeting.

We resist being observed in touching actions, perhaps mostly because we envision a sexual link to touching. Our cultural mores prohibit us from observing the most intimate form of touching—sexual intercourse. We extend our reluctance to being observed to many signs of affection, whether or not they are sexual in intent. As mature adults, we shy away from hugging or embracing in public, even for expressing friendship.

Modern psychologists have sought out ways through encounter group sessions to modify our behavior to allow us to feel more open to nonverbal touching behavior. Conflicting views have been presented. Some psychologists tell us that most touching techniques used in encounter groups are of little benefit, perhaps even harmful, since they foster defensiveness, produce stress, and have a potential for being psychologically disturbing. Their position underscores our cultural trait of little openness to touching strangers. It also points to a reluctance to have touching activities observed. I strongly recommend, however, that we consider a progressive, slowly developing, step-by-step pattern of touching behavior for specific purposes that would allow us to transcend the discomfort associated with touching strangers in general, while enabling us to relax just a bit about our touching behavior.

Understandably, most of us are not ready to embrace a complete stranger on the first meeting. If we are interested in developing a relationship, we want more information to go on. The information can generally be gained through verbal exchanges, which are more distant, less threatening, and more easily controlled than tactual contact. We can generally determine, through conversation, if we wish to move closer to others, and we can slowly assess their trustworthiness as they simultaneously determine ours.

If we are consistent in the meanings of our touching behavior, and others are similarly consistent with us, an unthreatening progression will follow. We will know, as will they, that a light touch by a hand on the arm is an act of friendliness and an expression of interest, not one of hostility or aggression. We can progressively work out understandings, such as whether a pat on the knee is used to show playfulness, to emphasize a point, or even to express a greeting. We can communicate that a hug or a full embrace means a warm greeting (a commitment of the entire self to it, so to speak), not sexual aggression. All touching transactions, in order not to threaten the relationship, must proceed with moderation and clearly expressed intentions.

BEGIN WITH THOSE CLOSEST TO YOU

A healthy improvement in the ability to be comfortable about touching might be brought about through slow, progressive, deliberate acts. This certainly doesn't mean that we become touching exhibitionists, ready to show everybody that we are the world's greatest touchers. A good place to begin could be in our homes. How many friends have confided that they never saw their parents hold hands, hug, or kiss each other? This state of affairs obviously encourages the children's future reticence to express themselves through touch. I suggest that couples begin to express their caring through touch in their homes freely, regardless of who is watching. Children or others who observe might be surprised or possibly ill at ease about what they see, viewing it as a departure from "dignified" behavior; but after several observations, they will probably be able to regard it as the honest expression of affection and caring it is. Don't hesitate on this; it is worth the risk. It can gradually make your life richer with meaning and expressed feelings.

Let's start with those people who are very significant in our lives. If they are a part of the family, very close friends, or loving mates, they will be more accepting of this new idea. . . . Without giving notice, take your mate's hand. Say nothing. Just hold the hand as unobtrusively as possible for a few minutes; then go back to doing whatever you were doing before. Or take your child lightly in your arms at intervals during the day. Let the child return to play or study without entering into verbal exchanges. The next time you are with a colleague you admire, dare to go over and give the associate a light pat on the back, saying, "You know, I really enjoy working with you" or "It's really great to be here with you." All these recommendations are designed to aid in improving interpersonal relationships. If our honest intent is to improve, we will do so. To gauge our progress, we might make "before" and "after" assessments of our relationships during a six-month period; a greater trust will surely emerge.

Touching behavior can have a significant impact on interpersonal relationships. Our touches and tactual expressions, when applied appropriately and tactfully, can carry with them a sense of warmth and companionship. Touches tend to improve interactions and communications. They cement our social and personal bonding with those people who are special to us.

PROBES

On a 10-point scale where 1 means "painfully awkward" and 10 means "utterly confident," where would you rank yourself on the following: (1) Your use of touch in your communication with family members? (2) Your use of touch in your job? (3) Your use of touch in your intimate relationships?

In a group of five to seven persons, discuss specific times when genuine feelings of caring or warmth were not communicated because of the person's inability to use touch appropriately and effectively.

What is your memory of touching in your family as you were growing up? What touch norms did you learn there?

Give an example from your own experience of the touch communication of a dentist, doctor, hair stylist, or other professional.

What are some specific differences that you've observed between white and non-white members of your community?

What is the most embarrassing experience involving touch that you can recall? (You don't need to share it with anyone, just recall it privately.) What did that experience reveal about the touch norms or values for touching that are most important to you?

How *consistent* is your touching? How might you increase its consistency?

PART 2

Openness
as "Inhaling"

CHAPTER 5

BEING
AWARE OF
YOURSELF

At first I thought that to "be myself" meant simply to act the way I feel. I would ask myself a question such as, "What do I want to say to this person?" and very often the answer was surprisingly negative, It seemed that when I looked inside, the negative feelings were the ones I noticed first. Possibly I noticed them because of their social unusualness; possibly they stood out because acting negatively was what I feared. But I soon found that behind most negative feelings were deeper, more positive feelings—if I held still long enough to look. The more I attempted to "be me" the more "me's" I found there were. I now see that "being me" means acknowledging all that I feel at the moment, and then taking responsibility for my actions by consciously choosing which level of my feelings I am going to respond to.

HUGH PRATHER

||||||||||||||||||||||||||||||||||||||||||||||||||||||||||||||||||||||||||||||||||||||||||||||||||||||||||||||||||||||||||||||||||||||||||||||||||||||||||||||||||||||||||||||||||||||||||||||||

Psychologist Carl Rogers has influenced many of the persons who have written selections in this book. I highly recommend that you read at least one of his books—for example, *On Becoming a Person, Person to Person: The Process of Becoming Human,* or *A Way of Being.*

This article is not an analysis of the self or a report of findings about it. Instead, it's a thoughtful comment by one individual about what's important to him. I especially resonate with the way he talks about the importance of "permitting" himself to understand another person and "opening channels whereby others can communicate their feelings, their private perceptual world, to me." I have also found it to be true for me, as it is for Rogers, that things work better when I avoid my tendency to "rush in to fix things." And I'm struck by the accuracy of the apparent paradox: "What is most personal is most general."

It seems to me that the attitudes and qualities Rogers is talking about here are those that enhance interpersonal communication. By getting to know which ones you cannot yet completely accept or achieve, you can get a clearer picture of what aspects of your own interpersonal communication could be improved.

Some Significant Learnings

Carl R. Rogers

I would like to make it very plain that these are learnings which have significance for *me.* I do not know whether they would hold true for you. I have no desire to present them as a guide for anyone else. Yet I have found that when another person has been willing to tell me something of his inner directions this has been of value to me, if only in sharpening my realization that my directions are different. So it is in that spirit that I offer the learnings which follow. In each case I believe they became a part of my actions and inner convictions long before I realized them consciously. They are certainly scattered learnings, and incomplete. I can only say that they are and have been very important to me. I continually learn and relearn them. I frequently fail to act in terms of them, but later I wish that I had. Frequently I fail to see a new situation as one in which some of these learnings might apply.

They are not fixed. They keep changing. Some seem to be acquiring a strong emphasis, others are perhaps less important to me than at one time, but they are all, to me, significant.

I will introduce each learning with a phrase or sentence which gives something of its personal meaning. Then I will elaborate on it a bit. There is not much organization to what follows except that the first learnings have to do mostly with relationships to others. There follow some that fall in the realm of personal values and convictions.

I might start off these several statements of significant learnings with a negative item. *In my relationships with persons I have found that it does not help, in the long run, to act as though I were something that I am not.* It does not help to act calm and pleasant when actually I am angry and critical. It does not help to act as though I know the answers when I do not. It does not help to act as though I were a loving person if actually, at the moment, I am hostile. It does not help for me to act as though I were full of assurance, if actually I am frightened and unsure. Even on a very simple level I have found that this statement seems to hold. It does not help for me to act as though I were well when I feel ill.

What I am saying here, put in another way, is that I have found it not to be helpful or effective in my relationships with other people to try to maintain a façade; to act in one way on the surface when I am experiencing something quite different underneath. It does not, I believe, make me helpful in my attempts to build up constructive relationships with other individuals. I would want to make it clear that while I feel I have learned this to be true, I have by no means adequately profited from it. In fact, it seems to me that most of the mistakes I make in personal relationships, most of the times in which I fail to be of help to other individuals, can be accounted for in terms of the fact that I have, for some defensive reason, behaved in one way at a surface level, while in reality my feelings run in a contrary direction.

A second learning might be stated as follows—*I find I am more effective when I can listen acceptantly to myself, and can be myself.* I feel that over the years I have learned to become more adequate in listening to *myself;* so that I know, somewhat more adequately than I used to, what I am feeling at any given moment—to be able to realize I *am* angry, or that I *do* feel rejecting toward this person; or that I feel very full of warmth and affection for this individual; or that I am bored and uninterested in what is going on; or that I am eager to understand this individual or that I am anxious and fearful in my relationship to this person. All of these diverse attitudes are feelings which I think I can listen to in myself. One way of putting this is that I feel I have become more adequate in letting myself *be* what I *am.* It becomes easier for me to accept myself as a decidedly imperfect person, who by no means functions at all times in the way in which I would like to function.

This must seem to some like a very strange direction in which to move. It seems to me to have value because the curious paradox is that when I accept myself as I am, then I change. I believe that I have learned this from my clients as well as within my own experience—that we cannot change, we cannot move away from what we are, until we thoroughly *accept* what we are. Then change seems to come about almost unnoticed.

Another result which seems to grow out of being myself is that relationships then become real. Real relationships have an exciting way of being vital and meaningful. If I can accept the fact that I am annoyed at or bored by this client or this student, then I am also much more likely to be able to accept his feelings in response. I can also accept the changed experience and the changed feelings which are then likely to occur in me and in him. Real relationships tend to change rather than to remain static.

So I find it effective to let myself be what I am in my attitudes; to know when I have reached my limit of endurance or of tolerance, and to accept that as a fact; to know when I desire to mold or manipulate people, and to accept that as a fact in myself. I would like to be as acceptant of these feelings as of feelings of warmth, interest, permissiveness, kindness, understanding, which are also a very real part of me. It is when I do accept all these attitudes as a fact, as a part of me, that my relationship with the other person then becomes what it is, and is able to grow and change more readily.

I come now to a central learning which has had a great deal of significance for me. I can state this learning as follows: *I have found it of enormous value when I can permit myself to understand another person.* The way in which I have worded this statement may seem strange to you. Is it necessary to *permit* oneself to understand another? I think that it is. Our first reaction to most of the statements which we hear from other people is an immediate evaluation, or judgment, rather than an understanding of it. When someone expresses some feeling or attitude or belief, our tendency is, almost immediately, to feel "That's right"; or "That's stupid"; "That's abnormal"; "That's unreasonable"; "That's incorrect"; "That's not nice." Very rarely do we permit ourselves to *understand* precisely what the meaning of his statement is to him. I believe this is because understanding is risky. If I let myself really understand another person, I might be changed by that understanding. And we all fear change. So as I say, it is not an easy thing to permit oneself to understand an individual, to enter thoroughly and completely and empathically into his frame of reference. It is also a rare thing.

To understand is enriching in a double way. I find, when I am working with clients in distress, that to understand the bizarre world of a psychotic individual, or to understand and sense the attitudes of a person who feels that life is too tragic to bear, or to understand a man who feels that he is a worthless and inferior individual—each of these understandings somehow enriches me. I learn from these experiences in ways that change me, that make me a different and, I think, a more responsive person. Even more important, perhaps, is the fact that my understanding of these individuals permits them to change. It permits them to accept their own fears and bizarre thoughts and tragic feelings and discouragements, as well as their moments of courage and kindness and love and sensitivity. And it is their experience as well as mine that when someone fully understands those feelings, this enables them to accept those feelings in themselves. Then they find both the feelings and themselves changing. Whether it is understanding a woman who feels that very literally she has a hook in her head by which others lead her about, or understanding a man who feels that no one is as lonely, no one is as separated from others as he, I find these understandings to be of value to me. But also, and even more importantly, to be understood has a very positive value to these individuals.

Here is another learning which has had importance for me. *I have found it enriching to open channels whereby others can communicate their feelings, their private perceptual worlds, to me.* Because understanding is rewarding, I would like to reduce the barriers between others and me, so that they can, if they wish, reveal themselves more fully.

In the therapeutic relationship there are a number of ways by which I can make it easier for the client to communicate himself. I can by my own attitudes create a safety in the relationship which makes such communication more possible. A sensitiveness of understanding which sees him as he is to himself, and accepts him as having those perceptions and feelings, helps too.

But as a teacher also I have found that I am enriched when I can open channels through which others can share themselves with me. So I try, often not too successfully, to create a climate in the classroom where feelings can be expressed, where people can differ—with each other and with the instructor. I have also frequently asked for "reaction sheets" from students—in which they can express themselves individually and personally regarding the course. They can tell of the way it is or is not meeting their needs, they can express their feelings regarding the instructor, or can tell of the personal difficulties they are having in relation to the course. These reaction sheets have no relation whatsoever to their grade. Sometimes the same sessions of a course are experienced in diametrically opposite ways. One student says, "My feeling is one of indefinable revulsion with the tone of this class." Another, a foreign student, speaking of the same week of the same course says, "Our class follows the best, fruitful and scientific way of learning. But for people who have been taught for a long, long time, as we have, by the lecture type, authoritative method, this new procedure is ununderstandable. People like us are conditioned to hear the instructor, to keep passively our notes and memorize his reading assignments for the exams. There is no need to say that it takes a long time for people to get rid of their habits regardless of whether or not their habits are sterile, infertile, and barren." To open myself to these sharply different feelings has been a deeply rewarding thing.

I have found the same thing true in groups where I am the administrator, or perceived as the leader. I wish to reduce the need for fear or defensiveness, so that people can communicate their feelings freely. This has been most exciting, and has led me to a whole new view of what administration can be. But I cannot expand on that here.

There is another very important learning which has come to me in my counseling work. I can voice this learning very briefly. *I have found it highly rewarding when I can accept another person.*

I have found that truly to accept another person and his feelings is by no means an easy thing, any more than is understanding. Can I really permit another person to feel hostile toward me? Can I accept his anger as a real and legitimate part of himself? Can I accept him when he views life and its problems in a way quite different from mine? Can I accept him when he feels very positively toward me, admiring me and wanting to model himself after me? All this is involved in acceptance, and it does not come easy. I believe that it is an increasingly common pattern in our culture for each one of us to believe, "Every other person must feel and think and believe the same as I do." We find it very hard to permit our children or our parents or our spouses to feel differently than we do about particular issues or problems. We cannot permit our clients or our students to differ from us or to utilize their experience in their own individual ways. On a national scale, we cannot permit another nation to think or feel differently than we do. Yet it has come to seem to me that this separateness of individuals, the right of each individual to utilize his experience in his own way and to discover his own meanings in it—this is one of the most priceless potentialities of life. Each person is an island unto himself, in a very real sense; and he can only build bridges to other islands if he is first of all willing to be himself and permitted to be himself. So I find that when I can accept another person, which means specifically accepting the feelings and attitudes and beliefs that he has as a real and vital part of him, then I am assisting him to become a person: and there seems to me great value in this.

The next learning I want to state may be difficult to communicate. It is this. *The more I am open to the realities in me and in the other person, the less do I find myself wishing to rush in to "fix things."* As I try to listen to myself and the experiencing going on in me, and the more I try to extend that same listening attitude to another person, the more respect I feel for the complex processes of life.

So I become less and less inclined to hurry in to fix things, to set goals, to mold people, to manipulate and push them in the way that I would like them to go. I am much more content simply to be myself and to let another person be himself. I know very well that this must seem like a strange, almost an Oriental point of view. What is life for if we are not going to do things to people? What is life for if we are not going to mold them to our purposes? What is life for if we are not going to teach them the things that *we* think they should learn? What is life for if we are not going to make them think and feel as we do? How can anyone hold such an inactive point of view as the one I am expressing? I am sure that attitudes such as these must be a part of the reaction of many of you.

Yet the paradoxical aspect of my experience is that the more I am simply willing to be myself, in all this complexity of life, and the more I am willing to understand and accept the realities in myself and in the other person, the more change seems to be stirred up. It is a very paradoxical thing—that to the degree that each one of us is willing to be himself, then he finds not only himself changing; but he finds that other people to whom he relates are also changing. At least this is a very vivid part of my experience, and one of the deepest things I think I have learned in my personal and professional life.

Let me turn now to some other learnings which are less concerned with relationships, and have more to do with my own actions and values. The first of these is very brief. *I can trust my experience.*

One of the basic things which I was a long time in realizing, and which I am still learning, is that when an activity *feels* as though it is valuable or worth doing, it *is* worth doing. Put another way, I have learned that my total organismic sensing of a situation is more trustworthy than my intellect.

All of my professional life I have been going in directions which others thought were foolish, and about which I have had my doubts myself. But I have never regretted moving in directions which "felt right," even though I have often felt lonely or foolish at the time.

I have found that when I have trusted some inner non-intellectual sensing, I have discovered wisdom in the move. In fact I have found that when I have followed one of these unconventional paths because it felt right or true, then in five or ten years many of my colleagues have joined me. and I no longer need to feel alone in it.

As I gradually come to trust my total reactions more deeply, I find that I can use them to guide my thinking. I have come to have more respect for those vague thoughts which occur in me from time to time, which *feel* as though they were significant. I am inclined to think that these unclear thoughts or hunches will lead me to important areas. I think of it as trusting the totality of my experience, which I have learned to suspect is wiser than my intellect. It is fallible, I am sure, but I believe it to be less fallible than my conscious mind alone. My attitude is very well expressed by Max Weber, the artist, when he says, "In carrying on my own humble creative effort, I depend greatly upon that which I do not yet know, and upon that which I have not yet done."

Very closely related to this learning is a corollary that, *evaluation by others is not a guide for me.* The judgments of others, while they are to be listened to, and taken into account for what they are, can never be a guide for me. This has been a hard thing to learn. I remember how shaken I was, in the early days, when a scholarly thoughtful man who seemed to me a much more competent and knowledgeable psychologist than I, told me what a mistake I was making by getting interested in psychotherapy. It could never lead anywhere, and as a psychologist I would not even have the opportunity to practice it.

In later years it has sometimes jolted me a bit to learn that I am, in the eyes of some others, a fraud, a person practicing medicine without a license, the author of a very superficial and damaging sort of therapy, a power seeker, a mystic, etc. And I have been equally disturbed by equally extreme praise. But I have not been too much concerned because I have come to feel that only one person (at least in my lifetime, and perhaps ever) can know whether what I am doing is honest, thorough, open, and sound, or false and defensive and unsound, and I am that person. I am happy to get all sorts of evidence regarding what I am doing and criticism (both friendly and hostile) and praise (both sincere and fawning) are a part of such evidence. But to weigh this evidence and to determine its meaning and usefulness is a task I cannot relinquish to anyone else.

In view of what I have been saying the next learning will probably not surprise you. *Experience is, for me, the highest authority.* The touchstone of validity is my own experience. No other person's ideas, and none of my own ideas, are as authoritative as my experience. It is to experience that I must return again and again, to discover a closer approximation to truth as it is in the process of becoming in me.

Neither the Bible nor the prophets—neither Freud nor research—neither the revelations of God nor man—can take precedence over my own direct experience.

My experience is the more authoritative as it becomes more primary, to use the semanticist's term. Thus the hierarchy of experience would be most authoritative at its lowest level. If I read a theory of psychotherapy, and if I formulate a theory of psychotherapy based on my work with clients, and if I also have a direct experience of psychotherapy with a client, then the degree of authority increases in the order in which I have listed these experiences.

My experience is not authoritative because it is infallible. It is the basis of authority because it can always be checked in new primary ways. In this way its frequent error or fallibility is always open to correction.

Now another personal learning. *I enjoy the discovering of order in experience.* It seems inevitable that I seek for the meaning or the orderliness or lawfulness in any large body of experience. It is this kind of curiosity, which I find it very satisfying to pursue, which has led me to each of the major formulations I have made. It led me to search for the orderliness in all the conglomeration of things clinicians did for children, and out of that came my book on *The Clinical Treatment of the Problem Child*. It led me to formulate the general principles which seemed to be operative in psychotherapy, and that has led to several books and many articles. It has led me into research to test the various types of lawfulness which I feel I have encountered in my experience. It has enticed me to construct theories to bring together the orderliness of that which has already been experienced and to project this order forward into new and unexplored realms where it may be further tested.

Thus I have come to see both scientific research and the process of theory construction as being aimed toward the inward ordering of significant experience. Research is the persistent disciplined effort to make sense and order out of the phenomena of subjective experience. It is justified because it is satisfying to perceive the world as having order, and because rewarding results often ensue when one understands the orderly relationships which appear in nature.

So I have come to recognize that the reason I devote myself to research, and to the building of theory, is to satisfy a need for perceiving order and meaning, a subjective need which exists in me. I have, at times, carried on research for other reasons—to satisfy others, to convince opponents and skeptics, to get ahead professionally, to gain prestige, and for other unsavory reasons. These errors in judgment and activity have only served to convince me more deeply that there is only one sound reason for pursuing scientific activities, and that is to satisfy a need for meaning which is in me.

Somewhere here I want to bring in a learning which has been most rewarding, because it makes me feel so deeply akin to others. I can word it this way. *What is most personal is most general.* There have been times when in talking with students or staff, or in my writing, I have expressed myself in ways so personal that I have felt I was expressing an attitude which it was probable no one else could understand, because it was so uniquely my own. Two written examples of this are the Preface to *Client-Centered Therapy* (regarded as most unsuitable by the publishers), and an article on "Persons or Science." In these instances I have almost invariably found that the very feeling which has seemed to me most private, most personal, and hence most incomprehensible by others, has turned out to be an expression for which there is a resonance in many other people. It has led me to believe that what is most personal and unique in each one of us is probably the very element which would, if it were shared or expressed, speak most deeply to others. This has helped me to understand artists and poets as people who have dared to express the unique in themselves.

There is one deep learning which is perhaps basic to all of the things I have said thus far. It has been forced upon me by more than twenty-five years of trying to be helpful to individuals in personal distress. It is simply this. *It has been my experience that persons have a basically positive direction.* In my deepest contacts with individuals in therapy, even those whose troubles are most disturbing, whose behavior has been most anti-social, whose feelings seem most abnormal, I find this to be true. When I can sensitively understand the feelings which they are expressing, when I am able to accept them as separate persons in their own right, then I find that they tend to move in certain directions. And what are these directions in which they tend to move? The words which I believe are most truly descriptive are words such as positive, constructive, moving toward self-actualization, growing toward maturity, growing toward socialization. I have come to feel that the more fully the individual is understood and accepted, the more he tends to drop the false fronts with which he has been meeting life, and the more he tends to move in a direction which is forward.

I would not want to be misunderstood on this. I do not have a Pollyanna view of human nature. I am quite aware that out of defensiveness and inner fear individuals can and do behave in ways which are incredibly cruel, horribly destructive, immature, regressive, and anti-social, hurtful. Yet one of the most refreshing and invigorating parts of my experience is to work with such individuals and to discover the strongly positive directional tendencies which exist in them, as in all of us, at the deepest levels.

Let me bring this long list to a close with one final learning which can be stated very briefly. *Life, at its best, is a flowing, changing process in which nothing is fixed.* In my clients and in myself I find that when life is richest and most rewarding it is a flowing process. To experience this is both fascinating and a little frightening. I find I am at my best when I can let the flow of my experience carry me, in a direction which appears to be forward, toward goals of which I am but dimly aware. In thus floating with the complex stream of my experience, and in trying to understand its ever-changing complexity, it should be evident that there are no fixed points. When I am thus able to be in process, it is clear that there can be no closed system of beliefs, no unchanging set of principles which I hold. Life is guided by a changing understanding of and interpretation of my experience. It is always in process of becoming.

I trust it is clear now why there is no philosophy or belief or set of principles which I could encourage or persuade others to have or hold. I can only try to live by *my* interpretation of the current meaning of *my* experience, and try to give others the permission and freedom to develop their own inward freedom and thus their own meaningful interpretation of their own experience.

If there is such a thing as truth, this free individual process of search should, I believe, converge toward it. And in a limited way, this is also what I seem to have experienced.

PROBES

Rogers's learnings become most useful when you ask yourself the questions he implies. Do *you* find it best not to act as though you were something that you aren't? Can you listen acceptantly to your self? Can you permit your self to understand another person? Can you reduce the barriers between your self and others? Do you trust your experience? Can you believe that persons have a basically positive direction? Can you see how your responses to those questions directly affect your communicating?

You might want to relate what Rogers says here about acceptance and listening to the ideas about empathic listening in Chapter 7.

Rogers's convictions that he can trust his experience also seem to relate to what Susan Campbell says about conflict in Chapter 10. Can you see the link?

> *The paradox of progress is that I grow each time I realize that I can only be where I am.*
>
> HUGH PRATHER

> *Some of the ways that I have kept myself out of touch with my body:*
> *Consulting a clock to see if I have had enough sleep.*
> *Trying to recall how much I have eaten in order to know how much I want to eat now.*
> *Putting on glasses when my eyes hurt (instead of resting them).*
> *Using aspirin and antacids.*
> *Wearing loose clothes so that I won't feel the objectional contours of my body.*
> *Putting thick soles and heels between me and the ground.*
> *Breathing through my mouth (which has no sense of smell).*
> *Using strong chemicals to prevent my body from perspiring and having its natural odor.*

Never brushing up against a stranger in a crowd.
Holding myself back from touching people when I talk to them.
Not looking at the parts of another person's body that I want to
look at.

HUGH PRATHER

I've included this reading because students in my interpersonal communication classes have told me that William Howell's notion of "internal monologue" is one of the most helpful ideas they encounter all term. This reading comes from Howell's book *The Empathic Communicator,* which I often use as a text.

Howell is an interpersonal communication and intercultural communication teacher at the University of Minnesota, and his book is based on his many years of experience with both those topics. By "internal monologue" he means the internal self-talk that's often going on. The central point of this excerpt is that your "covert" communicating is always affecting your "overt" communicating and that those effects can be damaging unless you learn to manage your internal monologue. Your internal monologue also affects the other person's communicating as he or she generates additional IM in response. That interactive, reciprocal feature of internal monologue is the point of the final model on page 115.

Howell also emphasizes that IM can act like a "power disc brake on internal and external adjustment to changing events." Our abilities to be flexible and to cope with change can be seriously undermined by internal monologue.

Whether internal monologue occurs in dyads, groups, or organizations, it is generally stressful, and it almost always reduces communication effectiveness. Howell discusses nine typical causes of this phenomenon and offers three suggestions for controlling it. In my experience, what Howell calls ego involvement, habit, and rationality are three of the most common causes. My internal monologue often peaks when I'm embarrassed because I've made what others might view as a simple mistake. I also engage in IM when some habitual expectations aren't met and when I can't make fully rational sense out of what's happening.

Howell's comments about how personal and social roles can contribute to IM echo part of what Maurice Friedman says in Chapter 12. Howell also broadens this point beyond male–female roles to those of parent–offspring, student–professor, boss–employee, and so on.

The first suggestion for controlling or managing your IM is to become aware of it and to recognize how it can work against you. The second is to learn to manage stress more effectively, for example, by maintaining physical relaxation. The third is potentially the most helpful; it is to refocus your attention from "inside" to "the between." This is a point Milt Thomas and I discuss in detail in Chapter 7, and it is crucial. The more you are actually concentrating on what's going on *between* you and the other person(s), the less you will be able to get tied up in your internal monologue.

The final section of the essay lists almost fifty questions you can ask yourself in order to begin controlling your IM. My students report that it's been worth the time they've invested in responding to these questions.

I hope that Howell's discussion will clarify how your *self*-awareness affects your *interpersonal* communicating. If you read this discussion along with Carl Rogers's "Significant Learnings," you should be ready to think seriously about your awareness of others (Chapter 6) and your listening (Chapter 7).

Coping with Internal Monologue

William S. Howell

The basic element in simple or complex relationships seems to be two people, a unit we term a *dyad.* . . . Since the basic human unit of interpersonal communication is the dyad, we can proceed to construct a dyadic model. This model should portray intrapersonal events as well as the interpersonal process.

Let us assume that the circles that follow represent two persons: A, a supervisor, and B, an employee supervised by A. As the interaction begins, A is approaching B, her purpose being to offer B a suggestion to improve the way he does his job.

A rushes up to B full of good intentions. She initiates the interaction by saying, "Hey, B, I want to talk to you about how you are doing your job."

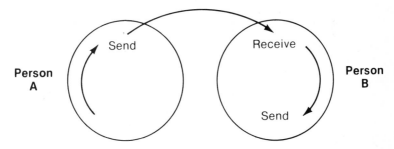

It happens that B, in addition to being A's subordinate, is also a timid soul, chronically insecure and apprehensive. When the boss hurries up with the abruptly expressed intent of discussing B's working methods, B is alarmed. He sends back a nonverbal message through a stiffened body, raised eyebrows, and compressed lips.

Fortunately, A is a sensitive communicator, and she picks up the nonverbal message. Many of us would pay no attention to B's reaction. We would simply go ahead and say what we had planned to say. A, however, not only interprets the cue as a sign that B is disturbed, but knows she must adapt to this reaction immediately. So, instead of continuing with her planned message, she changes her next verbal comment to "Hey, relax! It's not important, just a minor detail!"

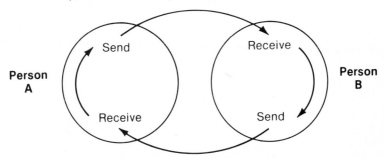

As the developing model shows, important events are happening intrapersonally. When B becomes alarmed and sends off the nonverbal cue of apprehension, this influences his reception of the next bit of communication from A. B at this point has only one interest, to find out how much threat there is in A's visit. And when A attempts reassurance, this conditions her reception of the next message from B. A's concern at this moment is to determine whether B has calmed down enough to go to work on the job suggestion, or whether she must provide more reassurance. When we represent these internal dynamics of A and B, the dyadic model is complete.

We should relieve suspense concerning the A and B episode. After A's reassurance, B responds by saying, "Well, you can't blame me for getting uptight! You came on real strong!" A must then either provide more reassurance or continue with her original message. She decides that B has indeed been reassured, and they proceed to interact about details of job modification.

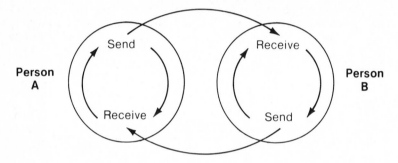

The model suggests that everything A does or says changes B's behavior. Further, whatever A receives modifies what she sends, and everything A sends changes the way she receives the next bit of communication. The same is true of B. Here is a dyadic interaction model of communication showing continuing intrapersonal and interpersonal feedback, and complete interdependence. This ongoing adjustment may be viewed as the process of *coping*. In John Keltner's words, "Coping with others is the essence of social interaction. Our ability to cope with others can develop only as we interact with each other in *our here and now*." . . . In this case, only when A was convinced that B was no longer upset did she mention her ideas and invite B to react to them. A made a wise decision in this instance. To see why, let us look more closely at B's internal state.

When B became apprehensive, a stream of uncontrolled thoughts raced through his mind. "Is A about to fire me?" "I must have been doing very poorly." "Perhaps I'll be transferred to something I don't like." "Probably I'll be demoted." "I'm really in danger," and so on. It is easy to see how sudden fear can generate compelling notions that displace or inhibit normal thinking. What was going on in B's head was the extraneous and obstructive conscious thinking known as *internal monologue (IM)*.

What happened to B happens frequently to everyone. People want to concentrate fully on a topic, but their minds wander. If they happen to be in an emotional state, the power of irrelevant thoughts is multiplied. Their attention is divided between what they should be doing and a stream of distractions. The more intense and constant the internal monologue, the lower a person's ability to pick up cues from the environment and respond sensibly to them. Apparently, A recognized this fact. Since she wanted B to consider her message thoughtfully, with a minimum of distraction, she made the relaxing of B's tension her top priority.

COMPLETING THE MODEL FOR INTERACTIVE COMMUNICATION

The whirling circle model can now be seen to be incomplete, simply because it assumes that people are capable of uniformly thoughtful, task-oriented communication. Actually, of course, two people interacting in a dyad are often distracted and inhibited by internal monologue. To be complete, the dyadic model must show the presence of internal monologue whenever it becomes sufficiently intense to interfere with an ongoing interaction.

The following model represents the communication between A and B immediately after A's opening comment, when B becomes emotional.

The appearance of "IM" suggests that normal effects of receiving or of sending are distorted wherever internal monologue is present. Not only is information processing affected in a person experiencing the disturbance, but the second individual generates internal monologue in adjusting to the effects of the first's internal monologue. A's efforts to calm B are "extraneous and obstructive" to her intended

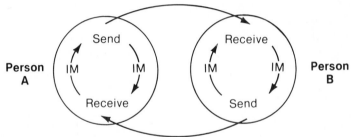

IM = Internal Monologue

purpose. Thus, a combination of B's internal monologue and A's countermonologue inhibits their working productively together. Until this extraneous and obstructive communication runs its course, the "IM" remains in the model. When it subsides to the point of insignificance, the "IM" is effectively removed and the circles of interaction and internal information processing can once again whirl freely.

To carry the whirling circle metaphor a step further, we can say that internal monologue acts like a power disc brake on external and internal adjustment to changing events. A sudden strong IM hits the brake pedal hard. Often the wheels lock, and adjustment to the other person and to events stops. Conversely, an interaction free of IM normally keeps the wheels rolling along at a good clip. In fact, speed of rotation becomes a measure of effectiveness. The faster the circles whirl, the more the resources of the persons involved are being combined in a joint venture. There seems to be no upper limit. In highly productive spoken interactions, greater speed of rotation is obtained by fragmentary verbalizing and increased reliance upon nonverbal codes.

A first step in controlling IM is to be aware of it and recognize its inhibiting effects. You can reduce the probability that IM will become a problem by avoiding topics likely to precipitate compelling, distracting thoughts. A mark of the highly proficient interpersonal communicator is the ability to "turn off" IM, or to not allow it to begin. This is an act of will that calls not only for self-discipline but lots of practice. It requires sufficient mastery of the mind that you can direct *all* your attention to the other person and stop being aware of self. A person who is "self-less" in this sense is unlikely to generate internal monologue—unless you choose to do so to avoid continuing an interaction!

To appreciate the impact IM has upon person-to-person communication, we need to look at it more closely. Specifically, we need to consider kinds of internal monologue and then probable causes.

KINDS OF INTERNAL MONOLOGUE

Extraneous and obstructive mental activity in interpersonal communication occurs in two markedly different forms—relaxing and stressful. Daydreaming while listening to a lecture is usually relaxing, for example. Worrying about the outcome of a job application interview, however, is normally stressful.

Relaxing IM often provides welcome relief. Recall a time you were trapped in conversation with a person who insisted on telling you, in seemingly endless detail, about happenings in which you were not interested. For you, IM was an escape hatch that permitted you to explore the fantasy of your choice or plan some coming event. But even though it eased your pain, this recreational IM did interfere with your listening. Thus, pleasant internal monologue can be just as extraneous and disruptive as the more stressful, less enjoyable forms.

Stressful IM is a somewhat frantic effort of the conscious mind to cope with the perplexing or with the unknown. In the example given earlier, Employee B was precipitated into an interaction with his boss that he did not understand. A flood of possible interpretations "took over" his conscious mind in an attempt to make sense out of a perplexing situation. The content of B's IM reveals why such monologue is usually stressful. Every question he asked himself and every possibility he considered pointed toward punishment for him. His IM could be said to be "disaster oriented."

The gloomy nature of B's internal monologue in this instance is entirely typical. Only a dedicated positive thinker can react to the unexpected appearance of a boss who says, "I want to talk with you about how you're doing your job," and infer that praise and a promotion are coming! Most people tend to think negatively in such circumstances, a tendency that is not only normal but necessary.

When people are placed in an enigmatic situation, one in which the outcome is unclear, why do they characteristically become concerned about what could go wrong rather than about what could go right? The answer is surprising: Because negative IM protects them from the unknown more efficiently than positive thinking. If you predict favorable consequences and they are in fact disastrous, you feel foolish and incompetent as well as sad. If you anticipate gloom and doom and disaster indeed strikes, however, you have softened the blow. You can say, "I knew it!" Being right is some small comfort. If events come to a happy conclusion, the fact that your prediction was wrong is quickly forgotten. Thus, uncertainty almost invariably produces an IM that is upsetting, depressing, and stressful.

What happens in individuals often occurs in groups. The tendency to assume the worst when in doubt is par for the course in organizations. The standard script for this scenario in a working organization develops when everyone knows that significant changes are on the way but no one has information about what the changes will be. Immediately, predicting the future becomes a major conversational pastime. Rumors quickly fill the gap of missing information. The most popular rumors, of course, are vivid descriptions of bad times ahead. Just as an individual becomes tense and emotional by contemplating unpleasant consequences, groups within an organization can become upset. Two results are loss of morale and lowered productivity.

In dyads, groups, and organizations, much stressful internal monologue can be avoided by supplying abundant information on plans, goals, purposes, and directions. People who know what is coming tend not to waste time and energy speculating about it and accordingly view the future less emotionally. Their time and energy become more available to do useful work.

The extent to which people are susceptible to internal monologue varies tremendously. Some persons produce IM whenever a situation becomes uncomfortable or unpleasant. Others have a greater ability to concentrate and focus their mental faculties upon the topic at hand. Usually they can keep IM from starting; if it does start, they can control it or "turn it off" at will. Because extraneous and obstructive thoughts are managed better by persons who control their IM, these people are able to get more done and be more creative than the rest of us.

ASSORTED CAUSES OF INTERNAL MONOLOGUE

An enormous number of distractions interfere with person-to-person communication. By now, you can call to mind dozens of situations in which IM generates spontaneously. To control compelling IM, however, you ought to be able to identify and classify its source. Here, then, are a few sources of internal monologue and, finally, a basic conflict in people's thinking that makes them vulnerable to IM.

Unexpected, Disturbing Events   One major source of IM is any surprising development. For example, you make a statement to a friend expecting automatic, total agreement and get vigorous dissent instead. "How can this be? What does he know I don't know? Does this mean I've offended this person?" Your IM is off and running. Very seldom does such a situation provide opportunity to explore the causes of your friend's unexpected behavior directly, so your internal monologue keeps speculating and getting in the way.

Often, unexpected happenings can change a familiar, predictable interaction into one clouded with uncertainty. The instructor of your class in nonverbal communication asks you to help him with his lecture on the ways familiar gestures are interpreted in various cultures. Your planned—and rehearsed—role is to make the illustrative gestures. When you come to class, you find that the instructor is ill and has requested that you conduct the class. For some time at the beginning of the class period, your internal monologue about what your friends are thinking, how well you are doing, whether you will be able to remember the most important points, and so on will probably interfere with your performance. As your attention shifts from concern with self to interaction with members of the class, the IM typically reduces and disappears.

Covert Forces   Everyone possesses **covert forces** that are powerful sources of internal monologue. These are consequences of being human. They are said to be covert because they operate out of awareness; that is, people feel their effects without knowing the cause. Many could be mentioned, but we will examine six covert forces and typical instances of the IM they generate.

1. *Ego involvement* is the tendency to feel that what one does is a projection of one's inner self. After the spring banquet, you are introducing the

speaker of the evening and forget her name. You feel ashamed, humiliated. The IM resulting from this insignificant mistake is energized by ego involvement. A sensible reaction would be to laugh at "goofing up," enjoy being kidded by members of the audience, and forget it. Many people, however, would suffer for days. They would be distracted by internal monologue, nagging thoughts of their public failure.

Ego involvement makes it difficult to be venturesome. Internal monologue plays the role of censor: "Will this cause people to admire me? If I say this, will I be criticized? This should be said, but it will not be approved of. Let someone else do it." When you withhold your resources because of what people will think or say, your ego involvement IM is at work. Ego involvement constantly frets over what other people think. The IM it produces attempts to protect your self-image.

2. *Emotion.* . . [is] a major component of the motivational complex. . . . When any emotion is active, people behave differently than when they are unemotional. The emotion of fear produced the internal monologue in Employee B. Any threatening situation makes people develop highly distracting thoughts. Fright changes perception of an interaction. Anger exaggerates and distorts. An angry IM will cause people to say and do things they later regret. The emotion of love, however, is associated with a different kind of monologue, one that makes us less critical of and more receptive to the loved person or object. These strong emotions fill the conscious mind with compelling fantasies, making it unlikely that rationality can prevail.

3. *Anxiety,* a third covert force, resembles the emotion of fear. People can be "anxious about" something without being "afraid of" it. Anxiety is a state of tension which causes people to try to make something happen instead of letting it happen. A salesperson may be unable to resist pressuring a customer to buy. A parent becomes anxious when a child is slow to talk. The youngster who has missed school because of illness is returned to classes too soon by an anxious mother. A guest shows up for dinner a half hour early. A batter swings early at a changeup pitch. Anxious IM says "Hurry up," "Do it now," "Don't think or talk it over," "Settle this once and for all." In group work, anxious IM increases tension, produces compulsive decision making, and reduces thoughtful deliberation.

4. Another covert force that increases internal monologue in person-to-person communication is *habit,* the internal pressure to complete processes in routine ways. When habitual expectations are not met, the owner of the habit tends to generate IM. When a meeting starts late or runs long overtime, some less flexible and adaptable members of the group are sure to be irritated. Their IM often centers upon the persons responsible for violating customary boundaries. Habit governs most people more than they like to admit. A significant amount of extraneous and obstructive fantasizing may well result from being forced into deviant patterns of speaking or acting. These patterns are uncomfortable simply because they are not habitual.

5. The next covert force is *sexuality.* Often members of a male–female dyad will combine discussion of a topic with distracting thoughts of their sexual relationship. In mixed groups, men and women relate to each other quite differently than in same-sex groups. This is not intentional and hence the behavior is influenced by a force that is truly covert.

6. Completing this arbitrary list is a covert force that may surprise the reader. It is *rationality.* How can rationality, which enables people to be logical, methodical, and accurate, be a covert force? Answer: It becomes covert

and a source of internal monologue when it produces a compulsion to fit everything into an orderly arrangement.

Rationality urges people to make sense of everything they participate in. Yet many worthwhile experiences *don't* make sense in any demonstrable and logical way. They have value in and of themselves, but it is a value that can't be articulated. Appreciation of a beautiful picture or of an exceptional musical performance are examples of worthwhile nonrational experiences. Yet people often feel compelled to explain—be logical about—such an experience. People in the Western world tend to believe that they should have a reason for every opinion. This conviction promotes much rationality-based internal monologue.

One IM that comes from the compulsion to be sensible about every-thing is rationalization. People enjoy a play and later, when they talk about it, make up "good reasons" why it was enjoyable. They feel pleasure, so they say, "The lighting was well done," "Stage movements were balanced," and "Costumes were colorful." These are interesting observations but amount to a completely inadequate description of the feelings of aesthetic experience. In fact, they are extraneous and disruptive and function as typical internal monologue.

Personal Relationships The final general cause of IM we will examine is the nature of personal relationships. Two factors that are *not* mutually exclusive are involved: (1) feelings people have about each other, and (2) roles emerging from position or status.

Think about yourself communicating with four sorts of associates: strangers, lovers, friends, and enemies. The relationship you have with any one of these will add to whatever you do together a "qualifying" IM. The monologue tends to be qualifying because it is used to interpret and evaluate whatever your partner does. Lovers and friends benefit from your enhancement of their contributions; strangers and enemies are made objects of suspicion and their comments are scrutinized critically, if not outright rejected. Your monologue rationalizes by manufacturing reasons for assigning credibility to one and mistrusting the other.

Position and status roles generate internal monologue that structures both the style and content of an interaction. On a social occasion, a plumber converses with a physician. Typically, their interaction is free and open until they mention their work. Then the conversation becomes relatively stiff, guarded, and limited to "safe" general topics. Each person's internal monologue is trying to instruct its owner about what to say and how to behave to meet the expectations of the other. This is certainly a good intention, but it removes from the conversation any sparkle that might have developed.

IM changes behavior whenever the roles that intersect differ in position or status. Here are some examples of role dyads that pose expectation-meeting problems: parent–offspring, student–professor, boss–employee, nurse–doctor, minister–member of the congregation, you and the President of the United States. Much of the position and status IM is triggered by a conscious or out-of-awareness realization that each role has boundaries that must not be crossed. The President has to act and sound like a president. Many of his habitual pre-Presidential ways of communicating are out of bounds. He can "stretch the presidential stereotype" slightly (thereby demonstrating a strong individualism), but if he goes too far, he will be pubished by adverse reactions in the media and by slumps in opinion polls. A President probably is pressured by internal monologue as much as anyone in our society.

Similarity in position and status contributes to reduction of IM. When you and a close friend of the same sex talk over a problem that is important to both of you, there may indeed be few if any extraneous and obstructive thoughts to interfere with your sharing of ideas.

CONTROLLING INTERNAL MONOLOGUE

IM, which represents unnecessary scripting that reduces effectiveness, seems to be a problem for everyone. We have examined assorted specific examples of IM in action. Now let us turn our attention to what we can do about it.

Two general classifications of internal monologue were discussed, the relaxing and the stressful. Relaxing IM is indeed a problem, but a minor one compared to the stressful kind with its deep roots in covert forces. Woolgathering and fantasizing to avoid less pleasant concentration upon a task show inability to control attention. People who daydream when they should be paying attention can do something about it, if motivated sufficiently. Training in listening comprehension and exercises to improve reading speed are useful. Practicing attention control by listening to difficult material on educational radio, identifying your internal monologue as soon as it begins and "turning it off" is a self-help method of gaining mastery of recreational relaxing IM. Regular practice of this simple exercise helps to reduce unwanted daydreaming and fantasizing.

Stressful internal monologue differs from the recreational variety by being based upon a feeling of discomfort, dis-ease, a sensation that something is about to go wrong or has already done so. This sensation creates mental and physical tensions that cause the conscious mind to become active. But since the resulting thoughts are extraneous and obstructive to the main flow of events, tension is usually increased rather than relieved. Left to run its course, IM often increases in a vicious spiral rather than slowing down to quiet extinction.

The sequence, then, is *stress-tension-accelerated* IM. Breaking the sequence is the best means of control. How is this accomplished?

Competent communicators break the chain by doing something to reduce tension. When they feel stress, they may talk about it. By refusing to become ego involved, they can remain relaxed. They can share their feeling with other persons, find out if it is mutual, and defuse it by analyzing it together.

Another technique is learning to maintain physical relaxation. It is a fact that mental tension cannot develop in a relaxed body. Mental and physical tension are closely connected; they grow and decline together. It is possible to learn to reverse the "natural" tendency to become tense under stress. Some athletes learn to be most relaxed when competition is keenest. Biofeedback sessions over a period of time are useful in developing ability to break the sequence by refusing to become tense.

A third way to slow the vicious spiral of IM under stress is the simplest and most difficult. You can turn off internal monologue by directing your attention away from it. Then it will die of malnourishment. When extraneous thoughts intrude, ignore them. Voluntarily devote all your energy to what is going on *between* yourself and another person. This is the natural method by which internal monologue is contained and conquered. In an earlier hypothetical example, you unexpectedly found yourself teaching a class. Your IM ran rampant until you found yourself highly involved in interaction with the students. IM then extinguished itself. You were too busy with more interesting matters to pay any attention to it.

Coping successfully with stressful IM eliminates most unnecessary and harmful scripting. Consequently, it is a "must" for the development of competence in interactive person-to-person communication . . .

SELF-ANALYSIS: YOU AND YOUR INTERNAL MONOLOGUE

Internal monologue (IM) is extraneous and obstructive conscious thinking. In the past few days, when has IM interfered with your person-to-person communication? Did you conquer it, or did it conquer you? Could it have been avoided by better management of the interaction? Did something within you start the IM, or did a happening outside yourself precipitate it? Did other persons in the interaction show effects of their internal monologue? If so, what were the symptoms? If not, why were the others free of IM when you were handicapped by it?

Explain to yourself precisely the consequences of your IM as it changed both your ability to adjust to changing circumstances and what you did—or did not—say. If you were to repeat this interaction, could you restrict or control your internal monologue? How would you go about preventing it? Once your IM has started, what techniques could you use to reduce or minimize it?

Why is it desirable that the circles in the whirling circle model rotate freely? Is it true that there is no upper limit to the speed of rotation, that faster is indeed better?

What is a greater problem for you, relaxing or stressful internal monologue? Think of a time you used IM as an escape mechanism. What are the favorite fantasies of your recreational internal monologue? Does your relaxing IM pretend to do useful work, like planning the future, or does it simply try to have fun?

Think of a time when a stressful, uncomfortable situation started your IM. Was your internal monologue script disaster oriented or optimistic? Did your IM predict an actual outcome? Can you recall being in a group under stress when the group monologue filled an information gap? Describe the incident. What, if anything, put a stop to the rumors that circulated? When one group monologue ended, did another begin?

Which of the six covert forces mentioned in this chapter energizes your internal monologue the most? Are you addicted to novelty or are you a creature of habit? Does this characteristic start an IM under certain circumstances?

What, if any, monologue tends to begin when you work with members of the opposite sex? Are your expectations of a woman conversationalist different from your expectations of a man? Is your style of speaking with a person of the other sex different from your manner of speaking with a person of the same sex? If so, list detailed differences.

How strong is your covert rationality? Do you feel a compulsion to put things in order, or do you enjoy disarray and impulsive decisions? Can you remember rationalizing a hasty conclusion? Was the rationalization for yourself, or for the benefit of others?

Think of an acquaintance with whom you communicate stiffly and with whom you rely upon scripting. Then think of another with whom you are relaxed and spontaneous. Decide which produces more IM for you and explain why that is the case.

Select three persons you know well, one of high status, one of your own status, and one well below yourself in status. What characterizes the role you play in communicating with each? Are any of these persons the same individuals you selected while reading the previous paragraph? Do you relate scripting to status differential?

What is your level of tension while talking to a group? What circumstances reduce this tension and what increases it? Are you less tense or more tense in talking to a group of strangers instead of people you know? Why?

Think of a time when you were ill at ease when talking with another person. Did you mention your discomfort and talk about it? Why or why not? Do you usually feel free to discuss feelings when interacting with friends? With strangers? Do you often reveal your feelings to your conversational partner? Would doing this reduce or increase internal monologue?

How much do you monitor your conversation? If you monitor a lot, why do you do so? Do you trust your out-of-awareness critical thinking to tell you what to say at moments of crisis?

When you are engaged in task-oriented activities with several other people, is your predominant style acting out or working through? Can you give examples of situations from work, family, or recreation where acting out is your preferred style? Can you cite other situations where working through would clearly be preferable?

Have you experienced one-to-one communication that approached Buber's ideal of dialogue? What requirements must two people meet if they are to attain a high level of working through?

Are the anticipated risks that hold people back from working through real or imaginary? Think about it.

PROBES

Give an example from your own experience of two persons' IM affecting each other. How is this phenomenon "like a power disc brake"? Do you agree with Howell that relaxing, pleasant IM can be as disruptive to your communication as stressful IM? How so?

In what situation do you experience the most ego involvement? Are there any communication *advantages* of this phenomenon?

Sexuality is a common and influential cause of IM, especially for adolescents. Can you recall a time from that period of your life when IM significantly affected your communication? What was the outcome?

Do you agree or disagree with Howell when he says, "Many worthwhile experiences *don't* make sense in any demonstrable and logical way"? Explain.

Based on your own observation, how does IM function at a typical party? Does it produce any positive effects? How do you cope with IM in a party context?

What are some concrete ways to follow Howell's third suggestion to "devote all your energy to what is going on *between* yourself and another person"?

When I first began trying to be myself, I at times felt trapped by my feelings. I thought that I was stuck with the feelings I had, that I couldn't change them, and shouldn't try to even if I could. I saw many negative feelings inside me that I didn't want, and yet I felt that I must express them if I were going to be myself.

Since then I have realized that my feelings do change and that I can have a hand in changing them. They change simply by my becoming aware of them. When I acknowledge my feelings they become more positive. And they change when I express them. For example, if I tell a man I don't like him, I usually like him better.

The second thing I have realized is that my not wanting to express a negative feeling is a feeling in itself, a part of me, and if I want not to express the negative feeling more than I do, then I will be acting more like myself by not expressing it.

HUGH PRATHER

CHAPTER 6

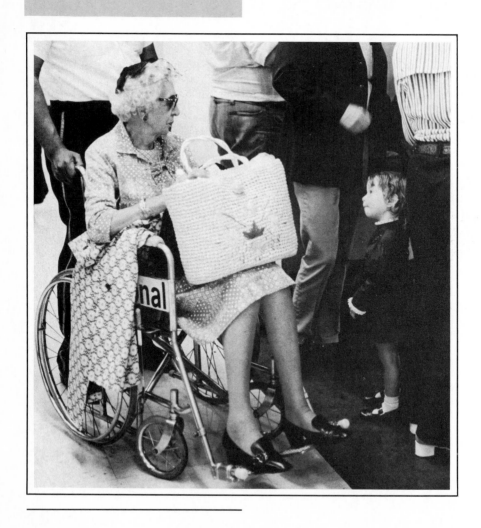

BEING
AWARE OF OTHERS

When I'm critical of another person, when I see his behavior as a "fault," my attitude includes these feelings: I think of him as one thing (instead of having many parts). I dislike him. I "just can't understand" his action. He seems unjustified. And I think he "knows better." If I feel this way I am in reality seeing my own self-condemnation. "Fault" means failure to meet a standard. Whose? Mine. Another person's behavior is "bad" or "understandable" according to my experience with myself. My criticism of him amounts to: If I had said that or acted that way I would think of myself as selfish, opinionated, immature, etc. A part of me wants to act that way or thinks of myself as acting that way and condemns this. If I understood why I act like that, or want to, and had forgiven myself for it, I wouldn't be condemning this person now. I'm getting upset with him because there is something in me I don't understand and haven't yet accepted.

HUGH PRATHER

|ı|ıı||ıı||ıı||ıı||ıı||ıı||ıı||ıı||ıı||ıı||ıı||ıı||ıı||ıı||ıı||ıı||ıı||ıı||ıı||ıı||ıı||ıı||ıı||ıı||ıı||ıı||ıı||ıı||ıı||ıı||ıı||ıı||ıı||ıı||ıı||ıı||ıı||ıı||ıı||ıı||ı|

This reading is a long one. Believe it or not, I cut about half of this essay and then decided that there was just too much good material here to cut it any further. Even though Jones' treatment is also a little "social scientific" for my taste, this is the most readable, complete, authoritative, and up-to-date account I have seen of the crucially important topic of person perception. That's why it's here.

Jones identifies his central purpose in the second paragraph, and in the fourth and fifth paragraphs he previews the whole article. His first main point is that the processes we call "stereotyping" are normal and unavoidable. As he puts it, there are "certain flaws in the way in which we process information about other people" that are not deficiencies or errors but are frequently shortcuts that simplify our perceiving. The first part of the essay describes person perception not as passive receiving but as a process of active choice-making. Then there are two sections where Jones discusses a generalization and an attribution that we characteristically make and that significantly affect the conclusions we draw about others. In the final section Jones talks about how our ways of perceiving others shape our interpersonal futures. His summary is a useful review of his main ideas.

In the section headed "Perception of Other People" Jones explains how person perception is really sense-making; at the most basic level, "taking in" information is really trying to understand, as he puts it, "what another person is up to." We do this in part by segmenting the stream of behavior we observe, and the ways we choose to segment it significantly affect what it means to us.

In the next section Jones discusses how it can appear that situations we experience control our perception by choosing *for* us what to attend to and treat as significant. That phenomenon affects the self-perception of minority persons who are "tokens" and the ways we perceive people directly in our line of sight as contrasted with those on the periphery of our vision.

Under the heading of "Categorization" Jones reviews how categories induce us to exaggerate similarities—for example, among racial or same-sex groups. As he summarizes, the problem is that once we have made a distinction between "us" and "them" on the basis of a single characteristic, "we may infer that 'they' possess additional characteristics for which we have no evidence."

The section called "Implicit Theories of Personality" discusses a widely recognized phenomenon that affects almost all our perceptions of others. When we perceive—or are told—that a person is, for example, "warm," we frequently attribute to him or her a variety of personality characteristics that we believe most "warm" people have—whether or not we have *any* evidence to support our attributions. This phenomenon is widespread enough to lead Jones to conclude that at least under some conditions, "Our implicit theories may play more of a role in our perception of others than the actual characteristics of the others."

In the following section Jones lays the foundation for and then explains what he sees as the single most significant characteristic of our processes of deciding what people are up to. He calls it the "fundamental attribution error," and it is our tendency to overemphasize personal factors and underemphasize situational ones. We tend, in other words, to make sense out of what we observe people doing by attributing their actions to their attitudes or to their personality instead of recognizing the significance of their environment—the situation they're in.

126

In the final section Jones discusses how our stereotyping can close us to new information about people and how we can "behave in ways that induce others to confirm our expectations of them" in a kind of self-fulfilling prophecy. His point here, as in the other sections, is twofold: (1) these are natural, "normal" processes that are to a considerable degree unavoidable; stereotyping is not a "disease" we can recover from. At the same time, (2) only when we recognize these tendencies and accept them as normal can we learn to modify them and to decrease their negative impact on our dealings with others.

You may want to read this selection more than once in order to get all of what's here. If you choose to do that, I think it will be worth the effort, because the ways you perceive the people you contact *significantly* affect how you communicate with them.

Perceiving Other People: Stereotyping as a Process of Social Cognition

Russell A. Jones

STEREOTYPES AND INFORMATION PROCESSING

Stereotypes are often claimed to be the result of illogical or faulty reasoning processes. It is seldom made clear exactly what and where the faults are, but the usual implication is that people who hold stereotypes are intellectually deficient. Archie Bunker, for example, with his myriad stereotypes of blacks, Jews, southerners, Californians, and almost every other group imaginable is clearly not too bright, and the revelations of his convoluted reasoning are filled with half-truths, inappropriate generalizations, malapropisms, and superstitions. Unfortunately, the Archie Bunkers of the world are not the only ones with stereotypes. We all have them, and it is very unlikely that increasing everyone's IQ by 20 or 30 points would change that fact. But is there any truth to the claim that stereotypes can result from faulty reasoning processes?

The purpose of this chapter is to examine some of the evidence bearing on that claim. In particular, we shall concern ourselves with evidence suggesting that stereotypes are in fact the normal result of certain flaws in the way in which we process information about other people. As we shall see, there are a number of imperfections in the ways in which we take in, manipulate, and try to make sense of the information about those we see and hear and interact with. However, far from being indications of abnormal or deficient functioning, these "imperfections" are in many cases information-processing shortcuts and procedures that usually serve us well and make our tasks easier.

For example, because of the tremendous amounts of information impinging on our eyes and ears in any given situation, we usually have to be quite selective about what we attend to. We simply cannot take it all in, so we pick out what we think are the most important aspects of a situation. But situations change, and our

Excerpt from *In the Eye of the Beholder: Contemporary Issues in Stereotyping*, pp. 41–85, Arthur G. Miller, ed. Copyright 1982. Reprinted by permission of Praeger Special Studies.

normal habits of attention may retard perception of those changes because we are looking elsewhere, at what we think is important. Similarly, once we have categorized another person in a particular way, we are likely to ignore the differences between that person and others who have been so categorized simply because categorization is, by definition, based on the perception of similarities. We tend to overgeneralize the bases of our categorizations and to act as if people categorized on the basis of similarity in one characteristic are likely to be similar in other respects, even when these "other respects" had no part in our initial categorization.

We shall explore these and a number of other information-processing biases in the pages to come. We begin with some basic issues in the perception of other people: how we go about attending to the behaviors of others, what sorts of things we are most likely to notice, and what is likely to happen once we make the leap from observation to categorization. We are seldom content with the simple perception of differences in behavior of different categories of people, however. We feel a need to explain those differences, to understand why they occurred. As we shall see, there is a fundamental error that we are likely to make in trying to explain why someone behaved as he or she did. We are likely to underestimate the extent to which that person's behavior was constrained by the situation, and to overestimate the extent to which it was due to his or her personal characteristics, to the sort of person he or she is.

Our explanations for behavior are also biased by several motivational forces. There is some evidence, for example, that we tend to blame victims for their misfortunes, even when the misfortune was entirely unpreventable. Such apparently irrational explanations serve to protect our sense of security. If we can convince ourselves that the victim failed to take certain precautions against disaster, all we have to do to prevent a similar disaster from occurring to us is to take those precautions. Once we have fleshed out our perceptual distinctions among people and groups with explanations for those differences, we are often in deep trouble, because we tend to rely on these internal representations. What we remember about a person or group becomes for us what they are, and what we can remember is often unrepresentative and distorted. We shall look at some of the reasons why this is so. . . .

PERCEPTION OF OTHER PEOPLE

Perception has to do with the "taking in" of information. As Erdelyi (1974, pp. 13–14) puts it, "Broadly conceived, perceptual processes may be best thought of as spanning the full sequence of events associated with information intake and consolidation, beginning just after stimulus input and ending prior to permanent storage in long-term memory." Thus, perception includes a number of different processes: attention, the encoding or interpretation of what we have just seen or heard or felt or tasted, short-term memory, and rehearsal of what we have encoded. Our encodings or interpretations, as well as what we choose to attend to and all other aspects of perception, are, of course, partially determined by what we have previously stored in long-term memory. Someone with an extensive knowledge of herbs and spices, for example, may get a great deal more enjoyment out of a gourmet meal because he or she will be more likely to be able to distinguish and name and remember the various tastes than someone without such knowledge. . . .

Segmenting the Stream of Behavior

If we want to find out what another person is like, one of the best ways to start is by simply observing that person: watching, listening, smelling, comparing what he or she does with what others do, and comparing what he or she does with what we would have done in the same situation. Our purpose in observing another's behavior is, first of all, to make sense of what the person appears to be doing. An intriguing line of research by Newtson and his colleagues has focused attention on the perceptual processes involved when we try to understand what another person is up to. The basic assumption behind Newtson's research is that the perceiver does not passively take in information about the behavior observed. Rather, the perceiver actively participates in the perceptual process by organizing the ongoing observed behavior into meaningful segments or actions. Thus, to a large extent the perceiver controls the amount and kind of information obtained when observing another's behavior, and may literally generate more or less information from a given behavioral sequence, depending on such factors as expectations and attentiveness.

In one of his first experiments, Newtson (1973) hypothesized that perceivers who break down an observed, ongoing behavior sequence into small units will subsequently be more confident of the validity of their impressions, and will have more differentiated impressions, than perceivers who break down the observed behavior sequence into larger segments. The idea is that when we break the behavior into small segments, we are attending to it more closely and, hence, obtain more information. The more information we have about another person, the more confident we are likely to be about our impression of the person and the more differentiated that impression is likely to be.

To check on this, Newtson asked first-year male students at the University of Wisconsin to observe a five-minute videotaped behavioral sequence. The subjects were furnished with a continuous event recorder, synchronized with the videotape, on which they were to mark off the behavior of the person on the videotape into meaningful segments. However, half the subjects were told to mark off the behavior into the largest units that seemed natural and meaningful, and half the subjects were told to mark off the behavior into the smallest units that seemed natural and meaningful. After watching the tape, subjects were asked to rate the observed person on a number of social and intellectual qualities, and to indicate how confident they were of their ratings.

Subjects instructed to use the smallest meaningful units did, in fact, divide the videotape into significantly more segments than those instructed to use the largest meaningful units (52.1 versus 21.3). As anticipated, subjects who broke the observed behavior into finer units—who attended more closely to what they saw—were more confident of their impressions. Further, the correlation between ratings of social and intellectual qualities was high and positive for subjects using large units, and virtually nonexistent for subjects using small units. In other words, subjects using small units had more differentiated impressions.

One other finding is of particular interest here. Following the confidence and impression ratings, subjects were asked to respond to four items, on each of which they were to imagine the person they had just observed on the videotape performing some additional action. For each of the items subjects were asked to choose between two explanations for the action: a dispositional explanation (he did that because of the type of person he is) and a situational explanation (he did that because of the situation he was in). Subjects who had broken down the videotaped behavior into small units made significantly more dispositional attributions on these items than did subjects who had employed grosser units and/or attended less closely to the behavior on the videotape. Thus, it appears that subjects who attend closely to another's behavior are more likely to perceive the other's subsequent behavior as personally caused—that is, as caused by traits, characteristics, and personality dispositions. . . .

In subsequent research Newtson, Engquist, and Bois (1977) have shown that observers segment the behaviors they are watching at break points, points in the ongoing stream of behavior where a noticeable change occurs in one or more of the features the observer is monitoring. Thus, the information we obtain from observing another's behavior is defined by changes. The unit of perception, as we have seen, is variable, and the observer has a great deal of choice in how the observed behavior is segmented. The usual purpose in observing another's behavior is, of course, to gain enough information to understand what the observed person is doing. As a sequence of behavior becomes predictable, Newtson has found, observers gradually begin to segment the behavior into larger and larger units. It is as if they feel they do not have to pay so much attention, because now they know what is going on. However, Newtson has also found that if an unexpected or unusual behavior occurs in the sequence being observed, perceivers quickly shift back to fine units and attend more closely to the person being observed, apparently in order to gain sufficient information about the person to reestablish predictability.

We attend most closely to the unusual in behavior, and we do so, apparently, in order to learn, to gain sufficient information about the person performing this unusual behavior so that we may anticipate how he or she is going to behave in the future. Further, one consequence of our focused attention is that we are more likely to see the behavior as being personally caused, as being due to some quality of the person we are observing, at least when the behavior is not constrained by a particular task. It should follow, then, that if there are certain situations in which particular people are unusual or salient, we are more likely to pay closer attention to them than to those around them and, perhaps, more likely to attribute their behaviors to their personality dispositions.

Tokens and Other Distinctive People

As noted above, in most situations there is simply more information available than we can handle. We are overwhelmed with sights, sounds, and smells, and have to select small portions of what is available to attend to and encode. The aspects of a situation that we choose to attend to are, of course, a function of many things, such as our interests and experience. There is some evidence, however, that in many situations we do not "choose" at all, at least not in a conscious, rational manner. Sometimes it seems as if situations "choose" for us by drawing our attention to certain of their features.

Consider the question of self-perception. There are literally thousands of things that each of us could tell another person if we were asked to describe ourselves. McGuire, McGuire, Child, and Fujioka (1978), however, suggest that what we notice about ourselves and what we choose to tell another person about ourselves are often those characteristics that are unusual in our customary environments. It follows that the only son of a couple who also have three daughters should be more conscious of his maleness than the son of a couple who also have one daughter. Similarly, a black child in a classroom with 29 white children should be more conscious of his or her identity as a black than would the same child in a classroom with 15 white and 14 other black children. Further, McGuire et al. argue that distinctiveness influences our conceptions of ourselves in two major ways: directly, in that we may define ourselves in terms of our distinctive or unusual features, and indirectly, in that others may perceive us and respond to us in terms of our distinctive attributes.

In support of the hypothesis that we define ourselves in terms of our distinctive attributes, McGuire et al. (1978) and McGuire, McGuire, and Winton (1979) report a study in which students in a predominantly white school system were interviewed and asked to describe themselves. Only 1 percent of the predominant white group spontaneously mentioned their ethnic group membership, while 17 percent of the black and 14 percent of the Hispanic students did so. Similarly, males were significantly more likely to mention being male when they came from households in which females were in the majority, and females were significantly more likely to mention being female when they came from households in which males were in the majority. Further, boys who came from homes where the father was absent were significantly more likely to mention being male than were boys who came from homes in which the father was present. Thus, there is some evidence that those characteristics we possess that are unusual in our normal environments are particularly salient in our self-perceptions.

It also seems to be the case that in perceiving other people, as in self-perception, we attend most closely to the unusual and the distinctive. Further, this focusing of attention on the distinctive has consequences for how we interpret what we have seen. "Distinctive" may, in fact, be too strong a word. In observing other people, we often seem to attend merely to whatever or whoever is easiest to attend to—the closest person, the person with the loudest (clearest) voice, the person we can see most easily. Taylor and Fiske (1975; 1978) prefer the term "salient" to "distinctive," and argue that, all too often, we unthinkingly devote the lion's share of our attention to whatever or whomever happens to be the most salient stimulus in our environment.

In a series of studies, Taylor and Fiske and their colleagues asked subjects to view simple interaction situations, such as a conversation between two people, and manipulated salience of the people conversing by varying the seating positions of the observers. Thus, some observers were seated so that they were looking directly at one of the two participants, but could see only the back and side of the second participant. Other observers were seated so that they were looking directly at the second participant, but could see only the back and side of the first participant. Still other observers were seated to the side of the participants, so that they could see both equally well. The two participants, actually confederates of the experimenters, carried on a five-minute conversation while being observed by groups of six who were seated as in Fig. 1.

Following the conversation, observers were asked a number of questions about what they had heard, and were asked to rate the participants on a number of scales. The major result was that observers 1 and 2 (who were facing participant A) rated A as having been significantly more responsible for the nature and direction of the conversation, while observers 5 and 6 (who were facing participant B) rated B as having been significantly more responsible for the nature and direction of the conversation. Observers 3 and 4, who could see both participants equally well, rated them as having been about equally responsible for the tone and topics of conversation. As Taylor and Fiske (1975, p. 445) note, "Where one's attention is directed in one's environment influences what information is perceptually salient. Perceptually salient information is subsequently overrepresented when one imputes social or causal meaning to one's perceptual experience."

It is true, of course, that our impressions of others are usually grounded in a

FIGURE 1

Seating Arrangement of Taylor and Fiske, in Which Two Participants Converse While Watched by Six Observers.

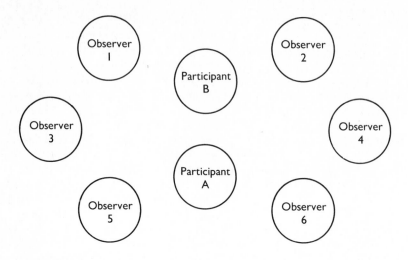

Source: Taylor and Fiske (1975), Fig. 1, p. 441. Copyright 1975 by the American Psychological Association. Reprinted by permission.

greater wealth of information than can be obtained by having observed them for five minutes while they sit in one position and converse with one other person. We typically see those about whom we form impressions in various settings, conversing with various people, and doing various different things. Under these circumstances how likely is it that mere perceptual salience plays such an important role in our impressions? Surely, when we have more meaningful information about a person, the distinctive or novel feature that at first caught and held our attention is no longer the keystone of our impression. Unfortunately, some field research on the experiences of token women in predominantly male organizations suggests otherwise.

Kanter (1977) defines a "token" as someone identified by ascribed characteristics such as race or sex, who carries with him or her a set of assumptions about status or likely behavior, and who is a member of a group in which all of the other members differ from the token on one such ascribed characteristic. Thus, a white in a group of blacks or a male in a group of females would be a token. In order to study the experiences of token women in ongoing social interaction, Kanter gained access to the sales division of a large industrial corporation, a division consisting of over 300 men and only 20 women. Further, since the sales division was geographically decentralized into a number of field offices, the skewed ratio of men to women in the sales force meant that each field office had only one female, or at most two, on the sales staff. Kanter spent hundreds of hours interviewing both male and female members of the sales division, observing their interactions in training groups, sitting in on their sales meetings, and participating in their informal social gatherings.

On the basis of her observations, Kanter argues that the proportional rarity of tokens in such groups is associated with three perceptual phenomena: (1) visibility—because of their differentness, tokens capture a larger share of attention; (2) polarization—the presence of the token, who has characteristics different from those of the other group members, makes the others more aware of their similarities to each other and their differentness from the token; and (3) assimilation—the token's attributes tend to be distorted to fit preexisting beliefs about the token's "social type." Each of these perceptual phenomena has consequences for the token. Visibility, for example, creates demanding performance pressures, because everything the token says or does is closely attended to. He or she cannot just slip into the shadows and relax. Polarization leads to an exaggeration of the dominant majority culture within the group and isolation of the token. Assimilation results in the token's being forced into limited roles within the group.

According to Kanter, the interaction dynamics accompanying the presence of a token in a group are heightened and dramatized when the token's social category is physically obvious. While it is true that such physically obvious stimuli as another's age, sex, or race do influence much of our social interaction, it seems to be the case that most of the discriminations we make among people are not based on physically obvious stimuli. We group people in many different ways—in terms of their intelligence, or friendliness, or arrogance, or modesty. We make such categorizations for our own convenience, of course, since they lessen the volume of information we have to retain. Once we categorize another person as, say, intelligent, we anticipate how he or she will react in certain future situations, even though we may never have seen him or her perform in similar situations. However, the very act of categorization may induce distortions in what we think we know about another person, distortions that may underlie what Kanter refers to as the polarization and assimilation processes that occur in groups with a token member of a race or sex different from that of the majority.

Categorization

The number of ways in which people are perceived to differ is enormous and, with the possible exception of sex, each of these individual differences varies along a continuous dimension. People are not, for example, simply intelligent or unintelligent, but vary in their degree of intelligence. We all know that. For convenience, however, we often break up these individual-difference dimensions into categories—such as "dumb," "average," and "smart." Transforming the gradual and continuous variations in intelligence into these three clear-cut categories makes life easier for us, in that it simplifies a tremendous amount of information and, for most everyday uses, such gross distinctions may suffice. The danger is that once we have classified two people or two groups into different categories, we may exaggerate the differences between them and ignore their similarities—or, conversely, once we have classified two people or two groups into the same category, we may exaggerate their similarities and ignore their differences. . . .

One way to look at this question of whether categorization induces us to exaggerate intracategory similarities is in terms of confusion. That is, if we have categorized people on the basis of attribute A—say, sex or skin color—are we more likely to confuse their standings on some other characteristic or on some behavior? If we observe a group of three males and three females interacting, for example, and are later asked to recall who said what during the interaction, what sorts of errors are we likely to make? If we do not categorize people by sex, we should be as likely to err by attributing something that a female said to a male as to another female, and vice versa. However, if we do categorize by sex, then we should be more likely to err by attributing something that a female said to another female than to a male, and something that a male said to another male than to a female.

Taylor, Fiske, Etcoff, and Ruderman (1978) provide some evidence on this point. Harvard undergraduates were asked to listen to tape-recorded discussions in which either six men or three men and three women took part. A picture of each speaker was projected onto a wall as he or she spoke, and subjects who listened to the six men found that three were white and three were black. Following the tape-slide presentation, subjects were asked to identify the participants who had made each of a number of suggestions during the discussion. Subjects who had heard the six-man discussion were more likely to err by attributing suggestions made by blacks to other blacks and by attributing suggestions made by whites to other whites than they were to err by attributing suggestions made by blacks to whites or vice versa. That is, the errors in attribution were more often intraracial than inter-racial. Similarly, errors made by subjects who listened to the discussion carried on by three males and three females were more often intrasex than intersex. As Taylor et al. (1978, pp. 790–791) note, subjects do "indeed process information about social groups using race and sex as ways of categorizing the group members and organizing information about them. . . . As a result of the categorization process, within-group differences tended to be minimized, whereas between-group differences remained clearer."

To avoid this sort of intracategory confusion, Hayakawa (1963) suggests that we should develop the habit of indexing our ideas, particularly our abstractions and categorizations. That is, we should constantly remind ourselves that two items or people or events that we have placed in the same category are not, thereby, the same. When dealing with people, we may categorize two people as similar with respect to one or even a dozen attributes, but they may differ with respect to thousands of attributes and items of personal history, interests, attitudes, values, and plans for the future. The problem is that once we have categorized or labeled someone, we tend to reify the label, to treat the word as if it captures the true essence of all that person is, when in fact the label at best designates the person's standing on one of thousands of personal attributes. . . .

The problem is that we know so much more about ourselves and others than the mere fact(s) of group membership. During the course of our experience with others, we learn to expect certain characteristics to co-occur. Having made a distinction between "us" and "them" on the basis of one characteristic, we may infer that "they" possess additional characteristics for which we have no evidence.

IMPLICIT THEORIES OF PERSONALITY

Everyone has a set of beliefs about what people are like. Further, casual observation suggests that these expectations about others differ in some respects from person to person, even though there may be large areas of overlap between the belief systems of any two people. But what do these "belief systems" realy entail? As Rosenberg and Jones (1972) point out, two things are involved: the categories we employ to describe the range of abilities, attitudes, interests, physical features, traits, and behaviors that we perceive in others, and the beliefs we hold concerning which of these perceived characteristics tend to go together and which do not. One way to sensitize people to the existence of such beliefs is to pose a question such as "What do you think of a wise, cruel man?"—a jarring inconsistency for most people. To most people, wise men are generally old, kindly—perhaps jaded—but never cruel. The categories into which we sort our perceptions of others and the beliefs about their associations constitute the rudiments of a theory of personality. Most people, however, are under little pressure to make explicit either the categories they employ or their beliefs about the relationships among categories— hence the term "implicit theories of personality."

The evidence for the existence of implicit theories of personality is relatively clear, and has been around for a long time. Asch (1946), for example, reported a study in which two groups of subjects were each read a list of characteristics that supposedly described a person. The two lists were identical except for one term. One group heard that the person was intelligent, skillful, industrious, warm, determined, practical, and cautious. The second group heard that the person was intelligent, skillful, industrious, cold, determined, practical, and cautious. Both groups of subjects were then asked to write brief sketches of the person described and to check (on a provided form) those additional qualities or characteristics that the described person would be likely to have. The resulting differences in impression were dramatic. Subjects for whom "warm" had been included on the list were much more likely to describe the stimulus person as generous, wise, happy, good-natured, humorous, sociable, popular, humane, altruistic, and imaginative.

Asch's basic demonstrations that we do infer additional qualities of a person from small initial amounts of information, and that changes in the initial information result in changes in the inferences made, have held up well through a series of replications. The next question one might ask about our implicit theories of personality, then, is whether there is any evidence that they influence the actual perception of other people—that is, whether they influence what we think we see other people doing and how we encode the behaviors of other people. . . .

Some findings come from a study by Rubin, Provenzano, and Luria (1974), in which the parents of newly born infants were asked to rate their young (less than 24 hours old) sons and daughters. Objective comparisons established that the male and female infants did not differ in weight, length, color, reflex irritability, or heart and respiration rates. Even so, the parents, especially the fathers, rated their sons as firmer, larger-featured, better coordinated, more alert, and hardier, and daughters as softer, finer-featured, more awkward, more inattentive, weaker, and more delicate. Thus it appears that the categories of our implicit theories and the interrelations among them may determine what we attend to and how we encode another person's behavior. Our implicit theories may play more of a role in our perception of others than the actual characteristics of the others, at least under some conditions.

What might some of those conditions be? One has to do with our own standing on the attribute in question. As an example of what is meant by this, consider a study by Benedetti and Hill (1960), in which students were selected, on the basis of test scores, as high, medium, or low in sociability. Each subject in each of these three groups was then asked to read a list of traits that were supposedly descriptive of another person, following which he or she selected from a list of 20 pairs the 20 traits that best fitted his or her impressions of the stimulus person. Half of the subjects in each of the sociability groups read the following list: "intelligent, skillful, industrious, sociable, determined, practical, cautious." The list read by the remaining subjects had "unsociable" substituted for "sociable." Of interest here is the finding that among those students who heard the person described as unsociable, those who were themselves low in sociability were more likely to attribute desirable characteristics to the person than were those who were high in sociability. . . .

Thus it appears that we do have implicit theories about what characteristics are likely to "go together" in other people; and once we have categorized another person on the basis of his or her standing on one attribute, we are likely to infer certain additional characteristics. It is important to note that such inferences are based on our beliefs about what characteristics are likely to be associated with the one that served as the basis for the initial categorization. The problem is that we then treat our inferences as facts, and believe that what we have inferred is the way things are (Nisbett & Ross, 1980). We shall return to the ways in which our implicit theories influence what we think we have seen.

But do we always behave in such an unscientific fashion? We often observe behavior for which we have no ready interpretation, and when we do, we may seek an explanation of why the person behaved as he or she did in what appears to be a relatively careful, analytic manner. There are several theoretical positions that assume we proceed in such a manner. But even when we honestly set out to understand why the person behaved in a certain way, there are traps for the unwary—traps that may induce and perpetuate stereotypical attributions.

EXPLANATIONS OF BEHAVIOR

In perceiving another's behavior, we tend to simplify as time passes. We start out observing discrete actions marked off by noticeable changes in the features we happen to be monitoring, and gradually organize these discrete actions into larger units. Zadny and Gerard (1974) have found that attributing a purpose or intent to an actor allows us to organize a behavioral sequence into larger units, and that, having done so, we tend to pay attention only to those aspects of the other's behavior that are relevant to the attributed purpose. If we are correct about our attributed intention, the accuracy of perception of the other's behavior will, of course, be enhanced. If we make a mistake, however, and attribute the wrong intention, the selectivity of our subsequent perceptions will make it quite difficult for us to realize the error. Even when we are correct about what the person is trying to do, we are rarely satisfied to stop at this point. We usually want to know why the person has a particular intention, why he or she is doing whatever we have observed.

Seeking the Causes of Behavior

Much of the research and theory on how we go about trying to pin down the cause of someone's behavior stems from the work of Heider (1958). The basic premise of Heider's work is that in order to understand the interpersonal world around us, we attempt to link the fleeting and variable interpersonal behaviors and events in which we find ourselves immersed to relatively unchanging underlying conditions or dispositional properties. According to Heider, any given behavior is dependent upon a combination of personal and situational forces. Further, the personal component can be broken down into ability and motivation. Heider's claim is that we tend to invoke these three general types of explanations (situation, ability, motivation), in varying degrees, whenever we want to understand why someone behaved in a particular way.

Building on Heider's basic premise, E. E. Jones and Davis (1965; also Jones, 1978) have developed a theory to explain some of the processes mediating the gap between observing someone perform a particular behavior and attributing a particular disposition to that person. The key to their conception is the idea that any given behavior represents a choice from among several that could have been performed, and that any effects of the behavior that are common to all of the alternatives could not be used to explain why the person behaved as he or she did. On the other hand, any consequences that are unique to a given behavior may provide some evidence on why the behavior was performed or why that particular course of action was chosen. Jones and Davis assume, as does Heider, that the more an act appears to be caused, or "called for," by the environment or situation, the less informative that act is about the person who performs it. Specifically, behaviors that are high in general social desirability, such as being polite, do not tell us much about a specific person because nearly everyone does these things. . . .

Thus, attribution theory, as formulated by Heider, Jones and Davis, and Kelley, assumes that we behave in a fairly rational, scientific manner when we try to understand or explain why a person behaved as he or she did. There is evidence, as we have seen, that under certain conditions we are as rational as attribution theory postulates. In spite of such findings, it is one of the ironies of modern social psychology that the overwhelming message of research on attribution processes is that in seeking to understand and predict behavior, we often, even usually, do not behave in the rational, analytic manner postulated by attribution theory. For example, consider the distinction between an outcome that is determined by skill and one that is determined by chance. In principle, this distinction can be easily made. In skill situations one presumably can influence the outcome; in chance situations one cannot. This distinction is basic to attribution theory, because if we are going to explain why someone behaved in a particular way, we must be able to separate those outcomes that are due to the person's ability and motivation and those outcomes that are due to situational factors such as luck. According to Langer (1975), however, in our day-to-day experience this distinction is often blurred, if not totally ignored. People often act as if things that can influence only skill-related outcomes can also influence chance outcomes.

For example, in skill-related competitive situations, the more competent one's opponent, the more likely one is to lose. The less competent one's opponent, the more likely one is to win. But what if the outcome is determined by chance, by the toss of a coin or the luck of the draw? Then, of course, the competence of one's opponent is completely irrelevant. However, if people do confuse skill and luck situations, they may let the characteristics of their opponent influence their behavior even in the latter. To check on this, Langer recruited male undergraduates at Yale to play a simple card game in which they and another "subject" drew for high cards after placing bets between 0 and 25 cents. For some subjects the opponent was neatly dressed, clean, and apparently competent, while for others the opponent was awkward, shy, and apparently incompetent. The major dependent measure was the average amount bet. As anticipated, subjects bet significantly less when their opponent was neat, clean, and confident than when he appeared to be a "schnook." . . .

Further, once we are aware of the outcome of a situation, we may not reconstruct the various possibilities inherent in the situation in the same way we would without such knowledge. Another issue concerns the *onset* of the attribution process. What factors—other than an experimenter making a formal request—are responsible for a person thinking about the causes of another's behavior and processing behavioral information in a deliberate, careful manner? Pyszczynski and Greenberg (1981) have suggested that people engage in more thorough attributional processing for behaviors which are unusual or unexpected. When expectancies *are* confirmed—as when a black person commits an act of aggression and the observer holds to a stereotype linking violence with blacks—one "may simply rely on the disposition prescribed by the stereotype without even considering other possible causal factors" (p. 37). There are a number of other ways in which we depart from the ideal in our attempts to explain behavior, but there is one that is so pervasive that it has come to be called the fundamental attribution error (L. Ross, 1977).

The Fundamental Attribution Error

When we observe someone's behavior, we observe that behavior in a context. Only in science fiction movies are we ever likely to see people behaving in a featureless environment, and then only for very brief periods—until they climb back into the spacecraft. Behavior usually occurs in complex, many-faceted situations, and quite often it is constrained by the situation in which it occurs. But, as noted before, we simply cannot take in and process all of the information available to us at any given time, and so we are likely to focus on the most salient aspects. When observing another person in a particular setting, the most salient aspect is likely to be the behavior of that person. Heider (1958) referred to this phenomenon as "behavior engulfing the field." Subsequent research has documented the fact that in making attributions about the causes of behavior, we often do give undue weight to what a person says or does, and too little attention to the conditions surrounding the person's behavior. The result is that we tend to see others' behavior as being due to their personal characteristics, to the sort of person they are; this is what L. Ross (1977) has termed the fundamental attribution error—that is, the tendency to underestimate the impact of situational factors in producing another's behavior and to overestimate the role of dispositional or personality factors.

The fundamental attribution error has been well documented in various areas. For example, E. E. Jones and Harris (1967) found that after having heard an unpopular attitude position being defended by another person, observers attributed belief in that position to the person, even when they knew the person had been assigned to defend the position by the debating team adviser. But the fundamental attribution error is not a mere laboratory phenomenon. It apparently plays a major role in our understanding of history, for example. As children we are told of the exploits of heroes and heroines. We learn of Caesar, Columbus, Florence Nightingale, and Robin Hood, but seldom are we told of the complex social circumstances surrounding these figures. As Carr (1961) puts it:

> It is easier to call Communism "the brainchild of Karl Marx" . . . than to analyze its origin and character, to attribute the Bolshevik revolution to the stupidity of Nicholas II . . . than to study its profound social causes, and to see in the two world wars of this century the result of the individual wickedness of Wilhelm II and Hitler rather than of some deep-seated breakdown in the system of international relations. [p. 57]

This does not mean, of course, that there are not great men and women who play crucial roles in various settings. It does mean that the perception of history is biased by what Boring (1963) referred to as the principle of "focus and margin." We focus on the most prominent and easily identifiable features, which are usually individual men and women, and we relegate to marginal status the elaborate and complex web of events surrounding those people. In short, we commit the fundamental attribution error.

In a similar manner the roles that we play in our day-to-day life may make us appear to have qualities and characteristics that we do not really possess. Interpersonal encounters are typically constrained by roles such as teacher–student, policeman–traffic offender, lecturer–audience. And, as L. D. Ross, Amabile, and Steinmetz (1977) point out:

> Roles confer unequal control over the style, content, and conduct of an encounter; such social control, in turn, generally facilitates displays of knowledge, skill, insight, wit, or sensitivity, while permitting the concealment of deficiencies. Accurate social judgment, accordingly, depends upon the perceiver's ability to make adequate allowance for such role-conferred advantages and disadvantages in self-presentation. [p. 485]

Again the point is that in forming an impression of another, we may not give sufficient weight to the situation in which we observe the other's behavior. . . .

There are also motivational sources of bias in our perceptions of others— that is, sources of bias that stem from our needs to protect and enhance our self-esteem. The false consensus effect seems to be on the border between motivational and nonmotivational biases. It may be a function of the vested interest we have in preserving our view of what is appropriate, or it may be a selective exposure effect due to the fact most of our friends and associates are basically similar to us and, hence, are likely to respond as we do in any given situation. . . .

SHAPING THE FUTURE

We have already seen, in the sub-section "Categorization," that the act of categorizing a person has certain definite cognitive consequences. We tend to exaggerate the similarities between people placed in the same category and the differences between people placed in different categories. These processes have consequences for the future, of course, but categorization of others may have even more direct and immediate consequences on how we behave toward them.

Ignoring New Information

One of the major ways in which stereotypes and categorization may shape our interpersonal futures is by interfering with appropriate utilization of new information about others. We often act as if the label we have applied to someone or our first impression of that person, which is usually based on quite superficial information, is all there is to the person. As a demonstration of this, Dailey (1952) asked subjects to read autobiographical sketches written by other people, and then to predict how those people would respond to specific items on a personality inventory. The criterion in each case was how the person had actually responded. Some subjects made predictions after reading half an autobiography and again after reading all of it. Other subjects made predictions only after reading an entire autobiography. The latter subjects were significantly more accurate in their predictions of how the stimulus person in each case would respond to the items on the inventory.

As Dailey points out, the premature decisions made after reading only half of an autobiography apparently prevented the subjects from fully profiting from the additional information in the second half of the autobiography. In subsequent research Dailey manipulated the importance of the material on which premature conclusions were based and, as expected, premature decisions were most detrimental when based on unimportant information. Also, simply allowing subjects to pause after reading some information (and think about it) had a biasing effect similar to asking for personality predictions on the basis of only a small amount of information. The decisions that subjects apparently made during the pause seemed, in effect, to close their minds to new information. . . .

The problems posed by premature conclusions about another person are complicated tremendously when the initial impression turns out to be negative— and, as we all know, many stereotypes are predominantly negative. One of the major things that differentiates negative from positive initial impressions is that negative impressions seem much more difficult to change. Briscoe, Woodyard, and Shaw (1967), for example, asked subjects to read a favorable and an unfavorable paragraph about a person, and to rate the person on a number of scales after reading each paragraph. When the unfavorable paragraph was read first, the changes from first to second ratings were significantly less than when the favorable paragraph was the basis of the initial impression.

Not only are negative first impressions likely to be more difficult to change, they are likely to result in less opportunity for change. According to Fishbein and Ajzen (1975), the beliefs we have about a person or group partially determine our affective orientation to that person or group. Our affective orientation, in turn, is the main determinant of our intentions about how to behave toward the person or group. When dealing with a group, of course, our beliefs about the group and its members are part of our stereotype, and our affective orientation, particularly if it is negative, is referred to as prejudice toward the group. Technically, "prejudice" can refer to positive or negative orientations, but in the realm of intergroup relations, it has come to mean, almost exclusively, a negative orientation. If a person has strong negative affect toward any ethnic group, it seems reasonable to suppose that exposure to that group might be avoided whenever possible. Such avoidance might explain why "All those (whites, blacks, Chinese) look alike" to the prejudiced person. He or she simply avoids them at every opportunity and, hence, never pays sufficient sustained attention to them to distinguish among them. There is, in fact, evidence (Malpass & Kravitz, 1969; Luce, 1974) that we recognize and remember faces of members of our own race better than faces of members of other social groups. Whites, for example, recognize and remember white faces better than black faces. . . .

Initial impressions and decisions about others, then, are likely to interfere with our ability to make intelligent use of subsequent information about those others. Further, if the initial impression we have of someone is negative, not only will it be relatively more resistant to change in response to new information, but it may make it quite likely that we will simply avoid obtaining additional information. We may just avoid further interaction with those about whom we have negative impressions. But what happens when circumstances dictate that we must interact with those about whom we have definite expectations and stereotypes? Is there any reason to believe that we behave in ways that increase the likelihood of having our expectations confirmed?

Behavioral Confirmation

There is evidence from various areas that we behave in ways that induce others to confirm our expectations of them. For example, many people have definite stereotypes about the physically attractive. Dion, Berscheid, and Walster (1972) have found that people attribute desirable personality characteristics to physically attractive others, and expect physically attractive others to lead better and more interesting lives than the unattractive. Of interest here is the possibility that because we believe attractive others have certain additional characteristics, we may behave toward them in ways that lead them to behave as we expect. That is, if we believe certain people have a number of socially desirable characteristics, we may treat them with more than average esteem and respect. When people are treated in such a manner, of course, they are more likely to behave in socially desirable ways. By giving the physically attractive the benefit of the doubt about their additional characteristics, we make it easier for them to be socially rewarding to us. Hence we confirm our initial assumption that they are more pleasant to interact with than the physically unattractive.

Snyder, Tanke, and Berscheid (1977) use the term "behavioral confirmation" to refer to how we may unknowingly induce others to treat us in such a way that our initial impressions of them are confirmed. For example, if we believe certain people are cold and hostile, we may be less friendly than if we believe them to be warm and generous. They, in turn, may be mildly offended by our coolness, and reciprocate in kind. Thus, our initial impression of their lack of warmth is confirmed, although the confirmation is brought about by our own behavior.

To see whether this sort of self-fulfilling prophecy occurs with stereotypes of the physically attractive, Snyder et al. designed an experiment in which male college students were to try to get acquainted with a female student over the telephone. The male–female pairs who participated in the research were not allowed to see each other prior to the telephone conversation. However, each male student was given some information about the woman he would be talking with and was shown a photograph that supposedly had just been taken with a Polaroid camera. All of the information furnished the males, except the photograph, was supplied by the actual person they were to talk with. The photographs were selected from one of two sets that had previously been rated as attractive or unattractive. After receiving this information, the male students indicated their initial impressions of their partners. Those who had just seen an attractive photo expected their partners to be, for example, more poised, more humorous, and more sociable than those who had just seen an unattractive photo.

Each male–female pair then engaged in a 10-minute phone conversation. The conversations were recorded with the male and female voices on separate tracks, and raters were later asked to listen to the tape tracks containing the female voices and answer a number of questions about the females. For example, they rated each female participant on a number of bipolar scales and answered questions such as "How much is she enjoying herself?" and "How animated and enthusiastic is this person?" Note that these raters heard only the females, who were just being themselves, but who were believed to be either attractive or unattractive by the person to whom they were talking. As anticipated, the females whose partners thought they were attractive were rated as sounding more poised, more humorous, more sociable, and generally more socially adept than the females whose partners thought they were unattractive. Data from another group of raters who listened to only the male voices revealed that those males who thought they were talking to an attractive female were themselves warmer, more sociable, and more interesting. It appears, then, that the beliefs of the males changed their behavior, which in turn induced changes in the behavior of the females . . .

Such interpersonal self-fulfilling prophecies are a pervasive part of our daily existence, and they play a major role in the perpetuation of stereotypes. Once we have a set of expectations about what members of a particular group are like and how they are likely to behave, we often induce those very behaviors. Rubovits and Maehr (1973), for example, note that many white, middle-class teachers expect lower-class blacks to perform poorly in academic subjects. To examine the effects of this expectation, they asked 66 white females enrolled in a teacher-training course to teach a brief lesson on television to groups of four seventh and eighth graders. In each group of four, two students were white and two were black. During the sessions an observer sat behind the students and coded the teachers' behaviors in terms of the amounts of attention, elaboration, encouragement, ignoring, praise, and criticism directed toward the individual students. Unfortunately, it was not possible to keep the observer blind as to the race of the student, and this may have biased the results. Even so, it is of interest that white students received significantly more attention than black students. Further, fewer statements were requested of black students, more statements of the black students were ignored, and black students were praised less and criticized more. All of these behaviors on the part of the teachers will, of course, eventually result in confirmation of their stereotype of poor academic performance by blacks.

An individual's behavior can be understood only as part of a system, a system that includes the behaviors of others and the expectations that those others hold about how the individual is going to behave. The ways in which such interpersonal expectancies and stereotypes can be communicated to the individual are manifold, running the gamut of verbal behaviors, nonverbal behaviors, and situational arrangements (Darley & Fazio, 1980). From mutual glances to avoidance of eye contact, from name dropping to name calling, from cooperation to competition— almost all aspects of behavior can be employed to let someone know what we expect from him or her. All too often the result is that we will have defined the situation so that the other person has little choice but to behave as expected and, thereby, confirm our stereotypes of him or her.

SUMMARY

We began this chapter by calling attention to the possibility that the existence of stereotypes may be in part a function of imperfections in the way we process information about others. In exploring that possibility we started by examining some data on how we perceive others' behaviors, and found that we do not passively take in information about behavior. Rather, we organize the observed behavior into meaningful segments. We also noted that the smaller the units we use, the more differentiated our impressions are likely to be, and under some conditions, the more likely we are to make dispositional attributions about the person we are observing. We also seem to attend more closely to the unusual, to that which is different.

This, of course, has implications for what we notice about ourselves and others. We saw that in groups, those members who are in the minority ("tokens") by virtue of some irrelevant, but highly visible, difference from the other group members are more constantly "visible" and, hence, under greater performance pressure. They also seem to produce polarization within the group and an exaggeration of the dominant majority culture. The token's own characteristics are likely to be distorted to fit preexisting beliefs about his or her "social type." The latter was seen to be an example of certain basic perceptual processes that accompany categorization—that is, we tend to exaggerate the similarities between objects or people placed in the same category, and to exaggerate the differences between objects or people placed in different categories.

Once we have categorized someone in a particular way, we often infer additional characteristics for which we have no evidence. Such inferences stem from our preexisting implicit theories of personality—the categories we employ to encode the various features and behaviors of others and the beliefs we hold concerning which of these categories tend to go together and which do not. We saw that our implicit theories influence how we encode another's behavior, and introduce a systematic distortion into what we remember about another's behavior. We are likely to "remember" that categories of behavior we believe to be associated both occurred, when in fact only one of them may have.

We usually are not satisfied with simple observation, however. We want to know why someone behaved as he or she did. We seek to explain behavior and, according to attribution theories, we do so in a relatively logical, rational manner. We seem to understand that behavior can be a function of ability, effort, situational factors, or any combination of these. We employ a covariation principle in our search for explanations—that is, we look for things that are present when the behavior is present and absent when the behavior is absent. Research on attribution processes, however, has found that we are not quite so rational as the theorists paint us. We confuse chance-determined and skill-determined outcomes. Once we know which of several possible outcomes did occur, we see it as being more inevitable than it really was. We are subject to the fundamental attribution error—that is, we tend to underestimate the power of situational constraints on behavior and to overestimate the role of dispositional factors. We are subject to a false consensus effect of seeing our own responses as typical and different responses as more revealing of the actor's personality quirks. We are also subject to egotism in explaining behavior. We give ourselves more credit for success and less blame for failure than we accord others. We apparently have a need to convince ourselves that we understand others when we anticipate having to interact with them, a need for effective control that again leads us to infer that we know more about them than we really do. . . .

Finally, we looked at how our beliefs about others may constrain future behavior toward them, and may even determine their own behavior. Once we have an impression of someone, we are less open to new information about that person. Our expectations may even lead us to behave in certain ways that have the effect of eliciting from others the very behaviors that will confirm our expectations.

References

Asch, S. E. "Forming Impressions of Personality," *Journal of Abnormal and Social Psychology* 41 (1946): 258–290.

Benedetti, D. T., and J. G. Hill. "A Determiner of the Centrality of a Trait in Impression Formation," *Journal of Abnormal and Social Psychology* 60 (1960): 278–280.

Boring, E. G. *History, Psychology, and Science.* New York: Wiley, 1963.

Briscoe, M. E., H. D. Woodyard, and M. E. Shaw. "Personality Impression Change as a Function of the Favorableness of First Impressions," *Journal of Personality* 35 (1967): 343–357.

Cantor, N. and W. Mischel. "Traits as Prototypes: Effects on Recognition Memory," *Journal of Personality and Social Psychology* 35 (1977): 38–48.

Carr, E. H. *What Is History?* New York: Vintage, 1961.

Cohen, C. E. "Cognitive Basis of Stereotyping." Paper presented at the 85th annual convention of the American Psychological Association, San Francisco, 1977.

Cohen, C. E. "Person Categories and Social Perception: Testing Some Boundaries of the Processing Effects of Prior Knowledge," *Journal of Personality and Social Psychology* 40 (1981): 441–452.

Dailey, C. A. "The Effects of Premature Conclusions upon the Acquisition of Understanding of a Person," *Journal of Psychology* 33 (1952): 133–152.

Darley, J. M. and R. H. Fazio. "Expectancy Confirmation Processes Arising in the Social Interaction Sequence," *American Psychologist* 35 (1980): 867–881.

Dion, K. K., E. Berscheid, and E. Walster. "What Is Beautiful Is Good," *Journal of Personality and Social Psychology* 24 (1972): 285–290.

Erdelyi, M. H. "A New Look at the New Look: Perceptual Defense and Vigilance," *Psychological Review* 81 (1974): 1–25.

Fischoff, B. "Hindsight/Foresight: The Effect of Outcome Knowledge on Judgment under Uncertainty," *Journal of Experimental Psychology: Human Perception and Performance* 1 (1975): 288–299.

Fishbein, M. and I. Ajzen. *Belief, Attitude, Intention and Behavior: An Introduction to Theory and Research.* Reading, Mass.: Addison-Wesley, 1975.

Hayakawa, S. I. *Symbol, Status, and Personality.* New York: Harcourt, Brace, & World, 1963.

Heider, F. *The Psychology of Interpersonal Relations.* New York: Wiley, 1958.

Jones, E. E. "Update of 'From Acts to Dispositions: The Attribution Process in Person Perception,'" in *Cognitive Theories in Social Psychology,* ed. L. Berkowitz. New York: Academic Press, 1978.

Jones, E. E. and K. E. Davis. "From Acts to Dispositions: The Attribution Process in Person Perception," in *Advances in Experimental Social Psychology,* vol. 2, ed. L. Berkowitz. New York: Academic Press, 1965.

Jones, E. E. and V. A. Harris "The Attribution of Attitudes," *Journal of Experimental Psychology* 63 (1966): 244–256.

Kanter, R. M. "Some Effects of Proportion on Group Life: Skewed Sex Ratios and Responses to Token Women," *American Journal of Sociology* 82 (1977): 965–990.

Kelley, H. H. "Attribution Theory in Social Psychology," in *Nebraska Symposium on Motivation,* vol. 15, ed. D. Levine. Lincoln: University of Nebraska Press, 1967.

Kelley, H. H. "The Processes of Causal Attribution," *American Psychologist* 28 (1973): 107–128.

Langer, E. J. "The Illusion of Control," *Journal of Personality and Social Psychology,* 32 (1975): 311–328.

McGuire, W. J., C. V. McGuire, P. Child, and T. Fujioka. "Salience of Ethnicity in the Spontaneous Self-Concept as a Function of One's Ethnic Distinctiveness in the Social Environment," *Journal of Personality and Social Psychology* 36 (1978): 511–520.

McGuire, W. J., C. V. McGuire, and W. Winton. "Effects of Household Sex Composition on the Salience of One's Gender in the Spontaneous Self-Concept," *Journal of Experimental Social Psychology* 15 (1979): 77–90.

Malpass, R. S. and J. Kravitz. "Recognition for Faces of Own and Other Race," *Journal of Personality and Social Psychology* 13 (1969): 330–334.

Newtson, D. "Attribution and the Unit of Perception of Ongoing Behavior," *Journal of Personality and Social Psychology* 28 (1973): 28–38.

Newtson, D. "Foundations of Attribution: The Perception of Ongoing Behavior," in *New Directions in Attribution Research,* vol 1, ed. J. H. Harvey, W. J. Ickes, and R. F. Kidd. Hilsdale, N.J.: Erlbaum, 1976.

Newtson, D., G. Engquist, and J. Bois. "The Objective Basis of Behavior Units," *Journal of Personality and Social Psychology* 35 (1977): 847–863.

Nisbett, R. and L. Ross. *Human Inference: Strategies and Shortcomings of Social Judgment.* Englewood Cliffs, N.J.: Prentice-Hall, 1980.

Pyszczynski, T. A. and J. Greenberg. "Role of Disconfirmed Expectancies in the Instigation of Attributional Processing," *Journal of Personality and Social Psychology* 40 (1981): 31–38.

Rosenberg, S. and R. A. Jones. "A Method of Investigating and Representing a Person's Implicit Theory of Personality: Theodore Dreiser's View of People," *Journal of Personality and Social Psychology* 22 (1972): 372–386.

Ross, L. "The Intuitive Psychologist and His Shortcomings: Distortions in the Attribution Process," in *Advances in Experimental Social Psychology,* vol. 10, ed. L. Berkowitz. New York: Academic Press, 1977.

Ross, L. D., T. M. Amabile, and J. L. Steinmetz. "Social Roles, Social Control, and Biases in Social-Perception Processes," *Journal of Personality and Social Psychology* 35 (1977): 485–494.

Rubin, J., F. Provenzano, and Z. Luria. "The Eye of the Beholder: Parent's Views on Sex of Newborns," *American Journal of Orthopsychiatry* 44 (1974): 512–519.

Rubovits, P. C. and M. L. Maehr. "Pygmalion Black and White," *Journal of Personality and Social Psychology,* 25 (1973): 210–218.

Snyder, M., E. D. Tanke, and E. Berscheid. "Social Perception and Interpersonal Behavior: On the Self-Fulfilling Nature of Social Stereotypes," *Journal of Personality and Social Psychology,* 35 (1977): 656–666.

Taylor, S. E. and S. T. Fiske. "Point of View and Perceptions of Causality," *Journal of Personality and Social Psychology,* 32 (1975): 439–445.

Taylor, S. E. and S. T. Fiske. "Salience, Attention, and Attribution: Top of the Head Phenomena," in *Advances in Experimental Social Psychology,* vol. 11, ed. L. Berkowitz, New York: Academic Press, 1978.

Taylor, S. E., S. T. Fiske, N. L. Etcoff, and A. J. Ruderman. "Categorical and Contextual Bases of Person Memory and Stereotyping," *Journal of Personality and Social Psychology* 36 (1978): 778–793.

Zadny, J. and H. B. Gerard. "Attributed Intentions and Informational Selectivity," *Journal of Experimental Social Psychology* 10 (1974): 34–52.

PROBES

Without thinking about it, we often talk and act as if perception were a passive rather than an active process. For example, we may say—and believe—"I *couldn't* understand that teacher; he was too confusing." Give an example from your own experience where you or someone else has done that. In the example you cite, what active processes were being overlooked?

How do you respond to Jones's point that stereotyping is not a "disease" we can get over but is an inherent part of everyone's perceptual processes?

Recall a recent conflict you've experienced with a friend or family member. What role did your "segmenting" of the other person's behavior play in your perception of the conflict?

When have you been a "token"? Did the experience affect you as it did the people Jones discusses? How so?

Compare and contrast what Jones says about female "tokens" with Judy Pearson's discussion of gender differences in communication in Chapter 11.

The research Jones discusses by Taylor, Fiske, Etcoff, and Ruderman provides some evidence for part of what I say about uniqueness in Chapter 1. Discuss the link between these two points.

Implicit personality theories often affect our perceptions of superiors. Give an example of how this phenomenon affected one of your early perceptions of (a) a supervisor or boss and (b) an instructor or professor.

One of the basic differences between our perception of objects and our perception of people is that we perceive people as choosing to do what they do. Jones argues that we overdo that process, that is, we underestimate the impact of situational factors on human behavior. Do you agree with Jones? Discuss.

How might you resist the tendency to "ignore new information" by relying on your categorizations? Be as specific as you can.

Give an example from your own experience of the kind of self-fulfilling prophecy Jones discusses.

This article also discusses how we perceive others, but Tournier's approach is significantly different from Russell Jones's. Tournier does not speak as a social scientist. He emphasizes our tendency to perceive people as if they were mechanisms or objects which can, as he says, "be confined within concepts, formulae, and definitions."

You and I depersonalize people whenever we treat them as if they could adequately be described by our stereotypes or generalizations. Tournier explains how seeing others as persons instead of as things can mean a "complete revolution" for some. Although he takes examples from his experience as a counselor and doctor, his ideas apply to your communication and to mine too. When we stop seeing only what Tournier calls "personages," or objectified others, and start seeing "persons," all kinds of changes are likely to take place. We can see teacher-student communication differently. Communication with family members can change. As Tournier puts it, "the atmosphere of office, workshop, or laboratory" can be "rapidly transformed when personal fellowship is established."

It goes without saying that we can't communicate person to person *all* of the time. Sometimes external factors—time, rigid roles, ignorance, fear—prevent it. Some situations call for idea-centered more than person-centered contacts. But, Tournier says, we should learn to "answer idea with idea but answer the person with the person." That is, we should know the difference between communicating interpersonally and noninterpersonally so we can strive for the former whenever it is possible.

The World of Things and the World of Persons
Paul Tournier

There are two worlds, or ways of looking at the world, of entering into relationship with it, depending on the spirit in which we approach it. We may see in it nothing but things, mechanisms, from those of physics to those of biology and even of psychology. Art, philosophy, religion can also become things, collections of concepts, formulae, definitions. On the other hand, one can lay oneself open to the world of persons, awaken to the sense of the person. By becoming oneself a person one discovers other persons round about, and one seeks to establish a personal bond with them.

The person always eludes our grasp; it is never static. It refuses to be confined within concepts, formulae, and definitions. It is not a thing to be encompassed, but a point of attraction, a guiding force, a direction, an attitude, which demands from us a corresponding attitude, which moves us to action and commits us. The world of things does not commit us. It is neutral, and leaves us neutral. We are cold, objective, impersonal observers, watching the operation of blind and inexorable mechanisms.

I am not claiming that we must shut our eyes to things, nor that we should cut ourselves off from intellectual objectivity, from the fascinating study of the ordinances and mechanisms of things. But I ask that we should not limit ourselves to the study of things, for they are only one half of the world, the static, impassible, unfeeling half. Even the heavenly bodies, moving with their unimaginable velocities, return in their orbits to the same position; this is the universal cycle of things, eternally starting again.

It is the person that has meaning, a birth and an end. The God of the philosophers is immutable; only the personal God has a purpose for history and for each being. To the scientist, man is but an episode in the universal dance of the atoms and the electrons. As the old French song says of the marionettes, "Three little turns, and off they go!" Off they go to dance elsewhere in a purposeless round.

From infant school to university we are taught to know things, to isolate them, identify them, count them, measure them and classify them. There is no need for me to dwell on the enormous development that has taken place over the centuries in this field, so that now specialization within the narrowest limits is the order of the day. This has not been without its effect on our minds. They are becoming incapable of perceiving what is not objective.

In this depersonalized state of mind man himself becomes a thing. Anatomy and physiology study his body as a thing, and psychology his mind as a thing, a mechanism. Economics studies him as a thing, an instrument of production and consumption, while sociology studies him as an element of society. He is a pawn on the chess-board of politics, a cog in industry, a learning-machine, everywhere a fraction of the mass.

. . . What I want to show now is how this unilateral view of the world and of man is completely upset by the awakening of the sense of the person. . . . When I turned from ecclesiastical activity to spiritual ministry, from technical to humane medicine, I was discovering the world of persons; I was discovering persons everywhere. Since that time, though I have not stopped being interested in things, I am much more passionately interested in persons.

I remember a visit paid to me by one of my former colleagues on the executive authority of the Church. I had fought him tooth and nail—that is to say, I had treated him as a thing, an adversary. The only thing about him that had mattered to me was his opinions, and the weight they might carry in the balance of our arguments. Ideas by themselves, detached from the person, are but things, abstractions, counters in the give and take of discussion.

And now here he was opening his heart to me. I too opened mine to him. He had come to talk to me about his personal life and his sufferings. I was making the discovery of his person, which I had never looked for before. I was so busy combating his ideas. I was discovering his person, his secrets, his solitude, his feelings. I even discovered that his ideas were not abstractions, but that they arose out of the sort of person he was, and protected his suffering like a shield. I talked with him about my own personal experiences, and realized that this former adversary had the same needs and the same difficulties as I, the same longing to find life and fellowship again. . . .

A man may spend years in an office, seeing in his employees only their work, their good qualities and their failings, and then, when personal contact is established, suddenly discover what lies behind the façade: the secret sufferings, the sequels of unhappy childhood, disappointed hopes, struggles to remain faithful to ideals. Then, too, he may understand the profound significance of the qualities and failings he has seen, and the meaning that work can have when it is no longer a thing but the activity of a community of persons.

It is as if a light had shown on life and shown it up in new colours. "We live," wrote Saint-Exupéry, "not on things, but on the meaning of things." The meaning of things is of the order of the person. When our eyes are open to the world of persons, things themselves become personal. It is just the reverse of the transformation of men into things of which we were speaking just now. Beasts, plants, and inanimate things take on the quality of persons. . . .

To become a person, to discover the world of persons, to acquire the sense of the person, to be more interested in people as persons than in their ideas, their party labels, their personage, means a complete revolution, changing the climate of our lives. Once adopted, it is an attitude which rapidly impregnates the whole of our lives. While at the Weissenstein conference I had occasion to congratulate one of my colleagues who had made an extremely good job of interpreting a talk I had given earlier in the day. "And do you know why?" he asked me. "It had been mentioned to me that one of our Scandinavian friends was finding it very troublesome following the speeches in foreign languages. So I interpreted for *him;* I never took my eyes off him, watching his face all the time to see if he had understood. And I found that through giving more attention to his person than to the ideas I was translating, I actually found it easier to express the ideas."

He had become an interpreter of the person, just as one can be a doctor of the person, or a teacher of the person, when one does not teach that impersonal thing, the class, but the persons of the pupils. In the same way, at a conference, one speaks quite differently if the audience is no longer an anonymous mass, if one seeks in it a few faces and exchanges glances with individuals, so that one's speech takes on the quality of a dialogue.

In the world of persons all one's professional relationships take on a new character. They become shot through with a joy that was absent when they were merely the fulfilling of a function. Everything becomes an occasion for personal contact, a chance to understand others and the personal factors which underlie their behavior, their reactions and opinions. It is much more interesting, as well as important, to understand why someone has a certain failing, than to be irritated by it; to understand why he maintains a certain point of view than to combat it; to listen to confidences than to judge by appearances.

The atmosphere of office, workshop, or laboratory is rapidly transformed when personal fellowship is established between those who previously criticized or ignored each other. In a recent lecture Professor F. Gonseth, professor of philosophy at the Zürich Polytechnic, the pioneer of the review *Dialectia,* spoke of the "law of dialogue" which he believes must govern the university of the future. By this phrase he means personal contact between teacher and student, so that the person is committed in the intellectual dialectic. The condition of this contact and commitment is that the teacher should not be so absorbed in his subject that he forgets all about the persons to whom he wishes to transmit it.

I was with some friends one day, and they were advising me to give more lectures and write less books, for, they said, in my writing they missed the personal accent of the spoken word. As you see, I am not following their advice. However precious one's friends are, one must not become their slave. Being a person means acting according to one's personal convictions, due regard of course being given to those of others. And my friends' observation is true. The living word remains the chief instrument of personal dialogue.

This is clearly seen in the case of those patients who send me beforehand—in writing—a long account of their lives. This is useful as information. But the point is that the purpose of a life-history is not so much to furnish information as to lead toward personal contact. Given by word of mouth it may be less intelligible, less systematic, but it is a method which calls for a much deeper commitment of the person.

I have my patients who write me letters after each consultation. They put in them the things they have not dared to say to my face. This has its value; it is for them a commitment, a way of forcing themselves to become more personal at the next consultation. But it is also a means of sparing themselves the intense emotion of a verbal explanation. It attenuates the dialogue, making it less direct because it uses a thing—paper—as an intermediary.

But even the spoken word itself can become a thing if it adopts the neutral and objective tone of information or discussion. Paradoxical though it may seem, the true dialogue is by no means a discussion. This is my answer to those of my colleagues who are perhaps afraid of not knowing what to reply to a patient who puts to them some moral problem that is on his conscience. It is important here to make a distinction between intellectual argument and personal encounter. Answer ideas with ideas, but answer the person with the person. Then often the heart's true response is silence.

Engaging in the dialogue, in the sense in which we understand it here, does not mean plunging into religious or philosophical theories about life, man, or God. The people who have helped me most are not those who have answered my confessions with advice, exhortation, or doctrine, but rather those who have listened to me in silence, and then told me of their own personal life, their own difficulties and experiences. It is this give and take that makes the dialogue.

If we answer with advice, exhortation, or theories, we are putting ourselves in a position of superiority, not equality. We are concerning ourselves with ideas, and not with the person, confining ourselves to the objective world of things, instead of entering the subjective world of persons. When someone lays bare to me the burning reality of his life, I am well aware that most of my replies could easily be only those of my personage. . . .

The moment the personage reappears, with its system of thought and its claim to possess and express truth, our sincerest efforts to help others will finish by crushing and repressing them instead of liberating them. The dialogue between persons is replaced by a moralizing or proselytizing discussion. "Those who impose upon us their ready-made solutions," writes one of my patients, "those who impose upon us their science or their theology, are incapable of healing us."

You will see now how wide of the mark are those who describe the medicine of the person as "religious psychotherapy," in the belief that it consists in the indoctrination of the patient, denunciation of his failings, in moral uplift, or in exhorting him to accept his lot, and forcing him into confession and prayer. That indeed would be acting as a personage and not as a person. Then we should really be in danger of usurping the place of the minister of religion, and attempting to perform a function which is not proper to us.

The medicine of the person demands unconditional respect for the person of others. That does not mean putting one's own flag in one's pocket, but rather that we must state our convictions in a way that is truly personal, not theoretical, having at the same time a sincere regard for the convictions of others. In this way dialogue becomes possible where previously it has been shipwrecked on the rocks of religious, philosophical, political, or social prejudice. . . .

PROBES

Do you think that Tournier's view is "antiintellectual"? Is he saying, in effect, that we should feel our way into a relationship rather than think our way into it?

The author Saint Exupéry, as you may know, wrote *The Little Prince*. What does his statement, "We live not on things, but on the meaning of things," say to you?

Would it be a revolutionary change for you to begin to look at the world as a world of persons rather than of things? How would your communication change?

> *I don't want to argue any more about how he "is." You see him one way, I see him another way, he sees himself a third way. Now if you want to talk about what how we see him indicates about us . . .*
>
> HUGH PRATHER

In these two excerpts from his book *Knots*, R. D. Laing captures the essence of how person perception affects interpersonal communication. Laing recognizes that all our communicating is continually affected by how I am seeing myself ("my me"), how I am seeing you ("my you"), how I am seeing you seeing me ("my your me"), and so on to theoretical infinity. I talked about these images in Chapter 2, and Dean Barnlund also mentioned them in his "meaning-centered" essay. Here Laing graphically illustrates how complex and convoluted the whole process of image creation, perception, and response can get. He also shows how communication that is based on distorted images can start to spiral; that is, to fall into repetitive circles, each of which is intensified by the one before it. In other words, Laing shows how misunderstandings can often be traced to distorted images and often can be overcome only when those distortions are clarified.

Laing is convinced that the kind of communication he sketches here can—and often does—drive people crazy. I suspect that he is right. But the key to escaping the spiral is being aware of what you're doing. Reading Laing's examples and relating them to your own experience can help.

Knots

R. D. Laing

I.

He can't be happy
  when there is so much suffering in the world
She can't be happy
  if he is unhappy

She wants to be happy
He does not feel entitled to be happy
She wants him to be happy
and he wants her to be happy

He feels guilty if he is happy
and guilty if she is not happy

She wants both to be happy

He wants her to be happy

So they are both unhappy

He accuses her of being selfish
   because she is trying to get him to be happy
   so that she can be happy

She accuses him of being selfish
   because he is only thinking of himself

He thinks he is thinking of the whole cosmos

She thinks she is mainly thinking of him
   because she loves him

She has turned to drink
   as a way to cope
   that makes her less able to cope

the more she drinks
the more frightened she is of becoming a drunkard

the more drunk
the less frightened of being drunk

the more frightened of being drunk when not drunk
   the more not frightened drunk
   the more frightened not drunk

the more she destroys herself
the more frightened of being destroyed by him

the more frightened of destroying him
the more she destroys herself

II.

Jack is afraid of Jill
Jill is afraid of Jack

Jack is more afraid of Jill
   if Jack thinks
   that Jill thinks
that Jack is afraid of Jill

Jill is more afraid of Jack
      if Jill thinks

    that Jack thinks
that Jill is afraid of Jack

Since Jack is afraid
   that Jill will think that
     Jack is afraid
  Jack pretends that
     Jack is not afraid of Jill
so that Jill will be more afraid of Jack

and since Jill is afraid
   that Jack will think that
     Jill is afraid
  Jill pretends that
     Jill is not afraid of Jack

Thus
   Jack tries to make Jill afraid
     by not being afraid of Jill
   and Jill tries to make Jack afraid
     by not being afraid of Jack

The more Jack is afraid of Jill
  the more frightened is Jack that
    Jill will think
      that Jack is afraid.

the more Jill is afraid of Jack
  the more frightened is Jill that
    Jack will think
      that Jill is afraid

the more afraid Jack is of Jill
  the more frightened Jack is
not to be frightened of Jill
because it is very dangerous not to be afraid when
faced with one so dangerous

Jack is frightened because Jill is dangerous
Jill appears dangerous because Jack is frightened

the more afraid Jill is of Jack
  the more frightened Jill is
not to be frightened of Jack

The more Jack is frightened not to be frightened
the more frightened he is to appear frightened

the more frightened Jill is
    not to be frightened
the more frightened Jill is
  to appear to be frightened

the more frightened each is,
    the less frightened each appears to be

Jack is frightened
   not to be frightened at Jill
and to appear to be frightened at Jill
and that Jill be not frightened at Jack

      Jill is frightened
      not to be frightened at Jack
   and to appear to be frightened at Jack
and that Jack be not frightened at Jill

Jack therefore tries to frighten Jill
by appearing not to be frightened
   that she appears not to be frightened
and Jill tries to frighten Jack
   by appearing not to be frightened
      that he appears not to be frightened

The more Jack tries to appear not to be frightened
   the more frightened he is that
      he is not frightened
   that he appears to be frightened
   that Jill is not frightened

the more Jill tries to appear not to be frightened
   the more frightened she is that
      she is not frightened
   that she appears to be frightened
   that Jack is not frightened

The more this is so
   the more Jack frightens Jill
   by appearing not to be frightened
and the more Jill frightens Jack
   by appearing not to be frightened

Can each become frightened of being
   frightened and of frightening
instead of being frightened
   not to be frightened
   and not to frighten?

Can Jack and Jill
   terrified that each and the other are not terrified
become
   terrified that each and other are terrified, and
eventually,
   not terrified that each and other not be terrified?

PROBES

Have you ever felt tied in "knots" as you tried to listen to and be understood by
others?

Can you identify in your own experience a spiral that's like the "drinking-to-cope-fearing-drunkenness-and-drinking-to-escape-fear" one Laing captures? How can you escape that kind of spiral?

What elements of your strongest love relationship are similar to the relationship between Jack and Jill?

How would you respond to the question Laing asks at the end of the Jack and Jill selection?

CHAPTER 7

LISTENING

*I am afraid of your silence
because of what it could mean. I
suspect your silence of meaning
you are getting bored or losing
interest or making up your own
mind about me without my
guidance. I believe that as long
as I keep you talking I can know
what you are thinking. But
silence can also mean confidence.
And mutual respect. Silence can
mean live and let live: the
appreciation that I am I and you
are you. The silence is an
affirmation that we are already
together—as two people. Words
can mean that I want to make
you into a friend and silence can
mean that I accept your already
being one.*

HUGH PRATHER

||||||||||||||||||||||||||||||||||||||||||||||||||||||||||||||||||||||||||||||||||||||||||||||||||||||||||||||||||||||||||||||||||||||||||

Good introductory treatments of listening have always been rare. Each time I've searched the books and magazines for materials for earlier editions of *Bridges Not Walls* I've had trouble finding a clear, fairly brief discussion that covers a broad range of listening topics, approaches its subject from a relational and nontechnical point of view, and includes some specific suggestions about how to do it better. This reading by Robert Bolton covers all those bases quite well. Bolton is the president of a communication consulting firm, and this material comes from his book *People Skills,* where he discusses how to assert yourself, listen, and resolve conflicts.

In the first section of this chapter Bolton introduces his topic by pointing out that we listen more than we do *anything* else, yet (1) most of us listen very poorly, partly because (2) we're never taught otherwise. Instead of listening, schools teach reading, writing, and some speaking, and at home many of us learn directly or indirectly to "pretend you don't notice" and to tune out or interrupt rather than listening effectively.

Bolton's alternative to this approach begins by distinguishing the physiological process of *hearing*—receiving sound waves—from the complex psychological and communicative process of *listening*—hearing plus interpreting, understanding, and checking your perceptions. Then he breaks the process down into three clusters of listening skills: Attending, Following, and Reflecting. I've reprinted his discussions of the attending and following skill clusters and some of his important introductory ideas about the skills of Reflecting or perception checking. There's more about the third skill cluster in the "Dialogic Listening" discussion by Milt Thomas and me later in this chapter.

One of the strong points of Bolton's essay is his discussion of Attending. When you think about it, it's kind of obvious that you can't listen without *focusing* on the other person, but we often take that important fact too much for granted. Bolton emphasizes the point that, "What a person wants most of all from a listener" is that "the listener really be there for him" or her, and that without this kind of presence "no attending technique will work." I count nine specific suggestions about how to translate your intent-to-be-present into action: lean toward the speaker, face her squarely, maintain an open posture, position yourself at an appropriate distance, let your body "be moved by the talker," avoid distracting motions, have good eye contact, cut environmental distractions, and minimize physical barriers. Bolton also notes that although most people already know how to attend, focusing on attending communication motivates us to do more often what we "know" but often neglect. At the end of the section he has some useful things to say about how we can work hard to improve and still "act naturally."

In his discussion of Following skills, Bolton continues to make helpfully explicit several communication behaviors that are usually left undiscussed. The first Following skill is called a "door opener," and Bolton notes how some of our most well-meaning responses—reassuring and advice-giving—often function to *close* the conversation door rather than to facilitate talk. He identifies the four elements of door openers and gives several examples of how they can work. "Minimal encourages" is Bolton's term for another skill you already have but may not always use. "Mm-hmm," "Then?" "Really," "Tell me more" are all simple but effective ways to Follow effectively. Bolton's discussion of questions emphasizes the importance of open rather than closed questions and the wisdom of asking fewer questions. As he notes in the final part of this section, the silence that can come when you rely less on questions can actually improve the quality of your listening. In his words, "Most listeners talk too much."

As I mentioned, I could not include all of Bolton's discussion of the Reflecting skill cluster, but I did want you to be able to read what he says about when to listen reflectively and when not to. This section reemphasizes the point that good listening *has* to begin with a commitment; without it no listening techniques are worth much. As he suggests, do listen fully and reflectively, for example, before you argue or criticize, when the other person is experiencing strong feelings, or when he or she just wants to sort out feelings and thoughts. But don't do it when, for example, you can't be accepting, when you feel the need to control the other rather than trusting her to find her own solution, when you can't separate yourself from the other person, or when you're feeling "pressured, hassled or depleted." I also like Bolton's last point: "The good news is that sometimes listening is a beautiful experience. The bad news is that it can be a heavy burden."

If you listen thoroughly to what Bolton says here, I think you'll have laid a good foundation for the rest of the readings in this chapter.

Listening Is More Than Merely Hearing

Robert Bolton

THE IMPORTANCE OF LISTENING

If you are at all typical, *listening takes up more of your waking hours than any other activity*. A study of persons of varied occupational backgrounds showed that 70 percent of their waking moments were spent in communication. And of that time, writing took 9 percent, reading absorbed 16 percent, talking accounted for 30 percent, and listening occupied 45 percent.[1] Other surveys underscore the large amount of time that people in different walks of life spend in listening.[2] It is important to listen effectively because of the sheer amount of it that you do each day.

Furthermore, many of the most important facets of your life are greatly influenced by your skills (or lack of skill) in listening. The quality of your friendships, the cohesiveness of your family relationships, your effectiveness at work—these hinge, in large measure, on your ability to listen.

Unfortunately, few people are good listeners. Even at the purely informational level, researchers claim that 75 percent of oral communication is ignored, misunderstood, or quickly forgotten. Rarer still is the ability to listen for the deepest meanings in what people say. How devastating, but how common, to talk with someone about subjects of intense interest to oneself only to experience the stifling

Excerpt from the book *People Skills* by Robert Bolton, Ph.D. © 1979 by Prentice-Hall, Inc. Published by Prentice-Hall, Inc., Englewood Cliffs, NJ.

realization that the other person was not really listening and that his responses were simply automatic and mechanical. Perhaps it was after an experience like this that Jesus was quoted as saying, "Thou hearest in thy one ear but the other Thou has closed."[3]

Dr. Ralph G. Nichols, who developed innovative classes on listening at the University of Minnesota, writes:

> It can be stated with practically no qualification that people in general do not know how to listen. They have ears that hear very well, but seldom have they acquired the necessary . . . skills which would allow those ears to be used effectively for what is called *listening*. . . . For several years, we have been testing the ability of people to understand and remember what they hear. . . . These extensive tests led to this general conclusion: immediately after the average person has listened to someone talk, he remembers only about half of what he has heard—no matter how carefully he thought he was listening. What happens as time passes? Our own testing shows . . . that. . . we tend to forget from one-half to one-third [more] *within eight hours.* . . .[4]

All too often the speaker's words go "in one ear and out the other."

A major reason for the poor listening in our society is that most of us receive a very rigorous early training in nonlistening. The therapist Franklin Ernst says that "from the earliest years of life, a person's listening activity is the most heavily trained of all activities. . . . The person's listening . . . is more attended to than his bowel training, his bladder activity, or his genital activity."[5] Ernst points out that the typical child, in his most impressionable years, receives a steady diet of anti-listening edicts. Parents say things like:

"We don't listen to those things in our family."

"Don't pay any attention to him."

"Pretend you don't notice."

"Don't take it so seriously."

"He didn't mean what he said."

"Don't give them the satisfaction of knowing that you heard them" (and that it bothers you).

The typical parent not only verbalizes these antilistening comments, he demonstrates them daily in his own life. He is inattentive to persons speaking to him, may interrupt frequently, and responds with numerous roadblocks. By word and deed we are taught to be nonlisteners in our childhood.

Our schooling also conspires against the development of effective listening skills. About six years of training is given to reading in most school systems; additional opportunities are often available for remedial reading and speed reading. In the vast majority of schools, however, there are no effective training programs for developing listening skills. This makes little sense in a society where the graduated student will have to spend at least three times as much time listening as he spends reading.

Rather than receiving training in effective listening, the student in a typical school receives further antilistening training. Like his parents, most of his teachers will not be good listeners. They, too, will demonstrate inattentiveness, interruptions, and the use of many roadblocks throughout the school day. Furthermore, the typical classroom is structured for a larger ratio of listening time to talking time than the human being is capable of achieving. Some experts say that we can only listen effectively from one-third to two-thirds of the time. Whatever the specific ratio, each of us can recognize that when we listen for a long time without doing any talking or responding, our listening efficiency begins to drop drastically and finally our minds drift off to considering other topics than those about which the speaker is talking. Because the student cannot possibly listen effectively to all the talking to which school subjects him, he learns to turn off his mind when other people are speaking. This problem is compounded by the repetitions and boring nature of much teacher talk.

Most of us have been trained to be poor listeners, yet ironically, we spend more time listening than doing anything else, and the quality of our listening greatly affects both the personal and the vocational dimensions of our lives. The remainder of this chapter is devoted to defining *listening,* outlining the major clusters of listening skills, and teaching the more elementary of the listening skills.

LISTENING DEFINED

It is helpful to note the distinction between *hearing* and *listening. "Hearing,"* says Professor John Drakeford, "is a word used to describe the physiological sensory processes by which auditory sensations are received by the ears and transmitted to the brain. *Listening,* on the other hand, refers to a more complex psychological procedure involving interpreting and understanding the significance of the sensory experience."[0] In other words, I can hear what another person is saying without really listening to him. A teenager put it this way: "My friends listen to what I say, but my parents only hear me talk."

I recall a time when I was talking with someone who seemed to ignore everything I said. "You are not listening to me!" I accused. "Oh, yes I am!" he said. He then repeated word for word what I had told him. He *heard* exactly. But he wasn't *listening.* He didn't understand the meanings I was trying to convey. Perhaps you have had a similar experience and know how frustrating it can be to be heard accurately by someone who isn't listening with understanding.

The distinction between merely hearing and really listening is deeply embedded in our language. The word *listen* is derived from two Anglo-Saxon words. One word is *hlystan,* which means "hearing." The other is *hlosnian,* which means "to wait in suspense." Listening, then, is the *combination* of hearing what the other person says *and* a suspenseful waiting, an intense psychological involvement with the other.

Listening Skill Clusters

Learning to be an effective listener is a difficult task for many people. Our approach simplifies the learning process by focusing on single skills or small clusters of skills so people can concentrate on one skill or one cluster at a time.

Focusing on a single skill when necessary, and on small clusters of skills when possible, enables people to learn most efficiently. This approach helps the reader master one cluster of skills, see himself readily improve in that area, and then move to a more advanced set of skills. When each of the separate listening skill clusters has been learned, the reader can integrate the various skills into a sensitive and unified way of listening.

The clusters of listening skills . . . include:

SKILL CLUSTERS	SPECIFIC SKILLS
Attending Skills	• A Posture of Involvement
	• Appropriate Body Motion

	• Eye Contact
	• Nondistracting Environment
Following Skills	• Door Openers
	• Minimal Encourages
	• Infrequent Questions
	• Attentive Silence
Reflecting Skills	• Paraphrasing
	• Reflecting Feelings
	• Reflecting Meanings (Tying Feelings to Content)
	• Summative Reflections

ATTENDING SKILLS

Attending is giving your physical attention to another person. I sometimes refer to it as listening with the whole body. Attending is nonverbal communication that indicates that you are paying careful attention to the person who is talking. Attending skills include a posture of involvement, appropriate body motion, eye contact, and a nondistracting environment.

The Impact of Attending and Nonattending

Effective attending works wonders in human relations. It shows the other that you are interested in him and in what he has to say. It facilitates the expression of the most important matters on his mind and in his heart. Nonattending, on the other hand, tends to thwart the speaker's expression.

Allen Ivey and John Hinkle describe the results of attending in a college psychology course. They trained six students in attending behavior. Then a session, taught by a visiting professor, was videotaped. The students started out in typical student nonattending classroom behaviors. The professor lectured, unaware of the students' prearranged plan. His presentation was centered on his notes. He used no gestures, spoke in a monotone, and paid little attention to the students. At a prearranged signal, however, the students began deliberately to physically attend. Within a half a minute, the lecturer gestured for the first time, his verbal rate increased, and a lively classroom session was born. Simple attending had changed the whole picture. At another signal, the students stopped attending, and the speaker, after awkwardly seeking continued response, resumed the unengaging lecture with which he began the class.[7]

It is an impressive experience to talk to a person who is directly and totally there for you. Norman Rockwell, the artist famed for his *Saturday Evening Post* covers, recounted his experience while painting a portrait of President Eisenhower:

> The general and I didn't discuss politics or the campaign. Mostly we talked about painting and fishing. But what I remember most about the hour and a half I spent with him was the way he gave me all his attention. He was listening to me and talking to me, just as if he hadn't a care in the world, hadn't been through the trials of a political convention, wasn't on the brink of a presidential campaign.[8]

Attending is often one of the most effective behaviors we can offer when listening to someone.

A Posture of Involvement

Because body language often speaks louder than words, a "posture of involvement" is extremely important in listening. In their book *Human Territories: How We*

Behave in Space-Time, Drs. Albert Scheflen and Norman Ashcroft note, "Each region of the body can be oriented in such a way that it invites, facilitates, or holds an interpersonal relation. Or it can be oriented in order to break off, discourage, or avoid involvement."[9] Communication tends to be fostered when the listener demonstrates a relaxed alertness with the body leaning slightly forward, facing the other squarely, maintaining an "open" position and situating himself at an appropriate distance from the speaker.

The good listener communicates attentiveness through the *relaxed alertness* of his body during the conversation. What is sought is a balance between the relaxedness that communicates "I feel at home with you and accept you" and the alertness or productive tension that demonstrates "I sense the importance of what you are telling me and am very intent on understanding you." The blending of both of these body messages creates an effective listening presence.

Inclining one's body toward the speaker communicates more energy and attention than does leaning back or sprawling in the chair. When a public speaker has his audience enthralled, we say, "He has them on the edge of their seats." The people are not only leaning forward, but are sitting forward in their chairs. By contrast, some listeners slouch back in their chairs looking like propped-up cadavers. How demotivating that posture is to the speaker!

Facing the other squarely, your right shoulder to the other's left shoulder, helps communicate your involvement. The common phrase "He gave me the cold shoulder" suggests the indifference or rejection that can be communicated by not positioning yourself to face the other person. Because homes and offices are seldom arranged for good attending, you may have to rearrange some furniture to be able to position yourself properly.

Another aspect of facing the other squarely is to be at eye level with the speaker. This is especially important if you are an authority figure—a parent, teacher, or boss—of the speaker. Sitting on the edge of a desk when the other is in a chair or standing when he is sitting can be a major barrier to interpersonal contact. Parents of young children often comment on how important this aspect of attending is in their homes.

Maintaining an open position with arms and legs uncrossed is another important part of the posture of involvement. Tightly crossed arms or legs often communicate closedness and defensiveness. Baseball fans know what to expect when an umpire makes a call that is disputed by a team manager. The manager runs toward the umpire shouting and waving his arms. The umpire typically crosses his arms in a gesture of defensiveness, communicating that he will not budge from his position and that any argument will be fruitless. The very young do this same thing: they commonly cross their arms when defying their parents, indicating a psychological closedness to their parents' comments.

Positioning yourself at an appropriate distance from the speaker is an important aspect of attending. Too much distance between persons impedes communication. C. L. Lassen studied the effect of physical proximity in initial psychiatric interviews. The psychiatrists sat either three, six, or nine feet away from their clients. The clients' anxiety levels were measured, both by observable behaviors and through the clients' self-reports. Lassen discovered that a client's anxiety increased as the distance between himself and the psychiatrist increased.[10]

On the other hand, when a listener gets too close to another person, anxiety also increases. Some psychologists have demonstrated that the typical American feels uneasy when someone with whom he is not intimate positions himself closer than three feet for an extended time. Long periods of close physical proximity during a conversation can cause discomfort even when the persons are spouses or close friends. Cultural differences affect the optimal distance for conversing, as do individual differences within a given culture. The distance between yourself and another person that most facilitates communication can be discovered by watching for signs of anxiety and discomfort in the speaker and positioning yourself accordingly. Normally, about three feet is a comfortable distance in our society.

Appropriate Body Motion

Appropriate body movement is essential to good listening. In his book *Who's Listening?,* psychiatrist Franklin Ernst, Jr., writes:

> To listen is to move. To listen is to be moved by the talker—physically and psychologically. . . . The non-moving, unblinking person can reliably be estimated to be a non-listener. . . . When other visible moving has ceased and the eyeblink rate has fallen to less than once in six seconds, listening for practical purposes, has stopped.[11]

One study of nonverbal listener behavior noted that the listener who remains still is seen as controlled, cold, aloof, and reserved. By contrast, the listener who is more active—but not in a fitful or nervous way—is experienced as friendly, warm, casual, and as not acting in a role. People prefer speaking to listeners whose bodies are not rigid and unmoving.[12] When watching videotapes of effective listeners, I discovered that they tend to have a rhythm of less activity when the speaker is talking and somewhat more activity when they are responding. Occasionally, the listener becomes so in tune with the speaker that his gestures synchronize with the speaker's.

The avoidance of distracting motions and gestures is also essential for effective attending. The good listener moves his body in *response* to the speaker. Ineffective listeners move their bodies in response to stimuli that are unrelated to the talker. Their distraction is demonstrated by their body language: fiddling with pencils or keys, jingling money, fidgeting nervously, drumming fingers, cracking knuckles, frequently shifting weight or crossing and uncrossing the legs, swinging a crossed leg up and down, and other nervous mannerisms. Watching a TV program, waving or nodding one's head to people passing by, continuing with one's activities, like preparing a meal, or reading the paper can be very distracting when someone is talking to you.

Eye Contact

Effective eye contact expresses interest and a desire to listen. It involves focusing one's eyes softly on the speaker and occasionally shifting the gaze from his face to other parts of the body, to a gesturing hand, for example, and then back to the face and then to eye contact once again. Poor eye contact occurs when a listener repeatedly looks away from the speaker, stares at him constantly or blankly, or looks away as soon as the speaker looks at the listener.

Eye contact enables the speaker to appraise your receptiveness to him and his message. It helps him figure out how safe he is with you. Equally important, you can "hear" the speaker's deeper meanings through eye contact. Indeed, if effective listening means getting inside the other's skin and understanding the person's experience from his perspective, one of the best ways to enter that inner world is through the "window" of the eyes. Ralph Waldo Emerson said, "The eyes of men converse as much as their tongues, but with the advantage that the ocular dialect needs no dictionary, but is understood the world over."[13]

Many people have a difficult time establishing eye contact. Just as some people have a hard time knowing what to do with their hands in social interactions, other people do not know what to do with their eyes. People sometimes look away from another's face at the moment they sense he will show emotion on his face. Part of the reason for that behavior may be a desire not to be intrusive or embarrass the other.[14] (As we will see later, however, the effective listener hears feelings as well as content and understands what the other says with his body language as well as through words.) Another reason for not looking into the speaker's eyes is that it is one of the most intimate ways of relating to a person, and the fear of escalation of affection has made it somewhat taboo in many societies.[15]

Despite the fact that some people find it difficult to look into another's eyes, few of us enjoy carrying on a conversation with a person whose glance continually darts about the room. When I am listened to by that kind of person, I am distracted from what I am saying. For example, when a person talking with me at a party keeps looking around the room at other people, I often interpret that to mean that he would rather be someplace else—and I personally wish he would find out where he would rather be and go there! Lack of eye contact may be a sign of indifference or hostility. It can be experienced as a put-down.

The ability to have good eye contact is essential for effective interpersonal communication in our society. Sometimes it cannot be used maximally because others are uncomfortable with it. Often, however, it is one of the most effective of the listening skills. People who are uncomfortable with eye contact can develop the ability to communicate through the eyes. Awareness of the importance of eye contact helps many people overcome the inhibition. Additionally, people with this problem may have to work at looking at a person's face more often until they become more comfortable with this way of relating.

Nondistracting Environment

Attending involves giving the other person one's undivided attention. This is virtually impossible in environments that have a high level of distraction. An undistracting environment, one without significant physical barriers between people and one that is inviting rather than ugly—these conditions facilitate conversation.

The attending listener attempts to *cut environmental distractions to the minimum.* At home, the TV or stereo may be turned off in the room to provide the interruption-free and distraction-free environment that is so important for human interaction. If need be, the telephone receiver can be taken off the hook or unplugged, and a "Do not Disturb" sign can even be placed on the door. In many offices, the door can be closed, the music or intercom turned off, and the secretary can hold telephone calls until the conversation is completed. In the factory, finding an undistracting setting is difficult but not impossible. Good attending in a manufacturing plant may involve using the feet before using the ears—to get to an office or some other place where you will not be disturbed and where the environment is not distracting.

Removing sizable physical barriers fosters better communication. In offices the desk typically intrudes between the speaker and the listener. A. G. White's study of medical case-history interviewing discovered that 55 percent of the patients initially sat at ease when no desk separated the patient and the doctor; only 10 percent were at ease when a desk separated the patient from the doctor.[16] For some people, a desk is associated with a position of authority and can trigger feelings of weakness or hostility. When a listener sits behind a desk, the interaction is more likely to be role-to-role rather than person-to-person. If an office is too small to place two chairs away from the desk for conversation, it is desirable to have the visitor's chair beside the desk rather than across the desk.

Good attending fosters improved observation of the other's body language, which is an important part of listening. When a desk or other large physical barrier stands between you and the speaker, it is extremely difficult to note what the other's body is communicating.

Psychological Attention

What a person wants most of all from a listener is a sense of psychological presence. He wants the listener to really be there for him. Physical attending fosters psychological presence. When I am in a good environmental setting, have comfortable eye contact, appropriate body motion, and maintain the posture of involvement, my psychological attending usually improves. My physical attending skill also helps the other feel my psychological presence.

However, if I try to fake attention when listening to another, I deceive only myself. The listener who is truly present to another displays a vitality that registers on the face and body his interest and concern for what the other is saying. The person who is not really "there," even though his body takes an attending position, is inevitably detected. The speaker notes the glazed eyes, and his "antenna" picks up other signals that reveal that the listener's heart and mind are not with him. Without psychological presence, no attending technique will work.

Consciously Working at Attending

Surprisingly, we find that most people have a fairly accurate informal knowledge of attending before we teach them any attending skills. In our seminars, the trainer often says, "Position yourselves to show me that you are really interested in what I am saying." Most people in the group assume a fairly good attending position. Then the leader says, "Show me by your body posture that you couldn't care less about me or about what I am telling you." Virtually everyone demonstrates a clear idea of what nonattending behavior is like. So why do we make such an effort to teach attending skills? There are basically two reasons.

First of all, because the teaching of these skills does sharpen understanding of attending. People raise to the level of their awareness some understandings that were previously vague and hazy. People invariably learn something new and/or develop a deepened insight into what they already know.

Secondly, and more important, we find that a focus on the methods and merits of attending motivates many people to do what they already know how to do but often neglect to do. A focus on attending serves as a consciousness-raising experience that often motivates people to utilize these skills. Once people start attending at appropriate times, they are rewarded by a new quality of interpersonal relationships. Allan Ivey puts it this way:

> Some may question the possible artificiality of attending behavior or other skills. . . .
> They validly object to seeing life as a series of exercises in which the individual constantly dredges into a "handbag of skills" so he can adapt to each life situation. Our experience has been that individuals may sometimes begin attending in an artificial, deliberate manner. However, once attending has been initiated, the person to whom one is listening tends to become more animated, and this in turn reinforces the attender who very quickly forgets about attending deliberately and soon attends naturally. A variety of our clients and trainees have engaged in conscious attending behavior only to find themselves so interested in the person with whom they are talking that they lose themselves in the other.[17]

People tend to think of communication as a verbal process. Students of communication are convinced that most communication is nonverbal. The most commonly quoted estimate, based on research, is that 85 percent of our communication is nonverbal! So attending, the nonverbal part of listening, is a basic building block of the listening process.

FOLLOWING SKILLS

Beatrice Glass's car collided with another auto. As soon after the accident as possible she telephoned her husband, Charlie, and reported that she had been in an accident. "How much damage did it do to the car?" was his immediate response. When he had that information, Charlie asked, "Whose fault was it?" Then he said, "Don't admit a thing. You phone the insurance company and I'll call our lawyer. Just a minute and I'll give you the number."

"Any more questions?" she asked.

"No," he replied, "that just about covers it."

"Oh, it does, does it?" she screamed. "Well, just in case you are interested, I'm in the hospital with four broken ribs!"

Charlie's responses may have been more callous and blatant than those of the average husband, but what he did is typical for many people. Because Charlie's wife had a problem (an automobile accident that resulted in her hospitalization), Charlie's role in the conversation should have been primarily that of a listener. But he did most of the talking.

One of the primary tasks of a listener is to stay out of the other's way so the listener can discover how the speaker views his situation. Unfortunately, the average "listener" interrupts and diverts the speaker by asking many questions or making many statements. Researchers tell us that it is not at all uncommon for "listeners" to lead and direct a conversation through the frequent use of questions. It is also common for the "listener" to talk so much that he monopolizes the conversation!

Four following skills foster effective listening: door openers, minimal encourages, open questions, and attentive silence.

Door Openers

People often send *nonverbal clues* when they are burdened or excited about something. Their feelings are telegraphed in facial expressions, tone of voice, body posture, and energy level. For example, Jerry, who is normally exuberant, had not laughed or entered into the family repartee for four days. When they were alone, his wife, Darlene, said, "You don't seem yourself these past few days. You seem burdened by something. Care to talk about it?" That was Darlene's way of sending a door opener.

A door opener is a noncoercive invitation to talk. There are times when door openers are not necessary. The speaker plunges right into his theme. Sometimes, however, you will sense that the other person wants to talk but needs encouragement as Jerry did. At other times, the speaker will be in the midst of a conversation and will show signs that he is unsure about continuing. A door opener like this may help him proceed: "I'm interested in hearing more about it."

People often send door closers (roadblocks) when door openers are much more appropriate. When a child comes home from school with dragging steps and an unhappy expression on his face, parents often respond in ways that tend to make the child withdraw into himself. *Judgmental* statements are apt to pour forth.

167

"What a sourpuss you have on today."

"What did you do this time?"

"Don't inflict your lousy mood on me."

"What did you do, lose your best friend?"

Sometimes, they try to *reassure:*

"Cheer up."

"Things will get better. They always do."

"Next week you won't even remember what happened."

At such times, *advice giving* is another favorite tactic:

"Why don't you do something you like to do?"

"Don't mope around all day. That won't help anything."

"I'm sure that whatever happened wasn't worth ruining your day over."

Instead of yielding to the temptation to use roadblocks, parents could send a door opener:

"Looks like things didn't go well for you today. I've got time if you'd like to talk."

"Something unpleasant happen to you? Want to talk about it?"

Door openers typically have four elements.

1. *A description of the other person's body language.* "Your face is beaming today." "You look like you are not feeling up to par."
2. *An invitation to talk or to continue talking.* "Care to talk about it?" "Please go on." "I'm interested in what you are saying."
3. *Silence—giving the other person time to decide whether to talk and/or what he wants to say.*
4. *Attending—eye contact and a posture of involvement that demonstrates your interest in and concern for the other person.*

All four parts are not necessarily present in every door opener. One day, a friend with whom I had shared a great deal of my thoughts and feelings saw that I was troubled. He motioned to a chair and said quietly, "Let's hear about it." On another occasion, he simply said, "Shoot." These brief door openers worked well because of the trust and frequent self-disclosure in the relationship. If other people had said those things to me, I might have clammed up. The personality of the listener, the nature of the relationship, and other factors will determine the most effective door opener in a given situation.

Silence and attending alone often constitute a strong inducement to talk. A housewife who complained that her husband seldom talked with her decided to try attending to him when *he* wanted to talk. She discovered, to her dismay, that he seemed most ready to converse when he got home from work—and that's when she was in the midst of dinner preparations! For years she had continued attending to her cooking while calling questions over her shoulder about how his day had gone—but received virtually no response. Her new approach was to serve dinner forty-five minutes later, to take fifteen minutes to relax before her husband came home, and to spend a half-hour talking with him alone. For that half-hour, both the children and her cooking tasks were excluded. She says her husband now engages in significant conversations with her.

Another housewife who found it inconvenient to postpone the dinner hour planned to cook much of the meal earlier in the day on three days a week so she could attend to her husband's conversation when he arrived home. She says, "What a difference that has made! Some days we talk the whole time. On other occasions, our conversations are quite brief—but even these are not the forced exchanges we had when I used to grill him with questions while I prepared dinner. Some days, of course, we do no more than exchange greetings. But the whole interpersonal atmosphere of our house is changing because of my quiet, attentive availability during those three half-hour periods a week before dinner."

A person sending door openers needs an awareness of and a respect for the other person's probable feelings of ambivalence—he may want to self-disclose, yet be hesitant to do so.

One way to deal with ambivalence is to recognize and reflect back to the speaker how difficult it is to talk about painful experiences. When the speaker seems to find it difficult to speak about the things he is saying, a listener can reflect:

"It's pretty hard to talk about."

Another way of dealing with a person who is feeling very ambivalent is to make sure your door opener is an invitation rather than a directive to talk. Door openers should always be noncoercive.

Unfortunately, some people not only open the door, they try to drag the other through:

Sam: You look sad, John. Feel like talking?
John: Not really.
Sam: I can tell you are troubled. You know you can talk to me.
John: I don't feel like it right now.
Sam: You really ought to get it off your chest, you know.
John: Yeah, I know. Later maybe.
Sam: But the time to talk is when you are feeling things . . .

The empathic person respects the privacy of other people and is careful not to be intrusive. He honors rather than violates the other individual's separateness. When appropriate, empathic listeners invite conversation. They do not try to compel it.

It is difficult to offer a door opener, not to be taken up on it, and still let it go. However, in relationships where there is little trust or where communication has not been flowing well for some time, door openers will probably find little response from the other person. It takes time, skill, and goodwill to rebuild trust. Use of listening skills can help nurture this trust once more. If and when the relationship is restored, the door openers will probably find a welcome response.

Minimal Encourages

We have already stated that one of the listener's responsibilities is to allow the speaker room to talk about a situation as he sees and feels it. Many people, in their effort to stay out of the speaker's way, lapse into nonparticipation. Simple responses that encourage the speaker to tell his story in his way yet keep the listener active in the process are called *minimal encourages*. Minimal encourages are brief indicators to other persons that you are with them. The word *minimal* refers to the amount the listener says, which is very little, and to the amount of direction given to the conversation, which is also very little. The word *encourages*

169

is used because these words and phrases aid the speaker to continue speaking. Just a few words can let the other know you are listening without interrupting the flow of talk or breaking the mood. Minimal encourages will be sprinkled throughout a conversation. In the early stages of an interaction, they may be used more frequently to help the conversation gain momentum.

The simple "mm-hmm" is probably the most frequently used of the minimal encourages. That brief phrase can suggest, "Please continue. I'm listening and I understand." There are many brief responses that the listener can use:

Tell me more.	You betcha!
Oh?	Yes.
For instance . . .	Really?
I see.	Gosh.
Right.	And?
Then?	Go on.
So?	Sure.
I hear you.	Darn!

You undoubtedly have your own favorites. Repeating one or two of the speaker's key words or the last word or two of the speaker's statement also constitutes minimal encourages. When the speaker says, "I can't figure out what to do. I guess I'm just confused," the listener may respond "Confused."

A skilled listener can communicate much empathy through voice and facial expressions even when only one or two words are said. I watched a film of one of America's leading therapists listening to a woman tell how furious she was at things her mother had done to her. His empathic "You betcha" seemed to give her the feeling, "He understands how angry I am and he still accepts me." When one of our children told my wife of a big disappointment at school, Dot simply said, "Darn!" but her tone of voice, facial expression, and other nonverbals made it a very feeling-ful response.

Minimal encourages do not imply either agreement or disagreement with what the speaker said. Rather, they let the other know he has been heard and that the listener will try to follow his meaning if the speaker chooses to continue. Thus, when I respond to a speaker with "Right," it does not mean that I agree with the speaker. Rather, it means, "Yes, I hear what you are saying—go on."

This kind of response has often been parodied. We hear tales of the psychiatrist who says nothing but "mm-hmm" for fifty minutes and at the end of the session says, "That will be fifty dollars, please." Obviously, these expressions can be overdone or used mechanically. However, when sensitively orchestrated with a variety of other responses, they assist the speaker's self-exploration.

Infrequent Questions

Questions are an integral part of verbal interaction in our society. As with many other kinds of responses, questions have their strengths and their limitations. Comparatively few people in our culture know how to question effectively. We often rely on questions excessively and use them poorly. Questions usually focus on the intent, perspective, and concerns of the listener rather than on the speaker's orientation. When that happens, questions are a barrier to communication.

We distinguish between "closed" questions and "open" questions. *Closed questions* direct the speaker to give a specific, short response. They are often answered with one word like "yes" or "no." *Open questions,* on the other hand, provide *space* for the speaker to explore his thoughts without being hemmed in too much by the listener's categories. Closed questions are like true/false or multiple-choice test questions, while open questions are like essay questions. When an employee walks into her boss's office, the latter could ask either a closed or an open question:

Closed question: "Do you want to see me about the Rumsford job?"

Open Question: "What's on your mind, Ann?"

The open question is usually preferable because it does not suggest the agenda to the person who initiated the interaction.

When used skillfully and infrequently, open questions may help the listener better understand the speaker without directing the conversation. In the report on their study of open and closed questions, Moreland, Phillips, and Lockhart write:

> Crucial to the giving of open-ended questions is the concept of who is to lead the interview. While the interviewer does ask questions while using this skill, his questions are centered around concerns of the client rather than around concerns of the interviewer for the client. Questions should be designed to help the client clarify his own problems, rather than provide information for the interviewer. . . . If the interviewer relies on closed questions to structure his interview, he usually is forced to concentrate so hard on thinking up the next question that he fails to listen to and attend to the client.[18]

In addition to asking open rather than closed questions, it is important to *ask only one question at a time.* When two or more questions are asked in quick succession, the latter questions are usually closed questions. The tendency to ask more than one question seems related to the questioner's inner uncertainty. It rarely facilitates the conversation.

My experience in teaching communication skills leads me to conclude that *most people ask far too many questions.* Putting several questions in a conversation is risky to the interaction; it tends to put the listener opposite rather than beside the speaker, dictating the direction the conversation takes rather than giving the speaker an opportunity to explore his situation in his own way. Almost everyone I have taught would have been a better listener if he asked fewer questions. Furthermore, I believe that most questions can be expressed as statements and that doing so generally is far more productive in a conversation than repeated questioning.

When people try to give up their overreliance on questions, they usually feel very uncomfortable. They may feel the conversation is floundering because of more periods of silence. Skills taught in this part of the book (and in Chapter 4) will help you refrain from asking too many questions and at the same time not feel too much of a void in the conversation.

Attentive Silence

The beginning listener needs to learn the value of silence in freeing the speaker to think, feel, and express himself. "The beginning of wisdom is silence," said a Hebrew sage. "The second stage is listening."

Most listeners talk too much. They may speak as much or even more than the person trying to talk. Learning the art of silent responsiveness is essential to good listening. After all, another person cannot describe a problem if you are doing all the talking.

Silence on the part of the listener gives the speaker time to think about what he is going to say and thus enables him to go deeper into himself. It gives a person space to experience the feelings churning within. Silence also allows the speaker to proceed at his own pace. It provides time to deal with his ambivalence about sharing. In the frequent silences, he can choose whether or not to continue talking and at what depth. Silence often serves as a gentle nudge to go further into a conversation. When an interaction is studded with significant silences and backed by good attending, the results can be very impressive.

Through the years, I have returned again and again to these words of Eugene Herrigel that describe why silence can be such a powerful force for a person whose emotions are intense:

> The real meaning of suffering discloses itself only to him who has learned the art of compassion. . . . Gradually, he will fall silent, and in the end will sit there wordless, for a long time sunk deep in himself. And the strange thing is that this silence is not felt by the other person as indifference, as a desolate emptiness which disturbs rather than calms. It is as if this silence had more meaning than countless words could ever have. It is as if he were being drawn into a field of force from which fresh strength flows into him. He feels suffused with a strange confidence. . . . And it may be that in these hours, the resolve will be born to set out on the path that turns a wretched existence into a life of happiness.[19]

Silence can be a balm for sufferers; it is also important in moments of great joy. How beautiful are the silences of intimacy. Thomas Carlyle and Ralph Waldo Emerson sat together for hours one night in utter silence until one rose to go and said, "We've had a grand evening!" I've had many experiences like that with my wife, Dot, when we sat quietly before a fire or gazed silently into each other's eyes, basking in each other's affection. As Halford Luccock says:

> This silence of love is not indifference; it is not merely poverty of something to say. It is a positive form of self-communication. Just as silence is needed to hear a watch ticking, so silence is the medium through which heartbeats are heard.[20]

More than half the people who take communication skills training with us are initially uncomfortable with silence. Even a few seconds' pause in a conversation causes many of them to squirm. These people feel so ill at ease with silences that they have a strong inner compulsion to shatter the quiet with questions, advice, or any other sound that will end their discomfort by ending the silence. For these people, the focus of attention is not on the speaker but rather on their own inner disquiet. They are like the character in Samuel Becket's *Waiting for Godot* who said, "Let us try to converse calmly since we are incapable of keeping silent."[21]

Fortunately, most people can increase their comfort with silence in a relatively short period of time. When people find out what to do in silence, they become far less uptight in the verbal lulls that are so important to vital communication. During the pauses in an interaction, a good listener does the following:

Attends to the other. His body posture demonstrates that he is really there for the other person.

Observes the other. He sees that the speaker's eyes, facial expressions, posture, and gestures are all communicating. When you are not distracted by the other's words, you may "hear" his body language more clearly.

Thinks about what the other is communicating. He ponders what the other has said. He wonders what the speaker is feeling. He considers the variety of responses he might make. Then he selects the one that he thinks will be most facilitative.

When he is busy doing these things, the listener does not have time to become anxious about the silence.

Some people are helped in their quest for comfort with silences by realizing that when the other person is conversing about a pressing need, the focus of attention is on him—not on the listener. If he does not want to talk further, that's his prerogative. Why should it bother a listener if the speaker doesn't want to continue the conversation? Many people believe that once a problem has been stated, it should be solved—in one sitting. Human behavior simply isn't that neat and efficient.

Before the birth of Jesus, the author of the Book Ecclesiastes said there is a "time to keep silent and a time to speak."[22] The effective listener can do both. Some people sit quietly during a whole conversation, pushing the other into a monologue. Excessive silence can be as undesirable as no silence. To sit mute like a "bump on a log" does not constitute effective listening. It is rarely possible to listen effectively for a long time without making some kind of verbal response. Soon the mind of such an unresponsive "listener" dulls, his eyes become glazed, and it becomes obvious to the speaker that the "listener" is not with him. Silence, when overdone, is not golden—it is then merely a lack of response to the person with needs.

The effective listener learns to speak when that is appropriate, can be silent when that is a fitting response, and feels comfortable with either activity. The good listener becomes adept at verbal responses while at the same time recognizing the immense importance of silence in creative conversation. He frequently emulates Robert Benchley, who once said, "Drawing on my fine command of language, I said nothing."

SUMMARY

Listening is a combination of hearing what another person says and involvement with the person who is talking. Its importance can be gauged by the fact that we spend more time listening than anything else we do in our waking hours and because our ability to listen directly influences our friendships, our family relationships, and our effectiveness at work. For ease of learning, this book treats listening in three skill clusters: attending skills, following skills, and reflecting skills. Attending is demonstrating by a posture of involvement, eye contact, appropriate body movement, and assurance of a nondistracting environment that the listener is psychologically present to the speaker. The skills of using door openers, minimal encourages, open questions, and attentive silence enable the listener to keep the focus on the speaker's communication. The cluster of reflective listening skills will be taught in the next chapter.

. . .

WHEN TO LISTEN REFLECTIVELY

There are many times when the skills of reflective listening can be used. Here are some of them.

Before You Act

Some business concerns have saved thousands of dollars by training all their employees to paraphrase before taking action. Interpersonal communication is often misleading. A simple paraphrase is one of the most efficient tools a person can use for an accuracy check when he has been asked to do a task.

Some companies program a time at the end of meetings so people can paraphrase the action steps they are expected to take or are responsible for as a result of the meeting. Some claim that this use of paraphrasing has greatly improved the results of the meetings.

Before You Argue or Criticize

Many arguments could be avoided if people really understood what the other person was saying. How often have you heard someone say during a heated argument, "That's what I was trying to say all along." People often argue because they don't realize they are both on the same side of the issue. Even when a person's opinion is different from mine, I may understand or learn from the disagreeement when, by reflective listening, I discover how he arrived at that position. More detail on this will be found in Chapter 10 on conflict.

When the Other Person Experiences Strong Feelings or Wants to Talk Over a Problem

When another person is very excited, enthusiastic, or joyful—that is a time to reflect what he is saying. Likewise, when a person is depressed, confused, angry, or edgy—that is a time to be a reflective listener. When another person comes to me with a problem he wants to talk over, that is the time to listen reflectively while he arrives at his own best solution to his problem.

When the Other Person Is Speaking in a "Code"

When you guess that the other is coding his message, it indicates that there are issues and/or feelings that are hard to express. The best way to help the person verbalize these feelings is to actively listen. Reflective listening can help at these times to decode the message and uncover the real point of what the speaker is struggling to say.

When Another Person Wants to Sort Out His Feelings and Thoughts

Sometimes people want a solution to their problem. At other times, they are not solution-oriented and only want to explore a situation with a friend. It can be quite helpful at times just to share a dilemma with a friend without reaching any specific action plan. Unfortunately, some listeners grow frustrated when a speaker leaves without completing his problem solving.

During a "Direct Mutual Conversation"

In many situations where listening is appropriate, the focus of attention is on the speaker. The resources of both parties are geared toward him. In direct mutual conversation, however, both parties share equally the focus of the dialogue. Both persons initiate conversation as well as reflect what the other says. In this case, a person shares his point of view after he reflects what the other has said. Direct mutual conversation is rarely appropriate for a light conversation. When talking about matters of great importance to one or both parties, or when conflict is involved, this type of conversation can be very meaningful.

WHEN NOT TO LISTEN REFLECTIVELY

Some people ruin a good thing by using it at the wrong time. This is particularly true about reflective listening. When there is no specific reason for reflective listening, don't work at doing it. There are times when the other's needs will signal you to discipline youself to reflect. Reflective listening is work, however. It is unhealthy for a relationship if one or both parties are always working at the relationship when they are together. Relationships flourish when there are many hearty, carefree moments. When a relationship is always work for one person, it soon becomes a "drag" for both parties.

When You Are Not Able to Be Accepting

When you listen reflectively, the other tends to let his guard down. He becomes more vulnerable to you. If you become moralistic or judgmental or in some way demonstrate nonacceptance, he will probably be hurt much more than if you had responded judgmentally right from the start. if you feel you must "zap" someone with your pronouncements, do it at the outset and without seeming to be in a helping mode.

When You Do Not Trust the Other to Find His Own Solution

One of the basic theories underlying reflective listening is that when the other person has a problem, he is usually the best person to solve that problem. The primary purpose of active listening is to facilitate his solution of his own problem. There are several reasons why each person should retain the responsibility for solving his own problems:

> The other person with the problem has most of the data. No matter how effectively he discloses and I listen, the other will have more data on his situation than I can ever have.
>
> The other person takes all the risks. If the solution isn't as good as it looked on the surface, the other must suffer the consequences.
>
> The other must implement the solution.
>
> The other's confidence and sense of self-responsibility are strengthened when he makes and implements his own solutions. He takes a significant step toward shaping his own destiny.
>
> The other and I both benefit when he becomes less dependent on me as the listener/helper.

Some people don't "buy" this theory. Parents, teachers, bosses, and others often think their greater experience and/or intelligence should provide the solution. Sometimes people agree in the top of their minds with the theory that the person with a problem is in the best position to solve it. In practice, however, they look on their solution as better than anything the other could possibly imagine. So they "push" their solution. When I am tempted to impose my solutions on the person with the problem, I try to recall the words of Clark Moustakas, a psychologist at Detroit's Merrill-Palmer Institute:

> Ultimately, I cannot be responsible for another person. I can only participate in his life, no matter what that participation may come to mean to him. But, in the end, he discovers his own meanings, his own resources, his own nature, his own being.[23]

When You Are Talking to Yourself

Medical specialists tell me that we all talk to ourselves. When you talk to yourself about a significant problem, it is important to listen carefully enough to yourself to arrive at a sound decision.

Commonly, when a person talks to himself, he scarcely listens at all. Or he sends himself some gigantic roadblocks. Moralizing, for example, he says to him-self, "You *should* do . . . " or he may give himself a put-down: "You'll never be able to do it." Or any other one of the dirty dozen.

More hopefully, you can reflect the content and especially the feelings of your conversations to yourself. You can summarize and psychologically attend to yourself during lulls and silences. It is simply amazing how helpful it can be to listen reflectively to yourself.

You can even listen to your body signals this way. A person getting a headache can reflect as though talking to his own body:

ME: You've had it with me working so frantically today. You are beginning to throb now.

NECK AND HEAD: *(Sends more signals of physical discomfort.)*

ME: This is just the beginning, you say? It will be much worse soon.

NECK & HEAD: *(The muscles are still tense from the day's emotional pressure.)*

ME: You want me to lay off and give you a rest before you develop into a full-blown headache. I bet you'd like a massage, too.

Now at least you have heard your body complain about the way you are abus-ing it. Simply taking a moment to listen sometimes helps. At other times, of course, change of behavior is required.

When Encountering New Ideas in a Book or Lecture or at Work

I find that as I encounter new ideas, it helps to use active listening skills to decode the author's meaning. *I call this intellectual empathy.* I learned it as a graduate student writing a paper on John Calvin, a thinker known for his deterministic phi-losophy. I surprised myself at the excellence of my logic in demolishing Calvin's arguments, and my professor agreed that my logic was outstanding; but he added, "You haven't wrestled with the problem Calvin was facing." The professor was absolutely right. It is easy to criticize ideas even of an intellectual giant as long as one never addresses the complex problems he is trying to understand. I still don't agree with Calvin, but I now realize that he was facing a much deeper and more complex set of issues than I was. I respect him for his questions and have since learned from him.

I have to continually work at intellectual empathy. It is so easy to dismiss the ideas that do not find instant hospitality in my mind. As I teach communication skills and other courses to managers, salespersons, educators, and others, I find it is a rare person who does not have to struggle to be open to unfamiliar ideas and methods.

When You Are Not "Separate" from the Other

The good listener is able to get inside the other person's experience and yet remain separate. A boy told his father about an older "bully" who beat him up on the playground. The father was infuriated and insisted on calling the boy's parents. He allowed himself to get overinvolved. He took over his son's problem. A mother listened as her unmarried daughter said she was pregnant. The mother sobbed and said to this daughter, "How could you do this to us?" These "listeners" were not able to keep a healthy distance in the listening relationship. They were emotionally "triggered" by the other person's disclosure, which made it impossible for them to listen effectively.

When You Use Listening as a Way of Hiding Yourself

Some people consistently fall into the listener's role. They rarely disclose. They rarely impact on other people. They are not real, and their listening is usually dysfunctional for them and for the speaker. Other people use reflection to shield themselves from another's "negative" emotions. If the speaker is angry, and the listener doesn't want to experience the other's fury—he might simply reflect manipulatively. This seems to demonstrate how "mature" he is in handling the situation. If the listener doesn't feel the force of the other's anger, if he reflects without getting at least partially into the other's frame of reference, he will probably be creating distance in the relationship. That kind of "cowardly" listening has no place in a genuine relationship.

When You Feel Very Pressured, Hassled, or Depleted

It is important to be able to recognize those times when you may not be the best person to listen to a particular person. Maybe your inner self is out of kilter so that you can't be a good listener to anyone at the present time. It has taken me some time, but I've gradually come to accept that reality. Each person needs several listeners in his life. There will be times when each of us will not be inwardly ready to listen. If the other feels he has no one else to talk to, that is really unfortunate. But that is his problem to solve, not mine. I will probably do more harm than good if I try to listen when I am not inwardly ready to be there for that person.

There is no reason why you have to actively listen to any person. As much as I love my wife and want to be present for her as a listener, there are times when I am unwilling or unable to pay the price of empathic listening. If she starts a "heavy" conversation at one of those times, I tell her that I am not prepared to listen well right now.

THE GOOD NEWS AND THE BAD NEWS

The good news is that sometimes listening is a beautiful experience. The bad news is that it can be a heavy burden. As one listener admitted, "each act of listening that is not purely mechanical is a personal ordeal."[24] . . .

Listening is intensely demanding and therefore should not be entered into lightly. The experienced listener enters the helping relationship cautiously knowing that it involves time, effort, and sacrifice on his part. George Gazda points out that it is more respectful of the person with the problem or need if the listener weighs carefully the decison to help. Listening should not be entered into halfheartedly or carelessly. Nor should the listener enter a situation where it is likely that he will be ineffective. Such efforts are doomed to fail, and are likely to harm the speaker as well as disappoint the listener.[25]

References

1. Ralph G. Nichols and Leonard A. Stevens, *Are You Listening?* (New York: McGraw-Hill, 1957), pp. 6–7.
2. Ibid., pp. 6–10.
3. Quoted in B. Harvey Branscomb. *The Teachings of Jesus: A Textbook for College and Individual Use* (New York: Abingdon, 1931), p. 23. This saying comes from an apocryphal "New Testament" book.
4. Ralph G. Nichols and Leonard A. Stevens, "Listening to People," *Harvard Business Review* (September–October 1957).

5. Franklin Ernst, Jr., *Who's Listening? A Handbook of the Transactional Analysis of the Listening Function* (Vallejo, Calif.: Addresso 'set, 1973).
6. John Drakeford, *The Awesome Power of the Listening Ear* (Waco, Tex.: Word, 1967), p. 17.
7. Allen Ivey and John Hinkle, "The Transactional Classroom," unpublished manuscript, University of Massachusetts, 1970.
8. Norman Rockwell, "My Adventures as an Illustrator," ed. T. Rockwell, *Saturday Evening Post* (April 2, 1960). p. 67. President John Kennedy had this ability, too. See Drakeford, *The Awesome Power of the Listening Ear,* p. 65.
9. Albert Scheflen with Norman Ashcraft, *Human Territories: How We Behave in Space-Time* (Englewood Cliffs, N.J.: Prentice-Hall, 1976), pp. 6, 42.
10. C. L. Lassen, "Effect of Proximity on Anxiety and Communication in the Initial Psychiatric Interview," *Journal of Abnormal Psychology* 18 (1973): 220–232.
11. Ernst, *Who's Listening?* p. 113.
12. Charles Truax and Robert Carkhuff, *Toward Effective Counseling and Psychotherapy: Training and Practice* (New York: Aldine/Atherton, 1967), pp. 361–362.
13. Quoted in Gerald Nierenberg and Henry Calero, *How to Read a Person Like a Book* (New York: Pocket Books, 1975), p. 28.
14. Paul Ekman and Wallace Friesen, *Unmasking the Face: A Guide to Recognizing Emotions from Facial Expressions* (Englewood Cliffs, N.J.:Prentice-Hall, 1975), pp. 14–16.
15. Silvan Tomkins, in *Challenges of Humanistic Psychology,* ed. James Bugental (New York: McGraw-Hill, 1967), p. 57.
16. Anthony G. White, *Reforming Metropolitan Governments: A Bibliography* (New York: Garland, 1975).
17. Allen Ivey, *Microcounseling: Innovations in Interviewing Training* (Springfield, Ill.: Thomas, 1975).
18. John Moreland, Jeanne Phillips, and Jeff Lockhart, "Open Invitation to Talk," manuscript, University of Massachusetts, 1969, p. 1.
19. Eugene Herrigel, *The Method of Zen,* ed. Herman Tausend and R. F. C. Hull (New York: Pantheon, 1976), pp. 124–125.
20. Halford Luccock, *Halford Luccock Treasury,* ed. Robert Luccock, Jr. (New York: Abingdon, 1963), p. 242.
21. Quoted in Nathan Scott, *Man in the Modern Theater* (Richmond, Va.: John Knox, 1965), p. 86.
22. Ecclesiastes 3:7.
23. Clark Moustakas, *Creativity and Conformity* (Princeton, N.J.: D. Van Nostrand, 1967), p. 23.
24. Quoted in Douglas Steere, *On Beginning from Within/On Listening to Another* (New York: Harper & Row, 1943), p. 197.
25. George Gazda et al., *Human Relations Development: A Manual for Educators* (Boston: Allyn & Bacon, 1973), pp. 81–82.

PROBES

Several research studies have concluded that most people listen effectively to only 25–33% of what they hear. Do those figures fit your experience? Is your listening efficiency about the same as that or different? How about those who listen to you?

What rules, norms, or habits did you learn as you were growing up that increased your listening effectiveness? What rules, norms, or habits decreased it?

In school, class periods typically run longer than the average person's attention span. Describe three additional features of your school experience that work against good listening. Do the same for your work situation. What characteristics of that environment make it harder to listen well?

In your experience, what is the difference between a posture of involvement that looks genuine and one that looks faked or phony?

What does Bolton mean when he says, in the words of Franklin Ernst, Jr., that the body of a person listening effectively is "moved by the talker"?

Give an example from your own experience of the importance of eye contact for good listening.

In the section "Consciously Working at Attending," Bolton addresses the question, "How can I work this hard and still be natural?" How do you respond to what he says there? Does it ring true for you?

After you read the "Dialogic Listening" essay in this chapter, it might be useful for you to refer back to Bolton's discussion of Following skills.

Do you agree with Bolton that most listeners ask far too many questions? How so?

What are the two most useful suggestions from Bolton's advice about when to listen reflectively and when not to?

> *I can listen to someone without hearing him. Listening is fixing my attention only on the other person. Hearing requires that I listen inside me as I listen to him. Hearing is a rhythm whereby I shuttle between his words and my experience. It includes hearing his entire posture: his eyes, his lips, the tilt of his head, the movement of his fingers. It includes hearing his tone of voice and his silences. And hearing also includes attending to my reactions, such as the "sinking feeling" I get when the other person has stopped hearing me.*
>
> HUGH PRATHER

Milt Thomas is a friend of mine and a Ph.D. candidate in our department. In this next reading he and I describe an approach to listening that's grown out of our reading and teaching over the last two or three years. I first wrote about this approach in the October 1983 issue of a journal called *Communication Education.* While I was writing that article, I discussed it in a class Milt was taking, and he really picked up the ideas and ran with them. He began applying them in his own teaching and encouraging me to do the same. So when I decided to include a discussion on this approach in *Bridges Not Walls,* I knew that Milt could contribute a great deal to that effort.

The most exciting thing about our collaboration on this piece—and we are both still smiling about it—is that our work together was an example of what we were writing about. Each time we talked, we seemed to get more evidence of the value of this approach to listening. In fact, after we were finished, when I discovered that I needed to cut thirty-five pages from this book before sending it to the publisher, I asked Milt to discuss the issue with me, because I knew that the ways we had learned to listen to each other would make that conversation very produc-

---

*John Stewart, "Interpretive Listening; An Alternative to Empathy," *Communication Education,* 32 (October 1983): 379–391.

tive. I wasn't disappointed; the difficult decisions that emerged from that discussion still strike me as right.

So we encourage you to give dialogic listening a try. It's different from the kind of listening that Robert Bolton discusses, but only in the sense that it broadens and goes beyond his advice. We feel confident about it because we know it's solidly grounded in some well-developed philosophy of communication. But more important, we also know it can *work*.

Dialogic Listening: Sculpting Mutual Meanings

John Stewart and Milt Thomas

The two of us have recently had a number of communication experiences that have led us to substantially rethink our attitudes toward listening. In conversations with each other and in many of our contacts with students, family, friends, and co-workers, we have rediscovered in a concrete and exciting way the *productive* quality of interpersonal communication. In other words, we've experienced how in the most fruitful and satisfying conversations, our listening is focused less on *re*producing what's "inside" the other person and more on co-producing, with the other person, mutual meanings *between* us. As a result, we've rediscovered how a good conversation can create insights, ideas, and solutions to problems that none of the conversation partners could have generated alone. It seems to us that a certain kind of listening has helped that happen.

For example, Milt was recently involved with two other people in an effort to design and conduct a training program for beginning university teachers. Jack, one of Milt's partners, came to the planning sessions with very definite ideas about the design and operation of the program. He assumed that Milt and Susan would also have their definite ideas and that their meeting times would be spent with each trainer bargaining for his or her own plan. You could say that Jack was mainly content-focused. Susan's primary concern was the quality of learning experienced by the beginning university teachers; she focused more on outcome or goals. She was willing to bargain with Jack, to advocate her own ideas, or to engage in whatever process seemed to lead to the outcomes she valued.

Although Milt wasn't fully aware of the contrast at the time, his main concern was neither the content of the program nor outcomes for the participants, but the quality of the contact among the three planners. He was *not* just functioning as a "pure process" person; he brought his own ideas—for example, about how the new teachers could learn to handle the grading and the cross-cultural communication problems they might encounter in their classrooms. But Milt found his ideas about content and outcomes entering the conversation somewhat like "counterpunches" in the sense that they were responses to Jack's or Susan's contributions. He seemed to use the momentum of the ongoing talk to create "holes" that his contributions helped fill.

Milt's efforts were not always greeted cheerfully. He often slowed down the planning process as he made sure that he understood the others, that they understood him, and that they comprehended one another. When Susan and Jack presented their ideas, he would often raise questions or offer countersuggestions in order to build more talk about the ideas. Milt wasn't merely playing "devil's advocate" to stir things up; he was trying to help engage all three persons in a mutual building process. They were building conversation-texts, "chunks" of talk that developed ideas and suggestions, teased out nuances, and helped mold incomplete suggestions into refined ones.

While Jack's strength was content and Susan's strength was her outcome-focus, Milt's contribution to this effort came primarily from the way he *listened*. His attitudes and expectations, the questions he asked, the way he paraphrased others' comments, and even his nonverbal behavior—posture, tone of voice, rate of speaking, and so on—were all aimed not just toward *reproducing* what Jack or Susan said but toward *producing* with them a full response to the issues they faced.

We've come to call the kind of listening Milt engaged in *dialogic listening*. We use that term to label listening that values and builds mutuality, requires active involvement, is genuine, and grows out of a belief in and commitment to synergy—the idea that the whole actually can be greater than the sum of its parts. There are some important differences between dialogic listening and what's usually called "active listening" or "empathic listening." Let's start by briefly reviewing them.

"ACTIVE" OR "EMPATHIC" LISTENING

Recall for a minute some of what you've read or heard about listening, perhaps from Robert Bolton's excellent essay reprinted earlier in this chapter, from a listening text,[1] from your teacher, or in a listening seminar or workshop. For one thing, you may well have read or discussed some of the ironies of listening. For example, we spend much more time listening than we spend speaking, reading, or writing, but we're taught the most about writing and reading, a little about speaking, and almost nothing about listening.[2] Another irony is that we are worst at the activity we engage in the most. As Bolton notes, researchers claim that we usually remember only about one quarter of what we hear, and many people miss almost 100% of the feeling content of spoken communication.

To help remedy this situation, most books and articles emphasize that listening differs from hearing. Hearing is the physiological part of the process—the reception of sound waves. Good listening is traditionally defined as effective sensing, interpreting, and evaluating the other person's meanings. That definition is reflected in the anonymous maxim, "I know you believe you understand what you think I said, but I'm not sure you realize that what you heard is not what I meant." The idea behind this maxim is that listening involves *one* person grasping the *other* person's meanings, and since we can't get inside the other person's experience, the listening process is inherently flawed.

When people discuss empathic listening, they generally begin from this same basic understanding. Empathy is the process of "putting yourself in the other's place," or as Carl Rogers puts it,

> It means entering the private perceptual world of the other and becoming thoroughly at home in it. It involves being sensitive, moment by moment, to the changing felt meanings which flow in this other person. . . . To be with another in this way means that for the time being, you lay aside your own views and values in order to enter another's world without prejudice. In some sense it means that you lay aside yourself. . . .[3]

One of the most important skills for achieving empathic understanding is paraphrasing. As Bolton puts it, "a *paraphrase* is a *concise response* to the speaker which states the *essence* of the other's *content* in the *listener's own words*."[4] Most traditional treatments of active or empathic listening also discuss several other parts of the process, including attending skills, clarifying skills, and perception checking.[5]

These traditional accounts are useful in several ways. For one thing, they call our attention to the fact that most of us don't listen as well as we could. We think of listening as a passive process, like "soaking up sense data," and as a result we often don't work at it. Good listening takes real effort and traditional listening texts and workshops almost always include helpful suggestions about how to do it better. There's also something intuitively appealing about discussions of empathic listening. Each of us knows what it's like to "walk a mile in the other person's moccasins," and we've also had the opposite experience where someone is so self-centered that he or she never really connects with any *else's* thoughts or feelings. Empathizing with someone's fear or pain—or having someone empathize with yours—can be very confirming and reassuring, and when it doesn't happen, it can hurt.

But there are also some problems with this view of listening. For one thing, it's based on a kind of fiction. As we mentioned, you cannot actually "get inside" the other person's awareness, and it can be confusing to try to think, feel, and act as if you could. It's also impossible to, as Rogers puts it, "lay aside your own views and values" or to "lay aside yourself." Any decision or effort to make that kind of move would be the decision or effort of a "self" and it would be rooted in that self's views and values. In other words, you cannot put yourself on the shelf because that move is an active choice that keeps yourself involved. "Laying aside yourself" is as literally impossible as lifting yourself by your ears—or your own bootstraps. So you may well decide to focus on the other person and to do your best to sense her meanings or feel his happiness, but those efforts will always be grounded in your own attitudes, expectations, past experiences, and world view. You *can't* "lay aside yourself." Neither can we.

A second problem is that empathic listening can get distorted into a frustrating or even manipulative process of parroting. The generally recognized "father" of empathic listening, Carl Rogers, often commented on how vulnerable to distortion the process can be. Consider, for example, how you'd feel if you were the client in this counselor–client conversation:

CLIENT: I really think he's a very nice guy; he's so thoughtful, sensitive, and kind. He calls me a lot. He's fun to go out with.
COUNSELOR: You like him very much, then.
CLIENT: Yeah, and I think my friends like him too. Two of them have asked me to double-date.
COUNSELOR: You are pleased that your friends accept him.
CLIENT: Yeah, but I don't want to get too involved right now. I've got a lot of commitments at school and to my family.
COUNSELOR: You want to limit your involvement with him.
CLIENT: Yeah. . . . Is there an echo in here?

When your conversation partner—whether counselor, lover, parent, or friend—is focusing only on sensing your meanings or feeling your feelings, it can begin to seem like you are talking to yourself. The contact between you is sacrificed to serve the other person's desire to "understand fully."

That brings us to a third shortcoming of many of the traditional approaches to active or empathic listening: They emphasize the "psychology" of the situation rather than the *communication*. By that we mean that these approaches make each person's "psyche" or internal state the focus of attention rather than the verbal and nonverbal transaction that's going on *between* them. As we've already said, it can be very helpful to try to sense another's feelings, and it is confirming and reassuring when someone does that for you. But we think there's more to effective listening than that. You definitely do not need to stop trying to listen actively or empathically, but we do think it can be helpful to broaden your repertoire by also learning to listen dialogically.

DIALOGIC LISTENING

In our thinking and talking we've identified four distinctive features of dialogic listening. In this section we want to outline them and to offer five suggestions for practicing this approach. We'll conclude with a brief discussion of some problems you might encounter as you try to apply what we suggest here.

Focus on "Ours"

The first distinctive feature of dialogic listening is that it focuses on "ours" rather than "mine" or "yours." Without listening training of any kind—and sometimes even with it—many of us fall into a pattern of communicating as if we were talking to ourselves—we focus on "mine." Sometimes this monologic communication "just happens"; we're not aware of the fact that we are only discussing our topic from our point of view, or we're not conscious of how long we've been talking or how few real questions we've asked. At other times we get caught up in our own agendas; we get so involved in and enthusiastic about our project or opportunity that we lose track of—and hence contact with—the other person. That happens often to one of John's friends. The friend's wife urges him to "be more sensitive," but he often can't seem to help himself. He gets going on his most recent idea or project and fifteen minutes pass before he takes a breath. Then he'll abruptly notice what he's done and apologize for "monopolizing the conversation—again."

Other persons concentrate on "mine" simply because they believe that their agenda is more significant than anyone else's. They fall into a "me focused" pattern when their excitement or worry about their own concerns overshadows everything else. And in still other cases a person sticks with his or her agenda because of the belief that "I can say it my way better than you can say it your way," and the possibility that *we* could say it even more effectively never occurs to them. In short, unconsciousness, honest enthusiasm, and a sense of superiority can all help us keep our communication focused on "mine."

The preceding quotations from Rogers and Bolton illustrate how treatments of empathic listening concentrate on "yours." A paraphrase states the essence of the *other's* content in the listener's own words, and empathizing means "entering the private conceptual world of the *other*." As we have already said, this can be a useful move for the very self-centered person, but it can also lead to the kind of communication illustrated in our counselor–client example.

The third alternative is to focus on *ours*. This is what we had in mind when we subtitled this discussion "Sculpting Mutual Meanings." The metaphor is Milt's and he uses it to suggest a concrete, graphic image of what it means to listen dialogically. Picture yourself sitting on one side of a potter's wheel with your conversation partner across from you. As you work (talk) together, each of you adds clay to the form on the wheel, and each uses wet fingers, thumbs, and palms to shape the finished product. Like clay, talk is tangible and malleable; it's out there to hear, to record, and to shape. If I am unclear or uncertain about what I am thinking or about what I want to say, I can put something out there and you can modify its shape, ask me to add more clay, or add some of your own. Your specific shaping, which you could only have done in response to the shape I formed, may move in a direction I would never have envisioned. The clay you add may be an idea I've thought about before—though not here or in this form—or it may be completely new to me. Sometimes these "co-sculpting" sessions will be mostly playful, with general notions tossed on the wheel and the result looking like a vaguely shaped mass. At other times, the basic shape is well defined and we spend our time on detail and refinement. Our efforts, though, are almost always productive and frequently very gratifying. Sometimes I feel that our talk helps me understand myself better than I could have alone. At other times we produce something that transcends anything either of us could have conceived separately. That's because the figure we sculpt is not mine or yours, but *ours,* the outcome of both of our active shapings.

Open-ended and "Playful"

The second distinctive feature of dialogic listening is its open-ended, tentative, playful quality. We notice that when we are listening dialogically, we actually do not know what the outcome of the conversation will be. For example, John initiated the collaboration on this chapter because he knew that Milt had done a lot of thinking about this approach to listening and had worked with these ideas in the interpersonal communication courses he teaches. Our first conversation about this essay occurred in the hallway outside the Speech Communication Department office, where we set a time to meet and talk about the project. At that point neither of us knew what the outcome of our longer conversation would be. One option was for John to write the essay and for Milt to read it and suggest changes and additions. Another possibility was that Milt would write it, based on his recent classroom experience, and then John would edit and polish it. A third is that each of us would draft different sections and then comment on what the other person wrote. In our meeting, we didn't discuss any of those options until after an hour and a half or so, when our tentative strategy emerged from our talk. We agreed that we would start by having John take the ideas that developed in our conversation—most of which Milt had initiated and given examples of—and would begin organizing the whole, and Milt would draft certain sections that he knew best. As the process has developed, Milt has written several sections, John has integrated Milt's contributions into the text, and Milt has critiqued, raised questions, and made additions to each draft. Our point is that this kind of open-endedness is one of the primary prerequisites for—and one of the greatest challenges of—dialogic listening.

It's a challenge especially because a great deal of what we learn in twentieth-century Western culture pushes us in the opposite direction, toward closure and certainty. For example, if you read John's "Interpersonal Communication—Contact Between Persons" essay in Chapter 2 of this book, you probably recall his discussion of the "Spiritual Child." Some people dislike that discussion because they think it is too "abstract" and "ambiguous"; they are impatient with it and want more "hard content." In his book on creativity, Roger von Oech addresses those concerns when he discusses "soft and hard thinking."[6] "Hard" thinking is logical, analytical, critical, propositional, digital, focused, concrete, and "left-brain." "Soft" thinking is speculative, divergent, symbolic, elliptical, analogical, ambiguous, metaphoric, and "right-brain." Both are vital to effective problem-solving. Yet von Oech describes how, especially in the twentieth-century Western world, we are taught that there is only one kind of *real* thinking that leads to *real* knowledge, and that's the "hard" kind. This same bias makes it difficult to practice the kind of openness and tentativeness that dialogic listening requires.

What von Oech calls "hard" thinking is thinking that values the three c's: certainty, closure, and control. Much of the "hard" sciences, like physics and chemistry, concentrate on the development of lawlike generalizations that apply with certainty in all situations.[7] Whether it's morning or evening, winter or summer, at General Motors or General Mills, H_2O is always water and, given one atmosphere of pressure, H_2O will always boil at 100°C and freeze at 0°C. If you know those laws you can confidently *control* the "behavior" of water, and you can be sure that on these matters inquiry is *closed;* we know what we need to know.

Obviously, the hard sciences and the hard thinking that develops them are enormously powerful and effective. Holography and the space shuttle, to say nothing of diet soft drinks and word processing, would be impossible without them. But certainty, closure, and control are not always possible, and especially where persons are involved, they're often not even desirable.

In order to listen dialogically you need, in place of the three c's, a combination of some modesty or humility and some trust. The modesty comes from remembering that persons are choosers, choice-makers. That means that you cannot predict with certainty what they will think, feel, or do in any situation. We just don't have that power over people, although habits and patterns sometimes make it seem as if we do. John's grandmother "always" cries at weddings, and politicians "always" like publicity. So it seems that we could predict what they'll do in those situations "every time." But all you have to do is pay attention to the people around you, and you will discover how those "always" predictions turn into" usually" or "sometimes." So there's an inverse relationship between this kind of humility and your desire for conversational certainty and control. When you can acknowledge and affirm your partner's power, as a person, to choose, you can relax your grip on two of the three c's.

There's also an inverse relationship between conversational trust and the two c's of closure and control. By trust we don't mean a naive belief that the world is a completely friendly place and that nobody in it means you any harm. That's obviously foolish. What we do mean is that you trust the potential of the conversation to produce more than you could on your own, and that, at least until you're proven wrong, you trust the other person's presence to you. For us, the cognitive part of this trust seems to be a decision to let the talk work, a choice in favor of what William S. Howell calls the "joint venture" quality of the conversation.[8] The feeling part seems to be a combination of a relaxing-letting-go and a deep-breath-leap-of-faith. That may overstate things a bit; the point is that you relax whatever white-knuckled grip you might have on the conversation's direction or outcome—"How can I be sure she doesn't think I am being silly?" "What if he won't give me the time off?"—and trust it to work.

Playfulness is the icing on the cake. If you and your conversation partner can manage to be tentative and experimental and can manifest a sense of open-endedness, you'll frequently find yourself literally playing with the ideas. In the past couple of decades scholars from several disciplines have emphasized the "seriousness" of play, the many senses in which play isn't just for fun. Psychotherapists discuss "games people play," defense analysts engage in war games, and play therapy is one way to help both troubled and normal children. Even a couple of philosophers have discussed the "playful" nature of conversation.[9] They emphasize that the "to-and-fro" is the basic form of everything we call "play," including sporting events, board games, and even the play of light on the water. Another characteristic is indeterminacy, that is, that play constantly renews itself. No Super Bowl or World Series game is ever the definitive or final instance of the play of football or baseball; these activities are constantly renewed in each playing. In addition, we don't completely control our playing; in an important sense we are played by the game as much as we play it. This quality becomes clear if you think of the way the rules, the tempo, the setting, and the spectators all affect your playing of racquetball, chess, baseball, or poker.

The point is, when we are engaged in spontaneous conversation, the form of the to-and-fro itself can generate insight and surprise—if we are listening dialogically. No un-self-conscious conversation is ever simply outward *replay* of your inner intentions and meanings. Instead, you and your partner actually play together; the two of you enter a dynamic over which you do not have complete control, and the outcome of your talk can be a surprise to you both, a creation of your play. It's difficult to write down an example of open-ended playfulness, but we think the following conversation at least points in the directions we mean:

KIM: Can I talk to you, Professor Carbaugh?

DON: Sure, "Student Wells," what's up? Oh, yes, you missed the exam on Friday, didn't you.

KIM: Yeah. That's why I came by. And since you said at the beginning of the term that you didn't have a set policy on makeups, I don't know what to do about it.

DON: Well, you're doing it exactly right! There's no set policy, because the situation is a little different in each case. So we definitely *do* have to do something about it, or you will end up with a zero. But I don't know yet what that should be. Sit down and let's talk about it.

KIM: Can I take the exam now?

DON: Right now? I don't know. . . . let's back off a little and talk about what happened when the rest of the class was writing the exam.

KIM: I was sick. Well, not exactly *sick,* sick, but I couldn't do it. I was really not physically or mentally able to do it.

DON: Keep talking. . . .

KIM: Well, I don't want to give you a pile of excuses.

DON: I don't want you to give me a pile either—*(smiling)* of anything. But I do want to hear what was happening with you.

KIM: We had a big party on Thursday at the house I'm in, and I was in charge of all the arrangements, and I stayed up most of Wednesday night getting ready for it, and then in the middle of the party my boyfriend and I had a big fight, and he left, and I fell apart that night and couldn't even get out of bed Friday until after noon. Actually, I knew the fight was coming; I wouldn't have gotten so upset except I was so tired. Anyway, I just blew it.

DON: Okay. I appreciate your honesty. Hmmm . . . so you didn't have a certified, diagnosed disease, but it sounds like you *were* fairly well incapacitated—and probably a little hungover too.

KIM: I don't drink.

DON: I apologize. A dumb assumption on my part. I'm sorry.

KIM: It's okay. So what are we going to do?

DON: Well, what do you suggest? Sounds like you ought to be able to take a makeup, but that you aren't exactly in the same position as somebody who had the flu or who had to attend a funeral.

KIM: I don't know; I think it's the same. I don't know why I should be penalized at all. But you're the teacher.

DON: Yeah, and *both* of us are involved in this—as is the rest of the class, indirectly. I'm concerned that the exam was Friday and now it's Monday.

KIM: And I could have talked about it with other people in the class.

DON: Yeah, that's possible; and that would be less fair to the others. I don't care to put you "on the stand" to testify about that; I don't like playing judge and jury. So what if I modify the exam, you take it this afternoon, and we knock fifteen points off the top because, as you put it, you did kind of "blow" it.

KIM: All of that's fine but the fifteen-point penalty. I think I was as sick as anyone who has the twenty-four-hour flu.

DON: Okay, let's run that part of it briefly by the class. I'll keep you anonymous and see how they feel about makeups under these general circumstances—whether they feel any unfairness.

KIM: Well, if you feel you have to do that.

DON: Sounds like you don't. What are you thinking?

Don's open-endedness is evident here in his unwillingness to set a rigid policy in advance, his concern that the two of them discuss the situation before arriving at a conclusion, and his willingness to admit his own errors and to acknowledge the validity of Kim's viewpoint. Obviously, he does have principles here, and the fact that he is open to play does not mean he's wishy-washy. In this case, his position is clear: "We definitely *do* have to do something about it, or you will end up with a zero," but he is willing to let the conversation guide the two of them toward their specific solution. There's also a little play here around titles—"professor" and "student"—and the "pile of excuses" metaphor. In addition, once Don enters into a discussion that is this open, he cannot not take Kim's arguments seriously. He has to at least listen to her; in that sense Don is "being played by the game." The same is obviously true for Kim. We end the example before a final resolution is reached to emphasize that even after this much talk it may still be important to stay open.

In Front of

The third distinctive feature of dialogic listening is that it emphasizes what's in front of or between the conversation partners rather than what's "behind" them. One influential definition of empathy includes this sentence: "It is an experiencing of the consciousness 'behind' another's outward communication, but with continuous awareness that this consciousness is originating and proceeding in the other."[10] That's the opposite of dialogic listening. Instead of trying to infer internal "psychic" states from the talk, when you are listening dialogically you join with the other person in the process of co-creating meaning *between* you.

Again, we don't mean to be making an artificial dichotomy. "Internal states" cannot be separated from external ones, and thoughts and feelings are obviously a part of all communication. But it makes a big difference whether you are *focusing* on those internal states, trying to make an educated guess about where the other person is coming from, or focusing on building talk between the two of you. In other words, it can make a big difference whether your metaphor is "figuring out where she's coming from" or "sculpting mutual meanings." When your focus is "behind" you spend your time and mental energy searching for possible fits between what you're seeing and hearing and what the other person "must be" meaning and feeling. In other words, you're engaging in a form of psychologizing, treating the talk as an indicator of something else that's more reliable, more important, more interesting.

On the other hand, when you're listening dialogically, your focus, as we said before, is on the communication not the psychology. We don't mean that you are insensitive to the other person's feelings. In fact, your sensitivity may well be heightened, but it is focused *between* rather than behind. You concentrate on the verbal and nonverbal text that the two of you are building together. In one sense you take the talk at face value; you attend to it and not to something you infer to be behind it. But that doesn't mean you uncritically accept everything that's said as the "whole truth and nothing but the truth." You respond and inquire in ways that make the mutual text as full and reliable as possible. You work to co-build it into a text you *can* trust. That leads us to the final distinctive feature we want to mention.

Presentness

When you're listening dialogically, you focus more on the present than on the past or future. Once again, please don't hear an absolute; the future is not irrelevant and neither is the past. When we met to discuss our collaboration on this essay, we felt the pressure of a future deadline, and we were encouraged by the success of past interactions. But as we talked, our attention was on the present; we were open to what *could* be co-built, we focused on the "ours" *between* us, and all that helped keep us in the here-and-now.

The philosopher of communication, Martin Buber, was once described by his friend and biographer Maurice Friedman as a person with a unique ability to be "present to the presentness of the other and able to call the other into presence with him." Friedman speaks of how, when he met Buber, he first noticed his eyes. Others mentioned too how Buber's look was penetrating but gentle. His gaze and his look seemed both to demand presentness and to reassure. One person said that the message from Buber's eyes was always, "Do not be afraid." And it was difficult not to respond in kind, with as much presentness as one could muster. This quality of Buber's communication is what we mean by this characteristic of dialogic listening.

Buber also had another way of making the point we are making here: he talked of the desirability of working toward a unity of one's saying, being, and doing. In one of his books, Buber wrote that human life can be thought of as consisting of three realms: thought, speech, and action. "Whoever straightens himself out in regard to all three will find that everything prospers at his hand."[11] Later in the same book he added, "The root of all conflict between me and my fellow man is that I do not say what I mean and I do not mean what I say."[12]

It seems to us that if you are going to work toward unifying your saying, being, and doing, you are going to have to focus on the present. You can't connect and coordinate your actions, speech, and be-ing in any other way. It also seems that when we focus on the present as a way toward unifying these three realms, our efforts tend to make it easier for the other person to do the same thing. So the whole process can spiral in a very positive way.

"But," you may be asking, "what if the other person is lying? What if the 'present talk' *cannot* be trusted? Isn't your advice a little naive?" Our response, as we mentioned earlier, is that we are not suggesting blind naiveté. If you allow us one other personal example, trust was an issue for us as we collaborated on this essay. John is clearly "one up" on the power scale in this partnership, because he's an associate professor and Milt is a teaching assistant. In order for us to be able to practice what we are preaching about dialogic listening, John has to be willing and able to participate in genuine power *sharing,* and Milt has to *trust* him to do that. It isn't enough for John just to "give Milt power" by letting him have his say while reserving the right to make the final decision. He has to actually share responsibility, to leave the outcomes genuinely open. Both of us also need to trust each other to work constructively with incomplete, fuzzy, and sometimes off-the-point ideas. Especially because he's power-down, Milt needs to trust John, first to criticize rather than just to superficially agree with everything, and second, to criticize in constructive ways and not to ridicule unfinished ideas. We've been excited by the power sharing and trust that's been generated. We think it's materially improved the finished product.

If you aren't that fortunate and find that you mistrust the other's presence or his truthfulness, you can make that fact part of your conversation. There are ways to raise that issue without ridiculing or rejecting the other person. You can describe your reservations or ask your questions in ways that keep the conversation going, and that brings us to our "how to do it" section.

APPLICATIONS

When we first began to think seriously about dialogic listening, we both moved almost immediately to this point. "What behavioral differences," we asked ourselves and each other, "are there between active or empathic listening and dialogic listening? What do you *do* differently?" For a while we felt like we'd run up against a brick wall. We could identify two or three important behaviors, "moves" or "techniques," but (1) there seemed to be much more to the process than just those behaviors and (2) strictly speaking, there was at least a mention in a "traditional" treatment of listening of each behavior on our list. After about two years of periodic thinking, discussing, and classroom experimenting, we began to understand our struggle. There are at least five ways of applying this approach to listening, but the most important element is the listener's *attitude, intent, awareness,* or *perspective.*

Remember the example Neil Postman uses in his "Minding Your Minding" essay in Chapter 2? Postman contrasts the experience of the churchgoer who is unaware of the structure and function of ritual in culture with the experience of the churchgoer who is aware of those dimensions. Postman's point is that *both* may participate fully in and profit from the event, but that the differences in awareness will make a real difference to the persons. We've found that to be true with dialogic listening. The first and most important application advice is that you define your specific listening situation as "ours," "open-ended," "between," and "present." Try not to focus your attention on "mine" or "his/hers," "control," "what's behind," or the past or future. When you're able to do that you will notice how "attitudes" and "behaviors" are not really separate. What you do—the behaviors— will *feel* different as your attitude or perspective shifts. At least that is our experience. For example, the ways we paraphrase (we'll discuss that skill in a minute) actually change as we shift from empathic to dialogic listening. We believe you may well discover the same. The point is, if you can genuinely achieve the mind-set we've discussed here, you'll have gone a long way toward listening dialogically.

"Say More"

One communication behavior that seems to be an application of that mind-set is the response, "Say more." As we explained when we discussed the sculpting metaphor, talk is tangible and malleable, and one of the primary goals of dialogic listening is to build more "chunks" of talk that develop ideas and suggestions, tease out nuances, and help define incomplete ideas. As a listener, you can most directly contribute to that process by simply encouraging your conversation partner to keep talking.

One common situation where "say more" can help is when someone makes a comment that sounds fuzzy or incomplete. Frequently, our inclination is to try to paraphrase what's been said or to act on that information even though we don't feel like we have the materials to do so. When Milt is in this situation, he finds himself feeling frustrated because he seems to have a disproportionate share of the burden to "make things clear." When he feels that frustration, he uses it as a signal to ask the person to "say more." The indirect message is that Milt wants the other person's help; he's saying, in effect, "I can't continue our sculpture until you add some definition to the form you began."

In this situation and in others, you might expect that your "say more" will just promote repetition and redundancy, but that's not been our experience. We find that if our encouragement is genuine, we frequently get talk that clarifies ideas, gets more specific, and substantially reduces misunderstanding. Like each of our suggestions, this one has to be used appropriately. It'd be pretty ridiculous to respond to "Could you tell me what time it is?" with "Say more about that." But each time you hear a new idea, a new topic, or an important point being made, we suggest you begin your listening effort at that moment not by guessing what the other person means but by asking them to tell you. "Say more," "Keep talking," or some similar encouragement can help.[13]

Run with the Metaphor

Our second suggestion is that you build more conversation-text, in part by extending whatever metaphors the other person has used to express his or her ideas, developing your own metaphors, or encouraging the other person to extend yours. As you know, a metaphor is a figure of speech that links two dissimilar objects or ideas in order to make a point. "My love is a red, red rose," "He's built like King Kong," and "The table wiggles because one leg is shorter than the other" all include metaphors. The first links my love and a rose in order to make a point. The second links his build and King Kong's, and the third links a table support with the appendage an animal uses to walk. As the third example suggests, metaphors are more common than we sometimes think. In fact, some people argue that virtually *all* language is metaphoric.[14]

We use the example, though, to encourage you to listen for both subtle and obvious metaphors and to weave them into your responses. We've found that when the other person hears his metaphor coming back at him, he can get a very quick and clear sense of how he's being heard. For example, notice how the process works in this conversation:

VICE PRESIDENT: This is an important project we're going after. Water reclamation is the wave of the future, if you'll pardon the pun, and we want to do as much of it as we can.

PROJECT MANAGER: I agree completely. But I am not sure the people from the other firms on our team are as enthusiastic as you and I are.

VICE PRESIDENT: Well, if they aren't, part of your job as quarterback is to get them charged up and committed. We can't go into this with a half-hearted attitude and expect to do well.

PROJECT MANAGER: Okay, I realize I am quarterbacking the effort, but it seems to me that the coach can also help "fire up the troops," and I haven't heard you doing much of that yet. Are you willing to help me increase their enthusiasm?

VICE PRESIDENT: Sure. What do you want me to do?

PROJECT MANAGER: I think part of the problem is they already think they've won the game. I don't. We haven't got this contract yet, and we won't get it unless we convince the city we *want* it. You could help by giving sort of half-time talk before the kickoff.

VICE PRESIDENT: Sure, no problem. I'll talk to everybody at the start of tomorrow's meeting.

In this situation the project manager develops his boss's "team" and "quarterback" metaphors by talking about what a "coach" can do with a "half-time talk." On the other hand, sometimes the process is more subtle.

CHIP: You look a lot less happy than when I saw you this morning. What's happening?

THERESE: I just got out of my second two-hour class today, and I can't believe how much I have to do. I'm really feeling squashed.

CHIP: "Squashed" like you can't come up for air, or "squashed" as in you have to do what everybody else wants and you can't pursue your own ideas?

THERESE: More like I can't come up for air. Every professor seems to think this is the only class I'm taking.

Again, the purpose of running with each other's metaphors (notice that "running with" is a metaphor too) is to co-build talk between you in order to produce as full as possible a response to the issues you face together. In addition, the metaphors themselves reframe or give you a new perspective on the topic of your conversation. A project manager who sees himself as a "quarterback" is going to think and behave differently from one who sees himself as a "general," a "guide," or a "senior-level bureaucrat." And the work stress that "squashes" you is different from the pressure that "keeps you jumping like a flea on a griddle." Listen for metaphors and take advantage of their power to shape and extend your ideas.

Paraphrase for Productivity

Our third suggestion is that you apply that most useful of all communication techniques, paraphrasing, but that you do it in a couple of new ways: Paraphrase not to *re*produce the other's meaning but to *pro*duce a fuller conversation-text between you, and ask the other person to paraphrase you. As we've noted, paraphrasing is usually defined as restating the other person's meaning in your own words. It's an enormously useful thing to do in *many* communication situations, including conflict, parent–child contacts, classroom, and on the job.

In a way, though, if you only spend your conversational time checking to see if you are following the same path as the other person, you aren't fully carrying your share of the conversational load. To do more of that, you can add to your paraphrase your own response to the question, "Now what?" In other words, you start by remembering that the meanings you are developing are created between the two of you, and individual perspectives are only a part of that. So you follow your perception—checking with whatever your good judgment tells you is your response to what the person said. The spirit of a paraphrase for productivity is that each individual perspective is a building block for the team effort.

When we suggest that paraphrasing can include new information—your contribution—we are not implying that the person listening dialogically has license to poke fun at or to parody the other person. Notice the difference among these three responses:

RITA: I like being in a "exclusive" relationship, and your commitment to me is important. But I still sometimes want to go out with other people.

MIKE'S RESPONSE: So even though there are some things you value about our decision not to date others, you're still a little uncertain about it.

TIM'S RESPONSE: Oh, so you want me to hang around like a fool while you go out and play social butterfly! Talk about a double standard!

SCOTT'S RESPONSE: It sounds like you think there are some advantages and disadvantages to the kind of relationship we have now. I like it the way it is now, but I don't like knowing that you aren't sure. Can you talk some more about your uncertainty?

Mike responded to Rita's comment with a paraphrase. That tells us that Mike listened to Rita, but not much more. Tim made a caricature of Rita's comment, masking an editorial in the guise of a paraphrase. Scott offered a productive paraphrase. He made explicit his interpretation of what Rita was saying, then he moved the focus of the conversation back to "the between," back to "the middle" where both persons could work on the problem together. Because of what Rita said, Scott may have felt hurt or mad or both, and maybe he wouldn't have been so constructive as we've made him sound, but the point is that he not only paraphrased but also interpreted and responded to her comments. When this happens both the paraphrase and the interpretation keep understanding growing between the individuals, instead of within them.

Another way to think about the paraphrase for productivity is that you're broadening your goal beyond "fidelity" or "correspondence." If you're paraphrasing for fidelity or correspondence, you're satisfied and "finished" with the task as soon as you've successfully reproduced "what she means." Your paraphrase is a success if it corresponds accurately to the other person's intent. We're suggesting that you go beyond correspondence to creativity, beyond reproducing to co-producing. It's the same point we've made before.

It's easy to see that this kind of listening takes energy, even more so if only one person in a conversation is committed to dialogue. One way to elicit help from the other participants in a conversation is to *ask for paraphrasing* from them. Whenever you're uncertain about whether the other person is listening fully, you can check their perceptions by asking them for talk. This works best if you don't demand a paraphrase, and if you don't say, "Ha! Gotcha!" if the other person cannot respond well. The other person's paraphrase can, however, let both of you check for mutual understanding, and it can also keep the other's interpretations and responses in the talk between you where they can be managed productively.

Context-Building

We've mentioned that your conversation partner(s) may sometimes not be as eager or as willing as you are to work toward shared understanding. Their indifference sometimes surfaces in semi-messages, such as a blank stare or a dirty look, an indistinct blob of words, or silence. Paraphrasing and asking for a paraphrase can help produce more talk to build on between you, but what else can you do? We've found that what we call context-building can help.

By "context" we mean the circumstances that surround or relate to a topic, idea, opinion, or statement. When someone says something, it is spoken in a particular context or situation, which is made up of at least the physical location, feelings and thoughts, and the comment it is a response to. When you are listening dialogically, you can thematize and help develop or flesh out this contextual information so it can become part of the material you are co-sculpting.

For example, often ideas come out initially as vague judgments such as, "That's stupid!" or, "What a jerk!" That's like slamming some clay down hard onto the potter's wheel. But there is potential value in a move like that, if you are willing to initiate talk that helps turn the clay from a blob into a more distinct shape. As difficult as it sounds, one of the best ways to respond to comments like these is to say, "What do you mean by 'stupid'?" or "Tell me more," or, "Where did that come from?" These contributions all help elicit additional talk.

Although many discussions of communication suggest that skillful communicators need to learn to describe their feelings, there is nothing particularly enlightening about, "I feel like hell!" thrown into the middle of a conversation. Feelings are accompanied by circumstances and desires—their context—and you can help sculpt mutual meanings by trying to find out what preceded the feelings, what they are a response to, and what desires accompany them. Try, "Are you disappointed by what she did to you or are you angry?" "I notice that whenever I offer a suggestion, you dismiss it. Do you see that happening too?" or, "What do you want to have happen?"

Of course, it's not always just the other person who offers de-contextualized comments. You too will catch yourself throwing out cryptic judgments and incomplete exclamations that contribute little to shared understanding. In fact, sometimes all of us do that on purpose. But when you are not trying to be vague, you can follow an "I'm bored," with talk about the parts of the context that you feel bored about and what you would like to have happen. These individual contributions can be part of a text of conversation that can help all the participants create shared meanings.

POTENTIAL PROBLEMS

We don't want to stop without at least mentioning some of the negative responses we've gotten to our efforts to listen dialogically. We assume that if you are actually going to try what we've outlined here, you may appreciate being forewarned about some potential difficulties.

Time   The first is most obvious: It takes *time*. Dialogic listening is not efficient. Open-endedness and play, a commitment to developing full conversation-texts and even presentness all extend and prolong talk-time. When you ask someone to "Say more," they usually do. Running with metaphors can fill up the better part of an afternoon. Be ready for that increased time commitment, and realize that when there just *isn't* time, most of your efforts to listen dialogically will be frustrated.

On the other hand, we've also found that the time issue becomes less important when we recognize (1) that the gain in quality of contact can more than balance the "loss" of time, (2) that dialogic listening generates "economies of clarity" that can increase subsequent communication efficiency, and (3) that it often doesn't take all *that* much time. By (1) we mean that yours and your conversation partner's feelings of confirmation, comfort, and even intimacy can be enhanced enough by dialogic listening that the time investment is more than worth it.

This kind of listening can also help a group handle misunderstanding before it gets serious and can help a couple build a firm foundation of mutual agreement under their relationship. Both those outcomes are examples of "economies of clarity." Our parallel here is the "economies of scale" that manufacturers get. As they get into larger-scale production—they build more widgets—their cost per widget goes down, and that's an example of "economy of scale." Similarly, as your listening builds clearer and clearer foundations, you can move through more fuzzy or problematic issues faster. That's what we mean by an "economy of clarity."

We've also found that though dialogic listening definitely takes time, it doesn't need to go on forever. A ten-minute conversation may be extended to fifteen minutes, and a one-hour meeting to an hour and twenty minutes. And usually that's not too much to pay for what you can get.

What Are You Up to?   After experiencing some openness, some presentness, a few "Keep talking'" and "Paraphrase what I just said" responses, some people want to stop the conversation to find what's going on. They perceive those communication behaviors as a little unusual, and they jump to the conclusion that we must be up to something. "Is this a study of some kind?" "Are you just answering every question with a question, or what?" Some people may perceive your efforts to co-build more talk as disruption just for the sake of disruption. Others may even hear this kind of listening as manipulative.

We believe there are two ways to respond to this challenge. The first is to examine your own motives. *Are* you "listening for effect?" *Are* you obstructing or manipulating? In order for this kind of listening to work, your attitude needs to be one of genuine open-endedness focusing on ours, and so on.

The second way is to give a brief account of what you're doing, to *meta*communicate. Metacommunication simply means communication about your communication, talk about your talk, and it can help facilitate your dialogic listening, especially where someone's feeling manipulated. Try, "I want us to talk about this more before we decide," or, "I'd really like to hear more talk; I don't think we've gotten everything out on the table yet and I'd like us to play with as full a deck as we can." You may even want to go into more detail about the value of focusing on the between and staying present—expressed in your own words, of course. Or in other situations you may want to begin a discussion with something like, "Let's just play with this question for a while. We don't have to come up out of this discussion with a solid decision or conclusion." The point is, if your motives are genuine and you can metacommunicate or give an account of your motives, you should be able to diminish much of the other person's defensiveness and sense of being manipulated.

"Give Me a Break!"   Sometimes when one of us asks another person to paraphrase what he just said or when we slow down a group discussion with metacommunication or a request for someone to "Say more," others respond with exasperation. "Ease up," they might say, "Give me a break," or "Get off my back." Dialogic listening both takes and demands effort, and sometimes people don't feel like they have the energy to invest in it. During the group experience Milt described at the beginning of this essay, his dialogic listening efforts were sometimes met with responses that indicated that Susan and Jack were just "tolerating Milt's little digressions." And that can be frustrating; it can even hurt. At other times people can simply refuse to engage with you—they ignore your request to "Say more" or they simply stop talking.

There is no easy solution to this set of problems. Another dose of self-examination can help: *Are* you coming across like a pushy true-believer? Have you let your efforts to listen dialogically become a new task that you're trying to force on the group? Sometimes "give-me-a-break" responses really mean, "Let me be lazy," and you need to gently persevere. But at other times you need to remember that all you can do is all you can do, and it's time to back off a bit.

CONCLUSION

We believe that dialogic listening is little different from some other approaches to listening. We experience the focus on "ours" as an actual shift of awareness, the open-ended playfulness as a real challenge, and the concentration on the between and on presentness as ways to highlight the productive, co-creating that we are engaging in with our conversation partners. We also notice some different communication behaviors, although they feel different mainly because of our shift from an empathic to a dialogic perspective, attitude, or point of view. Of the five we've discussed here, the commonest and most useful behaviors for us are "Say more," running with the other's metaphor, and productive paraphrasing.

But we don't want to overemphasize the differences. The communication attitudes and behaviors that are discussed under the headings of active and empathic listening can also promote genuine understanding. Even more important, though we've discussed these ideas and skills as an approach to dialogic *listening,* they can also serve as the guidelines for a complete approach to interpersonal communicating. That's because they are based on the works of two philosophers of dialogue, Martin Buber and Hans-Georg Gadamer. Buber's and Gadamer's writing and teaching offer an approach to all your communicating that is only partly developed and applied in what we say here about listening. It's the approach that's behind this entire book, and we hope that by the time you've read through all these materials, you'll see how these fit together. (We especially recommend that you compare this essay with the final one in the book, Buber's "Elements of the Interhuman.")

Listening is only part of the entire communication process. But if it's dialogic listening, it can promote the richest kind of interpersonal-quality contact. Listening dialogically involves focusing on what you share with the persons you are talking with, playing with the conversation in an open-ended way, concentrating mostly on the ideas talked about together, and maintaining an emphasis on "Here and now." Some ways to instill in your communication these aspects of a dialogic approach to listening are to encourage others to "Say more," to run with metaphors, to include new information in paraphrasing (and request paraphrasing from others), and to build in as much contextual information as you can to facilitate clarity. We encourage you to develop the attitudes and skills associated with a dialogic perspective in listening and see if you find them helpful.

References

1. See, for example, Lyman K. Steil, Larry L. Barker, and Kittie W. Watson, *Effective Listening: Key to Your Success* (Reading, Mass.: Addison-Wesley, 1983); Madelyn Burley-Allen, *Listening: The Forgotten Skill* (New York: Wiley, 1982); and Florence I. Wolff, Nadine C. Marsnik, William S. Tracey, and Ralph G. Nichols, *Perceptive Listening* (New York: Holt, Rinehart & Winston, 1983).
2. Steil, Barker, and Watson, p. 5.
3. Carl R. Rogers, *A Way of Being* (Boston: Houghton Mifflin, 1980), pp. 142–143.
4. Robert Bolton, "Listening Is More than Merely Hearing," in *People Skills: How to Assert Yourself, Listen to Others, and Resolve Conflicts* (Englewood Cliffs, N.J.: Prentice-Hall, 1979), p. 51.
5. See, e.g., Lawrence M. Brammer, *The Helping Relationship: Process and Skills,* 2nd ed. (Englewood Cliffs, N.J.: Prentice-Hall, 1979), Chapter 4.
6. Roger von Oech, *A Whack on the Side of the Head: How to Unlock Your Mind for Innovation* (Menlo Park, Calif.: Creative Think, 1982), pp. 29–39.
7. There is, however, a large and important "metaphoric" or "soft" side of physics, especially theoretical and nuclear physics, and of mathematics.
8. William S. Howell, *The Empathic Communicator* (Belmont, Calif.: Wadsworth, 1982), pp. 9–10.
9. We're thinking of Hans-Georg Gadamer and Paul Ricoeur. See, e.g., Gadamer's *Truth and Method* (New York: Seabury Press, 1975), pp. 91ff. and Ricoeur, "Appropriation," in *Hermeneutics and the Human Sciences,* ed. and trans. by John B. Thompson (Cambridge: Cambridge University Press, 1981), pp. 182–186.
10. G. T. Barrett-Lennard, "Dimensions of Therapist Response as Casual Factors in Therapeutic Change," *Psychological Monographs,* 76 (1962), cited in Rogers, *A Way of Being,* p. 144.
11. Martin Buber, "The Way of Man," in *Hasidism and Modern Man*, ed. and trans. Maurice Friedman (New York: Harper & Row, 1958), p. 155.
12. Ibid., p. 158.
13. Our suggestion here is similar to Step 2 of Robert Bolton's discussion of "door openers."
14. Paul Ricoeur, *The Rule of Metaphor: Multi-Disciplinary Studies of the Creation of Meaning in Language,* trans. Robert Czerny with Kathleen Mclaughlin and John Costello, SJ (London: Routledge and Kegan Paul, 1978).

PROBES

Paraphrase—describe in your own words—the difference we discuss between *reproductive* listening and *productive* listening.

"I know you believe you understand what you think I said, but I'm not sure you realize that what you heard is not what I meant." It strikes us that dialogic listening is a good *solution* to the *problem* that that quotation describes. Do you agree? Discuss.

Paraphrase our point that it's impossible to "lay aside yourself."

How well does the "sculpting" metaphor work for you? In what ways is it especially illuminating? In what ways does it seem inappropriate? What alternatives or additional metaphors would you suggest for the process we discuss here?

The idea that you can work with talk itself, that it is tangible and malleable and can be productively shaped, is a little unusual for some people. How is that idea different from some of what you've been taught in the past about human communication?

Do you agree that there are many pressures on us today pushing us toward the three c's—certainty, closure, and control? How do they affect your communicating?

Give an example from your own experience of conversational *play*. Discuss it with others. Which of the characteristics of play that we discuss do you notice in your own communicating?

Assume you are talking with a group of friends and one of them makes a racist or sexist remark that you don't like. In this situation how might you "unify your saying, being, and doing"?

What happens when you try the "say more" response we suggest?

Identify two metaphors in this essay that we did not discuss as examples of metaphorizing. Notice how many there are to choose from.

Explain what it means to shift your paraphrasing-goal from fidelity or correspondence to creativity. (And, if you want to, pinpoint which previous Probe in this set asks essentially this same question.)

Which of the three potential problems that we discuss seems to you to be the most difficult?

Malcom Brenner has been studying and writing about dolphins for several years. He has developed a close relationship with a female dolphin named Ruby. What follows is an account of an experience he and Ruby shared. I include this excerpt for a couple of reasons.

For one thing, I want to acknowledge that some people believe that some animals are "addressable." (I explain that term on pp. 19–20.) I do not share that belief. As I said in Chapter 2, I don't think that animals are capable of the reciprocal, mutual address-and-response that humans engage in continuously and naturally. But I also believe that the topic is worth discussing. In the spirit of what Milt and I said a few pages back, I think it can be useful to co-sculpt some conversation-text around the question, "What's distinctive or unique about *human* as contrasted with animal communicating?"

A second reason I include Brenner's description is that it highlights one of the most important elements of effective listening: acknowledging *otherness*. You can't listen effectively until you get outside yourself, until you recognize and really attend to the *other* who is not-you. Bolton indicates the importance of this move in his definition of listening and discusses its physical aspects as "Attending Skills." Milt and I made a similar point when we emphasized the importance of moving beyond "mine" to "ours." Brenner's story has always struck me as an excellent account of what it's like to be hit in the face with otherness. The climax of this story comes when he discovers that the dolphin, Ruby, really is an *other being*.

I have trouble reading this short piece without getting caught up in Brenner's excitement. Some people who read it, though, are skeptical about his account; they wish he had tapes, pictures, or other testimony to "prove" that what he said really happened. But whether or not you accept the accuracy of his observations, notice what happens when Brenner actually becomes aware of Ruby's otherness. As I said, that kind of awareness is the foundation of effective listening.

Say "Rooo-beee!"

Malcom Brenner

I went down to Ruby's pen. She was waiting, watching me out of one soft, slightly sad brown eye. I waded in up to my ankles and she swam to me. I rubbed her head and snout for a few minutes.

Then she pulled back. I reached out a little farther, and she pulled back still more, maintaining an infuriating six-inch space between the tips of my fingers and the tip of her snout. "Goddamn fish," I muttered, "trying to get me into the water with you, eh? . . . " She seemed so friendly, allowing me to rub her, and nuzzling up against my naked legs, that she finally convinced me.

I waded in up to my waist. She surfaced to breathe several feet away, then went under; there was no way to tell where she was. I felt her sonar in the water; it seemed to be coming from all around me. Suddenly Ruby was pushing her snout into my kneejoint, nuzzling me so that my knee folded up. Only her dorsal fin stuck out of water; I couldn't see or touch her, so I turned around.

She was gone. I heard her breathe behind me, and felt that snout in my knee again. The skin at the end of her snout was rough and it tickled. "Ruby, what the hell are you doing?" I asked her, but she was underwater, nuzzling my knee, so she could not hear the question.

Finally she surfaced in front of me, breathed, floated, and let me rub her, starting at her head. Her skin was smooth and finely ridged, and I was rubbing her carefully and gently. She would sink and nuzzle my knee some more, then return and let me rub her again.

She went down and didn't come up. I searched around, and she reappeared at the far end of the pool, sticking her head out of water and squawking at me. I understood it was her equivalent of, "Come on in, the water's fine!" By this time, the water felt absolutely freezing, but what can you expect from a creature with a built-in wet suit?

Underwater I could hear her whistles. I surfaced rapidly—it was cold!—and found her pushing my knees up to the surface, so that I was forced to float on my back. She swam around me, then under me, and began nuzzling my knees again! This knee fixation seemed inexplicable, and frustrating. It was hard to stay afloat in water that cold, so after a few minutes I swam over and hung onto the wire fence.

When she understood that I wasn't coming back, she returned to swim in tight circles around me, six or seven feet away, very, very fast. It was a little scary, and I realized I was not in control of the situation; in fact, I never had been since I had entered the water with her. She seemed concerned; her movements were extraordinarily swift, and I thought she'd gotten over-excited. She appeared at the far end of the pool, then raced back in my direction, heading straight for me at high speed. My stomach muscles involuntarily tightened and for the first time in my life I got an idea of what it would feel like to be rammed by a 450-pound dolphin traveling at twenty knots. Just before she hit me she swerved aside; but that little demonstration frightened me. I was certain Ruby wouldn't deliberately hurt me, but I thought that she might do so accidentally if she got over-excited. Dolphins

From Joan McIntyre (ed.), *Mind in the Waters*, © 1974 by Project Jonah. Reprinted with the permission of Charles Scribner's Sons. Thanks to Helen Martin Felton, who first introduced me to this story.

are very rough with each other in play, at least by human standards. I began to think about getting out.

As if she could read my mind, everything stopped. She swam over to me, slowly, peacefully, and began to nuzzle my feet on the bottom. Had she recognized my growing anxiety? The suddenness of her mood change was eerie. She began to rub her snout up and down my legs, and then she was nuzzling my crotch. I thought I knew what that meant! I thought she might want to swim beneath my legs, but she didn't; now she seemed to be trying to get me sexually aroused, and she was doing a pretty fair job of it, too.

By this time I was deathly cold. She broke off nuzzling me to swim to the other end of the pool, and I decided to use the opportunity to get out. I was out of the water before she could stop me. I hated to trick her like that, but my teeth were chattering uncontrollably. She immediately swam over, lay on her side, and gave me a big, sad eyeball. I remembered the ball.

I got the ball and tossed it into Ruby's pen. She immediately understood that this was catch, and after nosing the ball for a few seconds threw it back to me. We tossed it back and forth until Ruby convinced me that she was in the mood for a game.

It occurred to me that I could use this game of catch as a reward in an attempt to get Ruby to vocalize. It seemed like an ideal reward; we were both enjoying the game, and her participation was voluntary. I decided to try to get her to mimic her own name. "Ruby," I said. "Say, Rooo-beee!" All I got back at first was a bunch of delphinese, somewhere between a whistle and a squawk. I threw the ball, and she returned it. "All right, now, say 'Ruby'! Rooo-beee!" Again that squawk. "No, you're going to have to do better than that. . . . C'mon, say 'Rooo-beee'!" For several more repetitions all I could get was that squawky noise. I noticed that *she was repeating the same sound every time*; it wasn't just any old squawk, but one with recognizable characteristics. But it was delphinese, which might as well be gibberish to me. I wanted English out of her, or at least a reasonable facsimile, and I was going to withhold the reward until I got it.

Suddenly her vocalization changed. Her squawk came out in two distinct syllables, rather like the way I had been syllabificating "Rooo-beee!" I hurled the ball, and she returned it. Our progress became unbelievably rapid. In the space of five minutes, she began to copy the syllabification, rhythm, tone, and inflections of my pronunciation of the word "Ruby," and she did so with an accuracy and a speed I found amazing. Every time she came closer to my pronunciation I threw the ball, and she would return it to me. Each time her pronunciation was further away from mine I would withhold the ball until she improved. We became completely wrapped up in each other; the outside world ceased to exist. We stood a few feet apart in the water of her pen, staring at each other intently with bright eyes, and the excitement between us was palpable. Never in my life had I known such an intimate feeling of being in contact with an incredible nonhuman creature. It felt like it was what I had been created to do. Our minds seemed to be running on the same wave. We were together.

Sometimes she would break back down into delphinese, and then I would withhold the ball until she had improved. She put a consonant *R* sound on the beginning of her squawk; and then she put a *Y* sound at the end. The result was a startling, eerie mimicry that sounded like my "Rooo-beee!" yet wasn't. The *R* sound, the *Y* sound, the tone, rhythm, syllabification, were all there, but the middle of the sound was still this weird squawk. This all took place in about ten minutes.

I was overwhelmed with the speed and accuracy of her learning; I hadn't expected anything like this in response to a simple game of catch.

She repeated the word with this degree of accuracy a couple of times, then started babbling at me in delphinese, shaking her head up and down with her jaws open in that gesture, usually associated with pleasure, that I called "ya-ya-ing." I tried to get her to say "Rooo-beee!" again; more ya-ya-ing. Then she swam back a few feet and made a peculiar noise, a kind of "kee-orr-oop," but about three times faster than you pronounce it. It occurred to me—I don't know why—*to repeat that sound.* Ruby seemed to be expecting it of me. I did the best I could with it. She repeated it, but now it sounded slightly different; I mimicked her changes. God, she's doing to me what I was just doing to her! Where will this lead? By now the ball was forgotten; I was totally absorbed in listening to Ruby's vocalizations and attempting to mimic them as accurately as possible with my inadequate human lips and vocal cords. She repeated the sound again, changed still more, and I copied that; she repeated it again, and as I tried to mimic her I thought, this sounds vaguely familiar—"kee-orr-opp." The light in my head went on. *The sound I had just successfully imitated was the one she had been giving to me in the beginning,* in response to my first attempts to make her say "Ruby!"

This realization struck me as the sound was coming out of my lips. Several fuses in my mind blew simultaneously and I did an incredible double-take, nearly falling over, and staring at Ruby, who was watching me with great concentration. When she saw the double-take, and knew I knew, *she* flipped out, and went ya-ya-ing around the pool, throwing water into the air, very excited, and apparently happy that this two-legged cousin of hers was progressing so rapidly. I just stood there, watching her, trying to figure out exactly what had just happened between myself and this dolphin.

What do I think the meaning of that experience was? I don't really know. I have some *ideas,* however. In response to an English word, Ruby had given me a delphinese word or phrase, which I had ignored. She succeeded in taking control of the situation—*although I had been willing to relinquish control*—and had then tricked me into pronouncing the sound I had at first ignored! Our mutual reactions were so spontaneous, and so vivid, that there is no doubt of this in my mind. *I had been the one slowing down the communications between us!* I can't tell you with what force that realization struck me. But what was the meaning of that sound? I can only guess. Certainly Ruby was sophisticated enough to recognize her human name. It occurred to me that she was most likely either telling me her name for *me*—a straight turnabout—or telling me her name for herself. But these are just my projections. . . .

PROBES

If a dolphin could talk with you, what do you think the dolphin would say? (As you respond, try not to project *your* assumptions, beliefs, and so on, on the dolphin, but be open to its otherness.)

Have you ever felt like a dog or cat was *really* listening to you, aware of what you were saying? The look in their eyes sometimes seems almost human. But notice that the dog or cat never initiates a response-in-kind to you; that is, the animal doesn't try to teach *you* its name in barks or meows. Talking back, the demonstration of language ability seems to be what makes Ruby's behavior so remarkable. With that in mind, develop and explain this statement: "Language ability is the foundation of otherness."

Discuss the importance and function of *nonverbal* cues in the communication between Brenner and Ruby.

PART 3

Openness
as "Exhaling"

CHAPTER 8

Openness
as "Exhaling"

CHAPTER 8

SELF-DISCLOSURE

> *In order to see I have to be willing to be seen. If a man takes off his sunglasses I can hear him better.*
>
> HUGH PRATHER

I think/feel that it's important, before you read about how self-disclosure works, to be sure that you and I agree on what we're talking about. Self-disclosure is *not* interpersonal exhibitionism; it's *not* the communication equivalent of jumping onto the nearest desk or table and ripping your clothes off. People who fear the process or who want to attack the whole idea of communicating interpersonally often treat disclosure as if it were.

Self-disclosure is the act of verbally and nonverbally sharing with another some aspects of what makes you a person, aspects the other individual wouldn't be likely to recognize or understand without your help. In other words, self-disclosure is verbally and nonverbally making available information about your uniqueness, your choice-making, your addressability, and the unmeasurable or reflective parts of you—for example, your feelings.

It's really important, I think, to remember that self-disclosure is a process that can improve a *transaction,* that can positively affect what's happening *between* persons. Disclosure is not meant to meet just one person's needs, but rather to enhance the *relationship.* Consequently, effective self-disclosure is disclosure that's *appropriate,* appropriate to the situation and appropriate to the relationship between the persons communicating. A crowded theater or a football game is not the place to discuss a profound religious experience even with your closest friend. Intimate sexual fantasies are usually not appropriate topics for a teacher to discuss with a student or for an employer to discuss with an employee. In short, you don't disclose just to make *you* feel better, but to facilitate the relationship. So, some disclosures are appropriate and some are not.

Self-disclosure is also not necessarily negative and not necessarily profound. You can help another know you as a person by sharing your joy, your excitement, your anticipation, or enthusiasm, and it doesn't have to be about the most weighty topic in your life. Small joys, small compliments, small successes, or even small disappointments can help others know who you are.

You might look at my comments in the introduction to this book as an example of what I'm talking about. I do want you to know more about me than just that I'm "author" or "teacher." I do want you to see some of my personness. But I'm convinced that you would probably be bored, offended, or both by a detailed account of every heavy happening I've experienced in the past several years. So I want to tell you something, but not everything, of what distinguishes me from other persons, something of the choices I've made and the changes I've experienced recently, something of my feelings about what I'm doing. Since you're not here to respond in person, I'm not sure that what I've said is appropriate to the relationship between you and me, but I am working to make it that. I chose to disclose some of my self to you because I want our relationship to be more than just "writer–reader," but I also chose *what* to disclose because I know that our relationship cannot be imtinate or long-term. I would encourage you to treat self-disclosure in the same way: choose to do it because it will help others know you as a person, but base your choices on a clear understanding of what's desirable and what's possible for the *relationship.*

One more thing. Sometimes people fear self-disclosure because they feel that their self is their most precious possession and that if they give much of it to others, they are liable to run out, to end up without any self left. This fear is based on the assumption that selves are like money or the hours in a day—there is only so much and when it's gone, it's gone. But the assumption simply isn't accurate. Selves are not governed by the economic law of scarcity. Since each of us is continually growing and changing—becoming—the more we share, the more there is to share. To put it another way, when I give you something of myself, I don't give it "up"; I still "have" it, but as a result of my disclosure, now you "have" it too. As many couples who have enjoyed a long-term intimate relationship have learned, you can never succeed in disclosing everything about yourself. Similarly, the more you know about the other, the more clearly you realize how much more there is to know. Self-disclosure doesn't eliminate what Jourard calls the "mystery" of the other person; it can enhance it. In short, the fear that if you disclose you risk giving up all of your self is groundless.

It *is* true, though, that disclosure is risky. When I share something of my personness with you, I take the risk that you might reject it. That kind of rejection could hurt. But I take the risk because I know that if I don't, we cannot meet as persons. Although disclosing is risky, the relationship that can come with appropriate disclosure makes the risk, for me, worth it.

Fritz Steele's comments about self-disclosure come from his book *The Open Organization.* His book is especially valuable because it demonstrates that self-disclosure is not just a technique to use in encounter groups and intimate conversations; it is also a crucial part of the communication in every efficient and productive business organization. Steele is a professor of business communication and has served as a consultant for many manufacturing companies and industrial and service organizations. He draws his insights and examples from his experiences in business, and his ultimate aim is to help employees and managers become more aware of the dynamics of disclosure and nondisclosure so they can eventually change disclosure patterns in their organizations.

Regardless of your current major, interests, or job, you are or almost certainly will be working in *some* kind of organization. Notice what this writer is saying about the communication you'll experience there. Can you see how each organization has what Steele calls a "disclosure climate"? Notice the different kinds of threat that can hinder disclosure: evaluation, investment in maintaining the relationship, and the threat of loss of control. Notice too how your awareness of the content of disclosure and of the "sender," "receiver," and climate all determine how risky disclosure feels. I believe that this article, and especially Steele's summarizing table, can substantially increase your awareness of just how disclosure works. Moreover, the process obviously isn't limited to business settings; you can also apply these principles to your communication with your lover, spouse, family, and friends.

What Is Disclosure? and Basic Causes of Low Disclosure

Fritz Steele

WHAT IS DISCLOSURE?

I use this term rather than "being open" as my basic focus because it is a bit better at implying the fact that a *choice* is involved. Disclosure means sharing with another person, or persons, information which we have and which is at present hidden from others (at least as far as we know). We all know that there is much too much information in each of us to share everything with everyone. The time, energy, and chaos involved would prohibit doing anything else. Therefore, we must be selective, and one's disclosure choices constitute the selection process of what to share and what to keep to one's self, as well as when to share it.

Disclosure can be of ideas, information from other sources, feelings, or any other topics we can pass on to another person. Individuals can disclose opinions, descriptions of past behaviors, future intentions, feelings, or anything else that can be conceptualized or acted out. Organizations can also disclose, that is, make information available, and in different degrees to different people.

There are several levels to any act of disclosure. The simplest is the sharing of the *information* itself; after the disclosure, both the sender and receiver know what formerly was known only to the sender. A second level is concerned with *control* and *influence;* sharing information can be sender's attempt to influence the receiver and also the sender's sharing of potential influence over the content area, now that receiver knows about it, too. A third level is the building of *patterns* over time; each act of disclosure is part of a total experience that sender and receiver have with each other, and disclosure tends to build the relationship.

At yet another level, a disclosure is a *signal* about the sender's image of the *present nature* of the relationship—what he thinks it is in terms of intimacy, mutual roles, etc. Finally, disclosure is often either a *stimulus* to some kind of action or a signal that an action must be planned. In most work organizations, disclosures of one sort or another are the stimuli that fire people off in various directions, often in efforts to protect themselves in case things go wrong.

My focus will generally be on the forces that cause disclosure to be at a certain level in a system and the consequences of that level for the members and the performance of the system. Questions will arise about specific patterns: areas that people choose to disclose or not, what forces push them in either direction, and the resulting trade-offs for different choices. The emphasis on patterns is very deliberate. There will be less concern about the choice to disclose or not in a particular situation versus the pattern of choices over a period of time and for members of a whole group or organization. In other words, the main focus is on the *disclosure climate* of the system—the regular level of disclosure that is practiced and the effects of that level.

BASIC CAUSES OF LOW DISCLOSURE: THREATS

People don't usually go around hiding information because they have said to them-selves something like: "Wow, would it be fun to do some low disclosure today!" or "Why don't I go have a photograph taken of me not disclosing my feelings to someone else?" From the point of view of individual choices, a low-disclosure pat-tern is more the result of forces operating on the person. . . .

There are three major categories of threat to a person who decides to either share or withhold information from others. The first area is *evaluation*—the threat that the discloser will be evaluated negatively as a result of the disclosure. The main threat here is a loss of esteem, in the eyes of the discloser and others. Career safety and security are also important to the extent that a negative evaluation will have an effect on future opportunities for disclosure.

Examples of this threat show up frequently in manager interviews:

"If you speak up too much, people will think that you are trying to build your own image."

"Why should I let someone else see that I'm not sure? They'd just say that I'm weak and use it to steamroller me."

"Well, I didn't say that mainly because I felt like an ass for even thinking it; I would have been a double-ass if I had shared it."

The second area of threat is *investment in maintaining the relationship*. The risk is loss of social contact or satisfying relationships if the other person is alien-ated or angered by the disclosure. Paradoxically, people who take the risk of dis-closure often report that the relationship they feared destroying was actually strengthened by the sharing process, even if the content of the information was not pleasant for either party. Examples of protecting the relationship:

"I'm never too sure how the boss is going to react—he's a little unpredicta-ble—so I watch what I say when he's around."

"When I know that I'll be working with a person for the foreseeable future, I consciously screen what I say so that we don't blow the relationship and make it impossible to work together."

"I could have told her how I feel toward her, but it would have been so embarrassing to both of us that it probably would drive a wedge between us."

Third, there is the threat of *loss of control,* of the ability to influence a situ-ation. In the choice of whether to disclose future plans, this threat is felt primarily as a possible loss of *degrees of freedom* to act as you choose. For disclosure of past or present events, attitudes, or feelings, there is a similar potential loss of influence or dominance if information that is uniquely held is shared with others. In the lore of most American corporations and government agencies, to hold exclusive infor-mation is to feel as though one holds power. Examples of this type of threat are:

"Why kick sleeping dogs? The meeting might get out of hand if we talk about our feelings about past conflicts."

"If I had told her that I didn't intend to call about the shipment, she would have either pressured me or done it herself." . . .

LEVELS OF RISK

One way of thinking about the threats of disclosure is to consider the three areas of threats described above. However, these are categories that mean more to a researcher than to a person in the moment-to-moment process of making disclosure choices. At the level of individual experience, I think it is possible to make some general statements about the riskiness of specific kinds of disclosure. A particular disclosure can be roughly rated as to its riskiness on several dimensions: the nature of the *content* (time, topic, etc.), the nature of the *sender,* the sender's perceptions of the *receiver,* and the *social climate* in which the sender and the receiver are operating. The statements about riskiness that follow are meant to be generalizations, approximations that would be altered by particular cases and combinations with one another.

A. Content

A1. Time   In general, disclosures about *past* events are less risky than those about *future* plans, since disclosures about the past touch mainly evaluation threats, whereas those about the future involve both evaluation and loss of degrees of freedom. Disclosure of *present* actions, attitudes, etc., is the most risky of the three, since it raises threats in all three areas—evaluation, relationship, and control. Disclosure of information about the present is also the hardest to gloss over, since it makes statements that can be tested on the spot. Past and future statements, by contrast, can be neutralized by a challenge to accuracy that may not be testable right then, and so the test can be put off to some (unspecified) future time.

A2. Topic   On the average, disclosures that include the sender's *feelings* will be felt as more risky than those that disclose just the sender's *ideas.* This is because, as Argyris points out in his discussion of interpersonal competence, feelings disclosure must be "owned" by the person who is disclosing, whereas ideas can be spread and the source diffused by such comments as "they say," or "I heard yesterday that . . . ," and other ways of spreading responsibility beyond one's self. In our society, feelings are also riskier than ideas because of our norms about non-emotionality, i.e., not letting your feelings overpower you. However, these norms are really enforced in order to not let your feelings overpower the other person, since they refer to what feelings you should not *show,* not what feelings you should not *have.*

A3. Evaluativeness   Generally, topics that carry an explicit or implicit evaluation of yourself or others' abilities, competence, or general worth as a person are more risky than those that do not imply an evaluation. This relates directly to the evaluation threat and also the sender's and listener's internal feelings about what is evaluative. This judgment depends very much on what each person cares about and what self-image each is striving to maintain. A man who does not care about his skill at golf will not feel threatened by a friend's comment that he raises his head while putting. A person who *does* use golf skill as a measure of self-worth, however, may feel more evaluated by such a comment, and the sender is therefore taking a bigger risk in raising it. (This also relates to the receiver variables discussed below.)

A4. Cast of Characters   Most disclosures that relate to someone present at the moment are more risky than those related to someone who is not present; thus, the ease with which gossip about a third party flows and the difficulty in giving immediate, face-to-face feedback to the person receiving the disclosure. All three threats—evaluation, relational deterioration, and loss of control—are heightened when the disclosure is related to the person receiving it.

B. Sender

B1. Assumptions about the World   The sender's own personal style will affect the sense of risk. The sender who assumes that the world is a basically *hostile* place, with attack likely from any quarter, will find disclosure more risky than does the sender who feels that the world is generally *friendly,* with attacks being the exception.

B2. Task Definition   Similarly, for the sender who thinks of information as part of a tool kit in a process of *power struggle* and *political manipulation,* the act of disclosure becomes crucial, requiring careful decisions. On the other hand, if the sender approaches life in organizations as a *problem-solving process* and assumes that the more widely information is shared, the better the decisions will be, then any given disclosure will not seem very risky compared with its payoff in the problem-solving process.

B3. Personal Security   The sender who is relatively *defensive* about his or her self-image—is oriented toward *maintenance* of an image rather than *change and growth*—will tend to feel more threatened by the prospect of disclosing ideas and feelings.

B4. Job Security   If the sender's position in an organization is tenuous, that is, if he or she feels the need to avoid alienating co-workers (especially the boss) in order to remain employed, he or she will examine any disclosure more carefully for possibilities of loss of livelihood.

C. Receiver

The discussion above also suggests that there will be differences in risk depending on the sender's view of the nature of the receiver.

C1. Personal Security   For the receiver who tends to take things as personal evaluations, the risk of disclosure is greater.

C2. Commitment to the Relationship   Likewise, if the receiver is only tentatively involved in the relationship and can be easily put off, the chance of a break is greater.

C3. Power Orientation   If the sender sees the receiver as interested mainly in using whatever is disclosed as a basis for unilateral action (by the receiver), then the sender will see more threat of loss of degrees of freedom in disclosing information, especially information which the receiver is sure not to have.

C4. Receiver's Competence   If the sender perceives the receiver as not having the ability to listen and respond appropriately to new information, then disclosure will seem more risky with that receiver.

D. Climate

The social climate in which a disclosure is considered will increase or decrease the perception of risk.

D1. Norms   The more social norms support disclosure (or the fewer norms there are that punish openness), the less risky disclosure will seem.

D2. History   The more historical examples (in the system) there are of disclosures that went badly, the more risky present disclosure will seem. Conversely, the more positive experiences people remember, the more they will be encouraged to share information.

D3. Policies/Taboos   The more specific policies exist about prohibited information, the greater the institutional risk of violating the rules; the same is true for strongly held norms called *taboos*.

D4. Trust   The general level of trust between sender and receiver is a key factor in the sender's felt risk. If the sender believes that the receiver has no vested interest in using information maliciously, or if the sender has had previous experiences with the receiver's keeping confidences, then the sender feels a smaller risk in being open with that receiver.

SUMMARY

Taken as a whole, these different categories of risk factors provide a means of making general statements about the forces pushing toward and away from disclosure in particular cases. For example, consider a power-oriented, defensive sender pondering a disclosure about a present feeling related to a defensive receiver in a relational climate in which the historical pattern is low disclosure. Obviously, this is a loaded deck, since all the dimensions work toward disclosure being felt as very risky and likely to result in a bad outcome. At the other extreme, a secure sender, disclosing an idea about past actions of someone not present to a receptive receiver in a climate in which the norms support disclosure would feel very little risk in making the information available to the other person.

For purposes of analysis and change, however, the interesting cases are the mixed ones, in which some factors are favorable to disclosure and others are not. A secure sender contemplating disclosing present feelings about the receiver in a climate in which the norms and policies both prohibit free interchange is caught in a conflict situation that must be juggled somehow, usually based on the potential gains and the cues that the receiver gives about willingness to take a risk with the sender. (A summary of the perceived risks of disclosure is shown in Table 1 on page 214.)

AN INVESTMENT NOTE

A few more words need to be said about the influence on disclosure created by the degree of investment a person has in the relationship with the receiver. I talked about it before as if the influence were of only one kind—if I have a strong investment in maintaining the relationship, I feel that it is more risky to be open. But there are two other forces which tend to push us toward a level of lower disclosure: a *lack* of commitment to the relationship and a fear of developing an unwanted relationship.

When we do not care very much about how well a relationship or group process develops, we will be dissuaded from disclosure by our assumptions and fears about what might go wrong. In one organization, I found that many good managers were very frustrated and alienated by top management's overcontrolling climate. The frustrated managers were not even bothering to tell others how they felt. Their investment was so low that it was not worth the risk of further pressure being brought to bear on them; as a result, they were simply leaving the system. When we are strongly invested in staying with a system, on the other hand, it can be worthwhile to raise issues, even in the face of our own theories about the usefulness of Low Disclosure ("This is an emergency") and our fears about the consequences ("Discomfort will last only a while, and then it will be a better place to work.")

As one manager put it, "We used to level with one another, but not any more. I don't think we care enough about one another to be straight." Although people often justify holding back their real feelings on the grounds of caring for others, I believe that when we *really* care about someone, it can be demonstrated best by leveling with that person about our own actions, attitudes, and feelings.

Not only does actual psychological investment influence the level of disclosure, but so does our desired level of disclosure. The more we predict to ourselves that disclosure will lead to investment—in the sense of increased *commitment* to invest time and energy in a relationship—and the less we want this to happen, the less likely we are to operate in a high-disclosure manner. We all have had experiences in which openness (especially about feelings), far from destroying a relationship, tended to draw us closer to the other person. When you are not sure you want that closeness, this can indeed be a reason to think twice about being open.

PROBES

How does Steele's definition of disclosure compare to the one in the introduction to this chapter?

Which category of threat most often inhibits your disclosure? Evaluation? Investment in maintaining the relationship? Loss of control?

Recall the last time you felt comfortable sharing a strong feeling with a friend. Now use Table 1 to account for the success of that disclosure. In other words, consider each category on the table—content, sender, receiver, and climate—and see if you can determine why you felt relatively low risk.

Now recall the last time you decided *not* to disclose something to a person you work with. Again, use the table to account for what happened. What do you notice about your disclosure patterns and preferences?

What specific advice about encouraging disclosure can you draw from this article? Hint: Consider how you might encourage disclosure by changing an *evaluation*— "That was really stupid!"—to a *description*—"If you assemble those that way, they'll be harder to handle for the next person down the line." What other advice is here?

TABLE 1
A Summary of Felt Risks in Disclosure

DIMENSIONS	LOW RISK	MEDIUM RISK	HIGH RISK
A. Content			
A1. Time	Past events	Future	Present events
A2. Topic	Ideas, general concepts		Feelings, own concepts
A3. Evaluativeness	No evaluation components	Evaluation implied	Evaluation direct
A4. Cast	People who are not present		People who are present
B. Sender			
B1. Assumptions about the world	Basically friendly	Mixed bag	Basically hostile
B2. Task definition	Problem-solving	Mixture of politics and problem-solving	Power struggle
B3. Personal security	High self-acceptance, low defensiveness	Defensive depending on the content area	Low self-acceptance, high defensiveness
B4. Job security	High, very certain of position	Moderate security	Low, very tenuous
C. Receiver (As Perceived by Sender)			
C1. Personal security	High self-acceptance, low defensiveness	Defensive depending on the content area	Low self-acceptance, high defensiveness
C2. Commitment to relationship	High commitment	Some testing	Low commitment
C3. Power orientation	Collaboration with sender	Mixed orientation	Controlling the sender
C4. Receiver's competence	Very likely to handle new information well	Sometimes well, sometimes badly	Very unlikely to handle new information well
D. Climate (As Felt by Sender)			
D1. Norms	Support disclosure		Discourage disclosure
D2. History	Disclosure, went well		Few disclosures; bad experiences when happened
D3. Taboos/ policies	Few areas prohibited		Many areas prohibited
D4. Trust	High trust		Low trust

I want to say something to this person but the fear comes: "I'd better not" (he may misunderstand, he may be in a hurry, ad infinitum). These fears are not based on the present situation, they are based on the past, and I don't have to be governed by what once went wrong. The two of us are standing here in the present. What is the situation now?

HUGH PRATHER

One of the most important disclosure skills to learn is to *own* your feelings and to learn how to *express* them constructively. As I'm sure you've noticed, that's not easy to do, especially with negative feelings like anger. But it's crucially important.

In my classes and in my own life, owning feelings has taken time to teach and learn. It also takes a great deal of effort, because it requires you to publicly take on some responsibilities that most of use are very used to shoving off onto others. But when two or more persons are able to practice this skill, it has an amazing effect on their communicating. The skill is especially useful in dealing with conflict. It does more than any other single thing to enable each party in the conflict to make his or her own position clear without stomping on the other persons involved.

In order to own your feelings, you need to start with two "truths" that sometimes *feel* like "lies." The first is that feelings are not "involuntary"; they do *not* "just happen" to you regardless of what you do. Have you ever watched someone do this—or done it yourself? While you're in the middle of a heated argument with someone, the phone rings. One of you picks up the phone and says pleasantly, "Hello. Yes, this is _____. Oh fine, how are you? Good. Next week? That would be great; we'd like to come. Thanks for calling. Goodbye." Then the person hangs up and resumes the argument at its original intensity. If feelings were involuntary, that *couldn't* happen![1]

When you say, "I'm mad and I just can't help it!" you're really saying that you feel/think that you have a right to be angry under those circumstances and that you think/feel that anyone in the same situation would respond the same way. But you have chosen the space you are in. Feelings did not *force* you there.

As children we probably picked up from adults around us the idea that we were *supposed* to feel or even that we *had to* feel a certain way. Maybe your mom or dad responded to a loud thunderstorm with something like, "Are you afraid of the big noise?" Or maybe you "caught" a fear of bears or a love of cats from a parent or older sister or brother whom you depended on and who always strongly reacted that way. Whatever the case, although some "automatic" feeling reaction might have a strong hold on you, you can break it, and the first step is to recognize that feelings are *not* involuntary. It's a matter of learning that "I *decide* how to behave in any situation as I have learned to do. If I am to change how I behave, therefore, I have to learn some new options."[2]

The second "truth" is that feelings are our "inside" response to something "outside." They are *not* simply caused by something outside. Every time we say, "You make me so mad!" or "She's really boring," we're forgetting this truth. In the first instance we are actually saying something like this: "I feel anger and it's your fault. Change what you're doing so I won't have to be angry anymore." Obviously this "truth" is related to the first one.

My anger is just that—*mine.* I might have learned over the years to feel anger every time someone disagrees with me or every time a same-sex friend beats me at a game of skill, or every time a teacher grades a paper I've written with something lower than a B. But what I've learned is my property and my responsibility. You can't give me my anger—or take it away. It's mine, and I am ultimately the only person who can control it.

I'm not saying that we always have control over everything. There are some actions that can prevent us from doing something or force us to do something else—actions of a law-enforcement agency, an employer, a school or other institution. But how we *feel* is still up to us. It's part of the choice-making power we have that makes us human.

The more I can integrate this second "truth" into my communicating, the freer I feel. The day I realized that I didn't *have* to feel defensive and hurt when someone criticized my teaching was a red-letter day for me! Since I care about my teaching, I still listen to those comments and try to respond appropriately to them. But I don't feel like the *target* of the comment now, and consequently I don't feel so defensive. It's still really difficult for me to own a strong feeling of rejection or hurt, but I'm getting there. And what a difference it makes when I succeed!

In these excerpts from a chapter of his book *Caring Enough to Confront,* David Augsburger talks about the skill of owning your anger. He emphasizes the importance of seeing anger as one part of a whole person, not something evil or antisocial. He also explains how anger frequently is a thinly concealed demand— a demand that you recognize my worth or stop trying to control me. But the demand usually arises from fear of some sort. It's really helpful for me to remember that; fear is behind most anger, and when I can get in touch with the fear, it's much easier to handle the anger constructively. Finally, Augsburger suggests how anger can help, not hinder, a relationship. Listen especially to what he says at the end of this essay. The points he makes are fairly simple, but they can make a real difference in your communicating.

References

1. I am indebted for this example to John Narciso and David Burkett; see Chapter 4 of their book *Declare Yourself* (Englewood Cliffs, N.J.: Prentice-Hall, 1975).
2. Ibid., pp. 36–37.

Owning Anger: Let Both Your Faces Show

David Augsburger

You're standing in the living room, looking out the window at your son's back. You're replaying the last moment's conversation. "How stupid can you get?" you'd said. "You blew it again like a no-good kid. That's what you are, and you better shape up or you're shipping out."

There he goes, anger and rejection showing in the slump of his shoulders. "He blew it?" you ask yourself. "Well, I blew it even worse. I get angry, I attack him personally, I put him down, I chop away at his self-esteem. I'm getting nowhere. What else can we do? If I could just deal with what he's doing without attacking him. Maybe that would make a difference. I could try it."

When angry, are you likely to attack the other person, depreciating his personality, intelligence, skill, or worth? It doesn't get you what you want either, I'll bet.

Next time, try focusing your anger on the person's behavior. Express appreciation for the other as a person, even as you explain your anger at his or her way of behaving. It lets you stay in touch while getting at what you are angry about. . . .

Do you feel comfortable with the suggestion that anger is acceptable, that it can be openly owned, that anger is a normal, natural human emotion?

Dr. Ernest Bruder, an outstanding chaplain and counselor, writes, "Growing angry is a quite normal (though very bothersome) response in human relations, but it does cut the individual off from those who are important to him. For some this is so intolerable that the anger is never admitted to awareness and the individual tries to deny those feelings which are a part of his connection with the rest of humanity."[1]

Anger is not the essence of badness.

Hate is sin	Love is virtue
Anger is evil	Affection is good
Confronting is brutal	Caring is wonderful
Openness is questionable	Diplomacy is wise

Do you find yourself thinking in such clearly defined categories? Rejecting hate, anger, honest awareness, and expression of your true feelings and perspectives and clear confrontation with others? To cut off one-half of your emotional spectrum and reject all negative feelings is to refuse to be a whole person. To deny and repress everything on the negative side is to also stifle and crush the full expression of your positive side.

There is danger in abusing and misusing others with our positive emotions and actions—love, kindness, gentleness, tolerance, sweetness—just as there is the threat of cutting and destroying others with our negative responses—anger, harshness, criticism, irritation. To be engulfed and incorporated by a smothering love, all sweet gentleness, and I'm-only-trying-to-help-you-it's-for-your-own-good kindness is more treacherous than harsh, crisp frankness. You can at least reject it without fighting an affectionate, sticky mass of divinity-candy love.

I want to be a whole person in my relationships with you. I want to be in touch with both sides of you. Give me both your cold pricklies (honest anger) and your warm fuzzies (affirming love). Let both your faces show.

There are two sides in everyone. Both sides are important. Both are acceptable. Both are precious. Both can be loved.

Your wife made a cutting remark two days ago, and still no apology. Your daughter didn't thank you for the little gift you bought her. Your son forgot to put the tools back in their place in your shop. And you're feeling angry at all of them, at everything!

Anger is a demand. Like, "I demand an apology from you—an apology that suits me." "I demand you show appreciation for my gifts—in a way that pleases me." "I demand that you return my tools—perfectly—just the way I keep them." That's the real thrust of anger. A demand that also demands others meet your demands.

Even though you seldom put the demands into words, they are there inside your feelings. And you are resentful. "What if I said what I feel, if I really made my demands clear?" you ask yourself. "Then I could either stick to them, or laugh at them and forget them. . . ."

Get in touch with the demands you make of others. Recognize them. Start admitting them out loud. Then you have a choice: (1) you can negotiate the demands that matter, or (2) you can cancel the ones that don't.

Love is being honest and open about your demands. Love is canceling unfair demands. Love is freeing others to live and grow.

Underneath my feelings of anger . . .
   . . . there are concealed expectations.
   (I may not yet be aware of them myself.)

Inside my angry statements . . .
   . . . there are hidden demands.
   (I may not yet be able to put them into words.)

Recognized or unrecognized, the demands are there. Anger is a demand. It may be a demand that you hear me. Or that you recognize my worth. Or that you see me as precious and worthy to be loved. Or that you respect me. Or let go of my arm. Or quit trying to take control of my life.

The demands emerge whenever I see you as rejecting me, or foresee you as about to reject me as a person of worth.

Anger is a demand "that you recognize my worth." When I feel that another person is about to engulf or incorporate me (assuming ownership of me, taking me for granted, using me, absorbing me into his or her life-program), I feel angry.

Actually, I first feel anxious. "Anxiety is a sign that one's self-esteem, one's self-regard is endangered,"[2] as Harry Stack Sullivan expressed it. When my freedom to be me is threatened, I become anxious, tense, ready for some action. Escape? Anger? Or work out an agreement?

Escape may neither be possible nor practical. Agreement seems far away since I see you as ignoring my freedom, devaluing my worth, and attempting to use me. Anger is the most available option.

Anger is "the curse of interpersonal relations," Sullivan well said. A curse, because it is so instantly effective as a way of relieving anxiety. When a person flashes to anger, the anger clouds his recall of what just happened to spark the anger, confuses his awareness of what he is really demanding, and restricts his ability to work toward a new agreement.

But we chose—consciously or unconsciously—to become angry because:

"Anger is much more pleasant to experience than anxiety. The brute facts are that it is much more comfortable to feel angry than anxious. Admitting that neither is too delightful, there is everything in favor of anger. Anger often leaves one sort of worn out . . . and very often makes things worse in the long run, but there is a curious feeling of power when one is angry."[3]

Check the pattern: (1) I feel keen frustration in my relationship with another. (2) I see the other person as rejecting me—my worth, my needs, my freedom, my request. (3) I become suddenly and intensely anxious. (4) I blow away my anxiety with anger which confuses things even further. (5) I may then feel guilty for my behavior and resentful of the other's part in the painful experience.

Anger is a positive emotion, a self-affirming emotion which responds reflexively to the threat of rejection or devaluation with the messages (1) I am a person, a precious person, and (2) I demand that you recognize and respect me.

The energies of anger can flow in self-affirming ways when directed by love— the awareness of the other person's equal preciousness.

Anger energies become a creative force when they are employed (1) to change my own behavior which ignored the other's preciousness, and (2) to confront the other with his or her need to change unloving behavior. Anger energy can be directed at the cause of the anger, to get at the demands I am making, to own them, and then either correct my demanding self by canceling the demand, or call on the other to hear my demand and respond to how I see our relationship and what I want.

When I am on the receiving end of another's anger, I want to hear the anger-messages the other gives to me, and check out what I am picking up as a demand. Careful listening can discern what the other is demanding, clarify it in clear statements, and lead to clean confrontation. Then I have the choice of saying yes to the other's demands, or saying no. I may feel angry in return, but I want to experience my anger with honest "I statements," not with explosive "you statements."

Explosive anger is "the curse of interpersonal relations." Vented anger may ventilate feelings and provide instant, though temporary, release for tortured emotions, but it does little for relationships.

Clearly expressed anger is something different. Clear statements of anger feelings and angry demands can slice through emotional barriers or communications tangles and establish contact.

When angry, I want to give clear, simple "I messages." "You messages" are most often attacks, criticisms, devaluations of the other person, labels, or ways of fixing blame.

"I messages" are honest, clear, confessional. "I messages" own my anger, my responsibility, my demands without placing blame. Note the contrast between honest confession and distorted rejection.

I MESSAGES	YOU MESSAGES
I am angry.	You make me angry.
I feel rejected.	You're judging and rejecting me.
I don't like the wall between us.	You're building a wall between us.
I don't like blaming or being blamed.	You're blaming everything on me.
I want the freedom to say yes or no.	You're trying to run my life.
I want respectful friendship with you again.	You've got to respect me or you're not my friend.

"I just can't help it. It makes me angry."

"It just gets to me and touches off my temper."

"It's like something comes over me, and I can't do a thing about it."

"It's other people, that's what it is. They know I've got a quick temper and they're out to get me."

"It" is the problem. "It" causes untold irritation, anger, frustration, embarrassment, pain, guilt, and misery. "It's" not me. "It's" this something, or someone, or some situations.

When you find yourself using "it" as an explanation or as a scapegoat, stop. Listen to yourself. Recognize what you're doing. Avoiding responsibility. Sidestepping the real problem. Denying ownership of your feelings, responses, and actions.

Release comes not from denying, but from owning who—what—and where I am in my relationships.

I want to own what goes on in me and accept total responsibility for it.

I discover that as I own it, accepting full responsibility, I am then able to respond in new ways. I become response-able?

A great freedom comes as I own my thoughts, feelings, words, and emotions. (1) I become free to choose my actions. (2) I become free to choose my reactions.

My actions are mine. Your actions are yours. I am responsible for my behavior. You are responsible for yours.

I also accept responsibility for my actions.

"You make me angry," I used to say.

Untrue. No one can make another angry. If I become angry at you, I am responsible for that action. (I am not saying that anger is wrong. It may well be the most appropriate and loving response that I am aware of at that moment.)

But you do not make me angry. I make me angry at you. It is not the only behavior open to me.

There is no situation in which anger is the only possible response. If I become angry (and I may, it's acceptable) it's because I choose to respond with anger. I might have chosen kindness, irritation, humor, or many other alternatives (if I had been aware of these choices). There is no situation which commands us absolutely. For example, I have the choice to respond to another's threat with blind obedience, with silent passivity, with vocal refusal, with firm resistance, or with anger, if that seems appropriate.

When childhood experiences are limited, a person may mature with a limited set of behaviors open to him or her. Some have only two ways of coping with another's attack—anger or submission. If these are the only ways modeled by the parents or the family, they may be the only aware-choices in the person's behavioral repertoire.

If I have grown enough in life so that more than one pattern of behavior is available to me, then I can freely select the responses which seem most appropriate to the situation.

I want to be aware of a wealth of responses, and to have them available to me. Anger or patience. Toughness or gentleness. Clear confrontation or warm, caring support. I want to be able-to-respond in any of these.

I am responsible for choosing my responses to you.

I am responsible for the way I react to you.

I am responsible for how I see you. And from the way I see you—as either friendly or hostile; accepting or rejecting; welcoming or threatening—emerge my feelings. Feelings are the energies that power the way I choose to see you, or to perceive you.

I am responsible for how I see you—and from that for the way I feel about you.

You cannot make me angry. Unless I choose to be angry.

You cannot make me discouraged, or disgusted, or depressed. These are choices.

You cannot make me hate. I must choose to hate.

You cannot make me jealous. I must choose envy.

I experience all these and more on all too many occasions, but I am responsible for those actions or reactions. I make the choice.

I love me.	I also love you.
I love my freedom to be who I am.	I respect your freedom to be who you are.
I love my drive to be all I can be.	I admire your drive to be all you can be.

I love my right to be different from you.	I recognize your right to be different from me.
I love my need to be related to you.	I appreciate your need to be related to me.
The thoughts I think,	The thoughts you think,
The words I speak,	The words you speak,
The actions I take,	The actions you take,
The emotions I feel—They are mine, for them I am fully responsible.	The emotions you feel—They are yours, for them I am in no way responsible.
I am free to accept or to refuse 　your wants 　your requests 　your expectations 　your demands.	You are free to accept or to refuse 　my wants 　my requests 　my expectations 　my demands.
I can say yes.	You can say yes.
I can say no.	You can say no.
I am not in this world to live as you prescribe.	You are not in this world to live as I prescribe.
I am not responsible *for* you.	You are not responsible *for* me.
I will not be responsible *to* you.	You will not be responsible *to* me.
I want to be responsible *with* you.	You can be responsible *with* me.
I want to be your brother.	You may be a brother with me.

References

1. Ernest Bruder, *Ministering to Deeply Troubled People* (Englewood Cliffs, N.J.: Prentice-Hall, 1963), pp. 30–31.
2. Harry Stack Sullivan, *The Psychiatric Interview* (New York: Norton, 1954), pp. 218–219.
3. Ibid., p. 109.

PROBES

Is Augsburger's view of anger consistent with the relational view of communication presented in Chapter 2? How so?

Note how much owning your feelings depends on verbal cues. You start with a nonverbal attitude, but there is a world of *verbal* difference between what Augsburger calls "I" messages and "you" messages. When you use "I" messages, how are your words functioning? To reduce uncertainty? Bring people together? Evoke emotion? Refer or stand for? Affect perception?

Augsburger says that "my actions are mine. Your actions are yours. I am responsible for my behavior. You are responsible for yours." If this is true, why should we ever communicate with one another?

Do you believe anger is an acceptable feeling? Has anyone ever taught you that it isn't, that "nice" people don't get mad? What do your words and actions teach those around you about the acceptability of anger?

What are some *advantages* of "vented anger"?

> *Expressing anger is a very intimate act. And so, of course, it is very risky. It at once opens me up to a closer relationship, or to a verbal kick in the groin. I was irritated at Hank's denouncing every comment that anyone made at the meeting, but instead of telling him that, I argued against his logic. That was not expressing my irritation, it was reacting to it. Later, when I expressed it directly and told him how mad I was at his attitude, he made a very personal confession of how stupid he felt around all of us. He* could *have come back with a rebuff that would have hurt me.*

> *Again and again I am surprised at how often people appreciate my going to them with my negative feelings. I am afraid that my words will hurt our friendship, but it has turned out that they usually strengthen it.*

> HUGH PRATHER

In this reading Neil Postman presents the viewpoint of "the opposition." Postman offers a sensible and compelling argument *against* the notion that all we have to do to solve our problems is to communicate more effectively. Better communication, he says, is *not* a panacea, especially if by better communication we mean self-disclosing, that is, "saying what's on your mind," and "expressing your feelings honestly."

Postman reminds us, as do some communication researchers, that one of the important functions of speech communication is concealment.[1] Civility is a necessary part of society, he argues, and civility sometimes requires that we keep our feelings to ourselves. It's pretty hard to ignore the way he makes his point; as he puts it in one place, "There is no dishonesty in a baboon cage, and yet, for all that, it holds only baboons."

Postman maintains that when people disagree fundamentally—for example, about racial issues—"honest openness may not help at all." He writes, "There is no good reason . . . for parents always to be honest with their children."

You may find it tempting to dismiss Postman as some kind of fascist and to reject his remarks as inflammatory hate-mongering. Try not to take that easy way out. His main point is, as he puts it, "that 'authentic communication' is a two-edged sword," and I think that's an idea that's well worth thinking about and discussing.

I feel frustrated and disappointed when my students—or readers of this book—conclude that the main message in all of this is just that we need to "be open and honest." That's a vast oversimplification, and it's also a dangerous one. One of Postman's most important points is that in any given situation we do not have *an* "honest feeling" but a complex of often conflicting "authentic" feelings. So the expression of one may be no more or less "honest" or "dishonest" than the expression of another.

I hope this essay will prompt the kind of reflection and discussion that can move well beyond a simplistic belief in the universal value of "being open and honest."

Reference

1. Malcolm Parks, "Ideology in Interpersonal Communication: Off the Couch and into the World," *Communication Yearbook 5,* ed. Michael Burgoon (New Brunswick, N.J.: Transaction Books, 1982), pp. 79–107.

The Communication Panacea

Neil Postman

In the search for the Holy Grail of complete harmony, liberation, and integrity, which it is the duty of all true Americans to conduct, adventurers have stumbled upon a road sign which appears promising. It says in bold letters, **"All problems arise through lack of communication."** Under it, in smaller print, it says: "Say what is on your mind. Express your feelings honestly. This way lies the answer." A dangerous road, it seems to me. It is just as true to say, This way lies disaster.

I would not go so far as Oliver Goldsmith, who observed that the principal function of language is to *conceal* our thoughts. But I do think that concealment is one of the important functions of language, and on no account should it be dismissed categorically. As I have tried to make clear earlier, semantic environments have legitimate and necessary purposes of their own which do not always coincide with the particular and pressing needs of every individual within them. One of the main purposes of many of our semantic environments, for example, is to help us maintain a minimum level of civility in conducting our affairs. Civility requires not that we deny our feelings, only that we keep them to ourselves when they are not relevant to the situation at hand. Contrary to what many people believe, Freud does not teach us that we are "better off" when we express our deepest feelings. He teaches exactly the opposite: that civilization is impossible without inhibition. Silence, reticence, restraint, and, yes, even dishonesty can be great virtues, in certain circumstances. They are, for example, frequently necessary in order for people to work together harmoniously. To learn how to say no is important in achieving personal goals, but to learn how to say yes when you want to say no is at the core of civilized behavior. There is no dishonesty in a baboon cage, and yet, for all that, it holds only baboons.

Now there are, to be sure, many situations in which trouble develops because some people are unaware of what other people are thinking and feeling. "If I'd only *known* that!" the refrain goes, when it is too late. But there are just as many situations which would get worse, not better, if everyone knew exactly what everyone else was thinking. I have in mind, for example, a conflict over school busing that occurred some time ago in New York City but has been replicated many times in different places. Whites against blacks. The whites maintained that they did not want their children to go to other neighborhoods. They wanted them close at hand, so that the children could walk home for lunch and enjoy all the benefits of a "neighborhood school." The blacks maintained that the schools their children attended were run-down and had inadequate facilities. They wanted their children to have the benefits of a good educational plant. It was most fortunate, I think, that these two groups were not reduced to "sharing with each other" their real feelings about the matter. For the whites' part, much of it amounted to, "I don't want to live, eat, or do anything else with niggers. Period." For the blacks' part, some of it, at least, included, "You honky bastards have had your own way at my expense for so long that I couldn't care less what happens to you or your children." Had these people communicated such feelings to each other, it is more than likely that there could have been no resolution to this problem. (This seems to have been the case in Boston.) As it was, the issue could be dealt with *as if* such hatred did not exist, and therefore, a reasonable political compromise was reached.

It is true enough, incidentally, that in this dispute and others like it, the charge of racism was made. But the word *racism,* for all its ominous overtones, is a euphemism. It conceals more than it reveals. What Americans call a *racist* public remark is something like "The Jews own the banks" or "The blacks are lazy." Such remarks are bad enough. But they are honorifics when compared to the "true" feelings that underlie them.

I must stress that the "school problem" did not arise in the first place through lack of communication. It arose because of certain historical, sociological, economic, and political facts which could not be made to disappear through the "miracle of communication." Sometimes, the less people know about other people, the better off everyone is. In fact, political language at its best can be viewed as an attempt to find solutions to problems by circumventing the authentic hostile feelings of concerned parties.

In our personal lives, surely each of us must have ample evidence by now that the capacity of words to exacerbate, wound, and destroy is at least as great as their capacity to clarify, heal, and organize. There is no good reason, for example, for parents always to be honest with their children (or their children always to be honest with them). The goal of parenthood is not to be honest, but to raise children to be loving, generous, confident, and competent human beings. Where full and open revelation helps to further that end, it is "good." Where it would defeat it, it is stupid talk. Similarly, there is no good reason why your boss always needs to know what you are thinking. It might, in the first place, scare him out of his wits and you out of a job. Then, too, many of the problems you and he have do not arise from lack of communication, but from the nature of the employer-employee relationship, which sometimes means that the less money you make, the more he does. This is a "problem" for a labor organizer, not a communication specialist.

Some large American corporations have, of late, taken the line that "improved communication" between employees and management will solve important problems. But very often this amounts to a kind of pacification program, designed to direct attention away from fundamental economic relationships. It is also worth noting that a number of such corporations have ceased to hold "communication seminars" in which executives were encouraged to express their "true" feelings. What happened, apparently, is that some of them decided they hated their jobs (or each other) and quit. Whether this is "good" or not depends on your point of view. The corporations don't think it's so good, and probably the families of the men don't either.

The main point I want to make is that "authentic communication" is a two-edged sword. In some circumstances, it helps. In others, it defeats. This is a simple enough idea, and sensible people have always understood it. I am stressing it here only because there has grown up in America something amounting to a holy crusade in the cause of Communication. One of the terms blazoned on its banners is the phrase *real* (or *authentic*) feelings. Another is the motto "Get in touch with your feelings!" From what I have been able to observe, this mostly means expressing anger and hostility. When is the last time someone said to you, "Let me be *lovingly* frank"? The expression of warmth and gentleness is usually considered to be a façade, masking what you are really thinking. To be certified as authentically in touch with your feelings, you more or less have to be nasty. Like all crusades, the Communication Crusade has the magical power to endow the most barbarous behavior with a purity of motive that excuses and obscures just about all its consequences. No human relationship is so tender, apparently, that it cannot be "purified" by sacrificing one or another of its participants on the altar of "Truth." Or, to paraphrase a widely known remark on another subject, "Brutality in the cause of honesty needs no defense." The point is that getting in touch with your feelings often amounts to losing touch with the feelings of others. Or at least losing touch with the purposes for which people have come together.

A final word on the matter of "honesty." As I have said before, human purposes are exceedingly complex—multileveled and multilayered. This means that, in any given situation, one does not have *an* "honest feeling," but a whole complex of different feelings. And, more often than not, some of these feelings are in conflict. If anger predominates at one instant, this does not mean it is more "authentic" than the love or sorrow or concern with which it is mingled. And the expression of the anger, alone, is no less "dishonest" than any other partial representation of what one is feeling. By *dishonesty,* then, I do not merely mean saying the opposite of what you believe to be true. Sometimes it is necessary to do even this in the interests of what you construe to be a worthwhile purpose. But more often, dishonesty takes the form of your simply not saying *all* that you are thinking about or feeling in a given situation. And, since our motives and feelings are never all that clear, to our own eyes in any case, most of us are "dishonest" in this sense most of the time. To be aware of this fact and to temper one's talk in the light of it is a sign of what we might call "intelligence." Other words for it are discretion and tact.

The relevant point is that communication is most sensibly viewed as a means through which desirable ends may be achieved. As an end in itself, it is disappointing, even meaningless. And it certainly does not make a very good deity.

PROBES

Postman may sound like he is arguing against the other authors in this chapter, but I don't think that's accurate. What specific comments and suggestions by Fritz Steele and David Augsburger is Postman emphasizing and developing? Where is he underscoring points that they also make?

In your experience is what Postman calls "civility" more a function of keeping feelings to one's self or expressing them in "constructive" ways? How so?

Do you agree or disagree with Postman's characterization of the perceptions and feelings that are "really" behind racist remarks? Discuss.

What's an example from your own experience of the accuracy of Postman's claim that "sometimes, the less people know about other people, the better off everyone is"?

In what specific ways do you agree or disagree with what Postman says about parenting?

What does Postman mean when he says that authentic communication is a two-edged sword? What are the two "edges"? How can the sword "cut" two ways?

Discuss an example from your own experience where you felt a complex of inconsistent or perhaps contradictory "honest feelings." How did you handle them in that situation?

CHAPTER 9

CONFIRMATION

> The human person needs confirmation. . . . An animal does not need to be confirmed, for it is what it is unquestionably. It is different with [the person]. Sent forth from the natural domain of species into the hazard of the solitary category, surrounded by the air of a chaos which came into being with him, secretly and bashfully he watches for a Yes which allows him to be and which can come to him only from one human person to another. It is from one [person] to another that the heavenly bread of self-being is passed.
>
> MARTIN BUBER

‖ı‖ıı‖ııı‖

Confirmation means actively acknowledging a person as a person, recognizing him or her as a subject, a unique, unmeasurable, choosing, addressable human. As Cissna and Sieburg point out, Martin Buber was the first to use the term in this interpersonal sense.* As the quotation that begins this paragraph shows, Buber identifies confirmation as a phenomenon that distinguishes the human world from the nonhuman. His point is that we discover our personhood or humanness as we make contact with others. I learn that I am a person when I experience confirmation from another person. That's one of the crucial functions of communication; to confirm others and experience confirmation myself.

Ken Cissna and Evelyn Sieburg are two speech communication teachers who've been studying confirmation for several years. This essay is nicely organized into a section that defines and describes confirmation, a section that identifies its four main dimensions, and then a longer section that talks systematically about confirming and disconfirming behaviors.

The authors describe and illustrate how what they call indifferent responses, impervious responses, and disqualifying responses are all disconfirming. Indifference denies the other's existence, while imperviousness means responding only to my image of you, even if it contradicts your perception of yourself. We communicate indifference, for example, by avoiding eye contact or physical contact or by ignoring topics the other person brings up. Imperviousness can be communicated, for example, with "Don't be silly—of course you're not afraid," or, "Stop crying, there's nothing the matter with you!" Disqualification is the technique of denying without really saying "no," as we do when, for example, we utter the "sigh of martyrdom," respond tangentially to the other person, or say something like, "If I were going to criticize, I'd say your haircut looks awful, but I wouldn't say that."

Responses that confirm, the authors point out, are less clearly defined than disconfirming ones. However, they identify three clusters of communication, recognition, acknowledgment, and endorsement. They also emphasize that "confirming response is dialogic in structure; it is a reciprocal activity involving shared talk and sometimes shared silence." That echoes the points about contact and the between that I've made and that have been made by several other contributors to this book.

Patterns of Interactional Confirmation and Disconfirmation

Kenneth N. Leone Cissna and Evelyn Sieburg

The term "confirmation" was first used in an interpersonal sense by Martin Buber (1957), who attributed broad existential significance to confirmation, describing

---

*Martin Buber, "Distance and Relation," in *The Knowledge of Man,* ed. Maurice Friedman, trans. Maurice Friedman and R. G. Smith (New York: Harper & Row, 1965), p. 71.

it as basic to humanness and as providing the test of the degree of humanity present in any society. Although Buber did not explicitly define confirmation, he consistently stressed its importance to human intercourse:

> The basis of man's life with man is twofold, and it is one—the wish of every man to be *confirmed* as what he is, even as what he can become, by men; and the innate capacity in man to confirm his fellow men in this way. . . . Actual humanity exists only where this capacity unfolds. [p. 102]

R. D. Laing (1961) quoted extensively from Buber in his description of confirmation and disconfirmation as communicated qualities which exist in the relationship between two or more persons. Confirmation is the process through which individuals are "endorsed" by others, which, as Laing described it, implies recognition and acknowledgment of them. Though Laing developed confirmation at a conceptual level more thoroughly than anyone prior to him, his focus remained psychiatric: he was concerned with the effects of pervasive disconfirmation within the families of patients who had come to be diagnosed as schizophrenic. In such families, Laing noted, one child is frequently singled out as the recipient of especially destructive communicative acts by the other members. As Laing explained it, the behavior of the family "does not so much involve a child who has been subjected to outright neglect or even to obvious trauma, but a child who has been subjected to subtle but persistent *disconfirmation,* usually unwittingly" (1961:83). Laing further equated confirmation with a special kind of love, which "lets the other be, but with affection and concern," as contrasted with disconfirmation (or violence), which "attempts to constrain the other's freedom, to force him to act in the way we desire, but with ultimate lack of concern, with indifference to the other's own existence or destiny" (1967:58). This theme of showing concern while relinquishing control is common in psychiatric writing and is an important element in confirmation as we understand it. Although Laing stressed the significance of confirmation, he made no attempt to define it in terms of specific behaviors, noting only its variety of modes:

> Modes of confirmation or disconfirmation vary. Confirmation could be through a responsive smile (visual), a handshake (tactile), an expression of sympathy (auditory). A confirmatory response is *relevant* to the evocative action, it accords recognition to the evocatory act, and accepts its significance for the other, if not for the respondent. A confirmatory reaction is a direct response, it is "to the point," "on the same wavelength," as the initiatory or evocatory action. [1961:82]

In 1967, Watzlawick, Beavin, and Jackson located confirmation within a more general framework of human communication and developed it as a necessary element of all human interaction, involving a subtle but powerful validation of the other's self-image. In addition to its content, they said each unit of interaction also contains relational information, offering first, a self-definition by a person (P) and then a response from the other (O) to that self-definition. According to Watzlawick *et al.,* this response may take any of three possible forms: it may confirm, it may reject, or it may disconfirm. The last, disconfirmation, implies the relational message, "You do not exist," and negates the other as a valid message source. Confirmation implies acceptance of the speaker's self-definition. "As far as we can see, this confirmation of *P's* view of himself by O is probably the greatest single factor ensuring mental development and stability that has so far emerged from our study of communication" (p. 84). The descriptive material provided by Watzlawick *et al.* to illustrate disconfirmation includes instances of total unawareness of the person, lack of accurate perception of the other's point of view, and deliberate distortion or denial of the other's self-attributes.

Sieburg (1969) used the structure provided by Watzlawick as well as the concept of confirmation/disconfirmation to begin distinguishing between human communication which is growthful, productive, effective, functional, or "therapeutic," and communication which is not. She developed measurement systems for systematically observing confirming and disconfirming communication (1969, 1972); she devised the first scale which allowed for measurement of an individual's feeling of being confirmed by another person (1973). She has continued to refine the basic theory of confirmation (1975), and has recently used the concepts to describe both organizational (1976) and family (in preparation) communication systems. During this time, a growing body of theoretical development and empirical research has attempted to explore these important concerns (cf. Cissna, 1976a, 1976b). . . .

DIMENSIONS OF CONFIRMATION

In the few direct allusions in the literature to confirmation and disconfirmation, several different elements are suggested. Confirmation is, of course, tied by definition to self-experience; our first problem, therefore, was to identify the specific aspects of self-experience that could be influenced positively or negatively in interaction with others. Four such elements seemed significant for our purpose:

1. The element of existence (the individual sees self as existing)
2. The element of relating (the individual sees self as a being-in-relation with others)
3. The element of significance, or worth
4. The element of validity of experience

Thus, it was assumed that the behavior of one person toward another is confirming to the extent that it performs the following functions in regard to the other's self-experience:

1. It expresses recognition of the other's existence
2. It acknowledges a relationship of affiliation with the other
3. It expresses awareness of the significance or worth of the other
4. It accepts or "endorses" the other's self-experience (particularly emotional experience)

Each unit of response is assumed to evoke relational metamessages with regard to each of the above functions, which can identify it as either confirming or disconfirming:

CONFIRMING	DISCONFIRMING
"To me, you exist."	"To me, you do not exist."
"We are relating."	"We are not relating."
"To me, you are significant."	"To me, you are not significant."
"Your way of experiencing your world is valid."	"Your way of experiencing your world is invalid."

In attempting to find behavioral correlates of these functions, we acknowledge that it is not possible to point with certainty to particular behaviors that universally perform these confirming functions for all persons, since individuals differ in the way they interpret the same acts; that is, they interpret the stimuli and assign their own meaning to them. Despite this reservation about making firm causal connections between the behavior of one person and the internal experience of another, we have followed the symbolic interactionist view that certain symbolic cues *do* acquire consensual validation and therefore are consistently interpreted by most persons as reflecting certain attitudes toward them on the part of others.[1] Such cues thus have message value and are capable of arousing in the receiver feelings of being recognized or ignored, accepted or rejected, understood or misunderstood, humanized or "thingified," valued or devalued. This assumption was borne out in a very general way by our research to date (Sieburg & Larson, 1971). . . .

SYSTEMATIZING DISCONFIRMING BEHAVIOR

A variety of specific acts and omissions have been noted by clinicians and theoreticians as being damaging to some aspect of the receiver's self-view. We have arranged these behaviors into three general groupings, or clusters, each representing a somewhat different style of response:

1. Indifferent response (denying existence or relation)
2. Impervious response (denying self-experience of the other)
3. Disqualifying response (denying the other's significance)

These clusters include verbal/nonverbal and vocal/nonvocal behaviors. Since they encompass both content and process features of interaction, it meant that scorers must be trained to evaluate each scoring unit in terms of its manifest content, its transactional features, and its underlying structure. In either case, no single utterance stands alone since it is always in response to some behavior or another, and is so experienced by the other as having implications about his or her self.

Disconfirmation by Indifference

To deny another's existence is to deny the most fundamental aspect of self-experience. Indifference may be total, as when presence is denied; it may imply rejection of relatedness with the other; or it may only deny the other's attempt to communicate.

Denial of Presence   The absence of even a minimal show of recognition has been associated with alienation, self-destructiveness, violence against others, and with psychosis. Laing used the case of "Peter," a psychotic patient of 25 to illustrate the possible long-term effects of chronic indifference toward a child who may, as a consequence, come to believe that he has no presence at all—or to feel guilty that he *does,* feeling that he has no right even to occupy space.

> Peter . . . was a young man who was preoccupied with guilt *because* he occupied a place in the world, even in a physical sense. He could not realize . . . that he had a right to have any presence for others . . . A peculiar aspect of his childhood was that his presence in the world was largely ignored. No weight was given to the fact that he was in the same room while his parents had intercourse. He had been physically cared for in that he had been well fed and kept warm, and underwent no physical separation from his parents during his earlier years. Yet he had been consistently treated as though he did not "really" exist. Perhaps worse than the experience of physical separation was to be in the same room as his parents and ignored, not malevolently, but through sheer indifference. [Laing, 1961:119]

That such extreme indifference is also devastating to an adult is evident in the following excerpt from a marriage counseling session (Sieburg, personal audiotape). It is perhaps significant that throughout his wife's outburst, the husband sat silent and remote:

THERAPIST: . . . and is it okay to express emotion?

WIFE: Not in my house.

THERAPIST: Has he [the husband] ever *said* it's not okay to talk about feelings?

WIFE: But he never *says* anything!

THERAPIST: But he has ways of sending you messages?

WIFE: [loudly] Yes! And the message is *shut out*—no matter what I say, no matter what I do, I get no response—zero—shut out!

THERAPIST: And does that somehow make you feel you are wrong?

WIFE: Oh, of course not wrong—just *nothing!*

THERAPIST: Then what is it that makes you feel he disapproves of you?

WIFE: Because I get nothing! [tears] If I feel discouraged—like looking for a job all day and being turned down—and I cry—zero! No touching, no patting, no "Maybe tomorrow"—just *shut out.* And if I get angry at him, instead of getting angry back, he just walks away—just nothing! All the time I'm feeling shut out and shut off!

THERAPIST: And what is it you want from him?

WIFE: [quietly] Maybe sometimes just a pat on the back would be enough. But, no!—he just shrugs me off. Where am I supposed to go to feel real? [tears]

Avoiding Involvement   Extreme instances of indifference like those above are presumed to be rare because even the slightest attention at least confirms one's presence. Lesser shows of indifference, however, still create feelings of alienation, frustration, and lowered self-worth. Although recognition is a necessary first step in confirming another, it is not in itself sufficient unless accompanied by some further indication of a willingness to be involved.

The precise ways in which one person indicates to another that he or she is interested in relating (intimacy) are not fully known, but several clear indications of *unwillingness* to relate or to become more than minimally involved have emerged from research and have been included in our systemization of disconfirming behaviors. Of particular significance are the use of:

- Impersonal language—the avoidance of first person references (I, me, my, mine) in favor of a collective "we" or "one," or the tendency to begin sentences with "there" when making what amounts to a personal statement (as, "there seems to be . . . ")
- Avoidance of eye contact
- Avoidance of physical contact except in ritualized situations such as handshaking
- Other nonverbal "distancing" cues

Rejecting Communication   A third way of suggesting indifference to another is to respond in a way that is unrelated, or only minimally related, to what he or she has just said, thus creating a break or disjunction in the flow of interaction.

Totally irrelevant response is, of course, much like denial of presence in that the person whose topic is repeatedly ignored may soon come to doubt his or her very existence, and at best will feel that he or she is not heard, attended to, or regarded as significant. Perhaps for this reason Laing called relevance the "crux of confirmation," noting that only by responding relevantly can one lend significance to another's communication and accord recognition (Laing, 1961:87).

The most extreme form of communication rejection is monologue, in which one speaker continues on and on, neither hearing nor acknowledging anything the other says. It reflects unawareness and lack of concern about the other person except as a socially acceptable audience for the speaker's own self-listening. A less severe communication rejection occurs when the responder makes a connection, however slight, with what the other has said, but immediately shifts into something quite different of his or her own choosing.

Disconfirming by Imperviousness

The term "imperviousness" as used here follows Laing's usage and refers to a lack of accurate awareness of another's perceptions (Watzlawick *et al.,* 1967:91). Imperviousness is disconfirming because it denies or distorts another's self-expression and fosters dehumanized relationships in which one person perceives another as a pseudo-image rather than as what that person really is. Behaviorally, the impervious responder engages in various tactics that tend to negate or discredit the other's feeling expression. These may take the form of a flat denial that the other *has* such a feeling ("You don't really mean that"), or it may be handled more indirectly by reinterpreting the feeling in a more acceptable way, ("You're only saying that because . . . "), substituting some experience or feeling of the *listener* ("What you're trying to say is . . . "), challenging the speaker's right to have such a feeling ("How can you *possibly* feel that way after all that's been done for you?"), or some similar device intended to alter the feeling expressed. . . .

A slightly different form of imperviousness occurs when a responder creates and bestows on another an inaccurate identity, and then confirms the false identity, although it is not a part of the other's self-experience at all. Laing calls this pseudo-confirmation (1961:83). Thus a mother who insists that her daughter is always obedient and "never any trouble at all" may be able to interpret her daughter's most rebellious aggression in a way that fits the placid image she holds of her daughter, and the parents of even a murderous psychopath may be able to describe their son as a "good boy." Such a false confirmation frequently endorses the fiction of what the other is *wished* to be, without any real recognition of what the other is or how he/she feels. As noted earlier, this form of disconfirmation also appears as simply a well-meaning attempt to reassure another who is distressed, which too is usually motivated by the speaker's need to reduce his or her own discomfort.

"Don't be silly—of course you're not afraid!"

"You may think you feel that way now, but I know better."

"Stop crying—there's nothing the matter with you!"

"How can you possibly worry about a little thing like that?"

"No matter what you say, I know you still love me."

Such responses constitute a rejection of the other person's expression and often identity, raising doubts about the validity of his/her way of experiencing by suggesting, "You don't really feel as you say you do; you are only imagining that you do."

A subtle variation of the same tactic occurs when the speaker responds in a selective way, rewarding the other with attention and relevant response *only* when he or she communicates in an approved fashion, and becoming silent or indifferent if the other's speech or behavior does not meet with the responder's approval. This may mean that the speaker limits response to those topics initiated by self, ignoring any topic initiated by the other person.

Imperviousness is considered disconfirming because it contributes to a feeling of uncertainty about self or uncertainty about the validity of personal experiencing. Imperviousness occurs when a person is told how he or she feels, regardless of how he or she experiences self, when a person's talents and abilities are described without any data to support such a description, when motives are ascribed to another without any reference to the other's own experience, or when one's own efforts at self-expression are ignored or discounted unless they match the false image held by some other person. . . .

Disconfirmation by Disqualification

According to Watzlawick (1964) disqualification is a technique which enables one to say something without really saying it, to deny without really saying "no," and to disagree without really disagreeing. Certain messages, verbal and nonverbal, are included in this group because they (a) disqualify the other speaker, (b) disqualify another message, or (c) disqualify themselves.

Speaker Disqualification This may include such direct disparagement of the other as name-calling, criticism, blame, and hostile attack, but may also take the indirect form of the sigh of martyrdom, the muttered expletive, addressing an adult in a tone of voice usually reserved for a backward child, joking "on the square," sarcasm, or any of the other numerous tactics to make the other appear and feel too incompetent or unreliable for his message to have validity. This creates a particularly unanswerable put-down by evoking strong metamessages of insignificance or worthlessness. The following examples are spouses' responses from conjoint counseling sessions:

- "Can't you ever do anything right?"
- "Here we go again!" [sigh]
- "We heard you the first time—why do you always keep repeating yourself?"
- "It's no wonder the rear axle broke, with you in the back seat!" [laughter]
- "Why do you always have to get your mouth open when you don't know what you're talking about?"

Message Disqualification Without regard to their content, some messages tend to discredit the other person because of their irrelevance—that is, they do not "follow" the other's prior utterance in a transactional sense. (This is also a tactic of indifference and may serve a dual disconfirming purpose.) Such disjunctive responses were studied by Sluzki, Beavin, Tarnopolski, and Veron (1967) who used the term "transactional disqualification" to mean any incongruity in the response of the speaker in relation to the context of the previous message of the other. A relationship between two successive messages exists, they noted, on two possible levels: (a) continuity between the content of the two messages (are both persons talking about the same subject?), and (b) indication of reception of the prior message (what cues does the speaker give of receiving and understanding the previous message?). If a message is disjunctive at either of these levels, transactional disqualification of the prior message is said to have occurred.

A similar form of message disqualification occurs when a speaker reacts selectively to some incidental clue in another's speech, but ignores the primary theme. Thus the responder may acknowledge the other's attempt to communicate, but still appears to miss the point. This "tangential response" was identified and studied by Jurgen Ruesch (1958), who noted that a speaker often picks up on a topic presented, but then continues to spin a yarn in a different direction. The response is not totally irrelevant because it has made some connection, although perhaps slight, with the prior utterance. Because it causes the first speaker to question the value or importance of what he or she was trying to say, the tangential response is reported to affect adversely a speaker's feeling of self-significance, and is therefore included as a form of disconfirmation.

Message Disqualifying Itself
A third way in which a speaker can use disqualification to "say something without really saying it," is by sending messages that disqualify themselves. There are many ways in which this may be done, the commonest devices being lack of clarity, ambiguity, and incongruity of mode. These forms of response are grouped together here because they have all been interpreted as devices for avoiding involvement with another by generating the metamessage "I am not communicating," hence "We are not relating."

SYSTEMATIZING CONFIRMING BEHAVIORS
Responses that confirm are less clearly defined than disconfirming behaviors because there has been less motivation to study them. In fact, identification of specific acts that are generally confirming is difficult unless we simply identify confirmation as the absence of disconfirming behaviors. More research in this area is clearly needed, but, in general, confirming behaviors are those which permit people to experience their own being and significance as well as their interconnectedness with others. Following Laing (1961), these have been arranged into three clusters: recognition, acknowledgment, and endorsement.

The Recognition Cluster Recognition is expressed by looking at the other, making frequent eye contact, touching, speaking directly to the person, and allowing the other the opportunity to respond without being interrupted or having to force his or her way into an ongoing monologue. In the case of an infant, recognition means holding and cuddling beyond basic survival functions; in the case of an adult, it may still mean physical contact (touching), but it also means psychological contact in the form of personal language, clarity, congruence of mode, and authentic self-expression. In other words, confirmation requires that a person treat the other with respect, acknowledging his or her attempt to relate, and need to have a presence in the world.

The Acknowledgment Cluster Acknowledgment of another is demonstrated by a relevant and direct response to his or her communication. This does not require praise or even agreement, but simple conjunction. Buber (Friedman, 1960) recognized this aspect when he wrote that mutually confirming partners can still "struggle together in direct opposition," and Laing (1961) made a similar point when he said that even rejection can be confirming if it is direct, not tangential, and if it grants significance and validity to what the other says. To hear, attend, and take note of the other and to acknowledge the other by responding directly is probably the most valued form of confirmation—and possibly the most rare. It means that the other's expression is furthered, facilitated, and encouraged.

The Endorsement Cluster This cluster includes any responses that express acceptance of the other's feelings as being true, accurate, and "okay." In general, it means simply letting the other *be,* without blame, praise, analysis, justification, modification, or denial.

Confirming response is dialogic in structure; it is a reciprocal activity involving shared talk and sometimes shared silence. It is interactional in the broadest sense of the word. It is not a one-way flow of talk; it is not a trade-off in which each speaker pauses and appears to listen only in order to get a chance to speak again. It is a complex affair in which each participates as both subject and object, cause and effect, of the other's talk. In short, confirming response, like all communication, is not something one does, it is a process in which one shares.

References

Buber, M. "Distance and Relation," *Psychiatry* 20 (1957): 97–104.

Cissna, K. N. L. "Facilitative Communication and Interpersonal Relationships: An Empirical Test of a Theory of Interpersonal Communication." Doctoral dissertation, University of Denver, 1975.

Cissna, K. N. L. "Interpersonal Confirmation: A Review of Current/Recent Theory and Research." Paper presented at the Central States Speech Association Convention, Chicago, 1976, and the International Communication Association Convention, Portland, Oregon, 1976.

Cissna, K. N. L. *Interpersonal Confirmation: A Review of Current Theory, Measurement, and Research.* Saint Louis: Saint Louis University, 1976.

Cissna, K. N. L. "Gender, Sex Type, and Perceived Confirmation: A Response from the Perspective of Interpersonal Confirmation." Presented at the International Communication Association Convention, Philadelphia, 1979.

Cissna, K. N. L., and S. Keating. "Speech Communication Antecedents of Perceived Confirmation," *Western Journal of Speech Communication* 43 (1979): 48–60.

Friedman, M. S. "Dialogue and the "Essential We": The Bases of Values in the Philosophy of Martin Buber," *American Journal of Psychoanalysis* 20 (1960): 26–34.

Laing, R. D. *The Self and Others.* New York: Pantheon, 1961.

Laing, R. D. "Mystification, Confusion and Conflict," in *Intensive Family Therapy,* ed. I. Boszormenyi-Nagy and J. L. Framo. New York: Harper & Row, 1965.

Laing, R. D. *The Politics of Experience.* New York: Ballantine, 1967.

Laing, R. D. *The Self and Others.* 2nd ed. Baltimore: Penguin, 1969.

Laing, R. D. *Knots.* New York: Vintage, 1970.

Laing, R. D., and A. Esterson. *Sanity, Madness, and the Family.* Baltimore: Penguin, 1964.

Ruesch, J. "The Tangential Response," in *Psychopathology of Communication,* ed. P. H. Toch and J. Zuben. New York: Grune & Stratton, 1958.

Ruesch, J. and G. Bateson. *Communication: The Social Matrix of Psychiatry.* New York: Norton, 1951.

Sieburg, E. "Dysfunctional Communication and Interpersonal Responsiveness in Small Groups." Doctoral dissertation, University of Denver, 1969.

Sieburg, E. "Toward a Theory of Interpersonal Confirmation." Unpublished manuscript, University of Denver, 1972.

Sieburg, E. *Interpersonal Confirmation: A Paradigm for Conceptualization and Measurement.* San Diego: United States International University, 1975.

Sieburg, E. "Confirming and Disconfirming Organizational Communication," in *Communication in Organizations.* eds. J. L. Owen, P. A. Page, and G. I. Zimmerman, St. Paul: West Publishing, 1976.

Sieburg, E. *Family Communication Systems* (in preparation).
Sieburg, E. and C. E. Larson. "Dimensions of Interpersonal Response." Paper presented at the annual convention of the International Communication Association, Phoenix, 1971.
Watzlawick, P. *An Anthology of Human Communication.* Palo Alto: Science and Behavior Books, 1964.
Watzlawick, P., J. Beavin, and D. D. Jackson. *Pragmatics of Human Communication: A Study of Interactional Patterns, Pathologies, and Paradoxes.* New York: Norton, 1967.

PROBES

What makes the term "confirmation" appropriate for what's being discussed here? You can confirm an airplane reservation and in some churches young people are confirmed. How do those meanings echo the meaning of confirmation that's developed here?

Notice how, in the first paragraph under the heading "Dimensions of Confirmation," the authors emphasize the transactional or relational quality of the phenomenon. Paraphrase what you hear them saying there.

All of us experience disconfirmation, sometimes with destructive regularity. Give an example where you have given an *indifferent* response. Give an example of where you've received one. Do the same for *imperviousness* and *disqualification.*

When a person is "impervious," what is he or she impervious *to?* Discuss.

Create an example of well-meant imperviousness, that is, imperviousness motivated by a genuine desire to comfort or to protect the other person. Do the same with a disqualifying response.

Identify five specific confirming communication events that you experienced in the last four hours.

Maurice Friedman's comments about confirmation grow out of his life-long study and application of Martin Buber's ideas. In fact, Friedman's most recent book, which includes this excerpt, is called *The Confirmation of Otherness in Family, Community, and Society.* I especially like the way Friedman emphasizes that confirmation happens *between* persons. As he notes, one implication of that fact is that we cannot *make* confirmation happen; we cannot *will* it. We can, however, choose to be closed to it; we can shut out even the others who are genuinely trying to contact us. That's the point of Friedman's brief discussion of St. Francis of Assisi.

Another implication of the "between" quality of confirmation is that no one can offer or give a blanket of unconditional confirmation. We can only give as much of our personal selves as we can bring to the concrete situation, and we can only confirm the other in his or her uniqueness, as a person also conditioned by this concrete situation. Confirmation also differs from acceptance in that it can include a commitment to growth and change. At the end of this selection, Friedman discusses the dangers of the confirmation-with-strings-attached and the confirmation that smothers.

I hope that the combination of Cissna and Sieburg's quasi-social scientific treatment and Friedman's more philosophical discussion will give you a reasonably firm grasp of this crucial interpersonal phenomenon. Then Paul Rabinow's example in the final reading of this chapter should round out your understanding.

Confirmation and the Emergence of the Self

Maurice Friedman

Confirmation, as we have seen, is an integral part of the life of dialogue. Dialogue may be silent and monologue spoken. What really matters in genuine dialogue is my acceptance of the "otherness" of the other person, my willingness to listen to her and respond to her address. In monologue, in contrast, I only allow the other to exist as a content of my experience. Not only do I see her primarily in terms of her social class, her color, her religion, her IQ, or character neurosis; I do not leave myself open to her as a person at all. The life of dialogue is not one in which we have much to do with others, but one in which we really have to do with those with whom we have to do. . . .

Confirmation is central to human existence, but human existence is itself problematic, and the heart of its problematic is that of confirmation. This problematic can be grasped most clearly if we look at what we ordinarily take as a self-evident reality and as the foundation of our personal existence—our "I." The "I" is not an object or a thing. Indeed, it escapes all attempts to objectify it. But even as a subjective reality, it is not something continuous, secure, or easily discernible. It is elusive and insubstantial, paradoxical and perplexing to the point of illusion or even downright delusion. It cannot be understood as something taken by itself, outside of all relationship, but neither is it a part of a whole. It rests on the reality of the "between," the interhuman. I cannot regard my "I" as merely a product of social forces and influences, for then it is no longer an "I." There has to be that in me which can respond if I am going to talk about any true personal uniqueness. Therefore, I cannot say with George Herbert Mead, "The self is an eddy in the social current." I cannot turn the self into a mere confluence of social and psychological streams.

On the other hand, if I speak of the "I" as an "essence," that is misleading because it suggests something substantive that is within us as a vein of gold within a mountain waiting to be mined. Our uniqueness is our personal vocation, our life's calling that is discovered when we are called out by life and become "ourselves" in responding. We must respond to this call from where we are, and where we are is never merely social nor merely individual but uniquely personal. We need to be confirmed by others. Our very sense of ourselves only comes in our meeting with others. Yet through this confirmation we can grow to the strength of Socrates, who said, "I respect you, Athenians. But I will obey the god and not you." Socrates made his contribution to the common order of speech-with-meaning—he expressed his responsibility to his fellow Athenians precisely in opposing them. But if Socrates had not had seventy years in Athens in which he was part, first of his family of origin and then of his own family of wife and children, and if he had not been confirmed by the Athenian youth with whom he met in daily discussion, confirmed even when they opposed him, he would not have been able to stand alone.

The religious person sometimes imagines that one can be confirmed by God without any confirmation from one's fellow human beings. This is possible for a Jesus or a Buddha when they are adults. We are really set in existence, and existence is social existence. Once you have had real dialogue with human beings, you may then leave them for a desert island where you relate only to the chameleon, the Gila monster, or the waves lapping on the shore. But if you had no such relationship to begin with, you would not become a self. Or if you had such relations but were not confirmed or were even disconfirmed as an infant and young child, then your self will exist only in that impairment with which we are familiar in the schizophrenic, the paranoid, or the severe neurotic.

One of the paradoxes of confirmation is that, essential as it is to our and to all human existence, we cannot *will* to be confirmed. We cannot even *will* to confirm. When we do so we fall into what Leslie Farber has called willfulness, that sickness of the disordered will that seeks an illusory wholeness through trying to handle both sides of the dialogue. . . . Hence the futility and frustration of the love-lorn and the jealous who try to give up the beloved in order to receive her back and only make things worse in doing so. A large part of the pain of unrequited love as of jealousy comes from just this fact—that we cannot control others, that we must leave them really free to handle their side of the dialogue, to respond freely to our address rather than react as the effect of which *we* are the cause.

If we cannot *will* what the other side will give us, we *can* will not to receive. This is the other side of the coin. In a saying that Martin Buber has entitled ":Give and Take," one Hasidic master says: "Everyone must be both a giver and a receiver. He who is not both is like a barren tree." There are people who so habitually see themselves and are seen by others in the role of helper, responsible person, or giver, that they have never learned how to accept and still less how to ask for what they need. Once Rabbi Mendel sat motionless at his plate when everyone else at the Sabbath dinner was eating soup. "Mendel, why do you not eat?" asked Rabbi Elimelekh. "Because I do not have a spoon," Mendel replied. "Look," said Rabbi Elimelekh, "you must learn to ask for a spoon and if need be for a plate too." Rabbi Mendel took the words of his teacher to heart, and from that time on his fortunes mended.

I have always been deeply moved by St. Francis' prayer, which for many years I said every night before going to sleep:

O Lord,
Make me an instrument of Thy peace.
Where there is hatred, let me sow love;
Where there is despair, hope;
Where there is darkness, light;
Where there is sadness, joy.

O Divine Master
Grant that I may not so much seek
To be understood as to understand,
To be consoled as to console,
To be loved as to love.
For it is in giving that we receive,
It is in pardoning that we are pardoned,
And it is in dying that we are born into eternal life.

However, I have come increasingly to recognize that this prayer presents only one aspect of reality. A person has also to allow himself to be understood, to be consoled, to be loved. Toward the end of his life, St. Francis said, "I was too hard on Brother Ass," by which he meant his own body. Even by medieval standards, his asceticism was unbelievably harsh. St. Francis loved every person and every thing, but he did not love himself quite enough. There is a compassion for oneself which is the opposite of self-pity and self-indulgence because it arises from a distancing from oneself rather than from a wallowing in subjective emotions. Such compassion is a form of humility whereas being too hard on oneself is a form of pride. "Everyone must have two pockets to use as the occasion demands," said Rabbi Bunam. "In one pocket should be the words: 'For my sake the world was created,' and in the other, 'I am dust and ashes.'"

To exist as human beings we must, as long as we live, enter ever anew into the flowing interchange of confirming and being confirmed, of addressing and responding. This means that we must have that courage to address and that courage to respond which rests on, embodies, and makes manifest existential trust. It also means a new and deeper understanding of responsibility and of its relation to confirmation. Responsibility means to respond, and genuine response is response of the whole person. In every situation we are asked to respond in a unique way. Therefore, our wholeness in that situation is unique too, even though we become more and more ourselves through such response—hence, more and more recognizable by others in a personal uniqueness that extends beyond the moment.

Because confirmation is a reality of the between, no one can offer another a blanket of unconditional confirmation, regardless of what that other says, does, or is. We can only give what we have, and what we have, first of all, is not a technique of confirmation but our personal selves—selves which can make another present and "imagine the real" but selves which also respond from where we are. Further, because confirmation means a confirmation of our uniqueness, a blanket confirmation would be valueless. We need to be confirmed in our uniqueness as what we are, what we *can* become, and what we are called to become, and this can only be known in the give and take of living dialogue. Therefore, as Martin Buber stressed in his 1957 dialogue with Carl Rogers, that affirmation which says "I accept you as you are" is only the beginning of dialogue and must be distinguished from that confirmation which has to do with the development of the person over time. Rogers emphasized an unqualified acceptance of the person being helped, whereas Buber emphasized a confirmation which, while it accepts the other as a person, may also wrestle *with* him against himself. Rogers spoke of acceptance as a warm regard for the other and a respect for him as a person of unconditional worth, and that means "an acceptance of and regard for his attitudes of the moment, no matter how much they may contradict other attitudes he has held in the past." Buber, in response, said:

> I not only accept the other as he is, but I confirm him, in myself, and then in him, in relation to this potentiality that is meant by him and it can now be developed, it can evolve, it can answer the reality of life. . . . Let's take, for example, man and wife. He says, not expressly, but just by his whole relation to her, "I accept you as you are." But this does not mean, "I don't want you to change." But it says, "I discover in you just by my accepting love, I discover in you what you are meant to become."[1]

To Rogers' statement that complete acceptance of the person as he is is the strongest factor making for change, Buber countered with the problematic type of person with which he necessarily had to do. By this Buber meant the person whose very existence had run aground on the problematic of confirmation, a person whom simple acceptance could not help:

> There are cases when I must help him against himself. He wants my help against himself. . . . The first thing of all is that he trusts me. . . . What he wants is a being not only whom he can trust as a man trusts another, but a being that gives him now the certitude that "there *is* a soil, there *is* an existence." And if this is reached, now I can help this man even in his struggle against himself. And this I can only do if I distinguish between accepting and confirming.[2]

As babies we are really at the mercy of "significant others." Some people in their early years do not receive enough confirmation to enable them to be human. It is even possible that a nursery-school teacher could make all the difference for a deprived child's capacity to grow up human. Although once we are grown we imagine ourselves as independent "I"'s, as babies and little children we are totally dependent upon being called into existence as persons. Our notion of ourselves as separate consciousnesses that then enter into relation is an error produced by the individuation that we experience later. When we grow up, we think of ourselves as first and foremost "I" and imagine that we enter into relationship with others as one nation might send out ambassadors to foreign countries. Actually, as John Donne said, "No man is an island, entire of itself; every man is a piece of the continent," a continent that is based on the distancing and relating of our person-to-person relationships and of the "essential We" of family, group, community, and society.

To say that all men are created equal means, if anything, that each person may be and deserves to be related to as Thou. It does not mean, however, that this actually happens. There is a fundamental *inequality* insofar as the actual confirmation that each person receives is concerned. No one can ever change the fact of being an older brother or sister or a younger one or, for that matter, of being born with a gold, silver, lead, or copper spoon in his mouth. In every social group there is a sense of status, and in every social group there are those who have come out on the short end of the stick as far as confirmation is concerned.

What makes the emergence of the self still more problematic is that even where confirmation is given and given lavishly, it is usually with strings attached. It takes the form of an unspoken, invisible contract which reads: "If you are a good boy or girl, student, churchgoer, citizen, or soldier, we shall confirm you as lovable. If you are not, not only will you not be confirmed but you will have to live with the [introjected] knowledge that you are fundamentally unlovable." This is a contract that most of us buy, more or less, and there is no human way to be wholly free of it. This means that most confirmation is *not* unconditional, however much it may be "positive." As we grow older, this problematic is complicated still further by the need people have to fix each other in social roles. This is, if you like, a tragedy, but it is a well-nigh universal one. There are people who are made so anxious by not being able to put you in a given cubbyhole that they will never accept you. How many parents love their child but love him or her only as "my child" and will never allow that child to grow up—to become a person with a ground of his or her own. . . .

There is a distinction that must be made between a basic confirmation that gives us our ticket to exist and the confirmation along the road which has to do with the way in which we exist. If we are so fortunate as to have been confirmed in our right to exist, that does not mean that the confirmation then extends to everything we do. If, on the other hand, we have not been confirmed in our existence itself, then all the later confirmation we receive is not likely to fill the vacuum within.

Other people fix us in their images of us, and we in turn internalize those images and fix ourselves in them. Why is it so important to a child who goes to college not to be called by the nickname which his or her family and friends used when s/he was at home? It is because the young person wants to feel "I am growing up now." When such a young person goes home for vacation and the family calls him or her by the nickname he or she feels s/he has outgrown, they are imprisoning that young person in an image of him- or herself which has power over his or her self. It leads one to limit one's sense of what one can do. It gets in the way. Eventually, of course, one reaches the strength to say, "I am not this," and the still greater strength of standing one's own ground without being made anxious, defensive, or upset. If it remains a conflict situation, one can accept the tragedy for what it is. Unfortunately, some people never attain this courage and strength and, even if they succeed in getting their families to call them by different names, they remain bound to the roles in which their family has cast them.

References

1. Martin Buber, *The Knowledge of Man,* ed. Maurice Friedman, trans. Maurice Friedman and Ronald Gregor Smith (New York: Harper & Row, 1965), p. 182.
2. Ibid., p. 183.

PROBES

Paraphrase the last sentence of Friedman's first paragraph. What is he saying here?

Friedman says that you need others in order to be an I, a self. How do you respond to that point?

What are some practical implications of Friedman's point that we cannot *will* to be confirmed or to confirm?

What difference do you hear Friedman drawing between confirmation and acceptance? Is that consistent with Cissna and Sieburg's uses of those terms?

Have you experienced the *inequality* Friedman discusses?

What's the relationship between what Friedman calls the "basic confirmation that gives us our ticket to exist" and the confirmation "which has to do with the way in which we exist"?

The next selection comes from a small book that describes the experiences of a young, Jewish-American anthropologist who went to Morocco to live and study the culture there. I discovered this excerpt in a conversation with Tamar Katriel, an Israeli who was studying interpersonal communication in our department. Tamar noticed how the event Rabinow describes here is an excellent example of confirmation, which we were discussing in class.

One question we had discussed was whether confirmation is important in all cultures or just in Western ones. We know, for example, that the direct eye contact that can be so confirming to whites can often be inappropriate and uncomfortable for persons from Japanese or other nonwhite cultures. And there are many other differences.

Tamar noticed that Rabinow's description of his confrontation with Ali suggested that confirmation is also vital in nonwhite cultures but that it is communicated in radically different ways. Rabinow thought he could affirm Ali as a person by being passive, accepting, and deferent. When he blew up at Ali he thought he'd ruined their relationship. But he discovered that in Ali's culture it was more confirming to be confronted than to be treated gently and with total acceptance. It impressed me to read that only *after* their argument and the strong mutual confirmation it established were Rabinow and Ali able to talk about Ali's involvement in a radical religious group and prostitution, two very private topics. This article also introduces one of the main points of Chapter 12, "Communicating Across Cultures." As the readings there demonstrate, the basic elements of effective interpersonal communication—contact, confirmation, understanding, clarity, responsiveness—are important in all cultures, but the way you communicate each of these differs significantly from culture to culture. In other words, the mode of communicating described in this book is not restricted just to Western white majority cultures; it applies to all human contacts, so long as it is adapted to the cultural setting.

Confrontation with Ali
Paul Rabinow

Ali promised to take me to a wedding in the village of Sidi Lahcen Lyussi. I had already been to several urban weddings. The best Moroccan food, music, and ceremonial were displayed on these occasions. It was a nice change of pace, a break in the routine. The wedding would be an excellent opportunity for me to see the village, and for the villagers to see me.

That afternoon, Ali came by. I told him I wasn't sure I would be able to go with him because I was suffering from a stomach virus. The prospect of being in a strange and demanding situation where I wanted to please, for such a long period, seemed overwhelming, especially in my present condition. Ali expressed keen disappointment at this. He had clearly counted on transportation in my car and the mixed prestige of arriving with the most auspicious guest (if not the guest of honor).

When he returned the next day I was feeling a bit better. He assured me that we would stay only for a short time. He stressed all the preliminary politicking and arranging he had done; if I didn't show up it would not be good for either of us. So I agreed, but made him promise me that we would stay only an hour or so because I was still weak. He repeated his promise several times saying we would leave whenever I felt like it.

Paul Rabinow, *Reflections on Fieldwork in Morocco* (Berkeley: University of California Press, 1977), pp. 40–49. Reprinted by permission of the University of California Press.

Ali and Soussi came to my house around nine that evening and we were off. I was already somewhat tired and repeated clearly to Soussi, a renowned partygoer in his own right, that we would stay only for a short time and then return to Sefrou. *Waxxa,* O.K.?

It was already growing dark as we left Sefrou. By the time we turned off the highway onto the unpaved road which leads to the village, it was nearly pitch black, depriving me of a sense of the countryside, while adding to my feelings of uncertainty about the whole affair. Nonetheless, on arriving in the village I was exhilarated.

The wedding itself was held in a set of connected houses which formed a compound. A group of sons had built simple mud and mortar houses next to each other as they married, and by now these formed an enclosed compound. Each part of the enclosure was made up of a two-story building. The facilities for the animals and cooking areas were downstairs, the sleeping quarters were on the top level, connected by a rickety staircase. That night the center of the compound area had been covered with straw for the dancing. We were welcomed and ushered up the stairs into a long narrow room furnished with thin cushions along the perimeters. Perhaps five tables were arranged parallel to each other, running the length of the room. I told myself it was a good thing we had come, a wise decision. Everyone was friendly and seemed to know who I was. We had tea, then after perhaps an hour of chatting and banter, dinner was served on battered but polished metal trays. The hour of talk had passed amicably enough, even though my minimal Arabic did not permit much expansive conversation. I still had a beard at this point, and there was much friendly but insistent joking that this was improper for such a young man. The dinner was simple but nicely prepared, consisting of goat meat in a sort of olive oil stew with freshly baked bread, still warm from the oven.

After we ate and drank more tea, we went down to the courtyard, where the dancing began. I watched from a corner, leaning against a pillar. The dancers were all men, of course, and they formed two lines facing each other, their arms draped over one another's shoulders. Between the two lines was a singer with a crude tambourine. He sang and swayed back and forth. The lines of men responded in turn to his direct, insistent beat, answering his verses with verses of their own. The women were peeping out from another part of the compound where they had eaten their dinner. They were all dressed in their best clothes, brightly colored kaftans. They answered the various verses with calls of their own, enthusiastically urging the men on. Since I did not understand the songs and was not dancing, my excitement wore off rapidly. Ali was one of the most dedicated of the dancers, and it was difficult to catch his attention. During a break when the central singer was warming his tambourine over the fire to restretch the skin, I finally got Ali's ear and told him politely but insistently that I was not feeling well, that we had been here three hours already. It was midnight, could we leave soon after the next round of dances maybe? Of course, he said, just a few more minutes, no problem, don't worry, I understand.

An hour later I tried again and received the same answer. This time, however, I was getting angrier and more frustrated; I was feeling truly ill. The mountain air was quite cold by now, and I had not dressed warmly enough. I felt entirely at Ali's mercy. I didn't want to antagonize him, but neither did I want to stay. I continued to grumble to myself but managed to smile at whoever was smiling at me.

Finally, at three in the morning, I could stand it no longer. I was feeling terrible. I was furious at Ali but loath to express it. I was going to leave, regardless of the consequences. I told Soussi, let's go; if you want a ride, get Ali and that's it. Ali at this point was nowhere in sight. Soussi went off and returned to the car with a smiling and contented Ali. I was warming the engine up, publicly announcing my readiness to leave. They climbed in, Soussi in the front and Ali in the back, and we were off. The road for the first five miles is little more than a path—untarred, pitted, and winding and steep in places. I was a novice driver and unsure of myself, so I said nothing, concentrating all my energy on staying on the road and keeping the car going. I managed to negotiate this stretch of road successfully and heaved a sigh of relief when we reached the highway.

Soussi had been keeping up a steady flow of chatter as we bumped over the country road. I had kept my silence, ignoring Ali in the back, who said little himself. When we reached the highway and began rolling smoothly toward Sefrou, he asked in a nonchalant manner, *wash ferhan?,* are you happy? I snickered and said no. He pursued this. Why not? In simple terms I told him that I was sick, that it was three-thirty in the morning, and all I wanted to do was go home to bed—adding that I sincerely hoped he had enjoyed himself. Yes, he said, he had enjoyed himself, but if I was unhappy then the whole evening was spoiled, he was getting out of the car. Please, Ali, I said, let's just get back to Sefrou in peace. But why are you unhappy? I reminded him of his promise. If you are unhappy, he said, then I will walk back. This exchange was repeated several times, Soussi's vain attempts at mediation being ignored by both sides. Finally I told Ali he was acting like a baby, and yes, I was unhappy. He never offered any specific excuses but only insisted that if I was unhappy he would walk. He started to lean over and open the door on Soussi's side, scaring Soussi witless. We were traveling at forty miles an hour, and it scared me too, and I slowed down to ten. He challenged me again asking me if I was happy. I just could not bring myself to answer yes. My superego told me I should. But the events of the evening combined with the frustration of not being able to express myself fully to him in Arabic got the better of me. After another exchange and bluff on his part, I stopped the car to let him get out, which he now had to do. He did, promptly, and began striding down the dark highway in the direction of Sefrou. I let him get about one hundred yards ahead and then drove up alongside and told him to get in the car. He looked the other way. Soussi tried his luck with the same results. We repeated this melodrama two more times. I was confused, nauseous, and totally frustrated. I stepped on the gas and off we went to Sefrou, leaving Ali to walk the remaining five miles.

I went to sleep immediately, but woke from a fitful night saying to myself that I had probably made a grave professional mistake, because the informant is always right. Otherwise I was unrepentant. It was quite possible that I had ruined my relationship with Ali and that I had done irreparable damage to my chances of working my way into the village. But there were other things worth studying in Morocco, and it was something I would just have to make the best of. I took a walk through the tree-lined streets of the Ville Nouvelle and remembered a story a friend had told me before we took our doctoral exams; he had had nightmares for a week before the exams in which he saw himself as a shoe salesman. I mentally tried several occupations on for size as I drifted aimlessly among the villas. I felt calm; if this was anthropology and if I had ruined it for myself, then it simply wasn't for me.

The parameters seemed clear enough. I had to clarify for myself where I stood. If the informant was always right, then by implication the anthropologist had to become a sort of non-person, or more accurately a total persona. He had to be willing to enter into any situation as a smiling observer and carefully note down the specifics of the event under consideration. If one was interested in symbolic analysis or expressive culture, then the more elusive dimensions of feeling tone, gesture, and the like would be no exception. This was the position my professors had advocated: one simply endured whatever inconveniences and annoyances came along. One had to completely subordinate one's own code of ethics, conduct, and world view, to "suspend disbelief," as another colleague was proud of putting it, and sympathetically and accurately record events.

All of this had seemed simple enough back in Chicago (where, more accurately, no one paid more than lip service to these problems), but it was far from simple at the wedding. Ali had been a steady companion during the previous month and I had established a real rapport with him, more as a friend than as an informant; I was getting acclimated to Sefrou, and my Arabic was still too limited for us to do any sustained and systematic work together. I found the demands of greater self-control and abnegation hard to accept. I was used to engaging people energetically and found the idea of a year constantly on my guard, with very little to fall back on except the joys of asceticism, productive sublimation, and the pleasures of self-control, a grim prospect. . . .

At the wedding Ali was beginning to test me, much in the way that Moroccans test each other to ascertain strengths and weaknesses. He was pushing and probing. I tried to avoid responding in the counter-assertive style of another Moroccan, vainly offering instead the persona of anthropologist, all-accepting. He continued to interpret my behavior in his own terms; he saw me as weak, giving in to each of his testing thrusts. So the cycle continued: he would probe more deeply, show his dominance, and exhibit my submission and lack of character. Even on the way back to Sefrou he was testing me, and in what was a backhanded compliment, trying to humiliate me. But Ali was uneasy with his victories, and shifted to defining the situation in terms of a guest-host relationship. My silence in the car clearly signaled the limits of my submission. His response was a strong one: Was I happy? Was he a good host?

The role of the host combines two of the most important of Moroccan values. As throughout the Arabic world, the host is judged by his generosity. The truly good host is one whose bounty, the largesse he shows his guests, is truly never-ending. One of the highest compliments one can pay to a man is to say that he is *karim,* generous. The epitome of the host is the man who can entertain many people and distribute his bounty graciously. This links him ultimately to Allah, who is the source of bounty.

If the generosity is accepted by the guest, then a very clear relationship of domination is established. The guest, while being fed and taken care of, is by that very token acknowledging the power of the host. Merely entering into such a position represents an acceptance of submission. In this fiercely egalitarian society, the necessity of exchange or reciprocity so as to restore the balance is keenly felt. Moroccans will go to great lengths, and endure rather severe personal privation, to reciprocate hospitality. By so doing, they reestablish their claim to independence.

Later in the day, I went down to Soussi's store in search of Ali to try and make amends. At first he refused even to shake hands, and was suitably haughty. But with the aid of Soussi's mediation and innumerable and profuse apologies on my part, he began to come round. By the time I left them later that afternoon it was clear that we had reestablished our relationship. Actually, it had been broadened by the confrontation. I had in fact acknowledged him. I had, in his own terms, pulled the rug out from under him—first by cutting off communication and then by challenging his gambit in the car. There was a fortuitous congruence between my breaking point and Moroccan cultural style. Perhaps in another situation my behavior might have proved irreparable. Brinkmanship, however, is a fact of everyday life in Morocco, and finesse in its use is a necessity. By finally standing up to Ali I had communicated to him.

Indeed, from that point on, we got along famously. It was only after this incident that he began to reveal to me two aspects of his life which he had previously concealed: his involvement in an ecstatic brotherhood, and his involvement in prostitution.

PROBES

Notice how space is organized and used in the Moroccan village Rabinow describes. For example, how are the houses arranged and built? Where are the men and the women during the dancing? What messages about culture do you get from these uses of space?

How do you account for the radical response Rabinow first had to the argument with Ali—he actually considered having to become a shoe salesperson or something other than an anthropologist. Why do you suppose he responded so strongly?

What does Rabinow's experience say about the relationship between theory and practice?

Paraphrase Rabinow's explanation of the guest–host, dominant–submissive dynamic he found in Moroccan culture.

Notice that, for Rabinow, the key outcome of the confrontation with Ali was that "I had in fact acknowledged him." What does he mean by that?

PART 4

Bridging
Differences

CHAPTER 10

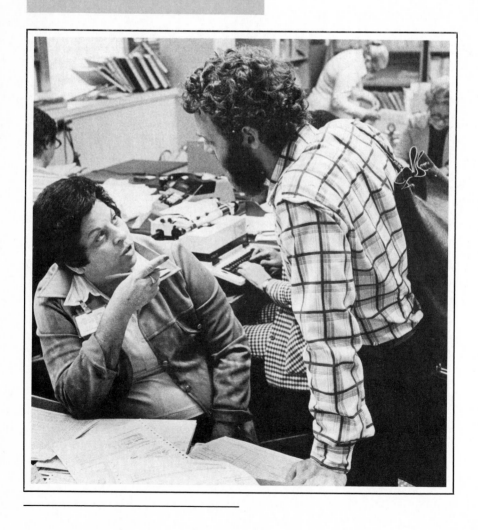

CONFLICT

> No one is wrong. At most
> someone is uninformed. If I think
> a man is wrong, either I am
> unaware of something, or he is.
> So unless I want to play a
> superiority game I had best find
> out what he is looking at.
> "You're wrong" means "I don't
> understand you"—I'm not
> seeing what you're seeing. But
> there is nothing wrong with you,
> you are simply not me and that's
> not wrong.
>
> HUGH PRATHER

All of us experience conflict; we disagree with our spouses, argue with our parents, dispute the merits of political candidates and issues with friends, and sometimes even quarrel with strangers at the bus stop. At times we lose sight of the fact that all this conflict is "normal" and "natural." So long as persons are individuals, there will be the potential for conflict each time they meet. In other words, conflict in and of itself is not evidence of a communication "failure" or "breakdown"; it just shows that two or more individuals happen to be in contact on a topic that reflects part of their individuality.

That's the first thing to learn about conflict: It isn't "wrong" or "bad," it's just part of being a person who's in contact with other persons. The only people who don't experience interpersonal conflict are hermits.

Since you can't prevent conflict, the important thing to learn is how to *handle* it in productive rather than destructive ways. Thus the second step is to determine how it happens and what you can do to help the conflicts you experience be useful and "clean" rather than spiteful and person-destroying. In the next selection, Jack Gibb shares some insights about how conflict happens and what you can do to promote a supportive rather than a defensive climate for communication.

As Gibb points out, when you anticipate or perceive that you are threatened by a person or a situation, you will usually react defensively and so will the other persons involved. When any combination of the six "defensiveness-producing" elements are present, a spiral usually begins, a spiral that starts with a little discomfort and often escalates into all-out conflict.

But, Gibb notes, you can also start a spiral in the other direction. The more supportive you can be, the less other people are likely to read into the situation distorted reactions created by their own defensiveness. So when you can manifest any combination of the six alternative attitudes and skills, you can help reduce the defensiveness that's present. You don't have to "give up" or "give in." You just have to stop trying so hard to demean, control, and impose your hard-and-fast superiority on the others.

Most of the people I work with find this article very useful. They discover that they can apply Gibb's analysis of the six characteristics of defensive and supportive communication climates to their own experience. They also find that Gibb is right when he says that most people are much more aware of being manipulated or deceived than the manipulators or deceivers think and that such awareness creates defensiveness. They are usually able to perceive quite accurately another's communication strategy or "gimmicks." When they learn that sometimes it's their own transparently manipulative behavior that creates defensiveness in others, they get one jump closer to communicating interpersonally.

Defensive Communication

Jack R. Gibb

One way to understand communication is to view it as a people process rather than as a language process. If one is to make fundamental improvement in communication, he must make changes in interpersonal relationships. One possible type of alteration—and the one with which this paper is concerned—is that of reducing the degree of defensiveness.

DEFINITION AND SIGNIFICANCE

Defensive behavior is defined as that behavior which occurs when an individual perceives threat or anticipates threat in the group. The person who behaves defensively, even though he also gives some attention to the common task, devotes an appreciable portion of his energy to defending himself. Besides talking about the topic, he thinks about how he appears to others, how he may be seen more favorably, how he may win, dominate, impress, or escape punishment, and/or how he may avoid or mitigate a perceived or an anticipated attack.

Such inner feelings and outward acts tend to create similarly defensive postures in others; and, if unchecked, the ensuing circular response becomes increasingly destructive. Defensive behavior, in short, engenders defensive listening, and this in turn produces postural, facial, and verbal cues which raise the defense level of the original communicator.

Defense arousal prevents the listener from concentrating upon the message. Not only do defensive communicators send off multiple value, motive, and affect cues, but also defensive recipients distort what they receive. As a person becomes more and more defensive, he becomes less and less able to perceive accurately the motives, the values, and the emotions of the sender. The writer's analyses of tape recorded discussions revealed that increases in defensive behavior were correlated positively with losses in efficiency in communication.[1] Specifically, distortions became greater when defensive states existed in the groups.

The converse, moreover, also is true. The more "supportive" or defense reductive the climate the less the receiver reads into the communication distorted loadings which arise from projections of his own anxieties, motives, and concerns. As defenses are reduced, the receivers become better able to concentrate upon the structure, the content, and the cognitive meanings of the message.

CATEGORIES OF DEFENSIVE AND SUPPORTIVE COMMUNICATION

In working over an eight-year period with recordings of discussions occurring in varied settings, the writer developed the six pairs of defensive and supportive categories presented in Table 1. Behavior which a listener perceives as possessing any of the characteristics listed in the left-hand column arouses defensiveness, whereas that which he interprets as having any of the qualities designated as supportive reduces defensive feelings. The degree to which these reactions occur depends

Jack R. Gibb, "Defensive Communication," *Journal of Communication* 11, no. 3 (September 1961): 141–148. Reprinted by permission of the *Journal of Communication* and the author.

TABLE 1

Categories of Behavior Characteristic of Supportive and Defensive Climates in Small Groups

DEFENSIVE CLIMATES	SUPPORTIVE CLIMATES
1. Evaluation	1. Description
2. Control	2. Problem orientation
3. Strategy	3. Spontaneity
4. Neutrality	4. Empathy
5. Superiority	5. Equality
6. Certainty	6. Provisionalism

upon the personal level of defensiveness and upon the general climate in the group at the time.[2]

Evaluation and Description

Speech or other behavior which appears evaluative increases defensiveness. If by expression, manner of speech, tone of voice, or verbal content the sender seems to be evaluating or judging the listener, then the receiver goes on guard. Of course, other factors may inhibit the reaction. If the listener thought that the speaker regarded him as an equal and was being open and spontaneous, for example, the evaluativeness in a message would be neutralized and perhaps not even perceived. This same principle applies equally to the other five categories of potentially defense-producing climates. The six sets are interactive.

Because our attitudes toward other persons are frequently, and often necessarily, evaluative, expressions which the defensive person will regard as nonjudgmental are hard to frame. Even the simplest question usually conveys the answer that the sender wishes or implies the response that would fit into his value system. A mother, for example, immediately following an earth tremor that shook the house, sought for her small son with the question: "Bobby, where are you?" The timid and plaintive "Mommy, I didn't do it" indicated how Bobby's chronic mild defensiveness predisposed him to react with a projection of his own guilt and in the context of his chronic assumption that questions are full of accusation.

Anyone who has attempted to train professionals to use information-seeking speech with neutral effect appreciates how difficult it is to teach a person to say even the simple "who did that?" without being seen as accusing. Speech is so frequently judgmental that there is a reality base for the defensive interpretations which are so common.

When insecure, group members are particularly likely to place blame, to see others as fitting into categories of good or bad, to make moral judgments of their colleagues, and to question the value, motive, and affect loadings of the speech which they hear. Since value loadings imply a judgment of others, a belief that the standards of the speaker differ from his own causes the listener to become defensive.

Descriptive speech, in contrast to that which is evaluative, tends to arouse a minimum of uneasiness. Speech acts which the listener perceives as genuine requests for information or as material with neutral loadings is descriptive. Specifically, presentations of feelings, events, perceptions, or processes which do not ask or imply that the receiver change behavior or attitude are minimally defense producing. The difficulty in avoiding overtone is illustrated by the problems of news reporters in writing stories about unions, communists, Blacks, and religious activities without tipping off the "party" line of the newspaper. One can often tell from the opening words in a news article which side the newspaper's editorial policy favors.

Control and Problem Orientation

Speech which is used to control the listener evokes resistance. In most of our social intercourse someone is trying to do something to someone else—to change an attitude, to influence behavior, or to restrict the field of activity. The degree to which attempts to control produce defensiveness depends upon the openness of the effort, for a suspicion that hidden motives exist heightens resistance. For this reason attempts of nondirective therapists and progressive educators to refrain from imposing a set of values, a point of view, or a problem solution upon the receivers meet with many barriers. Since the norm is control, noncontrollers must earn the perceptions that their efforts have no hidden motives. A bombardment of persuasive "messages" in the fields of politics, education, special causes, advertising, religion, medicine, industrial relations, and guidance has bred cynical and paranoidal responses in listeners.

Implicit in all attempts to alter another person is the assumption by the change agent that the person to be altered is inadequate. That the speaker secretly views the listener as ignorant, unable to make his own decisions, uninformed, immature, unwise, or possessed of wrong or inadequate attitudes is a subconscious perception which gives the latter a valid base for defensive reactions.

Methods of control are many and varied. Legalistic insistence on detail, restrictive regulations and policies, conformity norms, and all laws are among the methods. Gestures, facial expressions, other forms of nonverbal communication, and even such simple acts as holding a door open in a particular manner are means of imposing one's will upon another and hence are potential sources of resistance.

Problem orientation, on the other hand, is the antithesis of persuasion. When the sender communicates a desire to collaborate in defining a mutual problem and in seeking its solution, he tends to create the same problem orientation in the listener; and, of greater importance, he implies that he has no predetermined solution, attitude, or method to impose. Such behavior is permissive in that it allows the receiver to set his own goals, make his own decisions, and evaluate his own progress—or to share with the sender in doing so. The exact methods of attaining permissiveness are not known, but they must involve a constellation of cues and they certainly go beyond mere verbal assurances that the communicator has no hidden desires to exercise control.

Strategy and Spontaneity

When the sender is perceived as engaged in a stratagem involving ambiguous and multiple motivations, the receiver becomes defensive. No one wishes to be a guinea pig, a role player, or an impressed actor, and no one likes to be the victim of some hidden motivation. That which is concealed, also, may appear larger than it really is with the degree of defensiveness of the listener determining the perceived size of the suppressed element. The intense reaction of the reading audience to the material in *Hidden Persuaders* indicates the prevalence of defensive reactions to multiple motivations behind strategy. Group members who are seen as "taking a role," as feigning emotion, as toying with their colleagues, as withholding information, or as having special sources of data are especially resented. One participant once complained that another was "using a listening technique" on him!

A large part of the adverse reaction to much of the so-called human relations training is a feeling against what are perceived as gimmicks and tricks to fool or to "involve" people, to make a person think he is making his own decision, or to make the listener feel that the sender is genuinely interested in him as a person. Particularly violent reactions occur when it appears that someone is trying to make a stratagem appear spontaneous. One person has reported a boss who incurred resentment by habitually using the gimmick of "spontaneously" looking at his watch and saying, "My gosh, look at the time—I must run to an appointment." The belief was that the boss would create less irritation by honestly asking to be excused.

Similarly, the deliberate assumption of guilelessness and natural simplicity is especially resented. Monitoring the tapes of feedback and evaluation sessions in training groups indicates the surprising extent to which members perceive the strategies of their colleagues. This perceptual clarity may be quite shocking to the strategist, who usually feels that he had cleverly hidden the motivational aura around the "gimmick."

This aversion to deceit may account for one's resistance to politicians who are suspected of behind-the-scenes planning to get his vote, to psychologists whose listening apparently is motivated by more than the manifest or content-level interest in his behavior, or to the sophisticated, smooth, or clever person whose "oneupmanship" is marked with guile. In training groups the role-flexible person frequently is resented because his changes in behavior are perceived as strategic maneuvers.

In contrast, behavior which appears to be spontaneous and free of deception is defense reductive. If the communicator is seen as having a clean id, as having uncomplicated motivations, as being straightforward and honest, and as behaving spontaneously in response to the situation, he is likely to arouse minimal defense.

Neutrality and Empathy

When neutrality in speech appears to the listener to indicate a lack of concern for his welfare, he becomes defensive. Group members usually desire to be perceived as valued persons, as individuals of special worth, and as objects of concern and affection. The clinical, detached, person-is-an-object-of-study attitude on the part of many psychologist-trainers is resented by group members. Speech with low affect that communicates little warmth or caring is in such contrast with the affect-laden speech in social situations that it sometimes communicates rejection.

Communication that conveys empathy for the feelings and respect for the worth of the listener, however, is particularly supportive and defense reductive. Reassurance results when a message indicates that the speaker identifies himself with the listener's problems, shares his feelings, and accepts his emotional reactions at face value. Abortive efforts to deny the legitimacy of the receiver's emotions by assuring the receiver that he need not feel bad, that he should not feel rejected, or that he is overly anxious, though often intended as support giving, may impress the listener as lack of acceptance. The combination of understanding and empathizing with the other person's emotions with no accompanying effort to change him apparently is supportive at a high level.

The importance of gestural behavioral cues in communicating empathy should be mentioned. Apparently spontaneous facial and bodily evidences of concern are often interpreted as especially valid evidence of deep-level acceptance.

Superiority and Equality

When a person communicates to another that he feels superior in position, power, wealth, intellectual ability, physical characteristics, or other ways, he arouses defensiveness. Here, as with the other sources of disturbance, whatever arouses feelings of inadequacy causes the listener to center upon the affect loading of the statement rather than upon the cognitive elements. The receiver then reacts by not hearing the message, by forgetting it, by competing with the sender, or by becoming jealous of him.

The person who is perceived as feeling superior communicates that he is not willing to enter into a shared problem-solving relationship, that he probably does not desire feedback, that he does not require help, and/or that he will be likely to try to reduce the power, the status, or the worth of the receiver.

Many ways exist for creating the atmosphere that the sender feels himself equal to the listener. Defenses are reduced when one perceives the sender as being willing to enter into participative planning with mutual trust and respect. Differences in talent, ability, worth, appearance, status, and power often exist, but the low defense communicator seems to attach little importance to these distinctions.

Certainty and Provisionalism

The effects of dogmatism in producing defensiveness are well known. Those who seem to know the answers, to require no additional data, and to regard themselves as teachers rather than as co-workers tend to put others on guard. Moreover, in the writer's experiment, listeners often perceived manifest expressions of certainty as connoting inward feelings of inferiority. They saw the dogmatic individual as needing to be right, as wanting to win an argument rather than solve a problem, and as seeing his ideas as truths to be defended. This kind of behavior often was associated with acts which others regarded as attempts to exercise control. People who were right seemed to have low tolerance for members who were "wrong"—i.e., who did not agree with the sender.

One reduces the defensiveness of the listener when he communicates that he is willing to experiment with his own behavior, attitudes, and ideas. The person who appears to be taking provisional attitudes, to be investigating issues rather than taking sides on them, to be problem solving rather than debating, and to be willing to experiment and explore tends to communicate that the listener may have some control over the shared quest or the investigation of the ideas. If a person is genuinely searching for information and data, he does not resent help or company along the way.

CONCLUSION

The implications of the above material for the parent, the teacher, the manager, the administrator, or the therapist are fairly obvious. Arousing defensiveness interferes with communication and thus makes it difficult—and sometimes impossible—for anyone to convey ideas clearly and to move effectively toward the solution of therapeutic, educational, or managerial problems.

References

1. J. R. Gibb, "Defense Level and Influence Potential in Small Groups," *Leadership and Interpersonal Behavior,* ed. L. Petrullo and B. M. Bass (New York: Holt, Rinehart and Winston, 1961), pp. 66–81.
2. J. R. Gibb, "Sociopsychological Processes of Group Instruction," *The Dynamics of Instructional Groups,* ed. N. B. Henry (Fifty-ninth Yearbook of the National Society of the Study of Education, Part II, 1960), pp. 115–135.

PROBES

Does Gibb see defensiveness as a relational thing—something that's created *between* persons—or does he see it as something one person or group creates and forces on another person or a group?

Like Rogers in Chapter 5, Gibb cautions against evaluation. Is it possible to be nonevaluative? Or is that what Gibb is asking you to do?

Although most of Gibb's examples use verbal cues, each of the categories of defensiveness and supportiveness is also communicated nonverbally. Can you identify how you nonverbally communicate Evaluation? Control? Strategy? Superiority? Spontaneity? Empathy? Equality?

Self-disclosing is one way to communicate spontaneity. Can you identify communication behaviors that help create the other kinds of supportive climate?

Which categories of defensive behavior are most present in your relationship with your lover or spouse? Your employer? Your parents? Which categories of supportive behavior characterized those relationships?

> *I have two principal ways of discovering the areas where I fail to see myself. The first is acknowledging the qualities in others which irritate me. The second is recognizing the comments that make me defensive. All I have to do to discover what rankles me in other people's behavior is to review my latest encounters, but I have more difficulty recognizing when I am being defensive. I can identify it best by the following syndrome: I answer quickly. I feel in need of talking at length, and I feel impatient when interrupted. I explain. I try to persuade. But I feel frustrated even if I appear to succeed, as if the damage has already been done. I think hurriedly, and I feel a strong resistance to pausing and considering, as if something will be lost if I do this. My face feels fixed and serious. I usually avoid eye contact immediately after hearing the comment. I am incapable of taking the comment any way but seriously; the words never seem light or funny to me. When my reaction becomes apparent to the people present they often take the situation lightly. I feel somewhat misunderstood and misused.*
>
> HUGH PRATHER

Susan Campbell's message is important; I hope you can hear it clearly. At one level she is talking about the difference between cooperation and competition. She makes a point that you've probably heard before—at least it's something we've known for a long time: It's impossible to manage conflict productively when the participants are in a "dog-eat-dog" mindset, but as soon as people begin thinking cooperatively, conflicts almost immediately begin to dissolve. In other words, the participants' mindset can make all the difference. So if you really want to learn to cope effectively with conflict, begin with your mindset, your definition of the situation, or your point of view.

That's easy enough to say, but very difficult to do. You have to learn to *pause,* as Rollo May suggests in Chapter 4, actively to search for potential and actual points of commonality that are being obscured by the threat and heat of conflict, and then to muster the combination of trust and risk that are required for your mindset to change. You do not have to give up your own position. But you do have to trust that the "other side" has a legitimate position too. As I suspect you know, when you can manage all these steps, the payoff is worth it. But it isn't easy.

At another level, Campbell is making an even more fundamental and more significant point about paradox. It's a point that echoes some of what I said in Chapter 1, and it's an idea implicit in Laing's "Knots" in Chapter 6, and even aspects of Postman's "The Communication Panacea" in Chapter 8. It's also the point of Hugh Prather's comment at the end of the book. Campbell's point is that "contradiction" or paradox is part of the way things are with humans, and our efforts to overcome this phenomenon are often misguided.

This more fundamental point surfaces in Campbell's sections called "Reconciling the Irreconcilable" and "Power Struggle and Paradox." In the former, she recounts an experience where she *felt* that "either–or" was becoming "both–and." As she puts it, "My ambivalence had become two-sidedness rather than oppositeness, polarity rather than polarization." The effects were profound. Although she says she can't articulate them precisely, she tells how her acceptance of what she calls the "*natural messiness* of things" has had a significant impact on how she deals with conflict in her life.

In the final section of the reading the author applies this insight to four important paradoxes that we all experience. Each one can contribute to arguments and other kinds of conflict. The first has to do with power and control. "When I am terribly attached to having something happen a certain way," she reports, "that is usually when I will be frustrated. When I am relaxed about the outcome, I am more apt to be satisfied." The second deals with intimacy and indifference, paradoxical feelings of closeness and distance. The third paradox is about the relationship between diseases and cures, problems and solutions. As Campbell puts it, "The more skilled we become at solving problems, the more problems we have."

The fourth is, I think, the most important. I talk about it as the relationship between responsibility and response-ability. In her words, "You are responsible for the quality of your own state of mind, and at the same time you are responsible for the 'waves' you create around you, which influence others."

This excerpt offers some weighty chunks of wisdom, and I use that term advisedly. Even though you will find it easy to read and quite brief, I encourage you to go over it more than once. Campbell's message applies directly to your efforts to manage conflict and almost as directly to every other aspect of your interpersonal communicating.

From Either–Or to Both–And Relationships

Susan M. Campbell

The back door slammed a little harder than usual. In spite of her better judgment, Margie called out, "Daniel, did you wipe your feet?" After 13 years of marriage she knows how to read Daniel's door-slamming signals. She knows he is irritated about something. But she has needs too, and one of them is to keep her freshly-polished kitchen floor clean for tomorrow's dinner guests.

"How was your day?" she inquires as Daniel shuffles mechanically into the living room, unloading books and papers as he goes along.

"Huh?"

"You don't seem to be in a very good mood," she tries again.

"Look, don't tell me what kind of mood I'm in—I feel fine! And how many times do I have to tell you, I'm not one of the children—I *don't* need to be told when to wipe my feet!"

We're at it again, Margie thinks to herself. I just want to express myself, and I wind up putting him off. He never wants to hear about the things that concern *me*.

We're at it again, Daniel thinks to himself. She knows I've had a hard day and she can't wait to start badgering me.

Margie and Daniel *are* at it again. This is just a little incident, but it is typical of so many little incidents. They have learned to live with a certain level of tension in their relationship, but each wishes secretly that there were a way to get back the good feelings they once had together.

Have you ever tried and tried to get another person to understand your needs, and found that the harder you tried, the less understanding the other person became? Or that the more you asserted your interests, the more assertive the other became in response?

Many relationships reach a point where the partners have forgotten why they got together in the first place. This can happen at home, at work, in friendships. You may be slighted in some small way, so you return the slight. We do have the power to hurt one another, so to protect ourselves from being hurt, or to respond to a real or imagined hurt, we begin to *disconnect,* to pull the plug on our emotional connection.

From *Beyond the Power Struggle: Dealing with Conflict in Love and Work* © 1984 by Susan M. Campbell. Reprinted by permission of Impact Publishers, Inc.

Daniel and Margie reacted as most of us do when others seem unsympathetic to our needs: they escalated the situation, asserting their needs even more forcefully. As they felt increasingly disconnected from one another, they became more and more adversarial. They were creating a power struggle. . . .

Either–Or Thinking and the Power Struggle

"Seek no contract, and you will find union." This ancient Taoist maxim illustrates one of the great paradoxes of human relationships: the harder you try for agreement, accord, communion, the more these qualities elude you. When you are *trying* to be in harmony with others, your attitude belies the fact that you are not. If instead your actions are based on a feeling of connectedness with others, the question of agreement or disagreement becomes irrelevant.

Us and them. Yours and mine. Winners and losers. Some people go through life assuming that their interests are at odds with those of others. They spend a lot of time protecting their own interests. Those who see their interests as aligned with others' feel no such need for protection.

The desire for contracts or other legalistic agreements stems from fear or lack of trust. That same fear and lack of trust leads to *power struggles:* "Let's write it down so we know who is in control here!" Such insecurity is not resolved by avoiding contracts or suppressing fears, however. Those approaches simply treat the symptoms and not the cause of the disease. The answer lies in changing one's way of thinking about relationships with other people.

The fears that lead to power struggles are usually based on *either–or thinking.* It is either–or thinking which causes a mother to feel threatened if her son shows special affection for the mother of a friend—because "if he gives affection to her, he's taking affection from me." It implies a closed system, where the other mother's gain is her loss, since "there's only just so much love to go around." People believe that *either* you get your way *or* I get mine, and the world they create reflects this attitude.

If we are to have any chance at all of experiencing the world's abundance, we first need to change our thinking about the kind of world we live in. We need to change our habitual way of constructing what we think of as real. Most of us have been conditioned to think in either–or terms, to divide our world up into bits and pieces and parts, each segment having a separate and independent existence of its own. In childhood, we had your toys and my toys. In adolescence, we had the in-group and the out-group. In adulthood, we have success and failure.

In relationships, according to the either–or mind set, we have your needs and my needs, your way of doing or seeing things and mine. And when you assert yours, I feel threatened and protective of mine.

Do you tend to feel more comfortable with others when they agree with you and less so when they disagree with you? It's a common reaction, and it suggests a feeling of threat associated with differences or disagreement. Many people are unaware that they feel threatened by differences. They simply know they feel uncomfortable around certain people. But why should anyone feel threatened or uncomfortable when confronted with a difference in viewpoint? Because most of us were taught that *either* your way *or* my way is valid. We rarely consider the possibility that *both* may be!

The way out of the either–or trap, the way to get beyond the struggle-oriented mind set, is to begin to think in *both–and* terms. This expansion allows in more information. It is changing a camera's lens from standard to wide angle. You can see more all at once, and this allows you to see interconnectedness among things you once thought to be separate.

The Expanded View: Both–And in Action

I once owned a house in a "nicer" section of an old New England town. It was the custom in that neighborhood to keep the Cape Cod style homes neatly painted, the shrubbery well-groomed and the lawns freshly mowed. After I had been living there for about six months, I noticed that my next door neighbor, Shady Houlihan, had begun to neglect the upkeep of his property. The paint on his house had begun to peel noticeably. He had stopped mowing his lawn. And he was often seen sitting in his front yard in a rusty old lawn chair, unshaven, nursing a bottle of whiskey. My first impulse—and that of several other neighbors—was to somehow make him feel unwelcome in the neighborhood, in hopes that he would decide to move. We feared that the condition of his place would affect our property values.

During one neighborhood gathering, several of us were bemoaning the continued deterioration of Shady's place when someone mentioned that it had all started when he lost his job as a postman. He'd held the job for 15 years, had been unable to find another and had become depressed. As the discussion continued, someone else suggested that if anyone could help Shady find work, he might recover. We might all be spared continued concern over declining property values and deteriorating appearance of the neighborhood.

I remembered a Federal grant that had recently funded a teen drop-in center in a nearby town. One of the positions that had not yet been filled was that of caretaker. I decided to talk to Shady to let him know about this possibility of work. Shady showed considerable interest and aptitude for the position and eventually took the job. His depression lifted. He began to take care of his house and yard. And everyone in the neighborhood felt good about having a hand in Shady's recovery.

Like most stories, this one has a moral. When Shady's neighbors were seeing the world in *separative* terms, with us on the right side of the fence and him on the wrong side, all we could think of was how to get rid of Shady. This was a highly unrealistic solution because his was the only house in the neighborhood which was not owned mostly by the bank. His home was paid for. He'd lived in the neighborhood longer than any of us, and it was almost certain that he was there to stay. Thus, not only was the separative solution self-centered, it was also impractical. When our thinking shifted toward a view which emphasized our *connectedness* to Shady, as neighbors with a common interest and as fellow humans, then we were able to achieve a solution that was both practical and humane.

Seeing the world with an expanded view that shows how interconnected we are with our neighbors can help us bring new resources to bear on problems, resources we might never otherwise discover.

Seeing the world in separate parts, and yourself as separate from your fellow humans, can justify behaving in terms of narrow self-interest. When we step back to see the larger picture, we may find that it is ourselves we have hurt.

In close love and work relationships, the awareness of our interdependence usually comes naturally. The needs and views of *both* people seek harmonious expression—or at least peaceful coexistence. Without this, the relationship feels incomplete.

Yet most of us resist the experience of a deep and abiding harmony, even as we long for it. There seems to be a fear of what we may lose in merging with another, which can overshadow our hope of what we may gain. This simultaneous wish for harmony, alongside the fear of losing our individuality, leads to inner conflict. We seem unable to allow fear and hope to gracefully coexist within our psyches.

If we could break the habit of either–or thinking, which conditions us to pursue either harmony or individuality, we could see the larger picture—and perhaps recognize that both needs naturally occur together and can be satisfied together.

Reconciling the Irreconcilable

After spending the first 35 years of my life in a state of almost perpetual ambivalence, I began to search for relief. I was beginning to get awfully tired of the amount of energy I was wasting on this pattern of recurring inner conflict. Sometimes I seemed to feel peaceful and contented with my life, but I now believe that this was because the conflict had temporarily receded into the background of my awareness—I was simply busy with other things.

Do I express my anger or my hurt? Do I feel happy or sad? Do I love him or hate him? I was constantly plagued by questions such as these. I couldn't seem to settle on one way or the other to feel or to act.

Then one day I had an unexpected insight into another state of consciousness. I was co-leading a week-long encounter group at a Quaker retreat center in upstate New York. The theme of the workshop was "Encounter and Silence." By about the fifth day of the group, almost all of the 28 participants had experienced a significant catharsis or illumination. As the leader, I had not allowed myself the luxury of a deep emotional experience, however. I had been maintaining an air of composure and control as people all around me were having breakdowns and breakthroughs.

I began to notice that, although I could feel empathy with others' feelings, my own emotional sensitivity was becoming more and more blunted as the week wore on. It seemed as if I might be trying to armor myself against the intrusion of my own pain, so that I could pay attention to that of the others. Yet their pain was subtly stimulating similar feelings within me. I tried to pretend everything was all right with me. I played my role as group leader competently and effectively.

On the evening of the fifth day, the dam broke. Holding myself back from the group had led me to a stark awareness of my aloneness. I wept openly and told the group of my almost constant struggle with my inner ambivalence—a struggle which I had hidden from others since it first developed in my late adolescence. I seemed always to be of two minds, sometimes more. Everyone around me had always seemed so definite, so certain. I, on the other hand, could never decide what I felt because I always felt such a mixture of things. As I babbled and wept and allowed myself to be comforted, I slowly began to feel a strange and different sensation welling up within me, a feeling of utter despair entwined with a feeling of profound joy. It was a sensation that could not be called either despair or joy. I was neither happy nor sad, nor was I ambivalent. I was happy–sad: both grateful and despairing for my state as a human being, both trusting and insecure, both confident and helpless.

This experience is almost as vivid in my mind today as it was on that night, almost ten years ago. I will always remember the sense of wholeness, the freedom from inner conflict that I felt. My ambivalence had become two-sidedness rather than oppositeness, polarity rather than polarization. I experienced myself as *both–and* instead of *either–or*.

Somehow, and I can't say exactly how, my way of seeing things changed after that. I didn't demand of myself a choice between feelings like love and anger, fear and hope, joy and sadness. I let whatever was inside me be there, without trying to straighten things out or hide the messiness of my internal state. I still experienced mixed emotions, perhaps even more so than before. But they didn't feel so troublesome. I stopped trying to make myself "normal." And in the process I stopped feeling "crazy."

As time has passed and my lifework has come to focus on interpersonal relationships, I am beginning to see that many of the struggles that bring people pain in their relationships are similar to my struggle within myself. When you try to sort things out into neat little boxes, putting love over here and anger over there, fear in this box and trust in that one, you violate something about the *natural messiness* of things. When you expect B to follow A because it did once before, when you expect intentions to lead you in the intended direction, you ignore the absolute interconnectedness of everything alive.

I believe that this interconnectedness, mixed-upness or both–and-ness underlies the experience of what most people might call paradox or irony. You know the feeling: the harder you try to make something happen, the less likely it seems to occur. Or the more fully you come to know something, the more mysterious it seems. Or the more you come to love someone, the more they seem to provoke your anger. If experiences such as these cause you pain or puzzlement, perhaps it's time to learn more about both–and thinking. Many of our experiences don't seem to make sense when we think of them in the ordinary ways that we were taught. Our lives are full of paradoxes, or so it seems. But there is a more expanded, wide-angle view available to us. It is possible to relax and enjoy life's ironies!

POWER STRUGGLE AND PARADOX

I'd like to share with you some of the relationship paradoxes which I have encountered, and from which I have learned that life is to be experienced, not solved.

The Paradox of Surrender

Not long ago I began to notice that the harder I tried to achieve a particular type of relationship or to create a particular impression, the more these goals eluded me. Much to my surprise, when I *let go* of my attachment to how I wanted things to be, what I had been seeking did come to me!

- The more I tried to get my husband to *want* to make love with me, the more turned off he seemed to get. But when I accepted and appreciated the attentions he did give me, instead of concentrating on what *I* wanted, he "magically" became more loving.

- The more conscientiously I tried to ignore my husband's comments about former lovers (in the hope that he would soon stop doing this), the more he indulged his fantasies of the past. When I told him I was bothered by it, at the risk of making a big deal out of a minor irritation, he stopped. My "ignoring" it was actually making it into a bigger deal than mentioning it to him. When I let it go, he felt my relaxation and allowed himself to be influenced by my wishes—in a way that he could not when he felt my ill-concealed tension.

- When I tried to get my employees to work in the logical and organized way that I did, things in the office would get more and more chaotic and disorganized. When I came to know and trust each person's unique work style, after much discussion on the subject, I relaxed my concern with their sloppiness, and their work suddenly became more orderly.

Why do things often happen this way? Were people out to thwart my desires or teach me a lesson? Or was there another principle at work here? I believe the answer has to do with what I call "the paradox of surrender." When I am terribly attached to having something happen a certain way, that is usually when I will be frustrated. When I am relaxed about the outcome, I am more apt to be satisfied.

Attachment to having what I want seems to almost always be accompanied by a fear that I won't get it. This fear tends to inhibit the free exchange of energy between myself and another. We become less open to one another, less able to feel our natural empathy and connectedness with one another, less able to anticipate each others' needs. Thus, things often become discordant for no apparent reason. My lovers and co-workers were probably not intentionally resisting me. They just couldn't feel a clear, trustworthy connection to me anymore.

I have a friend, Harvey Bergdorf, whose situation clearly illustrates the paradox of surrender. Harvey is always saying to me, "I want so much to find a deep lasting love relationship that I seem to scare women away." This statement shows that Harvey already has a clue about why his lovers always leave him. It also contains a plea for deeper understanding of his situation.

As I think about my friend now, recalling the stories he has told me of the ups and downs of his love life, I'd like to speculate about what may be at the root of Harvey's unluckiness in love. Embedded in his wish for love is an even stronger *fear* that he won't find it. On top of this, he is angry at women in general because he has been hurt so often. And, as if that weren't enough to scare women away, he also feels a bit sorry for himself. Whenever he pursues the attentions of an attractive woman, he carries this negative emotional "baggage" with him. The woman can intuit the extra load Harvey is carrying, and although she may be attracted to him, she can't seem to get close to him. She herself may not even understand her negative response. It doesn't make rational sense. Harvey is an attractive guy. But there is something about the psychological space between the two would-be lovers that is cluttered. Harvey's baggage is in the way. He holds his fears and negative expectations so closely to him that there is no room for a woman's love.

Viewing the situation superficially, you'd think an attractive, eligible bachelor like Harvey could have his pick of women. But when we look at those relationships in more detail, we see not just Harry but the emotional climate between him and the women in his life. Only then do we see his fears—and her reactions to his fears—as important ingredients in the relationship.

If Harvey or his women friends could sense this interference with their mutual openness, they might then see themselves holding so tightly to how they want it to be, or how they fear it will be, that they cannot feel how it is. Usually conscious recognition and acceptance of a condition are necessary before change can occur. Harvey needs to admit how tightly he is holding on to his fears before he can begin to let them go. . . .

The Paradox of Understanding

[Another] relationship paradox involves the experience of knowing another person deeply. Often the more intimately I have come to know another, the more I can love and appreciate him, and in a sense, the more connected I feel to him. Yet at the same time, the more I know about another, the more I see our differences and areas of potential misunderstanding. The more I know him, the more reasons I find for loving him and at the same time the more reasons I see for leaving him. As I see him in greater depth and in a wider variety of situations, I see the ways in which he is absolutely himself, not an extension of me. This brings me to let go of needing him to be a certain way in conformity to my needs.

As this process of letting go is occurring, it has often felt at first as if I am becoming detached, indifferent or less loving toward my partner. This is not really the case, unless I am harboring anger about the realization that he is beyond my control. Ordinarily, the true appreciation of other-ness is accompanied by a calming and cooling down of the fire in the relationship, for much of the fire has to do with projections and fantasies.

Along with this cooling and calming comes a fullness, a sense of being satisfied with how it is, a letting go of the images and expectations of how it should be. I call this the paradox of understanding. The more I come to know another, the more I see the impossibility of completely understanding him. And as I accept this fact, my alienation dissolves into a deeper sense of understanding. I come to a point in the relationship where I realize that our differences, like our similarities, don't really make any difference when it comes to loving one another.

Realizations such as this can only come when I am able to remember to observe my reality through the wide-angle lens of past–present–future, as one continuity in time. The way I feel today may be altered radically by the day after tomorrow. The only way to get a consistent picture is to view things from the widest possible angle.

In the research I conducted for *The Couple's Journey,* I found that most couples need to experience ups and downs together before reaching the Stability Stage. After several years of loving and sharing and struggling, people begin to realize the source of their ups and downs. They see that sometimes their differences and disagreements cause pain and sometimes they do not. They become aware that it is not differences but one's *resistance* to differences that causes pain. And while it is true that the longer two people live or work together, the more differences they encounter, time can also bring a broadened perspective on these differences, and a lessening of the resistance to them.

Viewing your relationship from a broad time perspective allows you to see your differences in their context: a stable mosaic of experiences, somewhat changing, somewhat constant. Such a perspective is basic to the feeling of understanding.

The Iatrogenic Paradox

Medical researchers have found that new illnesses tend to occur in the population just as cures for these illnesses become available to medical science. Also, as the cure becomes more readily available, the incidence of an illness will increase. The more advanced the technology became for detecting and treating skin cancer, for example, the more cases of this disease were reported. As more people became trained as marriage counselors, more couples experienced problems in getting along.

In my own close loving and working relationships, I have observed that the better we become at resolving our interpersonal differences, the more differences we encounter. The more skilled we become at solving problems, the more problems we have. This seemed to me unfair at times. But as I became better able to solve problems, problems were no longer a nuisance. They were simply events calling for attention.

Thus, once again as my perspective expanded, as I was able to feel both my problem-solving capacities and my limitations needing corrective action, the apparent contradiction dissolved.

It is said that life never confronts you with any problem that is too big for you to handle. This statement may be simply a way of giving comfort to people in adversity. On the other hand, it reminds me that often it is the people who know best how to solve problems or face challenges that we find taking on even bigger challenges.

In ashrams or other centers for spiritual development, teachers always give the harder tasks to the more advanced pupils. This is true in most educational systems. Thus, if you pursue self-development because you think it will make your life easier, you may be surprised. Yet your surprise may not be altogether unpleasant, since you may find as you develop yourself that you no longer desire a problem-free life. You may even find yourself seeking out challenges that stretch your talents and capacities.

The Paradox of Responsibility

People who have been working for a while to develop their self-understanding realize that each of us is responsible for her or his own mental state or mood. Yet at the same time we see how affected we are by the moods of others close to us. Conversely, we know that the quality of our feelings and thoughts can profoundly affect those around us. You are responsible for the quality of your own state of mind, and at the same time you are responsible for the "waves" you create around you, which influence others.

When I am feeling anxiety, I radiate a dissonant or jagged energy field. When I am feeling calm, the waves around me are smooth and undisturbed. The subtle energy field that exists just surrounding my physical body sends out vibrations like electrical impulses through the air. People around me can feel my mood and level of tension.

We are all very good at nonverbal communication, whether we recognize this or not. Think of the times you have entered a gathering of people, not knowing what to expect. Do you remember how you could sense the mood in the room, the level of spontaneity or formality, of hostility or friendliness? You received this information through the airwaves, sort of the way a radar dish receives impulses from distant sources. Your senses are always scanning. And you are always sending. As the familiar saying goes, "You can't *not* communicate." No matter what we are doing, even in our sleep, our bodies are radiating some kind of vibratory information reflecting our inner state.

The closer my relationship is with another, the more that person will feel and perhaps be affected by my moods, for better or for worse. If my inner feeling state changes, this is apt to be picked up immediately by my mate, and his state may change accordingly. If I become more relaxed, he may become more relaxed. As I tense up, he may do likewise.

In my graduate school training to become a psychotherapist, I was taught how to intentionally alter my state of relaxation or tension, attention or inattention, to help a client experience varying degrees of openness or anxiety. I was also taught to notice how the client's openness or resistance affected my own feeling state.

These same principles may be applied in love and work relationships. As I come to know a partner or co-worker, I come to know how that person tends to react to certain changes in me. And if I want to, I can intentionally alter my inner state to effect a desired reaction. Yet the other is still responsible for how he responds to this change in me. It's his filter that determines how he will interpret my behavior.

At first, it may have seemed paradoxical to say that I am responsible for the quality of my mood *and* you are responsible for the effect your mood has on me. But as we expand our thinking to a *both–and* perspective, the contradiction is easily accepted. We are again reminded that the interactive air space between two people is as important as the individuals themselves.

As partners become willingly responsible for how they affect each other, as they become willing to accept and able to feel how they are influencing and being influenced by each other, a sort of "sixth sense" can develop between them.

My Aunt Ida and Uncle Frank have such a relationship. If he has had a bad day at work, she can sense this before he comes home. She'll make special preparations for his arrival, putting on a fresh dress, cooking his favorite pot roast and banana cream pie. Then she will await his homecoming, ready to offer him whatever caring or attention he needs. Frank's attunement to Ida's moods is equally refined. He can sense, for example, when Ida, a former smoker, is wishing for a cigarette. At such times he will go to her and take her hand or hold her in his arms and give her a kiss. He knows that this helps to relieve her craving for a smoke and sets her mind at ease again.

Aunt Ida and Uncle Frank feel some responsibility for each other's moods. They feel how their own moods affect each other; yet they never blame each other for their own moods. Ida says she always tries to prepare herself so she feels calm and relaxed before she talks to Frank about something he has done that bothers her. Frank tells me that when he feels irritable or moody, he tries to remember to let Ida know so that she won't take it personally.

Uncle Frank and Aunt Ida are in their 70's. They did not learn these things from encounter groups or self-improvement seminars. They paid attention over the years to the exchange of energy and emotion between them and gradually they learned how to keep their love alive. They learned that when either of them is in a bad mood, this can upset both of them. Likewise, when either radiates good humor, this can help both of them feel better. They learned also that they did not need to be the victims of each other's low moods, that they could (usually) choose to be open to their partner's positive influence, while letting the negative moods pass without undue notice. . . .

PROBES

Either–or thinking and its concomitant power struggles can characterize many different kinds of relationships. As I write this, for example, I'm involved in negotiations with the publisher of this book, and power struggles are part of what we're dealing with. Where do you encounter this challenge? At home? School? Work? In your social life? Which of the features that Campbell outlines also characterize your power struggles?

Which public institutions foster "either–or" thinking and which foster "both–and" thinking? For example, courts foster the former and in principle the United Nations is supposed to foster the latter. Which others can you identify?

What problematic situation in your own life might be eased by your "reconciling the irreconcilable" as Campbell reports she did at the "Encounter and Silence" gathering?

Frequently people are skeptical about the "paradox" point because they don't believe it's really possible to reconcile power and surrender, intimacy and indifference, and so on. In a group of five to seven persons, discuss actual examples of each of these paradoxes that have been personally experienced by members of the group. I believe you will find that they are more common than you might have thought.

Campbell uses the metaphor of a wide-angle lens to suggest how you can improve your "both–and" thinking. What is her point here? How does that metaphor help her clarify what she means? What is the relationship between her point and Postman's discussion of "metasemantics" in Chapter 2?

Discuss the relationship between Campbell's discussion of Uncle Frank and Aunt Ida and my discussion of a "relational" perspective.

⁞⁞

In this selection Ron Arnett develops the point I made at the start of this chapter— that conflict is inevitable and can be productive—and he outlines a "dialogic" or "interpersonal" approach to conflict management. He tells how conflict can enhance a relationship by infusing energy, promoting creative change, and helping all the persons involved develop a clearer understanding of the positions and belief systems they are forced to articulate.

Arnett also explains how Martin Buber's dialogic approach to conflict begins with a recognition of the other person and the potential legitimacy of his or her point of view. You don't have to give up your position or give in to the other, but you acknowledge his or her right to hold a position that's different from yours. That's what he and Buber mean by "standing your ground while being open to the other's view." The challenge is to walk that "narrow ridge" between conquering and capitulating. Buber also emphasizes the uniqueness of each person and stresses the importance of affirming that uniqueness, even in conflict. Again, you need to strive for a balance between blindly going along with others and refusing to have anything to do with them. That's another dimension of the "narrow ridge." As Arnett points out, a third key element of confronting in dialogue is being response-able. Buber views responsibility as literally the willingness and ability to respond, to actually take the other person into account and let your thinking, feeling, and acting be affected by him or her.

When conflicting persons can practice all three elements—standing one's ground without berating the other, balancing individuality and community, and practicing response-ability—they can productively handle almost any disagreement that arises.

The Inevitable Conflict and Confronting in Dialogue

Ronald C. Arnett

THE POSITIVE POSSIBILITIES OF CONFLICT

Conflict is seldom viewed as an enjoyable process . . . [yet it] can have positive possibilities. . . . Conflict is often necessary to clarify issues and concerns. To always avoid conflict eliminates the possibility for new insight and understanding that the conflicting situation may reveal. One person affirmed the need for the human conflict in order to clarify concerns and generate necessary discussion.

> I find myself in a fairly high level of conflict in this college setting, with a whole series of people. And it's usually not personal. I'm fairly conflictless in terms of interpersonal relations. But on the question of public policy and procedure and so on, I find myself frequently running a kind of conflict situation. I tend to think that's creative. I tend to think that social settings tend to be protective of themselves and that it's conflict that chases out, gets things out front that need to be out front. So I don't find that bad. I've been influenced to some degree by the school of thought which is related to Harold Lasky, who argues that the idea behind democracy is conflict, that democracy is a way by which to regularize conflict, but it's not inherently anticonflict. That is, they view this conflict as a kind of motor to get things going.

Another individual said he wanted to affirm conflict. It can strengthen people and encourage them to grow. Yet another stated, " . . . I think it's possible for an outsider to look at a conflict situation and say it is destructive, when actually the participants may grow together and stronger in the process. Conflict between humans can generate positive consequences that may go undiscovered without open disagreement."

The above comments describe conflict as potentially helpful and constructive. The presence of conflict may reveal a healthy, not a destructive relationship. The absence of conflict between opposing parties may indicate that some form of physical or psychological violence is being exerted in order to repress differences. Sometimes families, groups, or governments attempt to repress conflict in the public domain, but this action does not make a problem or concern disappear. Instead, secretive meetings and unexpressed feelings of resentment become the by-products of not dealing openly with conflicting interests. Kenneth Boulding, the Quaker economist and peace researcher, has stated that the "chronic disease of society" is the equating of conflict and violence. Society can then legitimize using increased violence in order to repress conflict. Whenever conflict arises, it is quickly brought under control by a show of force. This response to conflict is typified by the presence of the National Guard at Kent State University or the parent or authority who states, "You must do as I say, because I said it and for no other reason." In either case, the result is the same—conflict is repressed, not dealt with in a constructive manner. Boulding has stated that a violent response to conflict:

> . . . frequently inhibits settlement; for it leaves no path to settlement open but conquest, and this may not be possible." Short of complete annihilation, Boulding asserts, violence is able to end conflict by repressing it, driving it underground, but it can do

Ronald C. Arnett, *Dwell in Peace: Applying Nonviolence to Everyday Relationships* (Elgin, Ill.: The Brethren Press, 1980), eight pages of excerpts from pp. 68–76 and 113–124.

so only as long as it remains preponderant on the side of the victor. Such resolution as may occur must come from another quarter. Violence cannot affect it.[1]

An atmosphere without conflict is not always an indication of a healthy situation; it may be a sign of repression due to physical or psychological violence.

In America, the conflict between black and white was repressed for years through psychological and physical violence. Blacks were kept "in their place" and not granted the rights and freedoms of white Americans. Segregated schools, churches and rest rooms, literacy tests before voting in the South, and placement in the back seats of public transportation were but a few of the ways the conflict was repressed. As long as the black people were held in check with these measures, the conflict only simmered below the surface. In 1954, Martin Luther King, Jr., then a pastor in Montgomery, Alabama, aided the black people in nonviolent protest and resistance. A bus boycott was enacted that established massive noncooperation and a desire to ride the buses in dignity, rather than humiliation. And so began an intensive nonviolent campaign to reclaim the dignity of the black people.

King did not promote violence but he did encourage needed conflict. As William Puffenberger stated, "one of the great things about the techniques used by Martin Luther King, Jr. was his way of escalating the conflict but not escalating the violence." Martin Luther King, Jr. realized that violence repressed conflict and that in order for change to occur, conflict would have to surface. The white community would have to face the repressed tension and conflict between the races. The fact that human conflict can be destructive is undeniable, but not all conflict should be avoided. Conflict escalation without accompanying violence allows issues to be dealt with that may have been previously ignored. . . .

Conflict in interpersonal encounters is not only an inevitable element of human communication, but it can actually enhance a relationship. Conflict happens when dissimilar perceptions, ideologies, values or desires collide. Conflict can enhance a conversation or relationship as an opponent offers her view of a situation. In conflict, new ideas or new possibilities for viewing an activity may be opened to both parties. A relationship can quickly grow static and boring if each party is continually in agreement with the other. Ideally, each human relationship should manifest an optimal level of difference in which there is just enough dissimilarity to maintain interest without attempting to verbally destroy the other. Not only is conflict inevitable, it is essential to the maintenance of a healthy, growing, and interesting human relationship.

Some positive aspects of interpersonal conflict are also described by Richard Walton in *Interpersonal Peacemaking: Confrontations and Third Party Consultation.* Walton states that a moderate level of conflict may have the following helpful consequences: First, it may allow new motivation and energy to be discovered by the conflicting parties. Second, the innovation of individuals may be heightened due to a perceived necessity to deal with the conflict. Third, each individual in the conflict situation can develop an increased understanding of his own perceptions by having to articulate his views in a conflicting and argumentative situation. Fourth, each person often develops a firmer sense of identity; conflict allows values and belief systems to emerge into fuller view.[2] Bach and Wyden in *The Intimate Enemy: How to Fight Fair in Love and Marriage,* attempt to teach couples the rules for constructive and beneficial conflict. They contend that, "verbal conflict between intimates is not only acceptable, especially between husbands and wives; it is constructive and highly desirable."[3]

An example of the positive, but nevertheless difficult process of meeting a conflict situation is revealed in the following incident. An organization was having a major conflict over the abilities of one staff member. Some members accused this particular individual of incompetence. But when the accusers were asked who had ever shared negative comments with them about this staff member, only vague antecedents such as "they" or "a number of committed persons" were given. This process of criticism went on for about one year. The staff person under question offered no protest to the accusations. He simply sat back and allowed the criticism to mushroom and become distorted. Due to the staff member's decision not to confront accusations, other members began to doubt his ability to contribute a positive force to the organization. Comments such as, "He is incompetent," or "He is always in a fog," became estimates of the staff member's ability. Finally, the staff member began to challenge his accusers. He documented his sixty-hour work week and the large number of projects in which he was engaged. He then pushed his accusers for specifics, rather than general statements of criticism. He finally entered the conflict with those members that questioned his abilities.

The result of both parties grappling with the conflict was that fundamental issues of disagreement, rather than vague generalities regarding this staff member's ability, began to surface. Two significant happenings can be attributed to the conflict situation: (1) individuals clarified their concerns—the staff member was not assertive enough in his work, and (2) the staff member displayed late in the conflict situation that he could assert himself as a viable promoter of something he believed. Conflict opened the door for clarification of issues and potentially for reconciliation as the issues and demands on the staff member were made more explicit. . . .

CONFRONTING IN DIALOGUE

Resolving a conflict in dialogue requires the recognition of the humanity of both parties in the conflict. This method of dealing with conflict is an initial step toward dialogue. An individual voices his view while attempting to understand the other's perspective, which invites an exchange between two or more individuals to occur. Dialogue can be invited by one party, but it can only be given life by the efforts of all parties in conflict. . . .

In dialogue, each person is allowed to voice his view and finds that action affirmed by his opponent even in disagreement. An individual may attempt to persuade the other, but he does not use the kind of force that would ignore the other's right to a particular viewpoint.

Commitment Yet Openness

The above comments point to two important components in a dialogical encounter. First, an individual needs to stand her own ground, while being open to the other's view. A person is open to change, but only as he becomes convinced that another solution to a conflict is more acceptable. In dialogue as both parties stand firm in openness to the other, the final resolution may be a combination of the opposing views or one party may persuade the other to affirm the perspective he once opposed, or a previously unrecognized solution may emerge from the dialogue. Second, as a person stands her own ground in dialogue, she affirms the other's right to the same privilege. An individual may disagree with the other's view of a situation, but his right to hold that view is supported.

Martin Buber referred to dialogue as the unity of contraries, in that the human must stand her own ground yet be open to the other in a single movement. The human must walk with his partner in dialogue on a "narrow ridge" between two extremes: (1) refusing to attempt to understand the other's perspective of a situation, and (2) forsaking one's own ground and blindly following the other's opinion. A listener who does not attempt to hear her partner's view is closed to different views. Only material that is compatible with his previous expectations and past prejudices is comprehended. The opposite problem is the listener who is too easily directed by her partner. She has no ground of her own and quickly accepts the other's comments and opinions. According to Buber, to invite a dialogical encounter, the human must give up both extremes. An individual must participate in a "holy insecurity" that does not cling to either extreme. The person walks a narrow ridge in a holy insecurity that requires him to stand between the extremes of stubbornly standing his own ground and blindly following his partner's direction.[4]

The walking of the narrow ridge between standing one's ground and being open to the other's perception of the world is revealed through the actions of Martin Buber on September 27, 1953. At that time, Buber was awarded the Peace Prize of the German Book Trade in Paulskirche, Frankfurt, Germany. His acceptance speech was entitled "Genuine Dialogue and the Possibilities of Peace." When Buber gave his speech to the German audience, less than a decade had passed since the Jewish people had been so horribly deprived of their humanity [by the Nazis]. As Buber accepted his award, he openly stated his heartfelt belief that no previous historical event had ever been so systematically executed and organized as the cruelty the German people had inflicted upon his people. He said:

> I, who am one of those who remained alive, have only in a formal sense a common humanity with those who took part in this action. They have so radically removed themselves from the human sphere, so transposed themselves into a sphere of monstrous inhumanity inaccessible to my conception, that not even hatred, much less an overcoming of hatred, was able to arise in me. And what am I that I could here presume to "forgive"![5]

Martin Buber stood his own ground and delivered a message to his German audience that he had neither forgotten nor forgiven the actions of the German people.

Buber could have ended his speech at this point. He could have stood his ground without the accompanying movement of being open to the other. He could have rejected the difficult task of walking the narrow ridge between the extremes of a closed mind and acceptance of what many in the audience had implicitly and/ or explicitly sanctioned. But Buber was not a man to address another with either a closed focus or an optimistic naiveté. He stood his ground and allowed his own voice to be heard; and in an accompanying dual movement, he opened himself to establishing a common link between himself and his German audience. The following quotation, from later in Buber's address, dramatically reveals his openness to the other.

> When I think of the German people of the days of Auschwitz and Treblinka [Nazi death camps], I behold, first of all, the great many who knew that the monstrous event was taking place and did not oppose it. But my heart, which is acquainted with the weakness of men, refuses to condemn my neighbour for not prevailing upon himself to become a martyr. Next there emerged before me the mass of those who remained ignorant of what was withheld from the German public, and who did not try to discover what reality lay behind the rumours which were circulating. When I have these men in mind, I am gripped by the thought of the anxiety, likewise well known to me, of the human creature before a truth which he fears he cannot face. But finally there appears before me, from reliable reports, some who have become as familiar to me by sight,

action, and voice as if they were friends, those who refused to carry out the orders and suffered death or put themselves to death, and those who learned what was taking place and opposed it and were put to death, or those who learned what was taking place and because they could do nothing to stop it killed themselves. I see these men very near before me in that especial intimacy which binds us at times to the dead and to them alone. Reverence and love for these Germans now fills my heart.[6]

Martin Buber was firm and clear in his speech. He engaged in an authentic dialogue of walking a narrow ridge in the realm of holy insecurity, in which he neither failed to listen nor forsook his own ground. . . .

The task of the human is to confirm the individual uniqueness of her partner whether in friendly conversation or heated argument and conflict. An individual may still attempt to change her partner's viewpoint, but in dialogue the other's individual uniqueness and humanity is recognized. However, the uniqueness of each human is sometimes forgotten, even when agreement occurs. For instance, one may convince another that one's view of the world is correct and then be annoyed by the particular manner in which the other acts on that view of existence. The human often forgets that the other will give his own unique expression to the carrying out of a task. One must be careful not to ask the other to give up her distance and become a carbon copy of herself in action. The goal is to confirm the other and, if necessary, to also wrestle with opposing views. . . .

Confrontation and Reconciliation

Martin Buber viewed each human as unique; he contended that a person in dialogue should affirm her partner's uniqueness. Throughout his thought, Buber recognized that distance and difference between humans is a natural part of the living process. But Buber did not believe a person was personally whole if he did not bring his personal uniqueness into relation with others. Personal wholeness requires uniqueness of person meeting with his fellows.

A lack of personal wholeness is present when an individual does not have the courage to stand her own ground and bring her own unique response into relation with another. Many times a person is afraid of what others may think of his personal and unique response to a situation. He then escapes taking responsibility for his own unique response or personal ground of understanding by avoiding meeting or entering into relation with the other in one of two ways. First, an individual may leave his ground and blindly follow the other's understanding and perception of an event, thereby escaping responsibility for his own unique response. The other's concern becomes his direction. For example, a person could leave his own ground and only feel the other's pain or hurt. This apparent helping of another could be detrimental to what the other may need. An individual may need to become more independent and not rely so much on his fellows. If the human stands his own ground, he has a perspective on the situation that is unique and different, which may help in the solving of the problem. The second way a person can avoid responsibility is by "protecting" her unique viewpoint or ground by holding others at a distance. This defensive maneuver shields her from various viewpoints. Thus, she is locked in on her own opinion, unable to receive stimulation that could confirm, or change her perception.

The human must find an option between blindly giving himself to others and distancing himself from the rest of humanity. In both cases, the person does not bring his unique response to the relationship. He avoids really meeting the other by establishing a technique of groundless self-giving or self-protecting defensiveness. People often do not stand their ground in order to avoid conflict. One may attempt to console the other without presenting one's own view, which may do an injustice to the other. A person cannot gain another perspective on the situation if the other is always forsaking his ground for the safety of a consoling statement. Conflict sometimes needs to be overtly acknowledged in order for the possibility of dialogue or an authentic relationship to unfold.

One needs to be responsible to the other by voicing her unique response in the relation. An individual does not give up his personally unique way of viewing the world. One meets one's partner on one's own ground and confirms her by being open to her view, even in argument. The human has the responsibility in a dialogical encounter to engage in this dual movement with the other.

As one responds toward the other in the relation, he "turns toward" his partner and attempts to experience "the other side of the dialogue." The other person is allowed to be fully present in the relationship. According to Buber, one should attempt to see through the eyes of his partner, in order to learn what the other's perception of a particular happening may be. Responsibility means hearing one's partner in the concrete moment or immediate situation and then responding from the depth of his being. This does not mean that an individual simply "spills his guts" to another. The situation must call for how much he should reveal.

Buber's attention to the concrete situation means that different situations require their own particular responses. No one can tell another how she should respond before she enters the situation, according to Buber's view of responsibility in dialogue. As each person brings his uniqueness to the situation, his response will naturally be different than another person's answer to that happening. As each person offers her own unique response to a situation, some responses will be more appropriate than others. Some individuals may listen to the situation and the other more carefully. Then they answer the particular need of the situation that is announced with their own unique response. Thus, for Buber, responsibility means standing one's own ground and being open to the other *and* the situation. Each person and each situation makes its own demands. The listener then answers, but with his own personally unique response.[7]

The importance of responding to the other in the unique situation requires an authentic listening to and answering of the concrete moment. There is no technique or formula for such responsibility; it is the bringing of one's unique response to answer an address from a person and/or situation. Martin Buber states:

> Genuine responsibility exists only where there is real responding. . . . [There is] no knowledge and no technique, no system, and no programme; for now [we] have to do with what cannot be classified, with concretion itself. . . . We respond to the moment, but at the same time we respond on its behalf, we answer for it. A newly created concrete reality has been laid in our arms; we answer for it. A dog has looked at you, you answer for its glance, a child has clutched your hand, you answer for its touch, a host of men moves about you, you answer for their need.[8]

As the human stands her own ground and opens herself to establish contact with the other, she does not have the safety of a technique or formula that tells her how to respond. The human merely has the responsibility to answer with her own response to the address she has received. . . .

As previously stated, dialogue requires an individual to understand the other's world and simultaneously stand her own ground. Dialogue with another in a caring confrontation focuses attention on the issue of disagreement without forgetting the importance of others. This mode of confrontation may open the door for an eventual beneficial reconciliation. Through the announcement of one's own voice and caring for the other, the possibility of reconciliation may be open after the conflict encounter. Dale Brown states the importance of confrontation in conjunction with reconciliation.

> An easy peace without confrontation is often achieved by keeping the lid on basic injustice. Confrontation apart from the context of reconciliation eventuates in an unending cycle of retaliation. Only peace achieved through confrontation, involving grace and judgment, love and justice, will suffice.[9]

Caring confrontation of the opponent can embrace a dialogical movement of standing one's own ground and voicing one's own opinion and simultaneously being open to the other's view, even in disagreement. It is possible to confront the issue at hand and still attempt to care for one's opponent; it is this dual movement which may ultimately lead to reconciliation, rather than retaliation.

References

1. William Robert Miller, *Nonviolence: A Christian Interpretation* (New York: Schocken Books, 1972), p. 34.
2. Richard Walton, *Interpersonal Peacemaking: Confrontations and Third Party Consultation* (Reading, Mass.: Addison-Wesley, 1969), p. 5.
3. George R. Bach and Peter Wyden, *The Intimate Enemy: How to Fight Fair in Love and Marriage* (New York: Avon Books, 1973), p. 17.
4. Maurice S. Friedman, *Martin Buber: The Life of Dialogue* (Chicago: University of Chicago Press, 1976), p. 3.
5. Martin Buber, *Pointing the Way: Collected Essays,* trans. Maurice S. Friedman (New York: Harper & Brothers, 1957), p. 232.
6. Ibid., p. 233.
7. Maurice Friedman, "The Bases of Buber's Ethics," *The Philosophy of Martin Buber,* ed. Paul Arthur Schlipp and Maurice Friedman (LaSalle, Ill.: Open Court Press, 1967), pp. 171–172.
8. Martin Buber, *Between Man and Man* (New York: Macmillan, 1972), pp. 16–17.
9. Dale W. Brown, *The Christian Revolutionary* (Grand Rapids, Mich.: Wm. B. Eerdmans, 1971), pp. 129–130.

PROBES

Think of a conflict you experienced in the past where the outcome was positive— you gained a new understanding of the other's point of view, the relationship was strengthened by surviving the disagreement, or whatever. Let yourself actually feel some of the value of that event. Now think about a conflict you're having or about to have. Seriously consider the potential *value* of this current conflict. What happens?

What do you think Buber meant when he referred to dialogue as "the *unity* of *contraries*"?

What role does listening to "otherness" (see the article "Say 'Rooo-beee'" in Chapter 7) play in a dialogic approach to confrontation?

"Responsibility means response-ability." Explain.

You might profit from reading the final essay in this book—which is also by Buber—in conjunction with this one.

There is an important difference between expressing my antagonism and being critical. When I criticize I say in effect "You are wrong," and I leave unspoken the part I am playing in the condemnation. Criticism is thus "safer" than stating my feelings as mine because the other person will usually respond to the words and not to me. If, however, I say, "This is what goes off in me when you do such-and-such," I am admitting that all criticism requires a criticizer.

HUGH PRATHER

CHAPTER 11

COMMUNICATION BETWEEN WOMEN AND MEN

I do not want to insist that equality between the sexes depends on women's meanings predominating; I do want to insist that women's meanings should be allowed to coexist, that they should be accorded equal validity. In other words, I am seeking a radical solution: I want a woman's word to count as much as a man's, no more and no less.

DALE SPENDER

These are excerpts from a recently published book called *Gender and Communication*. Its author is a speech communication professor who has familiarized herself with just about all the research on female–male communication. That was a major task; the bibliography at the end of Pearson's book includes over 1200 references to books and articles written by anthropologists, psychologists, sociologists, linguists, and communication researchers and teachers.

The first section of this reading makes a case for studying gender and communication. Pearson points out that in the United States, and to some extent in at least the rest of the Western world, we are undergoing a "paradigm shift" in our attitudes about masculinity and femininity. The controversy over the Equal Rights Amendment, Geraldine Ferraro's historic vice presidential candidacy, the growing presence of women in traditionally male professions such as law and medicine, and the growing presence of men in historically female professions such as nursing and elementary education are relatively obvious features of this paradigm shift. Less obvious, more indirect evidences of the shift also abound in, for example, changing family patterns and parenting practices, arguments over abortion, and disputes about the roles of women in religious institutions.

Whatever its general features, the paradigm shift touches each of us individually as we communicate with same- and opposite-sex persons affected by it. We can cope with the shift most gracefully as we learn more about the characteristics of male and female communication. That is why the bulk of this reading reproduces Pearson's discussion of male–female language differences. I don't mean by my selection to imply that nonverbal differences are unimportant. Verbal differences, however, may be more subtle and less well known. In any case, this overview should work as an introduction to the topic.

Pearson identifies three kinds of language differences: substantive ones, "substantive differences merging into structural differences," and differences of structure. Substantive differences include variations in word choice, structural differences include how long or often a person talks, and the borderline category includes such features of a conversation as questioning and offering compound requests.

As you may have expected, there are significant differences in male and female vocabularies. Terms for colors, for genitalia and intercourse, and the use of profanity and expletives all differ, according to the research Pearson cites. In addition, women appear to engage more than men in what Pearson calls "hypercorrection" and to use more intensifiers, hedges, fillers, and qualifiers. At the same time, Pearson notes, the differences appear to be shrinking rather than growing; "Men and women appear to be using more similar forms."

The research Pearson reviews also indicates that women make more "compound requests" than men and use more tag questions. The difference between "Come here" and "Would you please come here" is the difference between a simple and a compound request. A tag question softens a declarative statement by adding, for example, an "isn't it?" or a "can't we?" Pearson points out that both forms of talk are considered nonassertive and that at least one study suggests that they significantly weaken the impact of the women who use them.

Pearson next discusses general questioning patterns, and in that discussion, as in others, she makes some suggestions about what you might do with your knowledge of the differences. For example, she suggests that if you are a woman you "consider the questions you are asked before responding freely, then try to determine the purpose of prefacing comments with a question." If you are a man you "consider the appropriateness of the questions which you would like to ask and your own sensitivity in responding to the questions asked of you."

Pearson's discussion of structural differences reviews talk time, interruptions, overlaps, and silence. Briefly, men and high-status persons talk more, interrupt more, and overlap the talk of women more, and women "fall silent more often when they are interacting with men than do women or men in same-sex dyads, or than men do in mixed-sex dyads."

In the final section of the reading, Pearson suggests some "corrective action." Despite some research findings to the contrary, Pearson does not advise women to adopt a male style. A feminine linguistic style has some positive attributes, but the wisest course of action is for both women and men to broaden their language repertoire. In the final paragraph of this section Pearson offers some specific suggestions about how we might do that.

The primary value of this information is that it teaches both women and men about the actual, as contrasted with the assumed differences that characterize male and female communicating. Knowledge of the differences can alert us to efforts by others to stereotype us and it can alert us to our own stereotyping, too. That can be one step toward the goal of contacting persons as *persons*, not ignoring the differences but also not exacerbating or unnecessarily emphasizing them.

Language Usage of Women and Men
Judy Cornelia Pearson

INTRODUCTION

A judge in Wisconsin claims that a 5-year-old girl involved in a sexual assault case was "promiscuous," and the case receives national attention as local citizens demand the recall of the judge. In 1977 a Massachusetts father is the first male to win child custody in that state, and the movie *Kramer vs. Kramer* shows a father in the role of single parent for his son. Betty Friedan authors a new book in 1981, *The Second Stage,* in which she implies that her first book, published in 1963, *The Feminine Mystique,* is out of date. In *The Second Stage* she puts forth a new challenge for women, overcoming the "feminist mystique."

The changing roles of women and men are inescapable. The contemporary women's movement, which had its auspices in Betty Friedan's *The Feminine Mystique,* has obscured the clear perceptions of women and men which once prevailed in our culture. New definitions of "male" and "female" in the psychological literature call into question traditional masculine and feminine sex roles. Consistent with this new approach, the changing sociological nature of the family requires flexibility and demonstrates that the "nuclear family" is obsolete.

The topic of "gender and communication" is relevant today because of the vast sociological and psychological changes which are part of our culture in the 1980's. Whether we choose to entertain ourselves with the movies, television, or the radio, we encounter this topic. In the best-selling books we select, the magazines or newspapers we read, we are confronted with the importance of "gender and communication." And, whether we focus on legal decision-making, governmental action, or religious tracts, we see the central, but often hidden, role of this newly emerging topic of consideration.

Why are we concerned with the issue of gender and communication *today?* Why are research studies that focus on the communication of women and men, nonexistent twenty years ago, now filling traditional journals and necessitating the creation of new journals which are devoted solely to this topic? Why are courses on sex differences in communication, female/male communication, and sex and communication being introduced on campuses throughout the country?

Thomas Kuhn, in *The Structure of Scientific Revolutions,* offers some theoretical explanation for the prevalence of the topic of gender and communication. Describing the stages through which people perceive knowledge, Kuhn suggests that when we believe a set of "facts," we have what is known as a *paradigm.* A paradigm may be thought of as a set of beliefs which are internally consistent and which are derived from an over-riding belief or "fact." For instance, at one time people thought that the world was flat and developed theories based on that central belief. Later, people believed that the world was round and replaced their outdated theories with contemporary views that were in line with their new paradigm. The time span between the two paradigms, when some people hold to one point of view and others maintain the other perspective, is known as a *paradigm shift.*

In the same way that scientific knowledge moves through differing paradigms, our belief systems also change. At one time, we believed that women and men had specific roles to play and that deviation from these roles was suspect. For instance, women have been viewed to be nurturers of children, while men have been perceived to be hunters, or providers of food. Today, these perceptions appear to a number of people to be unusual and impractical.

We are now undergoing a paradigm shift concerning women and men in our culture. In the United States the sharp divisiveness over the Equal Rights Amendment demonstrates the positions of the two bodies of belief. On the one hand, there are persons who support the traditional perspective in which men and women are viewed as more different than alike; on the other, there are those who propose a more contemporary view in which men and women are viewed as more alike than different. The traditionalists do not maintain that men and women are completely different, and persons with the contemporary perspective do not hold that men and women are completely alike. Nonetheless, a considerable gap exists between the perceived proportions of similarity and dissimilarity which are ascribed to persons who are labeled "female," and "male." . . .

The association of gender and communication is an important topic for you because of the frequency with which you communicate with members of the opposite and same sex and the difficulty of explaining and predicting successful communication interactions. Without a knowledge of the contrasting and similar communication styles of women and men, you are likely to encounter defeat in your interactions with others. It is less probable that you will have satisfying personal relationships, and your chances for success in your career are reduced. To the extent that you are able to understand the information in this text and to apply it to your interactions with others, you will be more likely to understand, predict, and have successful interactions with others. . . .

GENERAL LANGUAGE DIFFERENCES

In order to organize the language differences that appear to occur between women and men in a useful way, we have categorized them into substantive differences, structural differences, and a category of differences which appear to be hybrids of these two. We will call this third category substantive differences merging into structural differences and will consider it between the other two categories for proper placement. Substantive differences are those modifications or variations that occur within messages; they may be thought of as the differing words or vocabularies used by men and women. Structural differences include the frequency of times that someone talks, how long each person talks, how willing an individual is to yield the floor, and how each person was able to secure his or her turn to talk. When we refer to substantive differences merging into structural differences, we include such features of a conversation as questioning, controlling the topic of the conversation, and offering compound requests. Let us first consider substantive differences.

Vocabularies

Women and men appear to have different working vocabularies as they make distinctive lexical choices. A recent study added behavioral verification to Lakoff's (1975) hypothesis that men and women make differing lexical choices (Crosby & Nyquist, 1977). Men use more colloquial or nonstandard forms than do women (cf. Graves & Price, 1980).

Another difference in the language of women and men concerns color terms. Before you continue reading this chapter, ask a friend of the opposite sex to name the colors of ten items in the room. At the same time, when she or he is writing down her or his perceptions, write down your own color descriptors for the same items. Compare your lists. You may find that they conform to the research findings in this area. Lakoff (1975) noticed that women appear to have a far more discriminating set of names for colors than do men. Words like "puce," "chartreuse," "mauve," "ecru," and "teal" are more likely to show up in a conversation among women than among men. Specific career lines make great use of color, however, and it would not be surprising for a person in interior design, painting, or other creative fields to be sharply aware of these colors, regardless of this individual's sex. We may also see an alteration in the awareness of colors by men in the future. While women use more exotic or "fancy" words for colors than do men, younger men tend to use more discriminating or elegant words than do older men (Rich, 1977). In other words, younger men who at this time do not have the same vocabulary for colors as do women are making strides in learning and becoming aware of far more than were their predecessors.

Men and women do not discuss male and female body parts nor intercourse in similar language. Two researchers asked respondents to identify the terms that they would use to describe male genitals, female genitals, and copulation in each of four contexts—in informal conversation in a mixed-sex group, in informal conversation in a same-sex group, in private conversations with their parents, and in private conversations with a lover or spouse. They found that norms concerning sexual terminology did differ according to the context, with the most limited, most "clinical," terminology being used by both sexes in the "parent" context. Female subjects used a more limited vocabulary in all contexts than male subjects. Both sexes were more hesitant to name female than male genitals. Males used more "power slang" in discussing genitals and copulation, such as "my weapon," "my pistol," and "bolt action;" they were more verbal and employed greater variety in terms. Females used more clinical terms and more often manifested vagueness or made no response. The researchers speculate that the differences in terms between the two sexes may lead to confusion. In addition, women may feel more discomfort about their own sexuality and that of others than do men (Sanders & Robinson, 1979).

A more recent study replicated this investigation and provided more information. Simkins (1982) asked undergraduate students the terms they would use to describe female genitalia, male genitalia, and sexual intercourse in the same four settings used by Sanders and Robinson. Simpkins found that men and women tended to use formal terminology in mixed company and with parents. With same-sexed friends, males used colloquial terms for all three concepts, while females retained more formal terminology. In discussion with a spouse or lover, both males and females used formal terminology for the female genitalia; females retained a preference for formal terminology for male genitalia while men used more colloquial terms; both males and females used colloquial terminology for sexual intercourse.

A useful sidenote to this research is provided by Otto Jespersen, who wrote a classic text on language in 1922. Jespersen included a chapter on sex differences in language. Excerpts from the chapter are quoted, sometimes out of context, to illustrate how far we have come in eradicating language differences between women and men, or how little distance we have traveled in altering linguistic patterns between the sexes. Jespersen contends that men are the innovators of language and that they have far more words than do women. Although we can only speculate on the number of words which men and women each "possess," it is apparent that the two sexes tend to use different words.

Hostility, Profanity, and Expletives

Men appear more likely than women to use hostile words, profanity, and expletives. In 1975, Lakoff speculated that women are less likely to use profanity than are men. More recently Staley tested Lakoff's assertion and found significant results. She asked students who were ages 18–47 to respond to a questionnaire listing a series of emotional situations. For each situation, the respondents were to report the expletive they would use, the expletive which they predicted a member of the opposite sex would use, and to define each expletive they provided. Males and females averaged about the same number of expletives per questionnaire. A great difference in predicted response was observed; however, men predicted fewer expletives for women and women predicted more expletives for men. In addition, men predicted weaker expletive use by women. Both sexes judged female expletive use as weaker than male expletive use, even when the terms were identical. Both sexes viewed the expletives as devoid of literal meaning (Staley, 1978).

In the case of expletives, our stereotypes are not keeping pace with our behavioral practices. Men and women engage in similar behavior, yet they are judged to behave differently. The same situation may be true for modifications in hostile language since the most recent study was done in the early 1970's. At that time, females were found to use fewer hostile verbs than males. The researchers concluded that males are less inhibited in expressing hostility, although group pressure or social context may also influence the use of hostile verbs by men (Gilley & Summers, 1970). In the intervening 15 years since this study was completed, females may have increased their use of hostile language.

At the same time that Jespersen (1922) was describing male language as consisting of more vocabulary than female language, he was describing female language as that which included the most "decent words" and frequently included euphemisms. The notion that women would use more *euphemisms,* inoffensive words which are substituted for offensive terms, than men is parallel to the idea that men use more *dysphemisms,* offensive words which are substituted for inoffensive words. Although this conclusion is consistent with men using more expletives, more slang terms, and perhaps more hostile verbs, these findings are not stable. Instead, language may be changing in these areas for both men and women; in any case, we have little empirical verification for concluding that women do indeed use more euphemisms than do men.

Hypercorrection

Lakoff (1975) also hypothesized that women engage in *hypercorrection,* or reminding people of correct forms when they make errors. For instance, hypercorrection would occur if a person asked another, "You mean 'lie' instead of 'lay,' don't you?" "Do you mean *set* the glass on the table?" or "When are *she* and *he* coming?" Crosby and Nyquist (1977) demonstrated that women do tend to engage in hypercorrection more than men. We will note in Chapter 8 that women are more likely than men to pronounce words correctly and to use the complete "ing" ending of a word while men are more likely to mispronounce words and drop the final "g" of words which end with "ing." This correctness in pronunciation is parallel to women's greater likelihood to correct others; men's incorrectness in pronunciation makes them more likely candidates for correction.

Intensifiers, Hedges, Fillers, and Qualifiers

Women appear to use more intensifiers, hedges, fillers, and qualifiers than do men. Adverbs like "so," "such," "quite," and "awfully" are examples of *intensifiers* which women appear to use more than men (Key, 1972; Lakoff, 1975; Jespersen, 1922). One behavioral study which employed small groups of five to seven people found that women in all-female groups used six times more intensifiers than did men. In mixed sex groups, women used fewer intensifiers than women in same sex groups; however, in mixed sex groups, women used five times as many intensifiers than men in the mixed sex groups (McMillan, Clifton, McGrath, & Gale, 1977).

Hedges, or *qualifiers,* are words which modify, soften, or weaken other words or phrases. Hewitt and Stokes (1975) explain that hedges indicate the tentative nature of a statement or indicate some measure of uncertainty about the other person's response to it. Examples of such words and phrases are "maybe," "perhaps," "somewhat," "you know," "in my opinion," "it seems to me," and "let's see." When qualifiers or hedges are added to otherwise direct statements, such assertions become weakened and sound more tentative. For instance, imagine a parent scolding a child, "You should never touch a hot stove," compared to "Possibly you should never touch a hot stove." Or, contrast the woman who tells her date, "It's time to go," with her friend who states, "I guess it's time to go." Would you respond differently to your supervisor if she or he directed you to "Come into my office," than if the message was "Perhaps you could come into my office"? Crosby and Nyquist (1977) found that adult women use more hedges or qualifiers than do men, but Staley (1982) did not find any gender differences in the use of hedges by children aged 4, 8, 12, and 16. Staley observes that language behavior in society may be in the process of change and that linguistic sex role stereotyping may not be as predictable as it has been.

Disclaimers are a special class of hedges. Disclaimers are words or phrases which weaken or disparage the speaker's request or statement. The disclaimer suggests that the speaker is not serious, sincere, or very interested in his or her request. For instance, a person might say, "If you don't mind, could we . . . ," "I know this will sound unreasonable, but would you . . . ," "I hope you don't think I'm being unreasonable, but would you . . . ," or "Of course I don't know anything about politics, but I think. . . ." Persons who use disclaimers put the other person in an awkward position. The respondent does not know how he or she is to respond to the request or the information. If one acts upon it, he or she may be told later that the speaker said that it was unimportant or that one was being unreasonable; if the listener fail to act upon it, the speaker might say that he or she had made a request. Disclaimers confuse communication between two people and weaken the messages we send to others.

Verbal fillers and *vocal fluencies* frequently occur in our communication with others. Verbal fillers are those words or phrases that we use to fill in silences such as "like," "right," "okay," "well," and "you know." Vocal fluencies include uncodified sounds like "mmh," "ahh," and "eh" which are used for the same purpose. We are sometimes afraid of allowing a silence to occur when we are talking, so that we fill in the blanks with fillers or fluencies. Hirschman (1975) found that when women talk to men in two-person interactions, women use more fillers than do men. Women used fewest fillers when they were engaged in conversations with other women, although even here they used more fillers than did males in same-sex pairs.

Let us summarize the substantive language differences between women and men. First, they make different lexical choices or use different vocabularies. Women tend to use more formal terms, while men use more colloquial forms. Men use more hostile words, profanity, and expletives. Women engage in more hyper-correction than men. Women use more intensifying modifiers than do men, as well as more verbal fillers. In general, women appear to be more precise, more proper, and more polite than men. Although men and women exhibit substantive language differences, we may be perceiving far greater differences than those which actually occur. Our usage of language is constantly in flux, and men and women appear to be using more similar forms; at the same time, our perceptions of those forms tend to be somewhat outdated and stereotypical. Thus, our perceptions of language differences do not appear to be keeping pace with actual practice.

SUBSTANTIVE DIFFERENCES MERGING INTO STRUCTURAL DIFFERENCES

When we discuss structural differences in conversations, we are referring to a number of different components. Zimmerman and West (1975), for example, thought that the basic structure in a conversation must include the assumptions that usually one person speaks at a time and that generally people alternate as speaker and listener. We can thus discuss conversations from the point of view of "taking turns": how many turns each person took, how long each one's turn lasted, how willing each individual was to allow another to have a turn, and how each was able to secure his or her turn.

The notion of turns and taking turns is neither complex nor difficult to understand. At a noisy dinner table it is not unusual for children as young as two or three to tell others to be quiet because it is their turn. One of our children remarked to his garrulous grandmother that she had taken two turns when she had spoken and now was required to listen to him for two turns before she could again proceed. Although the notion of dividing conversations into turns is elementary, it is very useful.

When we examine taking turns in conversations, we find that all people do not take the same number of turns, that some tend to take far longer turns than others, that people challenge each other for turns, and that some people have definite ideas about who has the right to take a turn. Turns alternate very quickly. Anyone who has been associated with the theatre, radio, or television knows that silences generally do not occur after one person has spoken and before the next person begins to speak. When we are engaged in a conversation, we are typically ready to speak the moment the other person stops. Speakers generally provide us with transition cues which indicate that they are about to conclude their message and we can begin ours. Sometimes those cues are not present, however, or we do not notice them, so that two people are speaking at once, or no one is speaking.

When we examine language differences between women and men, we find that some variations are easily categorized as substantive differences while others are as readily classified as structural differences. At the same time, some differences appear to fall between these two categories. Substantive differences appear to merge into structural differences. For example, when sex differences are found on questioning-asking, are we considering structural or substantive differences? The substance of a comment is changed if it is phrased as a question rather than as a declarative statement; but the structure of the interaction is also affected as it calls for a comment from the other communicator. In this section . . . we will consider a number of such sex differences in communication, including compound requests, tag questions, the use of questions, the final word, and the control of the topic of conversation.

Compound Requests

When we make a request of another person, we may do so in a direct manner or we may add qualifiers and other terms to soften the request. If you wish to have someone come closer to you, you may simply say, "Come here." On the other hand, you may add, "Please come here," or "Would you please come here," or "If you don't mind, would you please come here." In each case, you are adding words and phrases which soften the request. If you use the command, "Come here," you are making a direct request or giving a direct order; if you use any of the other longer forms, you are making a *compound request.*

What are the effects of compound requests? They tend to sound more polite and less demanding than direct requests. At the same time, they sound tentative. If you ask someone to behave in a certain way, "If you do not mind," "If you would," or "If it would not inconvenience you," you appear to be asking them a question in which a choice is possible, rather than making a request of some action that you wish to have accomplished. Propriety and politeness are acquired at the expense of being misunderstood or not achieving your goal.

Compound requests are viewed as less assertive than direct requests or orders, and they are viewed as feminine linguistic forms (Newcombe & Arnkoff, 1979). Apparently women use compound requests more frequently than do men

(Thorne & Henley, 1975; Zimmerman & West, 1975). Women are more likely to ask others to do things for them with more words than their male counterparts would use. Though women may be viewed as more polite in their requests, they may find that they do not always obtain the action or response which they are seeking.

Tag Questions

Tag questions occur when we make a declarative statement, then follow it with a question relating to the same statement. For example, "It's really hot in here, isn't it?" "This is a good movie, don't you think?" and "They are all going out to dinner, aren't they?" are all tag questions. We sometimes use tag questions when we are not sure of information. If someone has told you something that you did not hear completely, or if you have reason to believe that a situation has changed, you might inquire, "You're going to attend U.S.C. this fall, aren't you?" We also use tag questions when we are trying to elicit information from another person, when we are attempting to obtain an answer to a question, or when we are trying to strike up a conversation. We might ask, "Texas is really lovely at this time of the year, isn't it?" "The game between Michigan State and Iowa was interesting, wasn't it?" or "This party is pretty dull, don't you think?" Finally, we use tag questions when we are attempting to persuade someone to accept or share a belief which we hold. You might suggest to your spouse. "Playing cards with the Millers tonight sounds like fun, doesn't it?" You might ask one of your parents, "The tuition at Georgetown is really expensive compared to Princeton, where I want to go, isn't it?" To a friend you might say, "I can borrow your brown suit for my job interview tomorrow, can't I?"

Tag questions are clearly less assertive than declarative statements; moreover, tag questions are viewed as being part of the female's linguistic repertoire rather than the male's language usage (Newcombe & Arnkoff, 1979). Early research in this area indicates that women make more frequent use of tag questions than do men (Zimmerman & West, 1975). In actual communication situations, women use twice as many tag questions as do men. In mixed sex groups, women use three times as many tag questions as men. Women in mixed sex groups also used three times as many tag questions as women in all-female groups (McMillan, Clifton, McGrath, & Gale, 1977).

Men in a professional meeting used far more tag questions than did the women who were in attendance. The context in which such questions are used should be considered in order to determine whether they are more likely to be used by men or by women. Tag questions do not necessarily indicate condescension; they may indicate simple requests, be used to forestall opposition to the speaker's statement, or function as requests for agreement or confirmation (Dubois & Crouch, 1975). Thorne (1981) also views tag questions as a contextual variable. She suggests that women may use tag questions in conversations with men in order to draw men out. Men are somewhat uncommunicative so that women may feel obligated to do the "embroidery" or "dirty work" in conversations. In other words, tag questions may not be a sign of uncertainty, but rather may indicate an interest in continuing a conversation. Women may ask tag questions in order to engage the other person in talking to them and give them an opportunity to look at the other person, listen actively, and contribute feedback.

A recent examination of tag questions yielded some disturbing results. In this investigation, tag questions were detrimental only when they were used by women.

In general, women who used certain devices, including tag questions and disclaimers, were perceived to have little knowledge, little intelligence, and little influence. The same negative effect was not produced by men who used tag questions and disclaimers (Bradley, 1981). This study implies that the linguistic devices which women have traditionally used may not be the significant elements in the devaluation of women's language; rather, the lower status of the women may be the relevant factor. Women who use tag questions are underestimated because of their biological sex rather than because of their linguistic style.

Tag questions may place the speaker in a subservient position or they may be functional in a conversation. Sometimes women appear to use tag questions to demonstrate concern for another person, and not because they perceive themselves as subservient. Nonetheless, others may perceive them to be subservient, even though this is not their intent.

Another linguistic style which is sometimes an appropriate, effective substitute for the tag question is the statement followed by a question relating to the other person's perceptions. Instead of using the tag question, "The University of Kansas really has a great number of courses in interpersonal communication, doesn't it?" a person may say, "The University of Kansas really has a great number of courses in interpersonal communication. Were you aware of that?" Instead of stating, "This is delicious lasagna, isn't it?" you might assert, "I think this lasagna is delicious. What's your opinion?" In each case, you clarify your own perceptions and still invite the opinion of the other person. At the same time, you are not compromising your own point of view; in other words, your perception of the university or of food may be different from that of your partners. The use of the statement followed by a question may be considered a useful addition to your behavioral repertoire. It is especially helpful when you are actually using tag questions to express your own opinions or feelings.

Questioning

Do women or men ask each other more questions? Sometimes men ask women more questions than women ask men. For instance, in a study of interaction among male-male dyads and female-female dyads, a greater proportion of the women's comments consisted of answers to questions than did the men's comments (Rosenfeld, 1966). In an analysis of the conversations of three middle-class couples between the ages of twenty-five and thirty-five, the women used three times more questions than did the men (Fishman, 1978). Thus, it is not clear which sex asks the other more questions.

Perhaps more useful than merely trying to determine whether questions are asked more frequently by one sex than the other is consideration of the rationale for asking questions. Eakins and Eakins (1978) state that asking questions and interrogating people are associated with behavior of the superior, while acquiescing or replying is often considered to be the behavior of a subordinate. We know that sharing personal information about ourselves, self-disclosure, which was discussed in Chapter 8, can be perceived as the loss of a resource, when viewed negatively. In other words, when we tell others about ourselves, we are providing them with information which they can use. . . . Women tend to provide more information about themselves than do men. The idea that women disclose more than men is related to the fact that they are asked more questions.

In those instances in which we determine that men ask more questions, we may hypothesize that this is done to gain information, and in a sense, to acquire power. On the other hand, men may be asking questions because they are interested in the other person. Similarly, either consciously or subconsciously women may answer questions in order to demonstrate subservience, or they may reply to questions because they enjoy interacting with others. Question asking and answering can be part of a power struggle in conversational interaction, or it may be a functional method of communicating, as in the interviewing process.

How can we explain the large number of questions women ask in established relationships compared to men? Fishman (1978) theorizes that women ask questions in order to elicit verbal responses from men. Frequently women preface their comments with phrases such as "Do you know what?" in order to gain a response from men. In these instances, they may be attempting to gain a "What?" or similar response which serves, in effect, as permission to speak.

The inconsistent findings on questioning and the alternative explanations for these differences disallow clear prescriptions regarding the use of questions in interactions. Nonetheless, to the extent that differences occur between men and women, we need to be cautious about behaving in traditional, stereotyped ways. If you are a woman, consider the questions you are asked before responding freely, then try to determine the purpose of prefacing comments with a question. If you are a man, consider the appropriateness of the questions which you would like to ask, and your own sensitivity in responding to the questions asked of you.

Control of the Topic

In *Through the Looking Glass,* this conversation between Alice and Humpty Dumpty occurs:

> "I don't know what you mean by 'glory'," Alice said.
>
> Humpty Dumpty smiled contemptuously. "Of course you don't—till I tell you. I meant there's a nice knockdown argument for you!"
>
> "But 'glory' doesn't mean 'a nice knockdown argument'," Alice objected.
>
> "When I use a word," Humpty Dumpty said, in a rather scornful tone, "it means just what I choose it to mean—neither more nor less."
>
> "The question is," said Alice, "whether you can make words mean so many different things."
>
> "The question is," said Humpty Dumpty, "which is to be master—that's all" [Carroll, 1965].

Although Humpty Dumpty was referring to the definition of words, his point is useful as we consider topic selection in conversations. Thorne (1981) asserts that the real power in controlling the topic of a conversation is the power to define reality.

Male–male, female–female, and male–female dyads have been investigated to determine patterns of topic change. Males, in male–female conversations, appear to assert strongly their claim to control topics (Zimmerman & West, 1975; Fishman, 1977, 1978). Male–female dyads in developing relationships do not talk as long about a topic as do two people of the same sex. In addition, male–female dyads use different strategies to change the topic. They tend to use more abrupt and direct methods, which may indicate that they are attempting to avoid over-commitment. Men, in male–male dyads, tend to use more indirect and gradual methods of topic change, that is, procedures which could be associated with a relational control process. Men may wish to avoid confronting the issue of who is to control the change of topics within conversation in male–male dyads (Ayres, 1980).

Associated with topic changes are the topics to which the conversation is changed. Four-, 8-, and 12-year-old males make more references to sports and specific locations while females of the same ages make more references to school, items they wish for, their needs, and their identity (Haas, 1981). Kelly, Wildman, and Ural (1982) contend that the use of male stereotypical topics may inhibit females from participating in conversations. Thus, both the content and the structure of the interaction encourage male control of the conversation.

Topic control is accomplished in a variety of ways. Among the more common are minimal responses to the other person's comment, silence, and interruptions. Delayed responses are also used to bring a topic to its conclusion, and if a theme is repeated too aggressively, you may decide to stop communicating with the other person: Walk away, say nothing, or look away from the other individual. In any event, keep in mind that in order for another person to control the topic, you must be willing to "relinquish the floor." The other person cannot control the subject of conversation unless you allow it to occur.

We can now summarize the material in this section on substantive differences merging into structural differences. Women make more compound requests than do men. Women tend to use more tag questions than men; although in some contexts, men tend to use this construction to a greater extent. Both women and men ask questions, but they appear to do so for different reasons. Males control the topics of conversations in male–female dyads, and may use abrupt and direct methods to do so. In male–male dyads, men use less abrupt and direct strategies to change the topic.

These linguistic forms tend to weaken or minimize women's statements, but they do not lessen or impair men's statements. At the same time, many of these forms serve necessary functions in the management of conversations. For instance, tag questions result in a woman being viewed as less knowledgable and less influential; however, tag questions may encourage another communicator to continue a conversation. When men use tag questions, they are not perceived as lacking in knowledge or influence. More than in the past, men and women may be using these linguistic forms in a similar way. Nevertheless, women are provided with negative sanctions when they use these forms, but men are not.

STRUCTURAL DIFFERENCES

We have considered substantive differences and the hybrid category of substantive distinctions merging into structural differences. In this section of the chapter, we will consider those language differences between men and women which appear to be purely structural. These include who dominates or talks more in a conversation, who interrupts, who overlaps, and how silence is used in conversational interactions.

Talk Time

Who talks more, men or women? If you ask people on the street their opinion on this question, you are more likely to receive consistently incorrect responses to this than to any other question discussed in this book. One of the most popular myths surrounding male/female communication is the notion that women talk more than men. In fact, men talk more than women (Eakins & Eakins, 1976; Wood, 1966; Swacker, 1975). In a summary of the research in this area, Thorne (1981) stated that most studies demonstrate that men either talk more than women, or there are no differences between the amount of talking men and women do. She points out that no studies have demonstrated that women talk more than men. Higher status women tend to talk more than lower status women. Boys are involved in more interactions than are girls. Male students talk more than female students, particularly when the teacher is female. Thorne's summary demonstrates that in a variety of contexts, and at various ages, men talk more than women.

An interesting study of parental interaction shows similiar findings. This study investigated mothers and fathers talking with their children. The parents and their children were placed in a room and told to play with each other. At first they were told to simply interact, but after a period of time a complex toy was introduced to the situation and the parents were told to explain it to the child. Women tended to adjust their speech when talking to the children, reducing their sentence length, making their ideas less complex, including more redundancy, and offering more pauses. When the parents were free to interact with the children, before the toy was introduced, the mothers and fathers talked about the same amount. When the toy was added to the situation, the women allowed the men to talk far more. The men were treated as "experts," even though they had no more information about the toy than did the women (Golinkoff & Ames, 1979). This study implies that one of the reasons that men may be allowed to talk more than women is that they are perceived as more knowledgeable, more competent, or in some way more credible.

Interruptions

Interruptions occur when the person who is listening begins to speak before the last word that could suggest the end of the speaker's statement, question, or comment. For instance, if one person were to state, "I can't wait to tell you what my mother said", and the second person began his or her comment, "Did you talk to Professor Fisher?" on the third word of the first person's statement, "wait," we would call the second person's comment an interruption.

Why do people interrupt each other? Some persons may interrupt because they are unaware of the implicit conversational rules which imply that one person waits for the other to complete expressing his or her thought before beginning to respond. Few people, however, are really unaware of this rule. More often, individuals interrupt because they are enthusiastic about something they have to share and are impatient about "waiting their turn," because they believe that what they have to offer is more important than the first person's message, or because they feel that they are personally more important than the other speaker.

Men interrupt others more than women do, and women are more frequently interrupted by others than men are interrupted by others (Zimmerman & West, 1975; Thorne & Henley, 1975; Baird, 1976; Kramer, 1974; Eakins and Eakins, 1978). Women appear to be less obtrusive and less forceful than men in conversational dominance (Frost & Wilmot, 1978; McMillan, Clifton, McGrath, & Gale, 1977). The pattern of interruptions between men and women might be anticipated, in view of our discussion of topic control. We noted that topic control occurs, to some extent, because people interrupt the speaker. We will see that this pattern is also consistent with overlaps which we will discuss in the next section.

The unequal distribution of interruptions between women and men should immediately cause us to be suspicious. Interruptions are generally perceived as attempts at conversational dominance, since they minimize the communicative role of the person being interrupted (Markel, Long, & Saine, 1976). Whether or not the interruptor is aware of this behavior, this individual is asserting relational dominance over the other person. Less pejoratively, interruptions are sometimes perceived as methods of controlling the interaction. In the same way that people control the topic of a conversation by "breaking in," they maintain control over the structure of the conversation by interrupting. Brandt (1980) demonstrated that the frequency of interruption is often correlated with a person's control over the direction of the conversation. In either case, interruptions serve to manage the interaction.

The same kinds of suggestions that were offered at the end of the section on topic changes apply here. If you are a person who is regularly interrupted, you should consider possible options. You can continue to talk even after you have been interrupted, you can ignore the interruption, or you can increase your volume. You can use the same tactics as the person who has interrupted you and allow him or her to talk but begin a new thought in the middle of his or her discourse. You can decide that you will not communicate with someone who continually interrupts you, say nothing, look away, or walk away from the other person. You can stop in order for the other person to present his or her message, then continue from the same point that you were interrupted, without responding to the interruption. You can describe to the other individual, in a non-evaluative manner what has occurred: "You have interrupted me three times in the last five minutes." Interruptions involve two people: the person who is doing the interrupting and the person whose statement or presentation is being interrupted. You are susceptible to being interrupted by others if you choose, or can indicate clearly that you will not be regularly interrupted by them if you find the practice dissatisfying to you. At the same time, you need to understand that your behavior will have consequences. To the extent that your communicative behavior is altered, the relationship between yourself and the other communicator is changed.

Overlaps

Overlaps occur when the individual who is listening makes a statement before the other person has finished speaking, but about the same time as the speaker's last word is uttered, or a word which could be perceived as his or her last word. For example, if someone states, "I would like to go to the movie at the Varsity tonight," and the second person responds, "Yes, me, too!" while the first person is verbalizing "tonight," the respondent's act would be considered an overlap.

Overlaps may occur for the same reason that interruptions occur: the second person believes what she or he has to add is more important than the message of the first person, or she or he is very enthusiastic about talking. Overlaps can be more easily justified than can interruptions. Often, the second speaker senses that the first speaker has about finished expressing his or her thought, and has simply begun talking a moment too soon. On the other hand, the person who overlaps may be attempting to shorten the first person's statement or to "gain the floor." Dominance and control are also possible reasons why people overlap each other. Whatever the rationale, men overlap women more than women overlap men (Zimmerman & West, 1975).

Silence

A final area in which sex differences occur is in the use of silences. Zimmerman and West (1975) examined the use of silence in female–female, male–male, and male–female dyads. They found that females in female–male conversations were silent more than any other person in the various combinations. In male–male and female–female conversations, the silences were scattered among the comments in a relatively equal manner. These researchers explained their findings by noting that most often the females who fell silent in the female–male dyads did so after one of three occurrences: a delayed minimal response by the male, an overlap by the male, or an interruption by the male. In these instances the female may have been uncertain about her partner's reaction to her comment or about the other person's feeling concerning the conversation. The less-than-positive response from the male partner appeared to affect the female's approval or enthusiasm about communicating.

Let us summarize these research findings. Men and persons of high status talk more than do women and low status persons. Men interrupt others more than women do, and women are the victims of more interruptions than are men. Men overlap women more than women overlap men. Women fall silent more often when they are interacting with men than do women or men in same-sex dyads, or than men do in mixed-sex dyads. The communicative patterns in this area imply that women are less competitive and aggressive in interactions; men appear to compete and win. Men talk, interrupt, and overlap more frequently, while women respond with silence. . . .

TAKING CORRECTIVE ACTION

We have determined in this chapter that far more restrictions and limitations are placed on women than on men in language usage, but men, too, have distinct ways of talking. One author writes that women are cautious about their language usage today because of the hold-overs from previous times (Haas, 1979). In other words, the role modeling provided by mothers and other groups or individuals influences our contemporary behavior to some extent. Differing language systems are detrimental to both men and women since they limit their behavioral options. In addition, the divergent language systems are conducive to misunderstandings between women and men.

Should women adopt a male style? Some authors have suggested that women use male structures (Lakoff, 1975). Specific research findings support this suggestion. Wright and Hosman (1983) determine that male or female witnesses in a courtroom setting were both perceived as more credible when they used a lower number of hedges. Stake and Stake (1979) posited that in women, confidence is followed by assertiveness. They imply that assertiveness is a characteristic which women should adopt.

All of the research does not encourage women to adopt male structures. While Wright and Hosman's investigation recommended the use of fewer hedges by both women and men, they also found that women were perceived to be more attractive when they used numerous intensifiers, a traditional form for women.

Another study shows that women who appear to be confident in small group interaction exert influence, but they are not viewed as positively as are confident men (Bradley, 1980). In other words, even when women adopt male strategies and behaviors, they may not succeed. Kramer (1978) notes that women find themselves in a paradoxical situation when they identify men as their oppressors but use a rhetoric which reflects a male-oriented culture that is being challenged. In other words, oppression is viewed as undesirable by women, yet they use the oppressive techniques on others to achieve their goals. Adopting a male style, then, does not appear to be the answer, since it does not necessarily assist women to attain their goals, and indeed tends to call into question the basic assumptions and values of women.

We observed in the last section that the female style has positive attributes. Kramer (1978) determined that many female language characteristics are rated as close to ideal speech. Baird and Bradley (1979) concluded that female managers were perceived as more effective than male managers. McMillan, Clifton, McGrath, & Gale (1977) questioned whether the qualities characterizing female speech are actually perceived negatively by listeners. Mulac and Lundell (1980) demonstrated that female speakers are rated as more pleasant and more attractive in aesthetic quality than males.

Bradac, Hemphill, and Tardy (1981) examined the effects of "powerful" and "powerless" speech on the attribution of blame to a defendant and a plaintiff in an artificial courtroom situation. The "powerless" style was comparable to the female style as it included hedges, intensifiers, polite forms, and hesitation forms. The "powerful" style included short or one-word replies. In one instance, respondents attributed greater fault to the individual who used the "powerful" style. These results imply that the "powerless" female style may be advantageous in eliciting less attribution of blame.

Though feminine linguistic style is not without positive attributes, it is more than questionable to recommend it as the style that should be adopted by all speakers. Earlier in this chapter, we determined that the feminine style may result in being devalued, may be less effective, and that it encourages dominance by others. The female style of communication has both positive *and* negative characteristics, so that it cannot be indiscriminatingly recommended. Men in positions of authority and power who acquired and maintained their status through "man talk" would tend to resist change. Other men may be discouraged from adopting a female style because of ridicule and denigration by others in the culture. Finally, persons who have strong instrumental inclinations, including women, would find that this style of communication was not suitable to their personality and individual style.

Women and men who wish to communicate with each other with minimal misunderstanding and with maximal effectiveness should consider a wide language repertoire, one which incorporated elements of the masculine and the feminine styles that have been outlined in this chapter. We should freely select from a variety of behaviors the appropriate cues for the situation. A woman who is dealing with a man who is attempting to control a conversation by interruptions, overlaps, and delayed responses might adopt a similar aggressive stance rather than submit to domination. A man conversing with a woman who is unusually silent might consider listening more than talking. Adopting a flexible stance and moving in and out of traditionally masculine and feminine behaviors is not a solution that will meet with immediate success. Men who behave in ways which are associated with stereotypical females and women who behave in a manner that is correlated with stereotypical males are still questionable characters in our culture. Nonetheless, this approach appears to hold the most promise for alteration of our language styles. To the extent that we can adapt new behaviors as necessary, we can eradicate the sexism which is harmful to all of us. Our language, as a symbol system, can move us from a social order in which discrimination is codified to a higher level of social organization in which distinctions between males and females are minimized.

References

Ayres, Joe. "Relationship Stages and Sex as Factors in Topic Dwell Time," *Western Journal of Speech Communication* 44 (1980): 253–260.

Baird, John E. "Sex Differences in Group Communication: A Review of Relevant Research," *The Quarterly Journal of Speech 62* (1976): 179–192.

Baird, John E., and Patricia Hayes Bradley. "Styles of Management and Communication: A Comparative Study of Men and Women," *Communication Monographs* 46 (1979): 101–111.

Bradac, J. J, C. H. Tardy, and L. A Hosman. "Disclosure Styles and a Hint at Their Genesis," *Human Communication Research* 6 (1980): 228–238.

Bradley, Patricia Hayes. "The Folk-Linguistics of Women's Speech: An Empirical Examination," *Communication Monographs* 48 (1981): 73–90.

Bradley, Patricia Hayes, "Sex, Competence and Opinion Deviation: An Expectation States Approach," *Communication Monographs* 47 (1980): 105–110.

Brandt, D. R. "A Systematic Approach to the Measurement of Dominance in Human Face-to-Face Interaction," *Communication Quarterly* 28 (1980): 31–43.

Carroll, Lewis. *Through the Looking Glass*. New York: Random House, 1965.

Crosby, Faye, and Linda Nyquist. "The Female Register: An Empirical Study of Lakoff's Hypotheses," *Language in Society* 6 (1977): 313–322.

Dubois, Betty Lou, and Isabel Crouch. "The Question of Tag Questions in Women's Speech: They Don't Really Use More of Them, Do They?" *Language in Society* 4 (1975): 289–294.

Eakins, Barbara Westbrook, and R. Gene Eakins. *Sex Differences in Human Communication*. Boston, Mass.: Houghton Mifflin Co., 1978.

Eakins, Barbara, and Gene Eakins. "Verbal Turn-Taking and Exchanges in Faculty Dialogue," *Papers in Southwest English IV: Proceedings of the Conference on the Sociology of the Languages of American Women,* ed. Betty Lou Dubois and Isabel Crouch, San Antonio, Tex.: Trinity University, 1976, pp. 53–62.

Fishman, Pamela M. "Interaction: The Work Women Do," *Social Problems* 25 (1978): 397–406.

Fishman, Pamela M. "International Shitwork," *Heresies: A Feminist Publication on Art & Politics* 2 (May 1977): 99–101.

Frost, Joyce Hocker, and William W. Wilmot. *Interpersonal Conflict*. Dubuque, Iowa: William C. Brown, 1978.

Gilley, Hoyt M., and Collier Summers. "Sex Differences in the Use of Hostile Verbs," *Journal of Psychology* 76 (1970): 33–37.

Golinkoff, Roberta Michnick, and Gail Johnson Ames. "A Comparison of Father's Speech to Mother's Speech with their Young Children," *Child Development* 50 (1979): 28–32.

Graves, Richard L., and Gayle B. Price. "Sex Differences in Syntax and Usage in Oral and Written Language," *Research in the Teaching of English* 145 (May 1980): 147–153.

Haas, Adelaide. "Male and Female Spoken Language Differences: Stereotypes and Evidence," *Psychological Bulletin* 86 (1979): 616–626.

Haas, Adelaide. "Partner Influence on Sex-Associated Spoken Language of Children," *Sex Roles* 7 (1981): 225–234.

Haas, L. "Determinants of Role-Sharing Behavior: A Study of Egalitarian Couples," *Sex Roles* 8 (1982): 747–760.

Hewitt, John P., and Randall Stokes. "Disclaimers," *American Sociological Review* 40 (1975): 1–11.

Hirschman, Lynette. "Female–Male Differences in Conversational Interaction," abstracted in *Language and Sex: Difference and Dominance,* ed. Barrie Thorne and Nancy Henley. Rowley, Mass: Newbury House, 1975, p. 249.

Jespersen, Otto. *Language: Its Nature, Development and Origin*. London: Allen and Unwin, 1922.

Kelly, Jeffrey A., Hal E. Wildman, and Jon K. Ureg. "A Behavioral Analysis of Gender and Sex Role Differences in Group Decision Making and Social Interactions," *Journal of Applied Social Psychology* 12 (1982): 112–127.

Key, Mary Ritchie, *Male/Female Language*. Metuchen, N.J.: The Scarecrow Press, 1975.

Kramer, Cheris R. "Women's Speech: Separate But Unequal?" *Quarterly Journal of Speech* 60 (1974): 14–24.

Kramer, Cheris, Barrie Thorne, and Nancy Henley. "Perspectives on Language and Communication," *Signs* 3 (1978): 638–651.

Lakoff, Robin. "You Are What You Say," *Ms.* 3 (1974): 63–67.
Markel, Norman N, Joseph, F. R. Long, and Thomas J. Saine. "Sex Effects in Conversational Interaction: Another Look at Male Dominance," *Human Communication Research* 2 (1976): 356–364.
McMillan, Julie R., A. Kay Clifton, Diane McGrath, and Wanda S. Gale. "Women's Language: Uncertainty or Interpersonal Sensitivity and Emotionality?" *Sex Roles* 3 (1977): 545–559.
Mulac, Anthony, and Luisa Lundell Torborg. "Differences in Perceptions Created by Syntactic-Semantic Productions of Male and Female Speakers," *Communication Monographs* 47 (1980): 111–118.
Newcombe, Nora, and Diane B. Arnkoff. "Effects of Speech Style and Sex of Speaker on Person Perception," *Journal of Personality and Social Psychology* 37 (1979): 1293–1303.
Rich, Elaine. "Sex-Related Differences in Colour Vocabulary," *Language and Speech* 20 (1977): 404–409.
Rosenfeld, Howard M. "Approval-Seeking and Approval-Inducing Functions of Verbal and Nonverbal Responses in the Dyad," *Journal of Personality and Social Psychology* 4 (1966): 597–605.
Sanders, Janet S., and William L. Robinson. "Talking and Not Talking about Sex: Male and Female Vocabularies," *Journal of Communication* 29 (1979): 22–30.
Simkins Rinck. "Male and Female Sexual Vocabulary in Different Interpersonal Contexts," *The Journal of Sex Research* 18 (1982): 160–172.
Staley, Constance. "Male–Female Use of Expletives: A Heck of a Difference in Expectations," *Anthropological Linguistics* 20 (1978): 367–380.
Staley, Constance. "Sex Related Differences in the Style of Children's Language," *Journal of Psycholinguistic Research* 11 (1982): 141–152.
Stake, Jayne E., and Michael N. Stake. "Performance—Self-Esteem and Dominance in Mixed Sex Dyads," *Journal of Personality* 47 (1979): 23–26 and 71–84.
Swacker, Marjorie. "The Sex of the Speaker as a Sociolinguistic Variable." in *Language and Sex: Difference and Dominance,* ed. Barrie Thorne and Nancy Henley. Rowley, Mass: Newbury House Publishers, 1975.
Thorne, Barrie. Public speech at Michigan State University, East Lansing, Michigan, 1981.
Thorne, Barrie, and Nancy Henley. "Difference and Dominance: An Overview of Language, Gender and Society," *Language and Sex: Difference and Dominance.* Rowley, Mass.: Newbury House Publishers, 1975, pp. 5–31.
Thorne, Barrie, and Nancy Henley. "Sex and Language Difference and Dominance," *Language in Society* 6 (1977): 110–113.
Wood, Marion M. "The Influence of Sex and Knowledge of Communication Effectiveness on Spontaneous Speech," *Word* 22 (1966): 117–137.
Wright, J. W., and L. A. Hosman. "Language Style and Sex Bias in the Courtroom: The Effects of Male and Female Use of Hedges and Intensifiers on Impression Information," *The Southern Speech Communication Journal* 48 (1983): 137–152.
Zimmerman, Don H., and Candace West. "Sex Roles, Interruptions and Silences in Conversation," in *Language and Sex: Difference and Dominance,* ed. Barrie Thorne and Nancy Henley. Rowley, Mass.: Newbury House Publishers, 1975.

PROBES

How do you respond to Judy Pearson's rationale for studying gender and communication? Do you agree that because of our "paradigm shift" it's a topic that needs study and discussion today? Or do you think that communication issues and problems are common to all humans and don't need to be narrowly treated as "female–male"?

Did you try the experiment about color vocabulary that Pearson suggests? If not, give it a try and see whether your findings support or contradict hers. How might you account for the difference?

I believe that there are fewer differences between women's and men's uses of profanity than Pearson suggests. That is, I believe that since 1970, females have, as she puts it, "increased their use of hostile language." What is your experience with this aspect of communication?

At several points in this reading (e.g., in the discussion of profanity and expletives) Pearson suggests that *actual* male–female communication differences are less important than our *perceptions* of those differences. For example, even when females use strong expletives, males still perceive their communication as weak. This same phenomenon appears to be true with tag questions. In your opinion, how significant is this part of the problem? Can this difference be changed? How?

Which of the substantive differences Pearson discusses has the most impact? Which does the most to weaken women's communication?

How do you generally interpret tag questions? Do you hear them as usually welcome efforts to continue the conversation or as signs of weakness and uncertainty?

To what extent do you think that a discussion like this one contributes to our sexual stereotypes? Is this effort helpful or harmful?

This brief excerpt from one of Maurice Friedman's books offers a "non-social-scientific" discussion by a male of some of the same issues Judy Pearson addresses in the immediately preceding reading. Friedman emphasizes the common *human* elements that can and, he believes, should underlie male–female communicating. Those elements come into play fully only when communication happens between persons rather than between fillers of social roles.

Friedman emphasizes that real improvements in communication between women and men will occur not because of generalizations about abstractions but as a result of everyday, concrete choices of individual persons. As he puts it, human equality and dignity "must be won in the dynamic of lived and living relationship." He also stresses that effective male–female communication does not occur when differences are dissolved but when the tensions of dissimilarity remain and the different persons nonetheless stay committed to genuine contact.

Friedman also suggests that the challenge of improving male–female communication is exacerbated by the subtlety and pervasiveness of the forces working against it. The unrealistically positive "Mother's Day idolization" that is part of a woman's *social* role can mask the genuine values and strengths of her as a person. Yet because the social role is positive, we are sometimes hesitant to challenge it.

The problem also affects men. Especially in their work lives, men feel the "tension between personal calling and social role." Here too the challenge is to personalize communication contacts.

Although Friedman's approach and style are significantly different from Judy Pearson's, I hope you will hear the strong agreement between these two authors on two central points: (1) many female–male contacts are unnecessarily depersonalized and objectifying and (2) changed attitudes can lead to genuine improvements for both women and men.

The Tension Between Personal Calling and Social Role

Maurice Friedman

The real thrust behind women's liberation, it seems to me, is the confusion and distortion that prevail in a province that should be that of the highest flowering of the human—the confusion about what it means to be a woman in relationship to a man in this particular historical situation. Somehow it tends to become a mere social role and, what is more, an imposed social role in which women are subject to the tyranny of both men's and women's notions of what it means to be "feminine." "The universal sway of the feminine stereotype is the single most important factor in male and female woman-hatred," writes Germaine Greer in *The Female Eunuch*. The battle for women's liberation is a battle for the wholeness of the human being, a battle for a woman's right to be a person.

Although much has changed in women's situation in the past years. the problematic tension between person and social role remains for them in a more aggravated form than for men. No one ever suggests that a career and fatherhood are incompatible, but, in the past at least, a woman has often been told that she must choose between career and motherhood. Most of the responsibility in the family structure is placed upon the woman, and neither men nor society in general are willing to provide women with the structural means of handling both roles with any ease. For many, a woman's choices are more restricted still: either she must marry and raise a family or face life with no identity at all, an "unwanted spinster." This too is changing with the advent of short-term commitments and "serial monogamy." But it still remains a dominant trend. Kate Millet holds that the rights of women to divorce, protection, citizenship, vote, and property have not affected their continued chattel status in name, residence, sex, domestic service, and economic dependence. Even in the academic world, women must seek survival or advancement from the approval of males who hold power.[1]

Basic to the cultural divisions of roles has been woman's reproductive role. The pill has modified this situation, but it has not fundamentally changed it. Society will not allow woman's reproductive role to be threatened; yet without freedom in this respect, all woman's other freedoms are in danger of being empty. "The real question is not, 'How can we justify abortion?' but 'How can we justify compulsory childbearing?'" At the same time, women are taught not to share love and sex but to use them for profit, for economic ascendancy and status acquisition. And by the same token, women are taught that they are of value when they are young: "Men may mature, but women just obsolesce."[2]

There is another, equally essential, and corollary aspect of this battle, however, and that is the realm of the "between." Equality and dignity cannot be won by women themselves, even by changing the attitude of any number of individual men. It must be won in the dynamic of lived and living relationship—in the concrete situations in which men and women meet and confirm one another as man or woman *and* as person, holding the tension between these two so that, if they can never be simply identified, neither can they ever be separated. If modern man in general knows anxiety, alienation, and exile, it is certain that modern woman knows it in still fuller measure—because she faces the simultaneous breakup of traditional values and of such traditional images of woman as might have satisfied her great-grandmother, grandmother, or even her mother. If the black man is invisible as *man* and *person* through his very visibility as black, woman is invisible as person and human being through her visibility as woman, as D. H. Lawrence has eloquently declared:

> Man is willing to accept woman as an equal, as a man in skirts, as an angel, a devil, a baby-face, a machine, an instrument, a bosom, a womb, a pair of legs, a servant, an encyclopedia, an ideal or an obscenity; the only thing he won't accept her as is as a human being, a real human being of the female sex.[3]

The invisibility of a woman is less obvious than that of a black because of the great respect, veneration, and Mother's Day idolization woman enjoys in our culture, not to mention her unquestionable power to seduce, manipulate, control, and dominate men through her feminine charms and "wiles." But the seduction and manipulation work both ways: Women have been taught to be devious and indirect because it is unladylike or unfeminine to be "too" outspoken, direct, demanding, angry, aggressive, or just plain enraged. Marya Mannes sees the pervasive anxiety in modern woman as the result of the shutting out of the *human* image by the imposed *social* image:

> What I call the destructive anxieties are not the growth of women's minds and powers, but quite the contrary: the pressures of society and the mass media to make women conform to the classic and traditional image in men's eyes. They must be not only the perfect wife, mother, and home-maker, but the ever-young, ever-slim, ever-alluring object of their desires. Every woman is deluged daily with urges to attain this impossible state. . . . The real demon is success—the anxieties engendered by this quest are relentless, degrading, corroding. What is worse, there is no end to this escalation of desire. . . . The legitimate anxiety—am I being true to myself as a human being?—is submerged in trivia and self-deception.[4]

One cannot legislate the removal of sexual differences arising from the culture just by recognizing that they are the product of the culture and not merely of biological inheritance, as Kate Millett seeks to do in *Sexual Politics*. Male and female, she says, are seen in our society as two distinct cultures, and this division and cataloguing reduce the human person to half of its potential in its struggle to fulfill "feminine" or "masculine" role expectations. This patriarchal system has probably exercised the most pervasive and insidious control of any other, innocently, wordlessly, installing itself as nature. To agree with this fully, as I do, is not to agree that one can easily get back to "nature" minus culture or that we know anything about the human person and society in a state of nature. The problem is no less real if it is borne by culture rather than by inheritance, though this may change our attitude toward it and give us some hope of changing it. One cannot will to see women as pure person or pure human being minus their variegated but nonetheless unmistakable feminine appearance and social role.

All we can do, here as elsewhere, is to hold the tension between the person and the social role, recognizing the necessity of both and moving in the direction of the freedom of every person to choose her own social role or roles and not have it imposed on her by others.

What is true of women in relation to men is also true of men in relation to women. But for many men in our culture the tension between personal calling and social role is felt most keenly in the world of work. Daniel J. Levinson in his perceptive study, *The Seasons of a Man's Life,* has delineated this tension with especial clarity in that phase of "Settling Down" which he calls "Becoming One's Own Man," a period which ordinarily extends from 35 or 36 to 40 or 41 and represents the peaking of early adulthood and the transition into what lies beyond. Levinson sees the goals of this phase as including not only advancing on one's ladder but also speaking more clearly with one's own voice, having a greater measure of authority, and becoming less dependent, both internally and externally, on other individuals and institutions. But Levinson also recognizes a built-in dilemma here, a dilemma which we have already glimpsed in the problem of the confirmation of otherness:

> On the other hand, a man wants to be more *independent,* more true to himself and less vulnerable to pressures and blandishments from others. On the other hand, he seeks *affirmation* in society. Speaking with his own voice is important, even if no one listens—but he especially wants to be heard and respected and given the rewards that are his due. The wish for independence leads him to do what he alone considers most essential, regardless of consequences; the wish for affirmation makes him sensitive to the response of others and susceptible to their influence.[5]

This dilemma is not just an internal one. As the man advances and comes in contact with senior men who have territories to protect, he receives a double message containing a subtle mixture of support and intimidation: "Be a good boy and you'll go far. Make trouble and you're dead." In the face of these, a man may discover that he is not as autonomous as he thought. "He wants to be his own man, but he also wants desperately to be understood and appreciated" and to have his talents affirmed. As a result, he may find himself in crucial situations too eager to please, too sensitive to criticism, too conforming to speak and act on the basis of his own convictions.

Levinson is also highly perceptive in his description of the "deillusionment" that sets in when at some point in his life a man confronts the omnipotent, fairy-tale quality of his fantasies about advancement and learns the degree to which his experience of success has been based upon illusion. The most poignant part of this illusion is the belief that one is advancing *for* oneself when actually it is often at the cost of one's self:

> Even when a man is doing well in an external sense, he may be gaining rewards that will turn out to have little meaning or value for him. His life may provide genuine satisfactions but at greater inner costs. In order to devote himself to certain goals, he may have to neglect or repress important parts of the self.[6]

The particular value for us of Levinson's periods of adult development is that, in contrast to Erik Erikson's eight stages, they are focused on the "between" and thus cast genuine light on the problem of the confirmation of otherness. Erikson's stages include, among others, Intimacy vs. Aloneness, Generativity vs. Stagnation, and Integrity vs. Despair, the stages of early, middle, and late adulthood. Each of Erikson's stages is governed by a crucial, problematic issue for the self in relation to the external world. "But their primary focus is *within the person.*" Levinson's concept of "life structure," in contrast, "is centered more directly on the *boundary between self and world,*" giving equal consideration to self and world as aspects of the lived life.[7]

References

1. Kate Millett, *Sexual Politics* (Garden City, N.Y.: Doubleday, 1970), pp. 25–26, 28–29, 31–35, 54, 58, 179, 189, 196.
2. Robin Morgan, ed., *Sisterhood Is Powerful: An Anthology of Writings from the Women's Liberation Movement* (New York: Vintage Books, 1970), pp. 45, 94. 181, 246, 278, 290–291, 172, 174–175.
3. Quoted in Morgan, *Sisterhood Is Powerful,* p. 564.
4. Marya Mannes, "The Roots of Anxiety in Modern Woman," *Journal of Neuropsychiatry,* 5 (1964): 412, quoted in Morgan, *Sisterhood Is Powerful,* p. 244.
5. Daniel J. Levinson et al., *The Seasons of a Man's Life* (New York: Knopf, 1978), p. 144.
6. Ibid., pp. 153–154.
7. Ibid., p. 323 and footnote.

PROBES

How important is Friedman's point about the general and the specific? Do you find general principles to be useful or in your experience is it the case-by-case specifics that make the most difference?

Friedman argues that it won't work to reduce the differences between the sexes— to look for more of the feminine in men and the masculine in women. He says we need to maintain the tension between the sexes and between personal and social role. Do you agree? How so?

Do you agree with Friedman that problems with male–female communication affect men as strongly as they affect women? Discuss.

Do you find Friedman's remarks to be less persuasive than Judy Pearson's or more so? How important is the fact that he does not cite research studies? How significant is the fact that he's male?

CHAPTER 12

COMMUNICATING ACROSS CULTURES

It's possible to view this chapter on intercultural communication as something that's "tacked on" to a book that doesn't really deal with this topic. But I don't think that's accurate; I believe there's a strong link between interpersonal and intercultural communication concerns. For one thing, intercultural communication situations confront all of us on an almost daily basis, regardless of whether we are at home or in some other country, state, city, or neighborhood. That's because, as the author of this essay points out, intercultural communication is not defined by national boundaries. Communication between a young person and an old person is often intercultural, as are contacts between a homosexual and a heterosexual, a born-again Christian and a Jew, and two Atlanta residents, one from Cambodia and the other a child of U.S. citizens born in Japan. The "prime discriminator," as Sarbaugh puts it, is heterogeneity or how dissimilar the persons are. Homogeneous or similar participants engage in *intra*cultural communication and heterogeneous participants communicate *inter*culturally.

Another reason I believe this chapter belongs in this book is that it emphasizes how effective communication attitudes and actions can be solidly grounded in what we know about the nature of persons, *all* persons. There are obviously significant differences among cultures, differences that can create a great deal of awkwardness and misunderstanding. But there are even more fundamental similarities, and the way to communicate well in intercultural contexts is to notice and build on the similarities.

Sarbaugh first illustrates the similarities among cultures by discussing conversational "openings" for greeting behaviors. He cites research that identified four elements that are present whenever people meet—in Taiwan, Saudi Arabia, or Mexico City; in Boston's Italian north side, Chicago's south side, or on Castro Street in San Francisco's gay community. The form or mode of each of the elements differs from culture to culture, but the elements themselves are similar. Thus the key to effective intercultural communication is to recognize which familiar functions are being performed in unfamiliar ways and to adapt to these differences.

The bulk of this reading discusses four general aspects of communication that vary in their specifics from culture to culture: language or code systems, beliefs about the world and the people in it, perceived relationships among participants, and perceived intent of the others in the transaction.

Language or code differences are often the most obvious obstacles. While some kinds of communication cannot occur unless the participants share at least minimal knowledge of grammar and vocabulary, nonverbal codes are actually more definitive of a culture than verbal language. Fortunately, as anyone who's spent time in a foreign culture knows, it is possible in a brief period of time to adapt your own nonverbal knowledge enough to make at least minimal contact with someone whose language you don't speak.

Different patterns of belief and overt behavior can create intercultural problems even between people who speak the same language. If you're going to communicate effectively you need to be open to, listen for, and adapt to the other's *world view*. Sarbaugh discusses two ways to do this, by "assimilation" or by "accommodation." He uses the example of the discovery in 1971 of the Stone Age

Tasaday tribe in the Philippine rain forest to illustrate the advantages and disadvantages of each.

Perceived relationships among participants are most likely to affect intercultural communication when a person accustomed to a strict hierarchical pattern encounters one accustomed to an egalitarian pattern. Sarbaugh's discussion of perceived intent underscores an obvious but important fact about intercultural communication: It won't work unless the persons *want* it to, and the single most important thing you can do to further understanding is to desire it genuinely. Finally, the reading illustrates how other differences in perceived intent can also affect intercultural understanding.

My intent is for this essay to provide an overview of intercultural communication in general terms and for the next reading to explore a specific example of interpersonal communication between people of two different cultures.

Some Boundaries for Intercultural Communication

L. E. Sarbaugh

The latter part of the twentieth century provided one of the most spectacular cases of intercultural communication in the recent history of mankind. It was the contact, in the Philippine rain forest, between the Tasaday* tribe and the party headed by Manuel Elizade, Jr. of the Panamin unit of the Philippine government. One of Elizade's party referred to it as a strange sensation of traveling through time . . . "a visit to my ancestors of 100,000 years ago." For the Tasaday, the shock of sudden exposure to twentieth century urban man and his tools must have been equally as great if not greater.

While the contrast in that case was both apparent and dramatic, the communication problems, in many ways, are similar to those among the inner city, surburbia, and a rural village in any country of the world. The task undertaken in this book is to identify and analyze the variables that affect the communication which we label intercultural, whether it occurs between individuals or groups, and in whatever geographic locale.

There appears to be a temptation among scholars and practitioners of communication to approach *intercultural* communication as though it were a different process than *intracultural* communication. As one begins to identify the variables that operate in the communication being studied, however, it becomes apparent that they are the same for both intercultural and intracultural settings. In all communication analysis, we are concerned with the characteristics of the participants, the relationships among them, their encoding and decoding behaviors, the channels by which they relay symbols to one another, the social and physical contexts within which they operate, and their intentions in the communicative act.

---

*The tribe discovered in the Philippine rain forest region in 1971.

Excerpt from *Intercultural Communication* by L. E. Sarbaugh, © 1979. Reprinted by permission of L. E. Sarbaugh, professor emeritus, Michigan State University.

INTERCULTURAL AND INTERNATIONAL COMPARED

Sometimes intercultural becomes equated with international. This, of course, is too restrictive a view of intercultural. In both examples previously cited—(a) the Tasaday and the Philippine government team; and (b) inner city, suburbia, and rural village—the comparison is between cultural sets within a nation. From this perspective, international becomes a subset of intercultural.

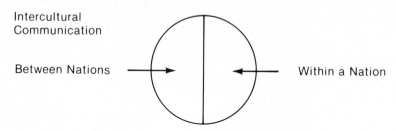

Intercultural
Communication

Between Nations   Within a Nation

There are two aspects of international communication which must be considered. One aspect is the communication which occurs between or among any two or more individuals of differing nationalities. The second aspect is that official communication, in which governmental representatives acting on behalf of their national government, exchange messages with governmental representatives of another nation, who also are authorized to act on behalf of their nation.

The level of interculturalness in any of these international transactions will depend on the kind and amount of expertise the participants have had with life in the other nation. It will be claimed here that some international transactions may well be categorized as intracultural, while others would be definitely intercultural. This could be true for either non-official or official communication.

Let's take an example in which international communication is not entirely subsumed within the intercultural. There are two school teachers from two different countries. Both have studied the same subjects under the same teachers in a third country; and both are now teaching agricultural irrigation in rural villages. Their cultural similarity has been further increased by extensive and intensive interaction as students so that they developed similar world views and beliefs while studying together. It is expected that their communication with one another will have higher fidelity and require less energy than will the communication of either of them with unschooled and unskilled workers in their respective countries.

The tendency to equate intercultural with international communication likely stems from the greater ease of identifying national boundaries. National boundaries somehow become more tangible than cultural boundaries; and, of course, there are noticeable differences in many aspects of behavior as one passes from one nation to another. There are noticeable differences also as one goes from a remote rural village in a country to metropolitan centers of that country. It's the differences between and among people, irrespective of geographical boundaries, that this text focuses on.

HETEROGENEITY—THE PRIME DISCRIMINATOR

A useful discriminator between intercultural and intracultural communication is the heterogeneity of the participants. The notion of "ideal types" (see Redfield, 1956) in regard to homogeneity-heterogeneity is helpful in developing this basis of distinguishing between intercultural and intracultural communication.

With the concept of ideal type, it is recognized that we would not expect to find two persons who were different on every characteristic; nor would we expect to find two persons who are alike on every characteristic. Yet it is useful to establish a continuum with the assumption of a pure homogeneous pair at one end and a pure heterogeneous pair at the other end.

Heterogeneous
Participants

Homogeneous
Participants

Intercultural

Intracultural

This view of intercultural and intracultural communication emphasizes that some communication events may rather easily be categorized as intercultural or intracultural. Others may be almost impossible to clearly classify as one or the other, i.e., those near the mid-point of the continuum. A perspective which classifies communication as either inter- or intracultural presumably does so using boundary criteria, either implicit or explicit.

The study and practice of communication can be approached with more precision if we classify it by level of interculturalness rather than as two dichotomous categories of intra- and intercultural. The initial difficulty will be to identify the critical dimensions of difference and to be able to specify the level among those dimensions a given transaction occurs at.

Another way of visualizing the inter-intracultural distinction (rather than the continuum) is to let two circles represent the life experiences of two persons (or groups). If the circles have minimal overlap (representing minimal similarity of experience), the two persons would be near the heterogeneous end of the continuum.

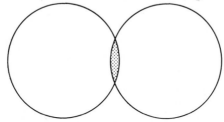

If the circles have maximum overlap, the two persons would be near the homogeneous end of the continuum, i.e., the intracultural communication end.

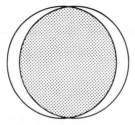

The homogeneity–heterogeneity distinction may lead to classifying communication across generations within the same village or town as highly intercultural communication. In societies where sex roles are quite distinct and clearly defined, there are aspects of intercultural communication in the communication between male and female. What is suggested here is that age or sex differences may or may not be intercultural. The classification of the communication as inter- or intracultural in this case will depend on what degree of homogeneity or heterogeneity of experiences the transactions of these persons have produced. . . .

The Tasaday tribesmen and the Elizade team would represent two groups whose life-experiences barely overlap. The members of a close-knit nuclear family would represent a group of persons where the overlap would be maximal. Also, the Tasaday tribesmen would be highly homogeneous among themselves while members of the Elizade team would be quite heterogeneous within the team. The Elizade team was composed of Elizade, Charles Lindbergh, an interpreter from a tribe close to, but outside the rain forest, a hunter-trapper who lived part-time outside the rain forest and at times went into the forest to hunt, a U.S. newsman, carriers and some other support staff.

If we look at all communication as a series of transactions . . . we then focus on the mutual involvement of the participants in delivering and receiving messages via whatever codes are available to them. The transactional view of communication emphasizes the mutuality of behaving either simultaneously or sequentially, the behavior of each influencing the behavior of the other. Speaking and listening generally are sequential, while behaviors involving nonverbal codes are more likely to be simultaneous.

If the focus is solely on speaking and listening, the act tends to be sequential in that one speaks, the other listens; the other speaks and the first listens. However, the production and reception of the nonverbal codes in a face-to-face situation will be occurring while the speaking and listening are occurring; and the parties may simultaneously produce and receive nonverbal codes with or without the production and reception of verbal codes.

As we describe and analyze transactions over time, we are dealing with communication as a process, not as a static event stopped in time. The interdependence of each participant with the other and with the environment is apparent in a process description.

Dan E. Miller, Robert A. Hintz, and Carl Couch at the University of Iowa have carefully studied what occurs in a variety of situations in which people initiate and carry on transactions. They started by watching what happens when two persons approach a door at the same time. How do these persons decide who goes through first? What are the various things that happen and in what order when two persons are in a room and only minimally aware of one another, then an emergency occurs outside the room? What are the elements of the communicative acts which follow? The assumption is that there are some universal principles here regardless of the level of interculturalness. Then, what are the differences in the operation or application of those principles with increasing heterogeneity (interculturalness)?

OPENINGS: FROM INDEPENDENCE TO INTERDEPENDENCE

Openings is the label which Miller, Hintz, and Couch (Couch and Hintz, 1975) give to the process by which transactions get initiated and move toward coordinated activity. For them, openings refer to the activities of two or more persons moving from a condition of behavioral independence to one of interdependence. It is thus the first necessary activity that two persons must successfully perform before they can do anything else together.

One of my African students told me that the most difficult thing for him to get accustomed to in the USA was the behavior of persons when meeting. In his country, if one person stopped, this was the signal for the other person coming toward him to stop for a talk. Here, he stopped and the other kept walking. This illustrates the necessity of the first element in the openings of Couch et al., i.e., reciprocally acknowledged attention.

The four elements of openings are:

1. Reciprocally acknowledged attention.
2. Mutual responsiveness.
3. Congruent functional identities.
4. Shared focus.

"Each of the elements must be constructed and maintained if concerted behavior is to occur," according to Miller, Hintz, and Couch.

We may use these categories in describing any communication transaction, whether intercultural or intracultural. It is a framework for studying communication as the process of two or more persons forming, maintaining, and dissolving unified lines of activity. These writers appear to have done what others have talked about, but few have done, i.e., study communication as a process.

If we were to look at intercultural communication from the perspective of "openings" we would expect that the heterogeneity among participants would complicate the efforts to carry out the four phases of openings. Work by Miller, Hintz, and Couch indicated that friend dyads accomplished openings in less than half the time that was required for stranger dyads. Three dyads of friends of long standing appeared to act simultaneously in accomplishing the four phases. In other instances the phases seemed to be sequentially produced.

When my African student is wearing the colorful dress of his country, other persons quickly and intensely attend to his presence. There is a high level of awareness, but the attention often is diverted away from the "opening" process in the transaction which he is attempting to initiate. The mutual responsiveness phase flounders. The African student and the other have difficulty anticipating each other. The transaction is different than intended by the student. They may find it virtually impossible to impute to the other sequences of behavior which are to follow, depending on the level of heterogeneity.

An Australian student reports that when he asks a question in class, all heads turn in his direction. He finds this very disconcerting, then has difficulty phrasing the question he intended to ask. As he speaks, the attention focuses on his Australian accent and the content of the question is missed. He reports that this has had a retarding effect on his asking questions about the content. There is an obvious lack of shared focus in this situation when the Australian starts his question. While the barrier may be overcome with increased time devoted to the transaction, it helps illustrate that the more intercultural the transaction, the more time one should allow for the satisfactory completion of it.

For any communicative acts to be established and to endure, a necessary first condition is that the parties attend to one another and acknowledge, either verbally or nonverbally or both, that they are attending. This is the first part of moving from a copresent social context to an interactive (or transactive) context. This is then a necessary condition for mutual responsiveness to occur; but as noted in the preceding illustration, it may not be a sufficient condition.

"One is responsive to another when he builds his acts off the prior, simultaneous or anticipated acts of another, and in the process of doing so informs the other participant(s) of that fact. Mutual responsiveness is obtained when each of the participants is in part organizing his activity on the basis of the other's activity and there is shared awareness that each is taking the other into account as they act toward each other and incorporate the other's activity into their own activity" (Couch and Hintz, 1975). Even to fight with another requires that each must be responsive to the activity of the other.

"Congruent functional identities (the third set of relationships) are present when 'both parties mutually impute to self and other sequences of forthcoming behavior.'" The functional identities refer to doing something in relation to another person. "The identities become congruent when they fit together to allow for completion of what both participants recognize as a unit of social activity." My Australian student has learned to anticipate the actions of his classmates; the classmates generally are unaware of his adaptation; his class participation has declined and the communication process in the class has been altered.

The labels used by Miller, Hintz, and Couch are reasonably descriptive of the behavior. Shared focus, the fourth condition for openings to be achieved, is an object or event attended to by two or more persons with each aware that they are attending to the same object or event. This shared focus is the basis for a social plan of behavior to be accomplished through coordinated behavior.

As noted earlier, the openings are expected to take less time; they are more likely to occur, and are more likely to be satisfactorily completed among friends than among strangers. Further, it is expected that homogeneity will be greater among friends than among strangers. Thus another difference between highly intercultural and highly intracultural communication would be the ease and speed with which "openings" may be accomplished. It will be recognized that strangers, after some interaction, may discover that they are relatively homogeneous on many dimensions. But they start with less predictability than do friends, hence strangers are more likely than friends to feel ill at ease in establishing openings.

When my African student appears in a group of persons in the USA who have had very limited or no contact with Africans, the colorful dress immediately focuses attention on the differences. The fact that the African student attended a Christian missionary school for his elementary and secondary schooling, and has lived and worked in close contact with middle-class families in the USA for the last three years is lost in the opening aspect of the communication process. Depending on the beliefs of the USA persons about Africans, the process may or may not move on from the reciprocally acknowledged attention to other aspects of the process—mutual responsiveness, congruent functional identities, and shared focus.

I would hypothesize that as visible heterogeneity increases, the reciprocally acknowledged attention will increase. That attention, however, may detract from the intended purpose of the transaction. Furthermore, it is expected that the communication difficulty would tend to increase as the heterogeneous participants proceed to each of the other three aspects of openings.

The participants may respond to one another, but the mutuality of those responses may be low as each misreads the prior acts of the other. The third aspect would likely be very difficult for highly heterogeneous participants as they attempt to impute to self and other sequences of forthcoming behavior. Each behavioral cue may suggest one type of forthcoming behavior to one participant and another type of forthcoming behavior to the other participant. The lack of fulfillment of the anticipated behavior likely would have a detrimental effect on the desire to continue the transaction.

When it comes to the fourth condition of openings, the shared focus, the difficulty experienced at the congruent functional identity phase likely will be further compounded. To have a basis for a social plan for accomplishing the desired coordinated action, the participants will need to have achieved a commonality of perspective about the way each should behave toward the other and toward objects required to achieve their goals.

One of the critical tasks is to identify the key variables (characteristics of participants and situations) which locate the communication along the homogeneous-heterogeneous continuum; i.e., the variables which influence the ease, speed, and fidelity with which the participants' move toward coordinated activity can be initiated and carried out.

SOME VARIABLES TO CONSIDER

Among the experiences of persons everywhere are some which are common to all. These may be taken as a base from which communication may be initiated; and they may form the base for "openings" at all levels of interculturalness and intraculturalness. Other experiences are unique to the members of each culture. These unique experiences are those which may be shared only through relating them to some common experience among the participants; this sharing takes longer and potentially is more likely to produce feelings of uneasiness among the participants.

Among the experiences which we would expect to be common to all humans are birth, growth, food, shelter, family, death, friendship, pain, happiness, motion, sleep, and natural elements—sun, moon, stars, plants, animals, land, and water.

Some elements, such as rain and snow, will be differentially experienced; and it is extremely difficult for one who has experienced snow to communicate something about snow to one who has not experienced it. Obviously, the full experience of snow, as with most other phenomena, cannot be communicated apart from the direct experience of it. The completeness of communicating the experience of snow will depend on the number of other similar phenomena which the two persons have shared.

While we have listed a number of experiences which are common to all persons, the way in which these are experienced will differ among persons from differing cultures and among persons within the same culture. Note that the claim is being made that no two persons ever have identical experiences; and that communicating about phenomena apart from directly experiencing them will always result in somewhat different perceptions and interpretations. The more homogeneous the participants, the more similar the perceptions and interpretations following a communicative act; the more heterogeneous the participants, the more dissimilar the perceptions and interpretations.

Again, the operations of basic communication principles at different levels of inter-intraculturalness of communication is emphasized. The difference is one of degree rather than one of kind. We must keep that notion in mind as we now look at the characteristics which differ among individuals, resulting in different perceptions and interpretations in the communicative efforts. Note that the amount of difference will increase as we move from the most intracultural to the most intercultural communication act.

Among the characteristics on which we expect differences among participants in a communicative act are:

1. Language or code systems.
2. The beliefs they have about the world, the people in it, and appropriate beliefs and behaviors.

3. The perceived relationship between or among the participants.
4. The perceived intent of the other(s) in the transaction.

CODE SYSTEMS

Language is often thought of first as a critical factor in intercultural communication. This is quite natural since all of our transactions involve some form of verbal or nonverbal code. A shared set of verbal and nonverbal codes is a necessary condition for communication to occur, but it certainly is not a sufficient condition. There is the possibility that the message, "we cannot achieve our intent," does come through when we have no shared code elements. Aside from that possibility, it seems defensible to say that some shared code elements is a necessary condition. The difficulty of concentrating on language differences is that the interdependence of language with other aspects of culture may be overlooked.

Every person who has had contact with persons from another language group has a repertoire of tales to tell; some innocent and humorous, and some of disastrous consequences. An often used example is that the O.K. sign in the USA means homosexual in some other cultures. Many nonverbal and verbal codes have perfectly acceptable denotations and connotations in one culture and may arouse offensive meanings among persons in another culture. There is no denying that language differences must receive special attention in intercultural communication, but one should also recognize that differences in beliefs about how people should behave are equally critical, if not more critical, in intercultural communication.

There is rarely, if ever, a one-to-one translation of codes from one language to another. Different cultures carve up the world in different ways and assign labels (codes or symbols) to the various elements in the physical and social environment. This will range from different categories of colors to different categories for ranking people within the group and different categories of roles.

Benjamin Whorf (1956) has claimed that one's language influences what one perceives and how it is interpreted. He has cited numerous examples to support that claim. One oft cited example is symbols for time in different cultures. Precise measures of time are very important to persons in highly technological cultures; while in the less industrialized societies there is less emphasis on time and the language codes are less precise for time.

Efforts to test the Whorf hypothesis with rigorous empirical research have not resolved the questions regarding the relation between language and perception of available stimuli. The more reasonable view would seem to be that there is an interdependence between language and what is in one's environment to sense.

We can observe that people create new elements in the language to label new categories of experience. Each of us also may note that we look at some aspects of our environment differently when our awareness is increased by new labels for events and relationships. For example, I became aware of different aspects of human relationship after being exposed to terms such as role, status, position, and norm in my first courses in sociology. Reciprocally acknowledged attention, mutual responsiveness, congruent functional identities, and shared focus also are having this effect as I work with those terms. They are suggesting a different way of looking at some aspects of communication.

Response to jokes is perhaps the best illustration of the inadequacy of learning the language of another culture group to insure effective communication with that group. We may notice the lack of response to jokes by two persons both of whom have learned the same vocabularies and grammatical structure but are from different cultures. The subtleties of intercultural communication are probably nowhere more apparent than in communication which involves humor.

For humor to be effectively communicated, the participants must share similar experiences in relation to the symbols being used. Since humor generally stems from a violation of expectations, the homogeneity of the participants in the communication must be sufficient to produce similar expectations about the object (or relationship) which is the subject of the humor. As the heterogeneity of the participants increases, the similarity of expectations aroused by a given set of symbols, tends to decline. Add to that, subtle (or not so subtle) differences in referent for a symbol used by both and the mutual responsiveness does not occur; one laughs but the other doesn't and can't see the humor in the message.

Within the consideration of symbol systems, we also must include beliefs and overt behaviors related to time and space. The literature abounds with examples of variations among cultures in regard to beliefs about and uses of time and space. Rather than take space here to provide another such inventory, some references will be included among the bibliographic items. Of course, one of the classics regarding time and space is Edward Hall's *Silent Language.*

PATTERNS OF BELIEF AND OVERT BEHAVIOR

Some of a person's beliefs may be unique to that person; others may be shared by all persons in the group or groups of which he is a member. In the latter case the beliefs take on normative characteristics with positive sanctions for adherence to the beliefs and overt behaviors accepted by the group; and there are negative sanctions for beliefs and behaviors not acceptable to the group.

One subset of beliefs will be given special attention, in the discussion of homogeneity-heterogeneity of participants. It will be called *world view.* As used here, world view encompasses that set of beliefs about the nature of life, the purpose of life, and the relation of man to the cosmos. The reason for handling this set separately is based on the assumption that this set of beliefs tends to develop more slowly and hence is more enduring that other beliefs. Further it is assumed that these world view beliefs are intertwined with beliefs about what is important or unimportant, what is appropriate or inappropriate.

World view encompasses the beliefs about where we came from, why we're here, and where we're going. It's the set of beliefs about how the human species fits into the overall scheme of things. It's the beliefs about death in relation to life; the belief or nonbelief in some kind of life after death; beliefs about controlling nature or being controlled by nature; and so on.

Another subset of beliefs singled out for additional treatment are those we call *values.* They include the beliefs about what is important or unimportant, good or bad, and right or wrong. They are broad and fundamental norms which are generally shared by groups. As such, they serve to guide, integrate, and channel the organized activities of the members. They are expressed in the norms of overt behavior and role expectations.

The role expectations are the anticipated ways for a person to perform in a given situation the behaviors associated with the position that person occupies in the social system. For example, it's the way others expect me to behave in my role as father, or teacher, or any of the other sets of behaviors for the positions I occupy within the social systems of which I'm a part. The normative patterns of overt behaviors under the heading of role expectations derive from the value orientations of the members of the group in which the behavior occurs.

If, for example, honesty is a strong value within myself and my group, and someone gives me too much money in payment for a service, then I'm expected to return the overpayment. It's part of the expectation of me in my role as a good member of the group.

When two or more persons are engaged in a transaction, they each may assume that they both know and both accept the same normative patterns of beliefs and overt behaviors. If they do indeed share the same patterns, the transaction has a better chance of proceeding efficiently than when they do not share the same patterns. When their beliefs about appropriate behaviors differ, there is a high probability of communication problems. One of my Ghanian friends provided a good example of this kind of problem.

This friend had told me that in several of the tribal cultures the authority figure is always accessible to all for whom he is an authority figure. A person who adheres to that belief may have difficulty adjusting to the Western bureaucratic cultural milieu where the authority figure is not readily accessible. An example of this occurred in my office.

A student came to see me in my role as assistant dean. The secretary told him that I was fully scheduled for the day and asked if he would like to make an appointment for the following day. The student said, "But, I'm here to see him now!" Each became very annoyed with the other. The student waited for an opportunity to be seen between the other appointments. The secretary later said, "I can't stand that Mr. Z; he's so demanding. He always thinks everyone else should stop and wait on him." The student also told me that he was having some difficulty with my secretary who was trying to keep him from seeing me. The secretary and the student had very different views of the appropriate behavior in this case.

Differences in patterns of behavior and belief among persons often are assigned stereotypically, based on what one has learned through all of his life experiences. People are responded to according to differences in age, sex, education, occupation, clothing, income level, etc., etc. There is a tendency to generalize that all assembly line workers, etc., will respond like all others in their category. There is some basis for such an expectation, since presumably they will have had an opportunity for similar experiences. However, this view overlooks the opportunities that individuals in each of those demographic categories have had for unique experiences.

Ideally, we would take into account the characteristics of each individual with whom we communicate; however, we often are forced to base our first predictions on some kind of general stereotype of the other person. Some of the old stereotypes that have interfered with effective communication and coordinated behavior are: all politicians are crooks; all French men are great lovers; all Indians are lazy and shiftless. In the process of interacting, reassessments occur among effective communicators so that more accurate judgments of and responses to the other person become possible. This assumes a dynamic, changing belief system, i.e., a process view of reality.

This view of the changes occurring during communication between two or more persons can be described by the concepts of assimilation and accommodation. These concepts are used in somewhat the same way as they are used by Piaget.

Assimilation is the process of exploring the environment, taking in parts of it, acting on those parts and transforming them into new forms which will fit into the existing structure. The messages in communicating represent the parts taken in. I may have been taught that good husbands are kind to their wives, but they don't do any work in the kitchen; that's "women's work." When I am in the Smith family home, I see Tom helping his wife Mary with the cooking and dishwashing. I can assimilate that experience into my belief structure which says that men should be kind to their wives. Certainly being helpful is being kind. There is some problem as far as the belief that men don't do kitchen work in their home. That requires making some accommodation in my belief system.

Accommodation, the complement of assimilation, is the process of adjusting the structure, the belief system, so that the individual's model of the world can accommodate each new acquisition. One's beliefs are built on these twin processes.

In transactions with heterogeneous others, there will be more new stimuli to be assimilated which in turn results in more accommodation of the belief system to new experiences. Both of the processes operating together produce progressively more stable equilibrium states of adaptation. Rigidity of the structure may inhibit the accommodation process, delaying the establishment of a new equilibrium, and thus interfering with intercultural communication.

If we reflect on the process of openings discussed earlier, it may be noted that the first three stages of that process are a necessary condition for the assimilation and accommodation to occur in transactions with any other persons; and that the process becomes more demanding with increasing heterogeneity between self and other. The shared focus is necessary for greater coordinated action and it also is more difficult to achieve with heterogeneity of the participants.

As one moves through life, even in a restricted physical and social environment such as that of the Tasaday, the assimilation-accommodation processes continue to produce new adaptations. Piaget states that life is a continuous creation of increasingly complex forms and a progressive balancing of these forms with the environment. For such as the Tasaday, these new adaptations may be more concentrated on experiences which we have listed as common to all humans.

When a party from Manila (or other urban center) enters the rain forest, many new stimuli are introduced to the Tasaday requiring a rapid change in the number and quality of events to be processed. As the accommodation is made, communication would become somewhat easier with those who have come from outside the rain forest.

The first efforts of the Manila party to communicate with the Tasaday achieved reciprocally acknowledged attention fairly soon, although the Manila party first saw the footprints and other signs of presence before a visible co-presence was established. The attention at first was focused on one another. Gradually as the co-presence in a mutually shared physical environment continued, there was reciprocally acknowledged attention; then it became possible to achieve mutual responsiveness, and finally some degree of congruent functional identity and shared focus. It required accommodation of belief structures by both parties before the new stimuli could be assimilated in the process of communicating. Much of the communication focused on those universal aspects of life noted earlier—food, shelter, family, etc.

One of the concerns of the Elizade party was the contamination of the Tasaday life style, a contamination which could never be retrenched. An ineradicable impact also had been made on the members of the Elizade party. In the few brief contacts between the two groups, some of the heterogeneity had been reduced; but it would take many extended contacts to change the world views of the two groups to the point that each could be reasonably certain that mutual perceptions and interpretations of phenomena were occurring. Throughout most of the world, the increasing access to mass media *is* expanding the range of contacts.

With the extension of television and other mass media, the potential for vicariously shared experiences becomes much greater for those persons who have access to the media. Industrialization has resulted in rather similar patterns of social organization and activities wherever it has occurred; thus, it has contributed to increasing the similarity of the beliefs.

Industrialization has made possible more rapid and more extensive travel with the concomitant opportunity for more persons to be exposed to more of the same phenomena. The process of industrialization and at least two of its products—high speed transportation and high speed communication over great distances for the masses—have contributed to a reduction of the heterogeneity of the participants in communication. But it would be unrealistic to assume that these processes would wipe out the difficulties of intercultural communication. It should help broaden the base within which effective communication can occur.

The beliefs about and attitudes toward persons from other cultures come from many kinds of exposure, both direct and indirect. If we begin listing how many of our beliefs are a result of our own direct experience, we find that many are relayed by other persons. Even the relaying may be indirect through printed or electronically recorded or transmitted messages. However acquired, these beliefs and attitudes serve to filter the stimuli to which we respond in our transactions with others and dictate the way in which we perceive and respond to those others.

Althen and Jaime (1971) in comparing Philippine and North American assumptions and values point out:

1. In North American culture, autonomy is encouraged; while in the Filipino culture, dependence is encouraged.
2. For the Filipino, there is a finite amount of good that can be divided and redivided but not augmented; thus, if one accumulates more wealth, he does so at the expense of others. For the North American, optimism exists that there is enough for everyone and the economics of self initiative is the arbiter of how much one accumulates.
3. For the North American, there is a dichotomy of work and play; for the Filipino, work and social life are not separated.
4. Confrontation in North America tends to be face-to-face; in the Philippines, it tends to be through an intermediary to avoid losing face.
5. The North American stresses the future; the Filipino stresses the present and the past, and life is lived from day to day.

These statements are based on some notion of modal characteristics of people of the two geographic areas. While we recognize that these comparisons will not hold for all persons in both areas, they illustrate some of the differences in values and assumptions about the world between two sets of persons from different geographic areas and different cultures, sets which are highly heterogeneous on some characteristics.

If Western time orientation and self advancement were relied on in efforts to encourage adoption of new technology in the Philippines, communication efforts would be very frustrating for both parties. The dictum of "know your audience," now broadened to "know the participants," which is referred to often in intracultural communication would be equally appropriate in this intercultural setting. The assumption is that if we will make the effort to know the beliefs and other characteristics of those with whom we are communicating, then we will be able to identify some shared foci for achieving coordinated action.

Different bases for assigning status and the violation of expectations as to how one responds to another of a different status often is a problem in intercultural

communication. The trauma from the violation of expectations may block receipt of any other messages in the system. In this way, it precludes or at least interferes with establishing mutual responsiveness, congruent functional identities, and the shared focus of the Miller-Hintz-Couch model.

PERCEIVED RELATIONSHIP AMONG PARTICIPANTS

One of the places where this violation of expectation is most likely to occur is where one person who is accustomed to a strict hierarchical pattern of relationships is attempting to communicate with another who is accustomed to an egalitarian pattern. They will find that each has quite different expectations about what is appropriate behavior for the other. Embarrassment likely will result and may preclude effective communication on the intended topic. It may result from the use or non-use of formal titles by the egalitarian oriented person in referring to the hierarchically oriented person.

The difficulty of predicting social position, roles, and norms increases as heterogeneity of the participants increases. This lack of predictability creates tension and discomfort for both parties leading to embarrassment, perhaps hostility and a tendency to avoid further communication with one another.

A teacher in the USA may have a student from a traditional culture, such as Thailand. If the teacher is unaware of Thai culture, he may be disturbed by the lack of participation and the reluctance of the Thai student to ask questions. Later, after some months of acculturation, the Thai student may tell the teacher that students in Thailand are taught not to ask questions of the teacher, lest the question might embarrass the teacher. Here a different norm produced some stress in the relationship as the communication effort was not producing the intended mutual responsiveness.

PERCEIVED INTENT

The intent of the participants also influences the outcome of communication, regardless of the level of intra-interculturalness. If both have a desire to understand, to be understood, and to achieve coordinated action, they likely will commit whatever energy is necessary and undergo discomfort to achieve that goal.

One example of high energy commitment to achieve coordinated action is that of two persons (or groups) from different cultural backgrounds attempting to put aside previous antagonisms and work together on a common community program. It may require several sessions to assure one another that they can trust each other. They may have to ask third parties to confirm the positive intentions of the other, and each may have to take some risks of being criticized by the other. Each may have to admit previous errors of belief and actions toward the other, then show the seriousness of their new intent. Such admissions may be embarrassing.

If the intent of either or both parties is to obstruct achieving commonness of feeling and understanding, then either or both may refuse to expend any energy in the transaction. Ignoring the other is in a sense a rejection message. If the person being ignored perceives the intent of the other as rejection, then the person ignored may respond with hurt feelings, anger, withdrawal, revenge, or similar behaviors. It may be that the person merely had other items demanding attention at the moment and was not aware of not attending to the person who was feeling ignored. If both ignore one another, then there is no opportunity for coordinated activity.

On the other hand, each of us can undoubtedly think of cases where someone expended tremendous effort in order to deceive and otherwise thwart mutual understanding and coordinated action. This calculated deception may require more knowledge of one's audience than does the intent for cooperative, coordinated action.

The intelligence operations of unfriendly national governments in relation to one another is often one of highly sophisticated deceptions. In the case of two persons or small groups, it may be that one feels inferior, but goes to great effort through dress, limousines, and other status symbols to communicate that they are wealthy and of high status. When both parties in a situation are engaging in this kind of deception, it often becomes very humorous to an observer. It even becomes the basis for situation comedy in the entertainment media.

Another interesting case for considering perceived intent is the tourist from the USA buying some item from a street vendor who is accustomed to price bargaining. The intent of the vendor is to lower his price to about half the initial asking price. The expectation of the tourist is to pay the price asked. When the tourist pays the initial price, the vendor is surprised and may even be disappointed to have missed the excitement of negotiating the price.

In office situations, one employee may tell a supervisor that some of the work is low quality and that some action needs to be taken to correct the situation. On the surface, this seems like a strong intent to improve quality of output. The supervisor may or may not perceive that the intent of the person is to criticize a fellow employee and perhaps have that person reprimanded or negatively evaluated.

The sample of situations cited herein presumably will suggest numerous cases from your own experience where intent was correctly perceived and cases where intent was incorrectly perceived; cases where intent was positive toward you and cases where it was negative. You also can no doubt remember cases where your intent toward the other was positive and cases where your intent was negative.

In all cases, my perception of your intent will influence how I structure my transactions with you, in my efforts to satisfy my needs in relation to your intent. The accuracy of my judgments of your intent is expected to be higher when we are highly homogeneous on the variables which we have been discussing than when we are highly heterogeneous. Anyone traveling in a strange country can report numerous cases of high uncertainty regarding the intent of persons with whom they were communicating. This is consistent with the general proposition that predictability of the other increases with homogeneity of the participants and decreases with heterogeneity of the participants; and that as predictability of the other increases, the possibility of achieving the intended outcome of the communication increases. . . .

References

Althen, Gary L., and Josephine Jaime. "Assumptions and Values in Philippine, American, and Other Cultures," in *Readings in Intercultural Communication,* vol. 1. Regional Council for International Education, University of Pittsburgh, Pittsburgh Pa. 15213, 1971.

Couch, Carl, and Robert A. Hintz. *Constructing Social Life.* Champaign, Ill.: Stypes Publishers, 1975.

Whorf, Benjamin. *Language, Thought and Reality.* New York: Wiley, and Cambridge, Mass.: MIT Press, 1956.

PROBES

Catalog the intercultural communication contacts you have experienced in the last 48 hours; try not to overlook the less obvious ones. In this time period virtually everyone has had at least a half dozen contacts with "heterogeneous" others.

Which of the elements Sarbaugh discusses—openings, codes, world views, relationships, or intent—were most obviously different in the contacts you catalogued?

In a discussion with a person from another culture, identify the differences between the four elements of openings or greetings in your culture and in hers or his. In other words, what are the different ways each of you accomplishes (1) reciprocally acknowledged attention, (2) mutual responsiveness, (3) congruent functional identities, and (4) shared focus?

Give an example from your own experience of the operation of "The Whorf Hypothesis."

What is an example of a difference in world view between the United States and the Soviet Union that appears to you to contribute to tensions between these two governments?

Reflect on your most lengthy experience in another culture and identify one instance when you assimilated part of the environment and one time when you accommodated to it.

▌▌

This reading focuses on two-person intercultural communication. The effects of television coverage on acts of terrorism, newspaper coverage of the Olympic Games, nuclear weapons reductions talks, and speeches at the U.N. are all instances of intercultural communication, but the type you and I are most likely to experience occurs as we meet face to face with one or perhaps two persons from another culture. In this excerpt from their interpersonal communication text, Don Cushman and Dudley Cahn discuss this kind of contact as it occurs between friends and within a business organization.

Although they use terminology that's different from what Sarbaugh uses in the preceding essay, Cushman and Cahn's approach is basically very compatible. They assert that we can best improve our intercultural communication competency by (1) becoming aware of and defining the world views that are operating in an intercultural context and (2) identifying the "conventions" or rules-for-behavior that manifest, apply, or embody the world views. Again, the point is that the *functions* are similar across cultures, but the world views that ground the functions and the behaviors that operationalize them are different.

Cushman and Cahn use the example of Japanese–U.S. communication. They identify three ways the world views of the two cultures differ, and then they discuss how those differences affect communication between friends in the two cultures. Despite the apparent differences in world views, U.S. and Japanese people agree on the importance to their friendships of togetherness, trust, warmth, and caring.

There are, however, significant differences in male–female ratios and conversation topics.

There are also similarities and differences in what Cushman and Cahn call "mateship" in the two cultures. At the end of this section of the reading they make some suggestions about how U.S. and Japanese dating partners might adapt to each other's world views and conventions.

The author's discussion of organizational communication reveals the differences in world views that characterize organizational life in each culture. Their intent, as they put it, is "to expand our choice of cultural influence (some people do choose to change cultures) and our choice of individual self-object relationships (some people adopt new sets of personal values)." I hope you'll find this discussion of one instance of intercultural communication to be illuminating and helpful.

Cross-Cultural Communication and Interpersonal Relationships

Donald P. Cushman and Dudley D. Cahn, Jr.

> *Cultures exist primarily to create and preserve common systems of symbols by which their members can assign and exchange meanings. Unhappily, the distinctive rules that govern these symbol systems are far from obvious. About some of these codes, such as language, we have extensive knowledge. About others, such as gestures and facial codes, we have only rudimentary knowledge. On many others . . . rules governing topical appropriateness, customs regulating physical contact, time and space codes, strategies for the management of conflict . . . we have almost no systematic knowledge.*
>
> D. BARNLUND (1975:7–8)

COMMUNICATION BETWEEN PEOPLE FROM DIFFERENT CULTURAL GROUPS

Increased mobility and access to the means of communication have made most Americans aware that their self-concepts are different from the self-concepts of people in other cultures. In the United States alone, over 20 million people visit from abroad each year (Samovar, Porter and Jain 1981). Tourists, businessmen, government officials, educators, students and athletes from America visit other countries each year. When we add to this the large number of intercultural marriages and friendships which develop from such visits, it becomes apparent that most Ameri-

Reprinted from *Communication in Interpersonal Relationships* by Donald P. Cushman and Dudley D. Cahn, Jr. by permission of the State University of New York Press.

cans will spend some time, and some Americans a great deal of time, in interaction with people from other cultures.

Above and beyond the problem of acquiring a common language, establishing, maintaining, and terminating interpersonal relationships at the cross-cultural level of interaction present the individuals involved with one very important problem. The consensus mechanisms by which communicators function as active participants in their respective cultures are unique to each culture. Thus both communicators must, if they are to understand and establish interpersonal relationships with one another, come to grips with their own cultural roles and with the cultural rules of those with whom they interact. Such reciprocal responsibilities do not normally arise when one communicates within one's own culture. Nor are these responsibilities easy to fulfill. How does a person in one culture indicate to a person from another the cultural pressures that govern his or her self-object relationships? Similarly, how does a person in one culture discover the cultural inclinations conveyed by the communication of a person from another culture?

Fortunately, there is a way to deal with the problems involved in communication across cultures. It is our position that control over this process comes from bringing to consciousness our own cultural tendencies or assumptive world views and those of others, and then defining the conventions that link what is perceived with what is communicated. It is the purpose of this chapter to clarify this process by examining the assumptive world view and conventions that link what is perceived with what is communicated in regard to (1) interpersonal communication between friends and mates and (2) organizational communication between supervisors and subordinates and decision makers in two divergent cultures.

The extent to which culture affects communication between people from different cultural groups is a function of the dissimilarity between the cultures, rules, or self-concepts (Samovar, Porter, and Jain 1983). As we indicated in the previous chapter, culture is a socialization process that influences one's self-concept or the way we relate to objects, other persons, and places. The extent of the difference in self-object relationships between members of two cultural groups depends on the uniqueness of each's socialization process. Two of the most divergent cultural traditions of mankind are the Eastern tradition associated with such countries as Japan, China, India, and Korea, and the Western tradition asociated with such countries as the United States, Great Britain, Italy, Germany, and France. We shall select Japan and the United States as representatives of these divergent traditions and examine the problems involved in cross-cultural communication between people in these diverse cultures at (1) the interpersonal and (2) the organizational levels of interaction.

INTERPERSONAL COMMUNICATION IN JAPAN AND THE UNITED STATES

Interpersonal communication in Japanese and American cultures differs, according to Naotsuka and Sakamoto (1981). In Japan most interactional occasions call for the ritualistic use of explicit statements of politeness, while there is a comparative lack of formalities in the United States. These differences are due to a Japanese emphasis on mutual dependence, self-depreciation, and use of mutual apology as a social lubricant to conversation. In America we tend to be mutually independent, self-asserting, and likely to employ confrontation as a lubricant for social interaction.

Mutual Dependence vs. Mutual Independence For the Japanese, interaction, activities, and accomplishments are viewed in terms of a group effort or of a dependence on others. Therefore, one is expected to demonstrate in communication an explicit awareness of others, their social status, and contribution to group harmony. For Americans, interaction, activities, and accomplishments are viewed as individual achievements. Members of a group are regarded as independent individuals in a voluntary, temporal association of equals.

Self-depreciation vs. Self-assertion The Japanese value self-depreciation as a sign of recognizing their cultural or group place. One should not stand out, but demonstrate through communication that one has no selfish delusions of independent grandeur. For Americans the opposite is the case. They value self-assertion, independence, and the importance of demonstrating through communication who they are and what they can do.

Mutual Apology vs. Mutual Confrontation as a Social Lubricant to Interaction Japanese employ mutual apology as the chief technique for encouraging interaction and for keeping things running smoothly. One is always expected to begin with an apology and respond to any awkwardness, regardless of personal responsibility, with an apology. Americans seldom apologize and encourage the smooth flow of interaction by confronting others in regard to their attitudes, values, and beliefs, as well as the evidential basis for those values and beliefs. Such confrontations invite and receive a response from others.

The communication of personal opinion is handled quite differently in each culture. In Japan personal opinions are avoided, and, when forced to present them, the Japanese convey them indirectly and implicitly through subtle nuances in tone and phrasing which rely on cultural resonance or non-verbal cues. In contrast, Americans are usually ready to express a personal opinion directly and frankly. These differences are due to the Japanese value of avoiding confrontation, avoiding personal explanations, and avoiding anything that will separate them out from the group. American thrive on and value direct confrontation, verbal explanations, and expressions of personal inclination.

Friendship and mate selection represent two of the most interpersonally intimate communication activities in any culture. Extensive research has been conducted on these interaction processes by scholars in Japan and the United States. Let's explore each in turn for similarities and differences. In so doing, we shall gain an insight into the problems and prospects for cross-cultural relationships in these areas.

Friendship in Japan and the United States

Atsumi (1980) maintains that the Japanese form two types of friendships: (1) *tsukiai,* or interpersonal relationships cultivated and maintained as a result of social obligation, and (2) *friends,* or close interpersonal relationships that develop from mutual liking, attraction, interest, or common values. Interpersonal relationships based on social obligation or *tsukiai* are usually tied to work or neighborhood contacts of limited duration. Interpersonal relationships based on mutual liking, attraction, interests, or values, or *friends,* are usually among same sex schoolmates and usually last a life time. Opposite-sex friends, according to Mochizuki (1981), are rare, with 20% of his survey reporting no known opposite sex friends prior to their engagement. Atsumi reports that the number of close friends one has is small, but these friends serve the important function of allowing one to talk freely about a broad range of mutual interests while being at ease. Japanese close interpersonal relationships are thus divided between those necessary for work and those rooted in common interests. Friendship interpersonal relationships tend to be with others of the same sex, are small in number, and allow for intimate interaction in which one feels at ease.

. . . In the United States, . . . friendship is based on common ideal and real values, authenticity or honesty and trust, and upon social/psychological support. . . . Americans frequently classify friendship relations along a dimension which includes social acquaintances, good friends, close friends, and best friends. Friendship is further classified into two roles, confidant and companion. A confidant is someone who respects and supports an individual's evaluative self-object relationships, while a companion is someone who supports an individual's behavioral self-object relationships. Americans tend to have numerous acquaintances, close and good friends from both sexes, but only a small number of best friends. American best friend relationships tend to involve both sexes, to be small in number, to be rooted in common interests, and to allow for evaluative and behavioral self-concept support.

While several studies have been conducted comparing Japanese and American friendship patterns, two are of particular interest to our present analysis. Takahara (1974) undertook a comparative study of Japanese and American synonyms for friendship. Thirty subjects from each culture evenly divided by sex listed the following terms with the highest frequencies:

JAPAN	(n)	AMERICA	(n)
1. Togetherness	25	1. Understanding	29
2. Trust	24	2. Respect	25
3. Warmth	23	3. Sincerity	24
4. Understanding	19	4. Trust	22
		Togetherness	22
		Helping	22
		Caring	22

Note the similarity in the two lists in regard to togetherness, trust, warmth, caring, and understanding. Gudykunst and Nishida (1983) explored similarities and differences in regard to Japanese and American friendships focusing on the degree and scope of their social penetration on specific topics of interaction. They found similarities in 16 out of 37 comparisons. The differences which emerged follow. Americans tend to talk more often and to penetrate deeper into such topics as marriage, love/dating/sex, and emotions. Japanese tend to talk more often about interests/hobbies, school/work, biographical matters, religion and money issues. They also tend to talk more about physical activities and to achieve greater social penetration on this topic.

In short, while Japanese and American friendships are very similar in regard to focus and function, they differ in regard to the male/female ratios of friendship and the topics of conversation. Americans tend to be more concerned with marriage, love/dating/sex, and emotion, while the Japanese are more concerned with physical activities, hobbies, work, religion and money issues.

Attention is now directed to an analysis of the mate selection process in both cultures.

Mateship in Japan and the United States

Japanese men marry between the ages of 25 and 28 while women do so between 23 and 25. There are two distinct types of mate selection processes in Japan, marriages which are arranged and those based on love. Seventy-five percent of the marriages follow the arranged pattern, 25% the love pattern. However, 50% of the men who were married reported that they married for love (*Japan Times* 1983). Mochizuki (1981) provides a detailed study of the two mate selection processes in Japan. Each of these mate selection patterns proceeds through three stages: (1) going steady, (2) getting engaged, and (3) marriage. There are some major differences regarding the length of time spent in each stage for each pattern. For arranged marriages the mean length of time from initial date to going steady was two months, initial date to engagement four months, and initial date to marriage five months. For love marriages the mean length of time from initial date to going steady was four months, initial date to engagement 12 months, and initial date to marriage 26 months. In terms of frequency and intimacy of interaction, 75% of both groups report dating more than once a week after the engagement, while 30% of the arranged marriages and 60% of the love relationships report being involved in premarital sex. The average number of close friends of the opposite sex prior to marriage was 3.5 for males and 2.7 for females. Twenty percent of the men reported their wives as their only friend of the opposite sex prior to marriage. Measures of consensus between partners on five topics ranging from where to live to how many children the family should have, yielded consensus in only 7.9% of the cases. These findings indicate that Japanese mate selection tends to vary in length of time and intimacy of interaction according to marital pattern; the quality of interaction seems to be relatively low in regard to the five topics considered; and 20% of the men selected mates from a sample of one.

. . . In the United States, . . . mateship is based on intelligence, physical attraction, and sex appeal and one's conformity to the other's view of what constitutes an ideal mate. . . . Progress through the mate selection process is a function of the lack of discrepancies between the male's real and ideal self and of reciprocated self-concept support. . . . Most Americans view love as an antecedent for sex and 80% of married couples report participating in premarital sex prior to marriage. Moreover, most engaged couples think they are in consensus on intimate topics when in fact they are not. Thus, we can conclude that American mate selection tends to involve a single pattern of love and physical attraction based on perceived similarities in intelligence, physical attraction, and sex appeal as well as considerable concern for the stability of the male as reflected in real-ideal self-concept similarity, and that sexual intimacy seems to be high and consensus low in such relationships.

Several important studies have been conducted comparing the Japanese and American mate selection processes. Takahara (1974) undertook a comparative study of Japanese and American synonyms for marriage. Thirty subjects from each culture evenly divided between the sexes reported the following terms with the highest frequency.

JAPAN	(n)	AMERICA	(n)
1. Trust	27	1. Love	30
2. Family	20	2. Respect	27
3. Understanding	18	3. Responsibility	24
4. Problem sharing	17	4. Understanding	23
5. Compromise	17	5. Helping each other	22
6. Love	16	6. Problem sharing	22
7. Endurance	16	7. Trust	21
8. Children	16	8. Encouraging	21

Cushman and Nishida (1984) examined each culture's views of an ideal mate. The following qualities emerged in order of importance by sex:

JAPAN

M	F
1. Common values	1 Sound health
2. Easy to talk to	2. Honest
3. Sound health	3. Easy to talk to
4. Intelligent	4. Common values
5. Affectionate	5. Intelligent
6. Honest	6. Affectionate
7. Handles money well	7. Handles money well

AMERICA

M	F
1. Sex Appeal	1. Sex Appeal
2. Respect	2. Affectionate
3. Affectionate	3. Respect
4. Supportive	4. Intelligent
5. Friendship	5. Friendship
6. Intelligent	6. Supportive
7. Attractive	7. Attractive

Note the considerable similarity among males and females in both cultures in regard to their conceptions of marriage and ideal mates. However, there are some major differences between the sexes in ranking those qualities. Japanese men seem to be more concerned with common values and affection, while Japanese women focus more on good health and honesty. American men are more concerned with affection, support, and friendship, while American women are more concerned with intelligence. Finally notice the considerable differences between Japanese and Americans in regard to an ideal mate: the Japanese require common values, sound health, and handling money well, while Americans seek sex appeal, physical attraction, and friendship. In short, there appear to be significant cultural differences between the Japanese and Americans in regard to the mate selection process itself, to some of the qualities of marriage, to many of the qualities of an ideal mate and, in particular, to the role love and sex are to play in marriage vs. good health, endurance, money, and children.

What then can we conclude regarding problems of communication arising from cultural differences in the friendship and mate selection process in these two countries? First, it appears that prospects for establishing cross-cultural friendships may be improved, by respecting cultural differences in regard to the scope of topics appropriate for discussion and the social penetration of these topics. Americans must minimize topics such as marriage, love/sex/dating, and emotions when communicating with Japanese. In turn, Japanese must minimize physical fitness and work when communicating with Americans. Prospects for trouble-free communication in regard to cross-cultural mateship are much less optimistic. Here several cultural barriers appear important. The American preoccupation with love and sex will create problems for the Japanese, and the Japanese concern for good health, children, and endurance will create problems for Americans. Thus, considerable caution is required between Japanese and American persons considering marriage.

Attention is now directed to an examination of cross-cultural similarities and differences between Japan and the United States in regard to organizational communication and interpersonal relationships.

ORGANIZATIONAL COMMUNICATION IN JAPAN AND THE UNITED STATES

Organizations come in many different sizes and shapes in both Japan and the United States. Similarly, organizational communication in these organizations involves a variety of activities and varies considerably according to each. Since it is not possible to examine all organizations nor all types of communication within organizations in one small section of this book, we shall restrict our analysis (1) to a consideration of large organization and (2) to such tasks as supervisor-subordinate communication and the process of decision-making.

Between 1970 and 1983 large Japanese corporations have come into world prominence in such areas as electronics, autos, computers, steel, industrial chemicals, and film. In fact, Japanese and American corporations rank among the most productive in the world in those areas. Ouchi (1981) provides a suggestive list of contrasts between the Japanese and American models of large organizations.

JAPANESE	AMERICAN
1. Lifetime employment	1. Short term employment
2. Slow evaluation and promotion	2. Rapid evaluation and promotion
3. Non-specialized career paths	3. Specialized career paths
4. Implicit control mechanism	4. Explicit control mechanisms
5. Collective decision-making	5. Individual decision-making
6. Collective responsibility	6. Individual responsibility
7. Holistic concern	7. Segmented concern

Let us explore in some detail how these differences manifest themselves in supervisors-subordinate communication and in decision-making.

Supervisor–subordinate communication. Yoshikawa (1982) provides an in depth analysis of the communication differences between Japanese and American corporations. He does this by first examining the cultural values in Japan which form the basis for the difference and then contrasting Japanese and American communication patterns which follow from the values. Four such values are highlighted.

First, the orientation of the Japanese culture is such that it is better to be harmonious than right or frank, and to achieve this end people will do everything to avoid appearing to oppose anyone directly. This value leads to a difference between Japanese and American supervisors. A Japanese manager has as his primary goal to be an effective mediator, the American manager an effective leader. A Japanese manager makes a key distinction between *tatemae* and *honne*. The former means in front; the latter means behind the scenes. In Japanese corporations, differences are handled behind the scenes, while commonalities are the only points of consideration at collective meetings. It goes without saying that at most organizational meetings in America it is the task of the manager to encourage an open and frank confrontation of competing ideas.

Second, the orientation of the Japanese culture is such that it prefers an effective communication style, while Americans prefer an instrumental communication style. The Japanese concentrate on how something is said, the Americans on what is being said. The Japanese supervisor tends to worry about the attitudes and feelings of his subordinates. The Japanese thus have planned informal get-togethers at bars or *otsukiai* where the chief task of the interaction is to get better acquainted. In America, supervisors seldom go out with subordinates, and when they do it is in addition to work. In *otsukiai* a subordinate can express all his concerns and oppositions, and the supervisor will listen and not use them against him, but rather will use them to further the interests of the subordinate involved.

Third, the orientation of the Japanese culture is to mistrust verbal language, the American culture to equate trust with living up to one's verbal commitments. Accordingly, 76% of Japanese believe a "silent man rather than an eloquent man will be the most successful" (Klopf et al., 1978). A good supervisor is thus a man of few words in Japan. A good supervisor in America defines rules and tasks clearly and gives frequent commands and evaluations.

Fourth, the orientation of the Japanese culture is to employ indirect-intermediate communication, while the Americans prefer a direct style. The Japanese find it very difficult and uncomfortable to talk face to face. They need something in between, whether it be *Otsukiai* or drink or lunch or sports activities such as golf. The Japanese also make extensive use of intermediaries, people who speak for them because they know better the person with whom they have to talk. American managers prefer a direct style and would seldom ask another subordinate to talk to someone rather than to talk themselves on important matters.

Harmony, personal concern, silence, and indirect intermediaries are all characteristics of Japanese supervisor–subordinate communication. Conflict, task-orientation, assertive and direct communication are characteristics of American supervisor–subordinate communication. Cross-cultural organizational communication between Japanese and American supervisors and subordinates thus becomes very troublesome. American subordinates view Japanese supervisors as lacking direction, being uncommunicative and indirect, and always avoiding conflict. Japanese subordinates view American supervisors as conflict prone, overbearing, talkative, and too direct.

Cross-cultural communication is important because it conditions our understanding of our own and others' cultures and of our own and others' unique self-concepts. This brief comparison between Japan and the United States helps to illustrate how such an awareness can expand our choice of cultural influence (some people do choose to change cultures) and our choice of individual self-object relationships (some people adopt new sets of personal values). While the similarities between Japanese and American cultures appear small and the differences appear large, particularly in regard to mateship, supervisor–subordinate relationships, and organizational decision-making, knowledge of the similarities and differences involved allows the actor in such situations to exert some measure of control over his or her communication behavior and thus become more effective in establishing, maintaining, and terminating interpersonal relationships. It is in this insight that the importance of communication and its effect upon interpersonal relationships reside in cross-cultural contexts.

References

Atsumi, R. "Patterns of Personal Relationships," *Social Analysis* 5 no. 6 (1980):63–78.

Barnland, D. *Public and Private Self in Japan and the United States: Communicative Styles in Two Cultures.* Forest Grove, Ore.: International Scholarly Book Services, 1975.

Cushman, D., and T. Nishida. "Mate Selection the United States and Japan." Unpublished manuscript, 1984.

Gudykunst, W., and T. Nishida. "Social Penetration and Japanese and American Close Friendships," in *Communication Yearbook,* vol. 7, ed. R. Bostrom. New Brunswick, N.J.: Transaction Books, 1983.

Hall, E. *Beyond Culture.* New York: Anchor Press, 1976.

Harris, Philip R., and Robert T. Moran. *Managing Cultural Differences.* Houston: Gulf, 1979.

"Husbands Should be Older than Wives: Poll," *Japan Times* (July 24, 1983).

Klopf, D., S. Ishii, and R. Cambra. "How Communicative are the Japanese?", *The Hawaii Times* (July 6, 1978).

Mochizuki, T. "Changing Patterns of Mate Selection," *Journal of Comparative Family Studies* 12, no. 3, (1981): 318–328.

Naotsuka, R., and N. Sakamoto. *Mutual Understanding of Different Cultures.* Tokyo, Japan: Taishukan, 1981.

Okabe, R. "Cultural Assumptions of Communication Theroy from Eastern and Western Perspectives: The Case of Japan and the United States," in *International and Intercultural Communication Annual,* vol.7, ed. W. B. Gudykunst. Annandale, Va.: Speech Communication Association, 1983.

Ouchi, W. *Theory Z.* Reading, Mass.: Addison-Wesley. 1981.

Saito, M. Nemawashi. *Et Cetera* 39 (1982): 205–218.

Samovar, L., R. Porter, and N. Jain. *Understanding Inter-cultural Communication.* Belmont, Calif.: Wordsworth, 1981.

Takahara, N. "Semantic Concepts of Marriage, Work, Friendship and Foreigner in Three Cultures," in *Intercultural Encounters with Japan,* ed. J. Condon and M. Saito. Tokyo, Japan: Simul Press, 1974.

Yoshikawa, M. "Japanese and American Modes of Communication and Implications for Managerial and Organizational Behavior." Unpublished paper, Second International Conference on Communication Theory: Eastern and Western Perspective. Yokohama, Japan. July 1982.

PROBES

Explain what Cushman and Cahn mean when they say, "It is our position that control over this [intercultural communication] process comes from bringing to consciousness our own cultural tendencies or assumptive world views and those of others, and then defining the conventions that link what is perceived with what is communicated."

Give a specific example from your own experience of your culture's position on mutual independence–dependence, self-assertion versus self-depreciation, and mutual apology versus mutual confrontation.

What is the parallel in your culture of the Japanese distinction between *tsukiai* and friend?

Do you agree with Cushman and Cahn's description of characteristics of friendship in the United States?

The frequency of arranged marriages in Japan is one of the most significant differences between that culture and U.S. culture. What aspects of the Japanese world view underlie that culture's acceptance of arranged marriages? If you are not Japanese, what does your reaction to the prevalence of arranged marriages in Japan tell you about your own world view?

How easy would it be for you to consider as a mate an opposite-sex person who holds the views of an ideal mate that are summarized on page 329? Which views would it be the most difficult for you to accept?

What are the most obvious differences between the Japanese business organization as Cushman and Cahn describe it and the business organization you currently work in?

PART 5

Approaches
to Interpersonal
Communication

CHAPTER 13

Photograph by John T. Wood.

LEO BUSCAGLIA'S APPROACH

I've never met Leo Buscaglia, but I've liked him ever since I heard a tape recording of one of his speeches in the early 1970s. The speech was about love, and Buscaglia was just beginning to be widely known as the professor from the University of Southern California who actually taught a course on the subject. It was obvious from the tape that Buscaglia was passionately involved with his subject matter and with the chance to share his ideas with others. He was an enthusiastic, dynamic presenter, and the applause and laughter on the tape told how much the audience loved him.

It's easy for some people to dismiss Buscaglia as a crazy Italian, some kind of unreconstructed flower child, or an example of all that's unstable in southern California. I have to admit I've even felt that way about him from time to time, and I *like* him. But I've also discovered that it's just about impossible to read his best-selling book *Living, Loving and Learning* without getting caught up in his enthusiasm and his love of life. Things may not be as simple as he sometimes makes them sound, but when you get right down to it, your attitude toward life *is* the foundation of everything else, and in a sense that is simple: It's either generally positive, ho-hum, or negative.

I chose this excerpt because it's about "togetherness." Buscaglia does not present an approach to interpersonal communication that you can logically outline or reduce to formal propositions. But his major ideas are pretty clear. The first one has to do with how we define the situations we find ourselves in: We can either see the positive or the negative side, and our choice helps determine the quality of life we experience. There are even advantages to being seen as a "crazy kook"; Buscaglia claims that when he's dancing in the leaves, "I'm having a ball and the sane ones are bored to death."

It's also important to have models and to model for others. Buscaglia tells how Tulio and Rosa, his mom and dad, didn't tell him how to enjoy life, they *showed* him. "Tactility" was one thing he was shown; Buscaglia loves hugging and, as he puts it, "I have never had an existential problem as to whether I exist or not. If I can touch you and you can touch me, I exist."

Another lesson he learned from his mother is that nondirective permissiveness is not the only way to love. His mama would say, "Shut up!" and as he puts it, "We always knew what that meant. It was a beautiful kind of interaction in the family. Not too amazing, none of us has ever had a mental problem."

Buscaglia's central theme is that "loving relationships, togetherness, away from 'I' and 'me' and to 'us' and 'we,' is where the joy really lies." How do you move toward togetherness? By risking, for one thing. "We need to reach out, we need to bring in, we need not to be afraid." We also need to reexamine our myth of romantic love. And to stay open to change. And to learn from our pain. And to exploit the therapeutic value of hugging and touching. And to live in the present.

In short, "Your relationships will be as vital and alive as *you* are. If you're dead, your relationship is dead. And if your relationships are boring and inadequate it's because *you* are boring and inadequate. Liven yourself up!"

Together with Leo Buscaglia

Leo Buscaglia

I'd like to talk to you about a concept that means a great deal to me, and that is the concept of togetherness. I really am concerned about how separated we all are. Everybody seems to be involved in what Schweitzer talked about so many years ago when he said we're all so much together in crowds and yet all of us are dying of loneliness. It's as if we don't know how to reach out to each other any more, to hold each other, to call to each other, to build bridges. And so I'd like to talk about togetherness, you and I, and some crazy ideas I have about building some of those bridges so that we can get a little bit closer.

I think it's personified, that separateness, loneliness, and despair, by what happened to me recently while I was traveling across country. So many things happen on airplanes. I just love airplanes. You meet old friends you've never seen, you make new friends because people know they may never see you again; it's like true confessions. They tell you about their wives and their husbands. I'm a real people person as you know, and I love to hear about wives, husbands, children, triumph, tears—all the wonderful things that make us human.

In a 747 jet another man and I were lucky to have the area with just two seats. At least *I* thought it was very lucky. He was at the window and as I walked to him I said, "Hello," which I always do, thinking we could start things going. If you're going to be together for five hours, you might as well say "hello," even though some people won't answer. I said, "Hello," and he said, "Oh, damn, I thought this seat next to me was going to be left empty so I could stretch out." And I said, "Oh I promise you that as soon as we get in the air, if there's an empty seat, I'll take it and let you have this one."

I sat next to him and got the seat belt tightened and a woman came on with a little baby. I couldn't help thinking, "Isn't it lucky to have airplane travel for women who have to travel with babies?" I think of Mama when she had little Vincenzo in her arms traveling across the country when she first came from Italy. It took seven days! And here this woman would make it to New York in just about five or six hours. I was thinking this positive thing when he said, "Oh damn. Look, there's a woman with a baby. The baby is going to squawk all the way to New York." That was number two. We hadn't even taken off yet! Number three occurred when the stewardess announced that there was a "no-smoking section" and he said, "Smokers should be shot!" I said, "All of them? I know some very nice smokers. I don't happen to be one, but I wouldn't want them all to be shot." Then we received the menu. Isn't it amazing that you can fly across the country and not only do they feed you, but they give you a menu with a choice of three entrées? That's phenomenal! He looked at everything and said, "Oh God, they never have anything good on these damn planes." Imagine, we still hadn't taken off yet. And then the stewardess got up and started pointing to the two exits in the rear, two exits in the front, you know how they do? They *have* to do that. He said, "Look at those stupid dames. You know, they don't do anything. They're only there to meet wealthy men. They don't work, they're just glorified waitresses." On and on he went. It was amazing me—all of this before the plane even left the ground.

When we were in the air (I couldn't move; I was stuck there; but I was determined he would be a lover before we arrived in New York), he turned to me and said, "What do you do?" I replied, "I'm a professor at a university." He said, "What do you teach?" And I said, "Courses in counseling and in loving people and relationships." He said, "Thank God, there's someone else who feels about people the way I do." Everybody thinks they are lovers! Before we got to New York I found out his wife had left him and he defined his children as "thankless bums." Isn't that amazing?

Reach out. Learn to reach out. Listen to yourself and hear how many times you say, "I am a lover." My question is, how many times a day do you hear yourself say, "I love," as opposed to "I hate, I hate, I hate." Very interesting phenomenon. I am sick of this kind of an approach to life, that's so centered on "I" and "me." I'm tired of hearing people say "I" and "me." I would love to hear people using "us" and "we" for a change. Isn't that nice? "us" and "we"? "I" is important, but my goodness, the strength comes from "us" and "we"! You and I together are much stronger than you or I alone, and I like to think that when we get together, I'm not only giving, I'm getting. I will now have four arms, two of yours and two of mine, two heads—that means we've got all kinds of new creative ideas—and two different worlds, your world and my world. And so I want you to come in.

I have learned some very interesting things that I believe are a result of people getting trapped in the concept of "I" and "me." This is from a book called *On an Average Day in America.* Get this: On an average day in America, 9,077 babies are born, and that's wonderful; 1,282 are illegitimate and not wanted. About 2,740 kids run away from home on an average day in America. About 1,986 couples divorce on an average day in America. An estimated 69 beautiful, incredible people will commit suicide on an average day in America. Someone is raped every 8 minutes, murdered every 27 minutes and robbed every 76 seconds. A burglar strikes every 10 seconds, a car is stolen every 33 seconds, and the average relationship in America today lasts three months. Now if that doesn't freak you out! And that's the world we're creating for ourselves! That's the world of I and me. Well, I don't want to be a part of that world, I want to create a different kind of world—and we can do it together. That's the wondrous thing.

I really have nothing to sell; I have a lot to share. And I'm positive that if we could relate, you could give me some ideas of how we can reverse this trend by recognizing that we can't survive alone and that aloneness and ego involvement leads to death and destruction.

Also we're learning a great deal about learning. I'm a teacher and I've been a teacher all my life and I love being a teacher, but I've only just recently found out that I teach nothing to no one. That's an ego trip if you believe that you can teach anything to anybody. All that I can be, at best, is an excited, wondrous, magical facilitator of knowledge. I can lay it out, but if you don't want to eat it, I can do nothing about it. But I also find that if I can make it attractive and exciting, that maybe a few people get hooked and wonder, "What is that kook talking about? Maybe if he's so crazy about life, maybe life is worth living." When I dance in the leaves, and I do it often, I find that other people get enough courage to go and dance in their leaves, too. And that's good. If I can teach someone to dance in the leaves, I'll run the risk of being called crazy. I love being called crazy because, as I said before, when you're called crazy it gives you a lot of leeway for behavior.

You can do damn near anything and everybody says, "Oh, that's crazy Buscaglia dancing in the leaves." And I'm having a ball and all the sane ones are bored to death.

You see, what we really need, the behavior modifiers tell us, are good *models*. We need models of love, people who can show us. Those of you who know my book *Love* know that I dedicated it to my parents, Tulio and Rosa Buscaglia, because they didn't teach me to love, they *showed* me how to love. And they had no idea about behavior modification. But people like Bandura at Stanford are showing us that the best way to teach is by modeling. Without telling anybody anything, without teaching anybody anything, you *be* what you want your children to be and watch them grow.

Many of you know that I grew up in a wonderful, great big, fantastic, loving Italian family and grew healthy and happy and wonderful on bagna calda and pasta fasule and polenta and all those marvelous dishes. But I also learned a lot of other things from these models, most of which was taught without my knowing. One thing they taught me is that we need to be touched and we need to be loved. And so I've been touching and loving all my life and I've been having a ball, touching and loving. It's been so nice and I didn't know that in "the outside world" you don't touch and you don't love—not without reservations. The first note I ever received from a teacher in America was a note written to Mama. You can imagine how sensitive this lady was if she wrote the following to a poor Italian immigrant woman who could barely speak English. "Dear Mrs. Buscaglia. Your son Felice is too *tactile.*" Can you believe that? I brought the note home to my mama who looked and said, "Hey what's this a-tactile? Felice, if you did something wrong, I'll smack your head in." I said, "I don't know what tactile is Mama, honest. I don't know what I did." So we went to the dictionary, which we did a lot of, and flipped to the word "tactile." It says, to feel, to touch. Mama says, "So what's wrong with that? That's a-nice. You gotta crazy teacher." I have never had an existential problem as to whether I exist or not. If I can touch you and you can touch me, I exist. So many people are dying of loneliness because they are not touched.

Also, they taught me how to share. We had a tiny house and a big family and boy, do you learn to share! Now we have enormous houses; everybody could get lost. Then we had lots of people and one toilet. Oh, do I remember! That was the center of the house. Everybody was in and out of the toilet all the time and the minute you'd get in there and sit down and relax for 30 seconds, "Get out of there, it's my turn." So you learned to give and you learned to share, you learned to get out and you learned to speed up and you learned to use the same sink and sleep in the same rooms. It's a wonderful thing to learn. I'm convinced that the family that goes to the toilet together, stays together. But now we have a toilet for Mary and a toilet for Sally and a toilet for Papa and a dressing room for Mama. That's too bad— we don't need all that space. It's so funny, but we build enormous houses and we work our fingers to the bone and we say it's for our children. But if you think about it, we bring them into these beautiful houses with lovely furniture and we don't let them live in them. "Don't touch this!" "Don't touch that!" "You're going to break that." For goodness sakes, who's the house for, the neighbors? Not in our house! The house was there for us to live in.

So I learned to share and I learned a wonderful sense of responsibility from Mama, who was a rugged lady. When she said something, it went. This always amused me when I got into the university and I studied theories of counseling and all this permissive stuff. Mama was the most magnificent nondirective, permissive counselor. She'd say, "Shut up!" We always knew what that meant. It was a beautiful kind of interaction with the family. Not too amazing, none of us have ever had a mental problem.

I remember as a kid, I wanted to go to Paris. She said, "Felice, you're too young for traveling." "But, Mama, I want to go." At that time, Jean Paul Sartre and Simone de Beauvoir were all involved in the wonderful concept of existentialism; and Felice wanted to go there because he heard that everybody was in misery and he wanted to go there and be miserable, too. I wanted to try everything. Mama says, "OK, you go, but if you do, you're declaring yourself an adult and don't ask me for anything after that. You're an adult. You're free, go." Oh, was it fantastic! I didn't have a lot of money, but I had a little bit and I went there and I lived everybody's dream. I had a tiny apartment. I could see from my skylight all the rooftops of Paris. I sat at the feet of people like Sartre and de Beauvoir—didn't understand a damn word they said—loved every minute of it. Suffered! Oh, did I suffer! And it was wonderful, on Camembert cheese and French wine. Pretty soon there was no money. I had no real concept of money. I was sharing with everybody, I was the last of the big spenders. I always had the bottle of wine, everyone came to my place to share it. This had been the way I grew up, the modeling I had learned. At our house the postman would come and Papa would pour him a glass of wine. "Eh, poor man, he's working all day. He needs a good glass of wine." We would say, "Papa, don't give him wine!" It would kill us when the teacher came to visit and Papa offered her wine. "The teacher won't drink wine." Then we were shocked when the teacher drank wine. She was no kook. It was good wine! But I remember getting to the point where I really had very little money—almost none. I thought I'd just wire home, that's all. I went to the telegraph office in Paris, and, to save money, just wrote, "Starving. Felice." One word but significant. Twenty-four hours later I had a telegram from Mama and *it* said, "Starve! Mama." The moment of truth! At long last I was an adult. What was I going to do now?

I'm going to tell you what that taught me. It taught me about hunger, it taught me about how cold a place can be, not only physically, but when you don't have the bottles of wine to share, the people who called themselves your "friends" don't come around anymore. It taught me a lot and I never would have learned it if Mama had relented and sent me a check. And I stayed there and stayed there, just to show her I could do it. When I went home many months later, she said to me one evening, "That was the hardest thing I ever had to do, but if I hadn't done it, you would never have grown to be Felice." And it was true. So through modeling, they taught me so much about living and loving together.

I'm often asked to be on talk shows. It always interests me that every other call, if not every single call, has to do with loneliness. "What do I do? I was married, I had kids and now I'm alone. I'm in an old apartment house, by myself. What happened? I would love to make friends with my neighbors, but I'm scared to knock at the door." "I walk down the street and I see attractive people and I try smiling at them, but I'm scared." We're teaching everybody everything there is except what is essential, and that is how to live in joy, how to live in happiness, how to have a sense of personal worth and personal dignity. Those things are taught, and they're learned. We need more people who teach that sort of thing by doing it, by risking, by saying hello, by sitting next to this man, by trying to show him that the stewardesses are people just like him, that this woman does have a baby and it's wonderful.

Recently on a talk show I heard a woman make an incredible statement. She said, "You know, I've spent the last 20 years trying to change my husband and I'm very disappointed in him. He's no longer the man I married." Isn't that marvelous?

I don't know how many of you know Rodney Dangerfield, but he says the craziest things. This is the zenith of what I'm talking about. He says, "We sleep in separate rooms, we have dinner apart, we take separate vacations, we're doing everything we can to keep our marriage together." Isn't that outrageous? And yet it's almost come to that.

Loving relationships, togetherness, away from "I" and "me" and to "us" and "we," is where the joy really lies. Eating a good dinner by yourself is fine, but sharing it with five or six people whom you love is heaven. Going in the park and looking at the trees by yourself can be lovely, but having someone on your arm who says "Look at the purple ones" while you're looking at the blue ones, and you don't miss the purple or the blue ones, is fantastic! Don't miss togetherness, because it's yours and it's available to you. Erich Fromm, who has written so many beautiful things about togetherness and love, said "The deepest need of man is to overcome his separateness. To leave the prison of his aloneness. The absolute failure to achieve this aim means insanity." And, he's a psychiatrist.

If you think about people who are mentally ill, they're the ones who have moved the farthest away from other people. The healthy ones dive right in the middle, no matter what it means. In love class we talked about risking and going out and I would say, "Why don't you do it?" "Oh, I'm afraid to be hurt." Good grief. What a crazy attitude. Being hurt occasionally can spice up your life. When you're crying, you're at least alive. Pain is better than nothing. We need to reach out, we need to bring in, we need not to be afraid. The biological sciences tell us this. I read something really interesting by Ashley Montague. He said, "Without interdependence, no living group of organisms could ever survive." Imagine—that's *all* forms of life! "And in so far as any group of organisms depart from their functioning, from their requirement of interdependence, to that extent does it then become malfunctional and inoperative." But, he adds, "Whenever organisms are interacting in a related manner, they are conferring *survival* benefits upon each other, giving each other *life.*" So, I'm involved in the process of *giving life.* It's the most incredible gift and it's yours to take.

Since all of these things are *learned,* what are some of the things that can bring us together, some of the things we need to know about togetherness, about relationships, about caring, about love? The first is so essential, because we have a very crazy concept in our culture called romantic love. That's why so many of us are disappointed! We really still believe what they tell us in musical comedies, that we look across a crowded room and there we see those special eyeballs that have been waiting for 20 years. You are drawn together, you embrace and walk out into the sunset and never have a problem. What a shame! And what about that wonderful courtship, when you are on your best behavior, she is on her best behavior? She always looks glorious every time you go to the door. You are always gallant. You even bring flowers and chocolates. You tell her how nice she looks and then you get married and the next day you say, "Who are you?" All of a sudden she appears in rollers. You say, "My God! I married someone from outer space!" "Wouldn't it be nice just once during courtship to answer the door and say, "Look, I wear rollers. So if that freaks you out, it's going to have to be." Why not? Presenting ourselves as we are, you recognize that if you are expecting a relationship to be a continual honeymoon of perfection you're going to be so disappointed.

But there are many kinds of honeymoons. I just love to talk to old people because they can tell you about the honeymoon transitions. Looking back, in order to learn. We don't do that, we're always looking ahead. But in looking back, they can tell you so many things. There was certainly a honeymoon of getting acquainted. Then there was a honeymoon of the first apartment and all that used furniture, maybe even boxes for bookcases, but in those times who the hell cared? You were so happy in that honeymoon. And then there was the honeymoon of the first kid coming. The honeymoon of watching everybody grow up, much to your amazement those 12, 15 years pass so fast and all of a sudden there you are, honeymoon after honeymoon after honeymoon. Elisabeth Kübler Ross tells us even that last honeymoon called "death" can be a glorious experience if we embrace it as we do all the other honeymoons, with no expectations. It's there, it's mine to experience and I want to know it when my time comes. I would like to live that way.

I don't want to harp on Mama and Papa, but since it's so close to me . . . do you know that my mother used to tell us the story that she had never seen my father until five days after they were married? It was an arranged marriage and in Italy when you arrange a marriage, the man comes over to the home and, of course, all the women there were waiting on the table, with him sitting at the table, but she would never dare look at him. She would ask her sisters, "What does he look like?" They'd say "Oooh, he's so handsome. You're really going to freak out on this one." She said she didn't dare look at him. At the wedding her eyes were always down, and that marvelous day about five days into the marriage where she actually turned around and faced him, she said, "I did good!" He already knew it. But isn't it amazing these two people who supposedly didn't go through this period of having to fall madly in love, managed to survive in a beautiful relationship that was constantly growing for over 55 years? If you had seen how close they were when they parted. You just had a feeling that death wasn't going to break them apart, there was some way that it would just be a transitional period and eventually they would be reunited, there's no question about it. So remember always, the most essential thing about a relationship is that one and one together always make two, and if you want to survive the relationship, you must always maintain who you are and continue to grow through change. You are two wonderful, magical individuals. You have your life, he has his life and you build bridges to each other; but you always maintain your integrity and your dignity because all relationships, no matter how magnificent they are, even if they last for 60 years, are temporary, and eventually you are going to be faced again with you. One of the saddest things is the person who has invested everything in a relationship and when the relationship ends they must ask, "What do I do now?"

If you love someone, your goal is to want them to be all that they are and you will encourage them every inch of the way. Everytime they do something that helps them to grow or learn something to help them to become more, you dance and celebrate the occasion. You're not growing apart, you are growing together, but hand in hand, not melting one into the other. You are a unique person, it's impossible to melt into somebody else.

Some of you know the beautiful poem by Gibran about relationships. I'm just going to quote a couple of sentences. It's so lovely. He says, "Sing and dance together and be joyous, but let each one also be alone. Even as the strings of a lute are alone, though they quiver to the same music." Isn't that nice? Go to someone and say, "I want to quiver with you." "Give your hearts, but not into each other's keeping, for only the hand of Life can contain your hearts. Stand together and yet not too near together for the pillars of the temple, in order to hold the temple up, stand apart. The oak tree and the cypress do not grow in each other's shadow." Don't ever grow in anybody's shadow, you cannot *grow* in someone else's shadow. You find your own sunlight and you get as big and wonderful and as glorious as possible. And you share, telling them, "Let's communicate, let's talk, let's let it happen." But it doesn't happen in someone else's shadow. There you wilt, you forget who you are, you lose you and if you've lost you, you've lost the most essential thing you have. So you're one and one but you're two and you're together. You're an "I." He's an "I" and you are together an "us."

Secondly, I think loving relationships and togetherness are made in heaven, but it has to be *practiced* on earth, and sometimes that is very difficult. In fact, I know of nothing that is more difficult. I'm preparing a book now on loving relationships and I've done an enormous amount of research on what I consider to be the most dynamic aspect of human behavior—and I can't find much. If you want to learn about loving relationships, you're hard pressed to do it. Sure, loving relationships may bring pain. Coming together and having to give some of yourself up may bring pain. But you can also learn from pain. It really annoys me when, in our society, nobody wants any suffering at all. The minute you begin to suffer, you start popping pills or drowning yourself in alcohol, not knowing that some of the greatest learning can take place in a state of pain and despair. The difference is, you experience it and you don't *cling* to it. It's sick to *cling* to despair. You experience it and you *let it go*. There are great moments in all of our lives that were despairing. If you think back and you used them well, they helped you to grow and become a far greater person.

I mentioned earlier about how estranged we are from each other. In this culture we learn that the way to meet people is to stand erect and say, "How do you do?" Talk about a distancing phenomenon! If you're really lucky, somebody will give their hand and say "How do you do?" It's usually very quick. It's no wonder that though we all crave each other, we don't have each other, we don't touch each other. In our culture, at the age of five and six, a boy child is told "No more of this hugging nonsense, you're a *man* now and men don't do these things." I'm glad I was in a home where people said, "Who said?" Nobody in my house said, "How do you do?" When the door opened and someone arrived, everybody kissed. Everybody! Nobody was ignored, everybody was touched. What a wondrous experience to be touched in love. And there are many ways of touching. Do you know the wonder of walking into a room and having people happy because you are there? That's the greatest thing. Instead of an expression on their faces saying "Oh my God, there he is again," a joyous smile appears because you've walked in. An aura comes with you that lights up the whole house. Know that feeling? Don't miss it!

What amuses me, is that now we're finding out that scientifically touching does make a difference in our lives, physiologically and psychologically. There is a Doctor Bresler at the UCLA pain clinic. He isn't writing regular prescriptions any more, he's writing a prescription that says, "four hugs a day." People will say the man is crazy. "Oh no," he says, "hug once in the morning, once at lunch, once in the evening and once before bed and you'll get well." Dr. Harold Falk, senior psychiatrist at the Menninger Foundation, said this: "Hugging can lift depression, enabling the body's immunization system to become tuned up. Hugging breathes fresh life into tired bodies and makes you feel younger and more vibrant. In the home, hugging can strengthen relationships and significantly reduce tensions." Helen Colton in her book, *Joy of Touching,* said that the hemoglobin in the blood increases significantly when you are touched, fondled and hugged. Hemoglobin is that part of the blood that carries the vital supplies of oxygen to the heart and to the brain—and she says that if you want to be healthy, you must touch each other, you must love each other, you must hold each other. One of the saddest things in our culture is that we stress the sexual aspect of a relationship way out of proportion. What a pity, because in those things we are often missing the tenderness, the warmth. The kiss when it's not expected, the touch on the shoulder when you really need it most—that's "sensual" gratification. Jim Sanderson, a syndicated columnist who writes for the *L.A. Times,* recently had a letter I just loved. It came from a woman who just gave her name as Margaret. She was 71 years old. Her son came to see her one night and burst into the house without knocking. What nerve! He burst into the house and there was Margaret on the couch really having a blast with one of her boyfriends from the Senior Citizens. Do you know that this man was so horrified to see his mother kissing a man on the couch that he turned on his heels, said, "That's disgusting," and left. What an ass! So poor Margaret writes, "Did I do wrong?" And you know what Sanderson answered her? I've got to read this because it's so beautiful. He said,

> The best things in life, Margaret, go on forever. Every human being requires conversation and friendship. Why do we assume that the needs of older people stop there? The body may creak a little but there is no arteriosclerosis of emotions. Older people literally hunger for caring and affection and physical touching, just like anybody. Adult children and other family members seldom provide anything more than starvation rations—an occasional kiss. We know that sex is perfectly feasible at any age, given good health, but even when this does not seem appropriate for various reasons, why should there not be a little latter day romance, a little love, a little innocent contact, a stolen kiss, a gentle massage, a caress on the cheek, one hand fondling another? Many women of your age, Margaret, often feel strange and alarming stirrings within themselves, feelings that may not have surfaced for years. This is the life force coming to your rescue to remind you that you are a male or a female, not just an all-purpose senior citizen. Rejoice in this, Margaret, you've had enough bad news.

You never cease needing to be recognized in a hundred different ways. Relationships and togetherness must be lived in the *present.* You have to live *now,* you have to enjoy it *now,* you have to do for people *now.* One of the saddest things I heard in the last year was a colleague of mine whose wife died suddenly, very young. Because death is an amazingly democratic thing, it never tells you when it's going to come. We just all know, believe it or not, someday it will come to *us.* And by living every moment you are ready for it. The only people who scream and yell at the moment of death are those people who have never lived at all. If you live now, when death comes you say, "C'mon, who's afraid of you?" But my colleague told me his wife had always wanted a red satin dress. He said, "I always thought that was really stupid and in bad taste." Then he said to me, with tears in his eyes, "Do you think it would be all right if I buried her in a red satin dress?" I felt like doing a Mama and saying, "Stupido!"

If your wife wants a red satin dress, get it now! Don't wait to decorate her casket with roses. Come in one day while she's sitting there alive and inundate her in roses. Throw them at her. We're always putting things off for tomorrow, especially, with people whom we love. Who cares what "people will say"? In reality they don't really care. "It's foolish for me to tell her I love her. She knows it." Are you sure? And do you ever get tired of having somebody say, "I love you"? Do you ever get tired of picking up your coffee cup and finding a little note underneath it that says, "You're incredible"? Do you ever tire of getting a card, not when it's your birthday or Valentine's Day, but a card that says, "My life is so much richer because you're in it"? The time to buy the dress is *now*. The time to give the flowers is *now*. The time to make the phone call is *now*. The time to write the note is *now*. The time to reach over and touch is *now*. The time to say "You're important to me, sometimes I seem to forget, but I don't. My life would be pretty empty without you," with no strings attached, is *now*. Losing a loved one is a hard way to learn that love is lived in the now. It's a hard way to learn that you buy the dress now, or write the note now. But *we* have another chance. That husband *doesn't*.

Loving relationships depend upon open, honest, beautiful communication. Never have a short argument. Never! The worst kind of argument in the world is when you walk in and say, "What's the matter honey?" "Nothing." "Oh, c'mon, there's something." "No, there's nothing." I've found a wonderful way to make the next argument a forever argument; you say "Oh, I'm so glad, it really seemed to me like there was something, and I'm glad to know that there is nothing. Bye." Next time you say, "What's the matter?" they're going to tell you. We don't listen to ourselves and the things that we say.

We need to listen to the way we say things because we've learned them from others. It's like teachers who say to kids, "I'm waiting for Sally!" It's no wonder Sally says, "Wait you old. . . ." But we say things that are just as obnoxious. You hear yourself saying, for instance, "The trouble with you is. . . ." Usually the trouble with me is *you*. "One of these days, you'll be sorry." Oh, *no* I won't. "If I've told you once, I've told you a thousand times." Then what the hell are you telling me *again* for? "I've given you the best years of my life." If these are the best years, what do I have to look forward to? "Do as you please, it's your life." Well, you know, if it is, will you let ME *live* it?

Togetherness. From "I" and "me" to "us" and "we." Your relationships will be as vital and alive as *you* are. If you're dead, your relationship is dead. And if your relationships are boring and inadequate, it's because *you* are boring and inadequate. Liven yourself up! Be aware that the world and the people in it are not created solely for *you*. Try making *someone else* comfortable. Assume that people are good until you *actually* and *specifically* learn differently. And even then, know that they have potential for change and that you can help them out. Practice using and thinking "us" and "we" rather than "I" and "me." Love *many* things intensely because the measure of you as a lover is how deeply you love how much. Remember that all things *change,* especially human relationships, and to maintain them, *we* must change with them. Make the change in growth. Make sure that you're constantly growing *together* but *separately*. Seek *healthy* people in your life who still remember how to laugh, how to love and how to cry. Remember that misery doesn't only love company, it *demands* it. Have none of it.

And lastly, I heard the Dalai Lama of Tibet last year. One of the things that he said was so poignant. He said, "We live very close together. So, our prime purpose in life is to *help* others." Then he sort of smiled and said, "And if you can't *help* them at least don't *hurt* them." If each of us promised ourselves that in terms of our human relationships and our togetherness, we were dedicated to the process of helping each other to grow, and that if we couldn't do that, we were at least not going to hurt each other, what a magical thing that would be. An Italian poet, Quasimodo, who won the Nobel prize for poetry, wrote a little poem that says: "Each of us stands alone in this vast world, momentarily bathed in a ray of sunlight. And suddenly it's night." The poem is called "Ed e' Subito Sera"—And Suddenly It's Night. If you stand together with me, we can share the sunlight, and believe me, the night won't seem so frightening.

PROBES

In a group of five to seven, share examples from your own experience of how your definition of the situation directly affected the quality of your life experience.

What do you think Buscaglia means by "getting trapped in the concept of 'I' and 'me'"?

How is the relationship Buscaglia discusses between "telling" and "showing" similar to the relationship between verbal codes (Chapter 3) and nonverbal codes (Chapter 4)?

What made Rosa Buscaglia's "Shut up!" a loving communication?

Buscaglia claims that mentally ill people are the "ones who have moved the farthest away from other people," whereas the "healthy ones dive right in the middle, no matter what it means." Do you agree or disagree? How so?

Buscaglia emphasizes, with the help of some lines from a book by Kahlil Gibran, the importance of separateness in a loving relationship. What implications does this point have for your communication with the people you love?

How do you respond to Buscaglia's references to the medical doctors who "prescribed" hugs? Could there be something to that? Or is this just another example of Leo's "craziness?"

)

CHAPTER 14

CARL R. ROGERS'S APPROACH

Like much of Carl Rogers's work, this talk was aimed at a specific audience. If you're not a guidance counselor—or a prospective one—you might feel that he's talking to somebody else here. But I don't agree. It seems to me that regardless of his intended audience, his writings speak to all of us. Rogers suggests that the *quality* of a counselor's relationship with his or her client or "counselee" is the key to successful counseling and that the best kind of relationship happens when the participants are congruent, empathic, and regard each other positively—unconditionally positively if they can.

Each of these three elements is a centrally important part of interpersonal communication. Congruence (i.e., accurately reflecting on the outside what you are experiencing on the inside) is a skill that's related to much of what is discussed in Chapter 8 of this book. Empathy is obviously what much of Chapters 6 and 7 are about. And the third element, positive regard, is the attitude that encourages you to apply just about everything in this book.

I'm not a counselor—except to the extent that we all are—and I have found that the quality of my interpersonal relationships improves to the degree that I am able to manifest most of the characteristics Rogers talks about. What I believe Rogers does here is successfully identify and describe in pretty concrete terms three of the hard-to-pin-down elements that separate objectified, impersonal talking *at* each other from real interpersonal communication.

The Interpersonal Relationship: The Core of Guidance

Carl R. Rogers

I would like to share with you in this paper a conclusion, a conviction, which has grown out of years of experience in dealing with individuals, a conclusion which finds some confirmation in a steadily growing body of empirical evidence. It is simply that in a wide variety of professional work involving relationships with people—whether as a psychotherapist, teacher, religious worker, guidance counselor, social worker, clinical psychologist—it is the *quality* of the interpersonal encounter with the client which is the most significant element in determining effectiveness.

Let me spell out a little more fully the basis of this statement in my personal experience. I have been primarily a counselor and psychotherapist. In the course of my professional life I have worked with troubled college students, with adults in difficulty, with "normal" individuals such as business executives, and more recently with hospitalized psychotic persons. I have endeavored to make use of the learnings from my therapeutic experience in my interactions with classes and seminars, in the training of teachers, in the administration of staff groups, in the clinical supervision of psychologists, psychiatrists, and guidance workers as they work with

Reprinted by permission from *Harvard Educational Review* 32 (Fall 1962): 416–429. Copyright © 1962 by the President and Fellows of Harvard College.

their clients or patients. Some of these relationships are long-continued and intensive, as in individual psychotherapy. Some are brief, as in experiences with workshop participants or in contacts with students who come for practical advice. They cover a wide range of depth. Gradually I have come to the conclusion that one learning which applies to all of these experiences is that it is the quality of the personal relationship which matters most. With some of these individuals I am in touch only briefly, with others I have the opportunity of knowing them intimately, but in either case the quality of the personal encounter is probably, in the long run, the element which determines the extent to which this is an experience which releases or promotes development and growth. I believe the quality of my encounter is more important in the long run than is my scholarly knowledge, my professional training, my counseling orientation, the techniques I use in the interview. In keeping with this line of thought, I suspect that for a guidance worker also the relationship he forms with each student—brief or continuing—is more important than his knowledge of tests and measurements, the adequacy of his record keeping, the theories he holds, the accuracy with which he is able to predict academic success, or the school in which he received his training.

In recent years I have thought a great deal about this issue. I have tried to observe counselors and therapists whose orientations are very different from mine, in order to understand the basis of their effectiveness as well as my own. I have listened to recorded interviews from many different sources. Gradually I have developed some theoretical formulations, some hypotheses as to the basis of effectiveness in relationships. As I have asked myself how individuals sharply different in personality, orientation and procedure can all be effective in a helping relationship, can each be successful in facilitating constructive change or development, I have concluded that it is because they bring to the helping relationship certain attitudinal ingredients. It is these that I hypothesize as making for effectiveness, whether we are speaking of a guidance counselor, a clinical psychologist, or a psychiatrist.

What are these attitudinal or experimental elements in the counselor which make a relationship a growth-promoting climate? I would like to describe them as carefully and accurately as I can, though I am well aware that words rarely capture or communicate the qualities of a personal encounter.

CONGRUENCE

In the first place, I hypothesize that personal growth is facilitated when the counselor is what he *is,* when in the relationship with his client he is genuine and without "front" or façade, openly being the feelings and attitudes which at that moment are flowing in him. We have used the term "congruence" to try to describe this condition. By this we mean that the feelings the counselor is experiencing are available to him, available to his awareness, that he is able to live these feelings, be them in the relationship, and able to communicate them if appropriate. It means that he comes into a direct personal encounter with his client, meeting him on a person-to-person basis. It means that he is *being* himself, not denying himself. No one fully achieves this condition, yet the more the therapist is able to listen acceptantly to what is going on within himself, and the more he is able to *be* the complexity of his feelings without fear, the higher the degree of his congruence.

I think that we readily sense this quality in our everyday life. We could each of us name persons whom we know who always seem to be operating from behind a front, who are playing a role, who tend to say things they do not feel. They are exhibiting incongruence. We do not reveal ourselves too deeply to such people. On the other hand each of us knows individuals whom we somehow trust, because we sense that they are being what they *are,* that we are dealing with the person himself, and not with a polite or professional façade. This is the quality of which we are speaking, and it is hypothesized that the more genuine and congruent the therapist is in the relationship, the more probability there is that change in personality in the client will occur. . . .

But is it always helpful to be genuine? What about negative feelings? What about the times when the counselor's real feeling toward his client is one of annoyance, or boredom, or dislike? My tentative answer is that even with such feelings as these, which we all have from time to time, it is preferable for the counselor to be real than to put up a façade of interest and concern and liking which he does not feel.

But it is not a simple thing to achieve such reality. I am not saying that it is helpful to blurt out impulsively every passing feeling and accusation under the comfortable impression that one is being genuine. Being real involves the difficult task of being acquainted with the flow of experiencing going on within oneself, a flow marked especially by complexity and continuous change. So if I sense that I am feeling bored by my contacts with this student, and this feeling persists, I think I owe it to him and to our relationship to share his feeling with him. But here again I will want to be constantly in touch with what is going on in me. If I am, I will recognize that it is *my* feeling of being bored which I am expressing, and not some supposed fact about him as a boring person. If I voice it as *my own* reaction, it has the potentiality of leading to a deeper relationship. But this feeling exists in the context of a complex and changing flow, and this needs to be communicated too. I would like to share with him my distress at feeling bored, and the discomfort I feel in expressing this aspect of me. As I share these attitudes I find that my feeling of boredom arises from my sense of remoteness from him, and that I would like to be more in touch with him. And even as I try to express these feelings, they change. I am certainly *not* bored as I try to communicate myself to him in this way, and I am far from bored as I wait with eagerness and perhaps a bit of apprehension for his response. I also feel a new sensitivity to him, now that I have shared this feeling which has been a barrier between us. So I am very much more able to hear the surprise or perhaps the hurt in his voice as he now finds *himself* speaking more genuinely because I have dared to be real with him. I have let myself be a person—real, imperfect—in my relationship with him.

I have tried to describe this first element at some length because I regard it as highly important, perhaps the most crucial of the conditions I will describe, and because it is neither easy to grasp nor to achieve. . . .

I hope it is clear that I am talking about a realness in the counselor which is deep and true, not superficial. I have sometimes thought that the word *transparency* helps to describe this element of personal congruence. If everything going on in me which is relevant to the relationship can be seen by my client, if he can see "clear through me," and if I am *willing* for this realness to show through in the relationship, then I can be almost certain that this will be a meaningful encounter in which we both learn and develop.

I have sometimes wondered if this is the only quality which matters in a counseling relationship. The evidence seems to show that other qualities also make a profound difference and are perhaps easier to achieve. So I am going to describe these others. But I would stress that if, in a given moment of relationship, they are not genuinely a part of the experience of the counselor, then it is, I believe, better to be genuinely what one is, than to pretend to be feeling these other qualities.

EMPATHY

The second essential condition in the relationship, as I see it, is that the counselor is experiencing an accurate empathic understanding of his client's private world, and is able to communicate some of the significant fragments of that understanding. To sense the client's inner world of private personal meanings as if it were your own, but without ever losing the "as if" quality, this is empathy, and this seems essential to a growth-promoting relationship. To sense his confusion or his timidity or his anger or his feeling of being treated unfairly as if it were your own, yet without your own uncertainty or fear or anger or suspicion getting bound up in it, this is the condition I am endeavoring to describe. When the client's world is clear to the counselor and he can move about in it freely, then he can both communicate his understanding of what is vaguely known to the client, and he can also voice meanings in the client's experience of which the client is scarcely aware. It is this kind of highly sensitive empathy which seems important in making it possible for a person to get close to himself and to learn, to change, and develop.

I suspect that each of us has discovered that this kind of understanding is extremely rare. We neither receive it nor offer it with any great frequency. Instead we offer another type of understanding which is very different, such as "I understand what is wrong with you" or "I understand what makes you act that way." These are the types of understanding which we usually offer and receive—an evaluative understanding from the outside. It is not surprising that we shy away from true understanding. If I am truly open to the way life is experienced by another person—if I can take his world into mine—then I run the risk of seeing life in his way, of being changed myself, and we all resist change. So we tend to view this other person's world only in our terms, not in his. We analyze and evaluate it. We do not understand it. But when someone understands how it feels and seems to be me, without wanting to analyze me or judge me, then I can blossom and grow in that climate. I am sure I am not alone in that feeling. I believe that when the counselor can grasp the moment-to-moment experiencing occurring in the inner world of the client, as the client sees and feels it, without losing the separateness of his own identity in this empathic process, then change is likely to occur.

Though the accuracy of such understanding is highly important, the communication of intent to understand is also helpful. Even in dealing with the confused or inarticulate or bizarre individual, if he perceives that I am *trying* to understand his meanings, this is helpful. It communicates the value I place on him as an individual. It gets across the fact that I perceive his feelings and meanings as being *worth* understanding.

None of us steadily achieves such a complete empathy as I have been trying to describe, any more than we achieve complete congruence, but there is no doubt that individuals can develop along this line. Suitable training experiences have been utilized in the training of counselors, and also in the "sensitivity training" of industrial management personnel. Such experiences enable the person to listen more sensitively, to receive more of the subtle meanings the other person is expressing in words, gesture, and posture, to resonate more deeply and freely within himself to the significance of those expressions.

POSITIVE REGARD

Now the third condition. I hypothesize that growth and change are more likely to occur the more that the counselor is experiencing a warm, positive, acceptant attitude toward what *is* in the client. It means that he prizes his client, as a person, with somewhat the same quality of feeling that a parent feels for his child, prizing him as a person regardless of his particular behavior at the moment. It means that he cares for his client in a non-possessive way, as a person with potentialities. It involves an open willingness for the client to be whatever feelings are real in him at the moment—hostility or tenderness, rebellion or submissiveness, assurance or self-depreciation. It means a kind of love for the client as he is, providing we understand the word love as equivalent to the theologian's term *agape*, and not in its usual romantic and possessive meanings. What I am describing is a feeling which is not paternalistic, nor sentimental, nor superficially social and agreeable. It respects the other person as a separate individual, and does not possess him. It is a kind of liking which has strength, and which is not demanding. We have termed it positive regard.

UNCONDITIONALITY OF REGARD

There is one aspect of this attitude of which I am somewhat less sure. I advance tentatively the hypothesis that the relationship will be more effective the more the positive regard is unconditional. By this I mean that the counselor prizes the client in a total, rather than a conditional way. He does not accept certain feelings in the client and disapprove others. He feels an *unconditional* positive regard for this person. This is an outgoing, positive feeling without reservations and without evaluations. It means *not* making judgments. I believe that when this nonevaluative prizing is present in the encounter between the counselor and his client, constructive change and development in the client are more likely to occur.

Certainly one does not need to be a professional to experience this attitude. The best of parents show this in abundance, while others do not. A friend of mine, a therapist in private practice on the east coast, illustrates this very well in a letter in which he tells me what he is learning about parents. He says:

> I am beginning to feel that the key to the human being is the attitudes with which the parents have regarded him. If the child was lucky enough to have parents who have felt proud of him, wanted him, wanted him just as he was, exactly as he was, this child grows into adulthood with self-confidence, self-esteem; he goes forth in life feeling sure of himself, strong, able to lick what confronts him. Franklin Delano Roosevelt is an example . . . "my friends. . . . " He couldn't imagine anyone thinking otherwise. He had two adoring parents. He was like the pampered dog who runs up at you, frisking his tail, eager to love you, for this dog has never known rejection or harshness. Even if you should kick him, he'll come right back to you, his tail friskier than ever, thinking you're playing a game with him and wanting more. This animal cannot imagine anyone disapproving or disliking him. Just as unconditional regard and love was poured into him, he has it now to give out. If a child is lucky enough to grow up in this unconditionally accepting atmosphere, he emerges as strong and sure and he can approach life and its vicissitudes with courage and confidence, with zest and joy of expectation.

> But the parents who like their children—if. They would like them if they were changed, altered, different; if they were smarter or if they were better, or if, if, if. The offspring of these parents have trouble because they never had the feeling of acceptance. These parents don't really like these children; they would like them if they were like someone else. When you come down to the basic fundamental, the parent feels: "I don't like *this* child, this child before me." They don't say that. I am beginning to believe that it would be better for all concerned if parents did. It wouldn't leave such horrible ravages on these unaccepted children. It's never done that crudely. "If you

were a nice boy and did this, that and the other thing, then we would all love you." I am coming to believe that children brought up by parents who would like them "if" are never quite right. They grow assuming that their parents are right and that they are wrong; that somehow or other they are at fault; and even worse, very frequently they feel they are stupid, inadequate, inferior.

This is an excellent contrast between an unconditional positive regard and a conditional regard. I believe it holds as true for counselors as for parents.

THE CLIENT'S PERCEPTION

Thus far all my hypotheses regarding the possibility of constructive growth have rested upon the experiencing of these elements by the counselor. There is, however, one condition which must exist in the client. Unless the attitudes I have been describing have been to some degree communicated to the client, and perceived by him, they do not exist in his perceptual world and thus cannot be effective. Consequently it is necessary to add one more condition to the equation which I have been building up regarding personal growth through counseling. It is that when the client perceives, to a minimal degree, the genuineness of the counselor and the acceptance and empathy which the counselor experiences for him, then development in personality and change in behavior are predicted.

This has implications for me as a counselor. I need to be sensitive not only to what is going on in me, and sensitive to the flow of feelings in my client. I must also be sensitive to the way he is receiving my communications. I have learned, especially in working with more disturbed persons, that empathy can be perceived as lack of involvement; that an unconditional regard on my part can be perceived as indifference; that warmth can be perceived as a threatening closeness, that real feelings of mine can be perceived as false. I would like to behave in ways, and communicate in ways which have clarity for this specific person, so that what I am experiencing in relationship to him would be perceived unambiguously by him. Like the other conditions I have proposed, the principle is easy to grasp; the achievement of it is difficult and complex.

SOME LIMITATIONS

I would like to stress that these are hypotheses. . . . They are beginning hypotheses, not the final word. I regard it as entirely possible that there are other conditions which I have not described, which are also essential. Recently I had occasion to listen to some recorded interviews by a young counselor of elementary school children. She was very warm and positive in her attitude toward her clients, yet she was definitely ineffective. She seemed to be responding warmly only to the superficial aspects of each child and so the contacts were chatty, social, and friendly, but it was clear she was not reaching the real person of the child. Yet in a number of ways she rated reasonably high on each of the conditions I have described. So perhaps there are still elements missing which I have not captured in my formulation. . . .

THE PHILOSOPHY WHICH IS IMPLICIT

It is evident that the kinds of attitudes I have described are not likely to be experienced by a counselor unless he holds a philosophy regarding people in which such attitudes are congenial. The attitudes pictured make no sense except in a context of great respect for the person and his potentialities. Unless the primary element in the counselor's value system is the worth of the individual, he is not apt to find himself experiencing a real caring, or a desire to understand, and perhaps he will not respect himself enough to be real. Certainly the professional person who holds the view that individuals are essentially objects to be manipulated for the welfare of the state, or the good of the educational institution, or "for their own good," or to satisfy his own need for power and control, would not experience the attitudinal elements I have described as constituting growth-promoting relationships. So these conditions are congenial and natural in certain philosophical contexts but not in others.

CONCLUSION

Let me conclude with a series of statements which for me follow logically one upon the other.

The purpose of most of the helping professions, including guidance counseling, is to enhance the personal development, the psychological growth towards a socialized maturity, of its clients.

The effectiveness of any member of the profession is most adequately measured in terms of the degree to which, in his work with his clients, he achieves this goal.

Our knowledge of the elements which bring about constructive change in personal growth is in its infant stages.

Such factual knowledge as we currently possess indicates that a primary change-producing influence is the degree to which the client experiences certain qualities in his relationship with his counselor.

In a variety of clients—normal, maladjusted, and psychotic—with many different counselors and therapists, and studying the relationship from the vantage point of the client, the therapist, or the uninvolved observer, certain qualities in the relationship are quite uniformly found to be associated with personal growth and change.

These elements are not constituted of technical knowledge or ideological sophistication. They are personal human qualities—something the counselor *experiences,* not something he *knows.* Constructive personal growth is associated with the counselor's realness, with his genuine and unconditional liking for his client, with his sensitive understanding of his client's private world, and with his ability to communicate these qualities in himself to his client.

These findings have some far-reaching implications for the theory and practice of guidance counseling and psychotherapy, and for the training of workers in these fields.

And, I think Carl Rogers would agree, they also have far-reaching implications for my day-to-day interpersonal communication, and for yours.[J. S.]

PROBES

How is Rogers's concept of congruence related to Steele's discussion of openness (Chapter 8)?

How do Rogers's comments about being congruent about negative feelings compare with what Augsburger says about owning your feelings (Chapter 8)?

Do you think congruence helps create a defensive climate or a supportive one (Chapter 10)?

How does Rogers's advice about empathy relate with what Jones says about perceiving persons (Chapter 6)?

Does Rogers believe that all people are basically good?

How would you compare and contrast the philosophy implicit in Rogers's comments and Barnlund's philosophy (Chapter 2)?

CHAPTER 15

ERICH FROMM'S APPROACH

''Love'' and ''interpersonal communication'' are *not* synonymous. But if you describe, as Erich Fromm does here, some of the key understandings, attitudes, and behaviors that make up mature human loving, you do find that you're saying a great deal about interpersonal quality communication.

Fromm's first main point speaks to the issue of *why* humans communicate. He argues that part of what it means to be a human is to be aware of one's self. Being aware of your self means being aware that you're different from and separate from others. That awareness, Fromm says, leads us to desire contact, unification, and relatedness with others. So at the most basic level, we are motivated to communicate by our awareness that we are unique, unlike all other persons and separate from them.

Fromm's second main point is that we have four ways of overcoming our separateness: indulging in orgiastic states, conforming, engaging in creative activity, or loving. The union that comes from orgiastic states—sex, alchohol or other drugs, and so on—is ultimately unsatisfactory, because it is temporary, is physically debilitating, and often produces anxiety and guilt feelings. Achieving union in conformity is not much better, because the tendency is to eliminate individual differences. Since each person is unique, a unity based on the assumption that we're the same as every other Republican, sorority member, Irishman, male, American, or whatever, is ultimately unsatisfactory. Separateness can also be overcome by way of creative activity, but the result of that effort is union with a thing—an art object of some sort—not with a person. So something is still missing.

Only love offers humans the opportunity to overcome our natural feelings of separateness in a satisfactory and lasting way. But, and this is Fromm's main point, you've got to realize that love is not a kind of ''symbiotic union'' based on two people *needing* each other. ''Love,'' he writes, ''is union under the condition of preserving one's integrity, one's individuality.'' That is a crucial point, I think. One of the most difficult and important things I've had to learn is how to encourage and participate in a relationship that is based on two independent persons choosing to grow together rather than on one person—or both—''needing'' the other.

Fromm's final main point is that each lover exerts his or her individual power in a loving relationship by giving, not by receiving, and that there are four attitude/actions each must learn to give effectively: care, responsibility, respect, and knowledge. Again, Fromm doesn't always discuss specific interpersonal relationships, and in a way that complements and to a degree completes much of what's in the other readings in Parts One, Two, Three, and Four.

This reading is a minor classic; it was first published over 30 years ago. That was before writers had come to recognize that ''humanity'' and ''humankind'' work much better than the words ''man'' and ''he'' when referring to all people, female and male. I hope that Fromm's outdated use of male terms won't keep you from perceiving his insights and wisdom.

The Theory of Love

Erich Fromm

Any theory of love must begin with a theory of man, of human existence. While we find love, or rather, the equivalent of love, in animals, their attachments are mainly a part of their instinctual equipment; only remnants of this instinctual equipment can be seen operating in man. What is essential in the existence of man is the fact that he has emerged from the animal kingdom, from instinctive adaptation, that he has transcended nature—although he never leaves it; he is a part of it—and yet once torn away from nature, he cannot return to it; once thrown out of paradise— a state of original oneness with nature—cherubim with flaming swords block his way, if he should try to return. Man can only go forward by developing his reason, by finding a new harmony, a human one, instead of the prehuman harmony which is irretrievably lost.

When man is born, the human race as well as the individual, he is thrown out of a situation which was definite, as definite as the instinct, into a situation which is indefinite, uncertain, and open. There is certainty only about the past—and about the future only as far as that it is death.

Man is gifted with reason; he is *life being aware of itself;* he has awareness of himself, of his fellow man, of his past, and of the possibilities of his future. This awareness of himself as a separate entity, the awareness of his own short life span, of the fact that without his will he is born and against his will he dies, that he will die before those whom he loves, or they before him, the awareness of his aloneness and separateness, of his helplessness before the forces of nature and of society, all this makes his separate, disunited existence an unbearable prison. He would become insane could he not liberate himself from this prison and reach out, unite himself in some form or other with men, with the world outside.

The experience of separateness arouses anxiety; it is, indeed, the source of all anxiety. Being separate means being cut off, without any capacity to use my human powers. Hence to be separate means to be helpless, unable to grasp the world—things and people—actively; it means that the world can invade me without my ability to react. Thus, separateness is the source of intense anxiety. Beyond that, it arouses shame and the feeling of guilt. This experience of guilt and shame in separateness is expressed in the Biblical story of Adam and Eve. After Adam and Eve have eaten of the "tree of knowledge of good and evil," after they have disobeyed (there is no good and evil unless there is freedom to disobey), after they have become human by having emancipated themselves from the original animal harmony with nature, i.e., after their birth as human beings—they saw "that they were naked—and they were ashamed." Should we assume that a myth as old and elementary as this has the prudish morals of the nineteenth-century outlook, and that the important point the story wants to convey to us is the embarrassment that their genitals were visible? This can hardly be so, and by understanding the story in a Victorian spirit, we miss the main point, which seems to be the following: after man and woman have become aware of themselves and of each other, they are

Abridged from pp. 7–31, "The Theory of Love," from *The Art of Loving* by Erich Fromm, volume 9 in the World Perspective Series edited by Ruth Nanda Anshen. Copyright © 1956 by Erich Fromm. Reprinted by permission of Harper & Row, Publishers, Inc.

aware of their separateness, and of their difference, inasmuch as they belong to different sexes. But while recognizing their separateness they remain strangers, because they have not yet learned to love each other (as is also made very clear by the fact that Adam defends himself by blaming Eve, rather than by trying to defend her). *The awareness of human separation, without reunion by love—is the source of shame. It is at the same time the source of guilt and anxiety.*

The deepest need of man, then, is the need to overcome his separateness, to leave the prison of his aloneness. The *absolute* failure to achieve this aim means insanity, because the panic of complete isolation can be overcome only by such a radical withdrawal from the world outside that the feeling of separation disappears—because the world outside, from which one is separated, has disappeared.

Man—of all ages and cultures—is confronted with the solution of one and the same question: the question of how to overcome separateness, how to achieve union, how to transcend one's own individual life and find at-onement. The question is the same for primitive man living in caves, for nomadic man taking care of his flocks, for the peasant in Egypt, the Phoenician trader, the Roman soldier, the medieval monk, the Japanese samurai, the modern clerk and factory hand. The question is the same, for it springs from the same ground: the human situation, the conditions of human existence. The answer varies. The question can be answered by animal worship, by human sacrifice or military conquest, by indulgence in luxury, by ascetic renunciation, by obsessional work, by artistic creation, by the love of God, and by the love of Man. While there are many answers—the record of which is human history—they are nevertheless not innumerable. On the contrary, as soon as one ignores smaller differences which belong more to the periphery than to the center, one discovers that there is only a limited number of answers which have been given, and only could have been given by man in the various cultures in which he has lived. The history of religion and philosophy is the history of these answers, of their diversity, as well as of their limitation in number.

The answers depend, to some extent, on the degree of individuation which an individual has reached. In the infant I-ness has developed but little yet; he still feels one with mother, has no feeling of separateness as long as mother is present. Its sense of aloneness is cured by the physical presence of the mother, her breasts, her skin. Only to the degree that the child develops his sense of separateness and individuality is the physical presence of the mother not sufficient any more, and does the need to overcome separateness in other ways arise.

Similarly, the human race in its infancy still feels one with nature. The soil, the animals, the plants are still man's world. He identifies himself with animals, and this is expressed by the wearing of animal masks, by the worshiping of a totem animal or animal gods. But the more the human race emerges from these primary bonds, the more it separates itself from the natural world, the more intense becomes the need to find new ways of escaping separateness.

One way of achieving this aim lies in all kinds of *orgiastic states*. These may have the form of an auto-induced trance, sometimes with the help of drugs. Many rituals of primitive tribes offer a vivid picture of this type of solution. In a transitory state of exaltation the world outside disappears, and with it the feeling of separateness from it. Inasmuch as these rituals are practiced in common, an experience of fusion with the group is added which makes this solution all the more effective. Closely related to, and often blended with this orgiastic solution, is the sexual experience. The sexual orgasm can produce a state similar to the one produced by a trance, or to the effects of certain drugs. Rites of communal sexual orgies were a part of many primitive rituals. It seems that after the orgiastic experience, man can go on for a time without suffering too much from his separateness. Slowly the tension of anxiety mounts, and then is reduced again by the repeated performance of the ritual.

As long as these orgiastic states are a matter of common practice in a tribe, they do not produce anxiety or guilt. To act in this way is right, and even virtuous, because it is a way shared by all, approved and demanded by the medicine men or priests; hence there is no reason to feel guilty or ashamed. It is quite different when the same solution is chosen by an individual in a culture which has left behind these common practices. Alcoholism and drug addiction are the forms which the individual chooses in a non-orgiastic culture. In contrast to those participating in the socially patterned solution, such individuals suffer from guilt feelings and remorse. While they try to escape from separateness by taking refuge in alcohol or drugs, they feel all the more separate after the orgiastic experience is over, and thus are driven to take recourse to it with increasing frequency and intensity. Slightly different from this is the recourse to a sexual orgiastic solution. To some extent it is a natural and normal form of overcoming separateness, and a partial answer to the problem of isolation. But in many individuals in whom separateness is not relieved in other ways, the search for the sexual orgasm assumes a function which makes it not very different from alcoholism and drug addiction. It becomes a desperate attempt to escape the anxiety engendered by separateness, and it results in an ever-increasing sense of separateness, since the sexual act without love never bridges the gap between two human beings, except momentarily.

All forms of orgiastic union have three characteristics: they are intense, even violent; they occur in the total personality, mind *and* body; they are transitory and periodical. Exactly the opposite holds true for that form of union which is by far the most frequent solution chosen by man in the past and in the present: the union based on *conformity* with the group, its customs, practices, and beliefs. Here again we find a considerable development.

In a primitive society the group is small; it consists of those with whom one shares blood and soil. With the growing development of culture, the group enlarges; it becomes the citizenry of a *polis,* the citizenry of a large state, the members of a church. Even the poor Roman felt pride because he could say *"civis romanus sum"*; Rome and the Empire were his family, his home, his world. Also in contemporary Western society the union with the group is the prevalent way of overcoming separateness. It is a union in which the individual self disappears to a large extent, and where the aim is to belong to the herd. If I am like everybody else, if I have no feelings or thoughts which make me different, if I conform in custom, dress, ideas, to the pattern of the group, I am saved; saved from the frightening experience of aloneness. The dictatorial systems use threats and terror to induce this conformity; the democratic countries, suggestion and propaganda. There is, indeed, one great difference between the two systems. In the democracies non-conformity is possible and, in fact, by no means entirely absent; in the totalitarian systems, only a few unusual heroes and martyrs can be expected to refuse obedience. But in spite of this difference the democratic societies show an overwhelming degree of conformity. The reason lies in the fact that there *has* to be an answer to the quest for union, and if there is no other or better way, then the union of herd conformity becomes the predominant one. One can only understand the power of the fear to be different, the fear to be only a few steps away from the herd, if one understands the depths of the need not to be separated. Sometimes this fear of non-conformity is rationalized as fear of practical dangers which could threaten the nonconformist. But actually, people *want* to conform to a much higher degree than they are *forced* to conform, at least in the Western democracies.

Most people are not even aware of their need to conform. They live under the illusion that they follow their own ideas and inclinations, that they are individualists, that they have arrived at their opinions as the result of their own thinking— and that it just happens that their ideas are the same as those of the majority. The consensus of all serves as a proof for the correctness of "their" ideas. Since there is still a need to feel some individuality, such need is satisfied with regard to minor differences; the initials on the handbag or the sweater, the name plate of the bank teller, the belonging to the Democratic as against the Republican party, to the Elks instead of to the Shriners become the expression of individual differences. The advertising slogan of "it is different" shows up this pathetic need for difference, when in reality there is hardly any left.

This increasing tendency for the elimination of differences is closely related to the concept and the experience of equality, as it is developing in the most advanced industrial societies. Equality had meant, in a religious context, that we are all God's children, that we all share in the same human-divine substance, that we are all one. It meant also that the very differences between individuals must be respected, that while it is true that we are all one, it is also true that each one of us is a unique entity, is a cosmos by itself. Such conviction of the uniqueness of the individual is expressed for instance in the Talmudic statement: "Whosoever saves a single life is as if he had saved the whole world; whosoever destroys a single life is as if he had destroyed the whole world." Equality as a condition for the development of individuality was also the meaning of the concept in the philosophy of the Western Enlightenment. It meant (most clearly formulated by Kant) that no man must be the means for the ends of another man. That all men are equal inasmuch as they are ends, and only ends, and never means to each other. Following the ideas of the Enlightenment, Socialist thinkers of various schools defined equality as abolition of exploitation, of the use of man by man, regardless of whether this use were cruel or "human."

In contemporary capitalistic society the meaning of equality has been transformed. By equality one refers to the equality of automatons; of men who have lost their individuality. *Equality today means "sameness," rather than "oneness."* It is the sameness of abstractions, of the men who work in the same jobs, who have the same amusements, who read the same newspapers, who have the same feelings and the same ideas. In this respect one must also look with some skepticism at some achievements which are usually praised as signs of our progress, such as the equality of women. Needless to say I am not speaking against the equality of women; but the positive aspects of this tendency for equality must not deceive one. It is part of the trend toward the elimination of differences. Equality is bought at this very price: women are equal because they are not different any more. The proposition of Enlightenment philosophy, *l'âme n'a pas de sexe,* the soul has no sex, has become the general practice. The polarity of the sexes is disappearing, and with it erotic love, which is based on this polarity. Men and women become the *same,* not *equals* as opposite poles. Contemporary society preaches this ideal of unindividualized equality because it needs human atoms, each one the same, to make them function in a mass aggregation, smoothly, without friction; all obeying the same commands, yet everybody being convinced that he is following his own desires. Just as modern mass production requires the standardization of commodities, so the social process requires standardization of man, and this standardization is called "equality."

Union by conformity is not intense and violent; it is calm, dictated by routine, and for this very reason often is insufficient to pacify the anxiety of separateness. The incidence of alcoholism, drug addiction, compulsive sexualism, and suicide in contemporary Western society are symptoms of this relative failure of herd conformity. Furthermore, this solution concerns mainly the mind and not the body, and for this reason too is lacking in comparison with the orgiastic solutions. Herd conformity has only one advantage: it is permanent, and not spasmodic. The individual is introduced into the conformity pattern at the age of three or four, and subsequently never loses his contact with the herd. Even his funeral, which he anticipates as his last great social affair, is in strict conformance with the pattern. . . .

A third way of attaining union lies in *creative activity,* be it that of the artist or of the artisan. In any kind of creative work the creating person unites himself with his material, which represents the world outside of himself. Whether a carpenter makes a table, or a goldsmith a piece of jewelry, whether the peasant grows his corn or the painter paints a picture, in all types of creative work the worker and his object become one, man unites himself with the world in the process of creation. This, however, holds true only for productive work, for work in which *I* plan, produce, see the result of my work. In the modern work process of a clerk, the worker on the endless belt, little is left of this uniting quality of work. The worker becomes an appendix to the machine or to the bureaucratic organization. He has ceased to be he—hence no union takes place beyond that of conformity.

The unity achieved in productive work is not interpersonal; the unity achieved in orgiastic fusion is transitory; the unity achieved by conformity is only pseudo-unity. Hence, they are only partial answers to the problem of existence. The full answer lies in the achievement of interpersonal union, of fusion with another person, in *love.*

This desire for interpersonal fusion is the most powerful striving in man. It is the most fundamental passion, it is the force which keeps the human race together, the clan, the family, society. The failure to achieve it means insanity or destruction—self-destruction or destruction of others. Without love, humanity could not exist for a day. Yet, if we call the achievement of interpersonal union "love," we find ourselves in a serious difficulty. Fusion can be achieved in different ways—and the differences are not less significant than what is common to the various forms of love. Should they all be called love? Or should we reserve the word "love" only for a specific kind of union, one which has been the ideal virtue in all great humanistic religions and philosophical systems of the last four thousand years of Western and Eastern history?

As with all semantic difficulties, the answer can only be arbitrary. What matters is that we know what kind of union we are talking about when we speak of love. Do we refer to love as the mature answer to the problem of existence, or do we speak of those immature forms of love which may be called *symbiotic union?* In the following pages I shall call love only the former. I shall begin the discussion of "love" with the latter.

Symbiotic union has its biological pattern in the relationship between the pregnant mother and the foetus. They are two, and yet one. They live "together" *(symbiosis),* they need each other. The foetus is a part of the mother, it receives everything it needs from her; mother is its world, as it were; she feeds it, she protects it, but also her own life is enhanced by it. In the *psychic* symbiotic union, the two bodies are independent, but the same kind of attachment exists psychologically.

The *passive* form of the symbiotic union is that of submission, or if we use a clinical term, of *masochism*. The masochistic person escapes from the unbearable feeling of isolation and separateness by making himself part and parcel of another person who directs him, guides him, protects him; who is his life and his oxygen, as it were. The power of the one to whom one submits is inflated, may he be a person or a god; he is everything. I am nothing, except inasmuch as I am part of him. As a part, I am part of greatness, of power, of certainty. The masochistic person does not have to make decisions, does not have to take any risks; he is never alone—but he is not independent; he has no integrity; he is not yet fully born. In a religious context the object of worship is called an idol; in a secular context of a masochistic love relationship the essential mechanism, that of idolatry, is the same. The masochistic relationship can be blended with physical, sexual desire; in this case it is not only a submission in which one's mind participates, but also one's whole body. There can be masochistic submission to fate, to sickness, to rhythmic music, to the orgiastic state produced by drugs or under hypnotic trance—in all these instances the person renounces his integrity, makes himself the instrument of somebody or something outside of himself; he need not solve the problem of living by productive activity.

The *active* form of symbiotic fusion is domination or, to use the psychological term corresponding to masochism, *sadism*. The sadistic person wants to escape from his aloneness and his sense of imprisonment by making another person part and parcel of himself. He inflates and enhances himself by incorporating another person, who worships him.

The sadistic person is as dependent on the submissive person as the latter is on the former; neither can live without the other. The difference is only that the sadistic person commands, exploits, hurts, humiliates, and that the masochistic person is commanded, exploited, hurt, humiliated. This is a considerable difference in a realistic sense; in a deeper emotional sense, the difference is not so great as that which they both have in common: fusion without integrity. If one understands this, it is also not surprising to find that usually a person reacts in both the sadistic and the masochistic manner, usually toward different objects. Hitler reacted primarily in a sadistic fashion toward people, but masochistically toward fate, history, the "higher power" of nature. His end—suicide among general destruction—is as characteristic as was his dream of success—total domination.

In contrast to symbiotic union, mature *love is union under the condition preserving one's integrity,* one's individuality. *Love is an active power in man;* a power which breaks through the walls which separate man from his fellow men, which unites him with others; love makes him overcome the sense of isolation and separateness, yet it permits him to be himself, to retain his integrity. In love the paradox occurs that two beings become one and yet remain two.

If we say love is an activity, we face a difficulty which lies in the ambiguous meaning of the word "activity." By "activity," in the modern usage of the word, is usually meant an action which brings about a change in an existing situation by means of an expenditure of energy. Thus a man is considered active if he does business, studies medicine, works on an endless belt, builds a table, or is engaged in sports. Common to all these activities is that they are directed toward an outside goal to be achieved. What is *not* taken into account is the *motivation* of activity.

Take for instance a man driven to incessant work by a sense of deep insecurity and loneliness; or another one driven by ambition, or greed for money. In all these cases the person is the slave of a passion, and his activity is in reality a "passivity" because he is driven; he is the sufferer, not the "actor." On the other hand, a man sitting quiet and contemplating, with no purpose or aim except that of experiencing himself and his oneness with the world, is considered to be "passive," because he is not "doing" anything. In reality, this attitude of concentrated meditation is the highest activity there is, an activity of the soul, which is possible only under the condition of inner freedom and independence. One concept of activity, the modern one, refers to the use of energy for the achievement of external aims; the other concept of activity refers to the use of man's inherent powers, regardless of whether any external change is brought about. . . . Envy, jealousy, ambition, any kind of greed are passions; love is an action, the practice of a human power, which can be practiced only in freedom and never as the result of a compulsion.

Love is an activity, not a passive affect, it is a "standing in," not a "falling for." In the most general way, the active character of love can be described by stating that love is primarily *giving,* not receiving.

What is giving? Simple as the answer to this question seems to be, it is actually full of ambiguities and complexities. The most widespread misunderstanding is that which assumes that giving is "giving up" something, being deprived of, sacrificing. The person whose character has not developed beyond the stage of the receptive, exploitative, or hoarding orientation, experiences the act of giving in this way. The marketing character is willing to give, but only in exchange for receiving; giving without receiving for him is being cheated. People whose main orientation is a nonproductive one feel giving as an impoverishment. Most individuals of this type therefore refuse to give. Some make a virtue out of giving in the sense of a sacrifice. They feel that just because it is painful to give, one *should* give; the virtue of giving to them lies in the very act of acceptance of the sacrifice. For them, the norm that it is better to give than to receive means that it is better to suffer deprivation that to experience joy.

For the productive character, giving has an entirely different meaning. Giving is the highest expression of potency. In the very act of giving, I experience my strength, my wealth, my power. This experience of heightened vitality and potency fills me with joy. I experience myself as overflowing, spending, alive, hence as joyous. Giving is more joyous than receiving, not because it is a deprivation, but because in the act of giving lies the expression of my aliveness.

It is not difficult to recognize the validity of this principle by applying it to various specific phenomena. The most elementary example lies in the sphere of sex. The culmination of the male sexual function lies in the act of giving; the man gives himself, his sexual organ, to the woman. At the moment of orgasm he gives his semen to her. He cannot help giving it if he is potent. If he cannot give, he is impotent. For the woman the process is not different, although somewhat more complex. She gives herself too; she opens the gates to her feminine center; in the act of receiving, she gives. If she is incapable of this act of giving, if she can only receive, she is frigid. With her the act of giving occurs again, not in her function as a lover, but in that as a mother. She gives of herself to the growing child within her, she gives her milk to the infant, she gives her bodily warmth. Not to give would be painful.

In the sphere of material things giving means being rich. Not he who *has* much is rich, but he who *gives* much. The hoarder who is anxiously worried about losing something is, psychologically speaking, the poor, impoverished man, regardless of how much he has. Whoever is capable of giving of himself is rich. He experiences himself as one who can confer of himself to others. Only one who is deprived of all that goes beyond the barest necessities for subsistence would be incapable of enjoying the act of giving material things. But daily experience shows that what a person considers the minimal necessities depends as much on his character as it depends on his actual possessions. It is well known that the poor are more willing to give than the rich. Nevertheless, poverty beyond a certain point may make it impossible to give, and is so degrading, not only because of the suffering it causes directly, but because of the fact that it deprives the poor of the joy of giving.

The most important sphere of giving, however, is not that of material things, but lies in the specifically human realm. What does one person give to another? He gives of himself, of the most precious he has, he gives of his life. This does not necessarily mean that he sacrifices his life for the other—but that he gives him of that which is alive in him; he gives him of his joy, of his interest, of his understanding, of his knowledge, of his humor, of his sadness—of all expressions and manifestations of that which is alive in him. In thus giving of his life, he enriches the other person, he enhances his own sense of aliveness. He does not give in order to receive; giving is in itself exquisite joy. But in giving he cannot help bringing something to life in the other person, and this which is brought to life reflects back to him; in truly giving, he cannot help receiving that which is given back to him. Giving implies to make the other person a giver also and they both share in the joy of what they have brought to life. In the act of giving something is born, and both persons involved are grateful for the life that is born for both of them. Specifically with regard to love this means: love is a power which produces love; impotence is the inability to produce love. This thought has been beautifully expressed by Marx: "Assume," he says, *"man* as *man,* and his relation to the world as a human one, and you can exchange love only for love, confidence for confidence, etc. If you wish to enjoy art, you must be an artistically trained person; if you wish to have influence on other people, you must be a person who has a really stimulating and furthering influence on other people. Every one of your relationships to man and to nature must be a definite expression of your *real, individual* life corresponding to the object of your will. If you love without calling forth love, that is, if your love as such does not produce love, if by means of an *expression of life* as a loving person you do not make of yourself a *loved person,* then your love is impotent, a misfortune."[1] But not only in love does giving mean receiving. The teacher is taught by his students, the actor is stimulated by his audience, the psychoanalyst is cured by his patient—provided they do not treat each other as objects, but are related to each other genuinely and productively.

It is hardly necessary to stress the fact that the ability to love as an act of giving depends on the character development of the person. It presupposes the attainment of a predominantly productive orientation; in this orientation the person has overcome dependency, narcissistic omnipotence, the wish to exploit others, or to hoard, and has acquired faith in his own human powers, courage to rely on his powers in the attainment of his goals. To the degree that these qualities are lacking, he is afraid of giving himself—hence of loving.

Beyond the element of giving, the active character of love becomes evident in the fact that it always implies certain basic elements, common to all forms of love. These are *care, responsibility, respect* and *knowledge.*

That love implies *care* is most evident in a mother's love for her child. No assurance of her love would strike us as sincere if we saw her lacking in care for the infant, if she neglected to feed it, to bathe it, to give it physical comfort; and we are impressed by her love if we see her caring for the child. It is not different even with the love for animals or flowers. If a woman told us that she loved flowers, and we saw that she forgot to water them, we would not believe in her "love" for flowers. *Love is the active concern for the life and the growth of that which we love.* Where this active concern is lacking, there is no love. This element of love has been beautifully described in the book of Jonah. God has told Jonah to go to Nineveh to warn its inhabitants that they will be punished unless they mend their evil ways. Jonah runs away from his mission because he is afraid that the people of Nineveh will repent and that God will forgive them. He is man with a strong sense of order and law, but without love. However, in his attempt to escape, he finds himself in the belly of a whale, symbolizing the state of isolation and imprisonment which his lack of love and and solidarity has brought upon him. God saves him, and Jonah goes to Nineveh. He preaches to the inhabitants as God had told him, and the very thing he was afraid of happens. The men of Nineveh repent their sins, mend their ways, and God forgives them and decides not to destroy the city. Jonah is intensely angry and disappointed; he wanted "justice" to be done, not mercy. At last he finds some comfort in the shade of a tree which God has made to grow for him to protect him from the sun. But when God makes the tree wilt, Jonah is depressed and angrily complains to God. God answers: "Thou hast had pity on the gourd for the which thou has not labored neither madest it grow; which came up in a night, and perished in a night. And should I not spare Nineveh, that great city, wherein are more than sixscore thousand people that cannot discern between their right hand and their left hand; and also much cattle?" God's answer to Jonah is to be understood symbolically. God explains to Jonah that the essence of love is to "labor" for something and "to make something grow," that love and labor are inseparable. One loves that for which one labors, and one labors for that which one loves.

Care and concern imply another aspect of love; that of *responsibility*. Today responsibility is often meant to denote duty, something imposed upon one from the outside. But responsibility, in its true sense, is an entirely voluntary act; it is my response to the needs, expressed or unexpressed, of another human being. To be "responsible" means to be able and ready to "respond." Jonah did not feel responsible to the inhabitants of Nineveh. He, like Cain, could ask: "Am I my brother's keeper?" The loving person responds. The life of his brother is not his brother's business alone, but his own. He feels responsible for his fellow men, as he feels responsible for himself. This responsibility, in the case of the mother and her infant, refers mainly to the care of physical needs. In the love between adults it refers mainly to the psychic needs of the other person.

Responsibility could deteriorate into domination and possessiveness, were it not for a third component of love, *respect*. Respect is not fear and awe; it denotes, in accordance with the root of the word (*respicere* = to look at), the ability to see a person as he is, to be aware of his unique individuality. Respect means the concern that the other person should grow and unfold as he is. Respect, thus, implies the absence of exploitation. I want the loved person to grow and unfold for his own sake, and in his own ways, and not for the purpose of serving me. If I love the other person, I feel one with him or her, but with him *as he is,* not as I need him to be as an object for my use. It is clear that respect is possible only if *I* have achieved independence; if I can stand and walk without needing crutches, without having to dominate and exploit anyone else. Respect exists only on the basis of freedom: *"L'amour est l'enfant de la liberté"* as an old French song says; love is the child of freedom, never that of domination.

To respect a person is not possible without *knowing* him; care and responsibility would be blind if they were not guided by knowledge. Knowledge would be empty if it were not motivated by concern. There are many layers of knowledge; the knowledge which is an aspect of love is one which does not stay at the periphery, but penetrates to the core. It is possible only when I can transcend the concern for myself and see the other person in his own terms. I may know, for instance, that a person is angry, even if he does not show it overtly; but I may know him more deeply than that; then I know that he is anxious, and worried; that he feels lonely, that he feels guilty. Then I know that his anger is only the manifestation of something deeper, and I see him as anxious and embarrassed, that is, as the suffering person, rather than as the angry one.

Knowledge has one more, and a more fundamental, relation to the problem of love. The basic need to fuse with another person so as to transcend the person of one's separateness is closely related to another specifically human desire, that to know the "secret of man." While life in its merely biological aspects is a miracle and a secret, man in his human aspects is an unfathomable secret to himself—and to his fellow man. We know ourselves, and yet even with all the efforts we may make, we do not know ourselves. We know our fellow man, and yet we do not know him, because we are not a thing and our fellow man is not a thing. The further we reach into the depth of our being, or someone else's being, the more the goal of knowledge eludes us. Yet we cannot help desiring to penetrate into the secret of man's soul, into the innermost nucleus which is "he."

There is one way, a desperate one, to know the secret: it is that of complete power over another person; the power which makes him do what we want, feel what we want, think what we want; which transforms him into a thing, our thing, our possession. The ultimate degree of this attempt to know lies in the extremes of sadism, the desire and ability to make a human being suffer; to torture him, to force him to betray his secret in his suffering. In this craving for penetrating man's secret, his and hence our own, lies an essential motivation for the depth and intensity of cruelty and destructiveness. In a very succinct way this idea has been expressed by Isaac Babel. He quotes a fellow officer in the Russian civil war, who has just stamped his former master to death, as saying: "With shooting—I'll put it his way—with shooting you only get rid of a chap. . . . With shooting you'll never get at the soul, to where it is in a fellow and how it shows itself. But I don't spare myself, and I've more than once trampled an enemy for over an hour. You see, I want to get to know what life really is, what life's like down our way."[2]

In children we often see this path to knowledge quite overtly. The child takes something apart, breaks it up in order to know it; or it takes an animal apart; cruelly tears off the wings of a butterfly in order to know it, to force its secret. The cruelty itself is motivated by something deeper: the wish to know the secret of things and of life.

The other path to knowing "the secret" is love. Love is active penetration of the other person, in which my desire to know is stilled by union. In the act of fusion I know you, I know myself, I know everybody—and I "know" nothing. I know in the only way knowledge of that which is alive is possible for man—by experience of union—not by any knowledge our thought can give. Sadism is motivated by the wish to know the secret, yet I remain as ignorant as I was before. I have torn the other being apart limb from limb, yet all I have done is to destroy him. Love is the only way of knowledge, which in the act of union answers my quest. In the act of loving, of giving myself, in the act of penetrating the other person, I find myself, I discover myself, I discover us both, I discover man. . . .

References

1. "Nationalökonomie und Philosophie," 1844, published in Karl Marx's *Die Frühschriften*, Alfred Kröner Verlag (Stuttgart, 1953), pp. 300, 301. (My translation, E. F.)
2. I. Babel, *The Collected Stories* (New York: Criterion Books, 1955).

PROBES

Do you agree with Fromm that each human has a basic need to overcome separateness? Or do you think that it's possible to live a fully human life as a hermit?

What are some of the ways you achieve union via conformity? How do you nonverbally communicate your conformity?

How do Fromm's comments about male and female equality relate to the discussion in Chapter 11 about communication between women and men?

What's the difference, in Fromm's view, between *needing* to be in relationship with another person and *wanting* to?

What does Fromm mean when he says that "love is an activity, not a passive affect; it is a 'standing in,' not a 'falling for'"?

How might your communication behavior change when you view "responsibility" as "ability to respond"? (See page 371.)

How would you paraphrase the final sentence in this selection?

CHAPTER 16

MARTIN BUBER'S APPROACH

Martin Buber, a Jewish philosopher, teacher, and theologian, was born and raised in what is now part of the Soviet Union, and died in 1965 in Israel. Throughout his life, Buber was both a "scholar" or "intellectual" and an intensely practical person interested in everyday life experiences. As an intellectual, he was hungry to learn and to write all he could about how humans relate with one another. As a practical person, he was determined to keep all of his theorizing and scholarship firmly based in and applicable to the concrete events he experienced every day. Because he was raised by his grandparents in Europe during the late nineteenth and early twentieth centuries (Buber's parents were separated), lived through both world wars, was active in several political movements, and was a well-known, even famous, citizen of Israel, his life experiences are different in many ways from yours and mine. But for me, Buber's peculiar genius is that he can sense that part of his experience that is universal and can project that universal knowledge about human meetings through his European heritage and his "foreign" native language in such a way that he talks to me directly. In other words, even though he is in many ways very different from me, he says, "this is my experience; reflect on it a little and you might find that it's your experience too." Sometimes I stumble over Buber's language, the way he puts things. But when I listen to him and do what he asks, I discover that he's right. It *is* my experience, only now I understand it better than I ever did before.

I don't know whether this one excerpt from Buber's writing will work that way for you. But the possibility is there if you will open yourself to hear him.* That's one thing about Buber's writings. Although he's a philosopher, he has been criticized because he doesn't state philosophical propositions and then try to verify and validate them with "proof." Instead, Buber insists that his reader try to meet him in a *conversation,* a dialogue. The main thing is for the reader to see whether his or her life experiences resonate with Buber's. This resonance is the only "proof" of the validity of Buber's ideas that the reader will receive. So far, millions of persons have experienced that resonance. Books by and about Buber, especially his *I and Thou,* have been translated into over twenty languages and are read around the world.

In almost all his writing, Buber begins by observing that each of us lives a twofold reality. He describes the two "folds" in the section of *I and Thou* I paraphrased in my essay in Chapter 2. To be an *individual,* we need only to interact with other objects—human and otherwise—in the world. To function effectively as an individual, we merely need to develop and maintain our ability to be "objective," to explain ourselves and the world with accurate theories and valid cause-and-effect formulations. But we become fully human *persons* only in genuine relationships with others, only when we meet another and "make the other present as a whole and as a unique being, as the person that he is."

*You might also be interested in other things written by or about Buber. For starters I recommend Aubrey Hodes, *Martin Buber: An Intimate Portrait* (New York: Viking, 1971); or Hilary Evans Bender, *Monarch Notes: The Philosophy of Martin Buber* (New York: Monarch, 1974). Maurice Friedman has written the definitive Buber biography, and I'd especially recommend the third volume, *Martin Buber's Life and Work: The Later Years, 1945–1965* (New York: Dutton, 1983). Buber's most important and influential book is *I and Thou,* trans. Walter Kaufmann (New York: Scribner, 1970).

This genuine relationship Buber talks about is the "highest form" of what I've been calling interpersonal communication. You've probably heard of Buber's term for it—an "*I-Thou* relationship."* According to Buber, the individual lives always in the world of *I-It;* the *person* can enter the world of *I-Thou.* Both worlds are necessary. You can't expect to communicate interpersonally with everyone in every situation. But you can become a fully human person only by sharing genuine interpersonal relationships with others. As Buber puts it, without *It* the person cannot live. But he who lives with *It* alone is not a person.

This article is taken from a talk Buber gave when he visited the United States in 1957. It's especially useful because it is a kind of summary of much of what he had written in the first seventy-nine years of his life (he died when he was eighty-seven).

I've outlined the article to simplify it some and to show how clearly organized it actually is. As you can see from the outline, Buber's subject is interpersonal relationships, which he calls "man's personal dealings with one another," or "the interhuman." Like the rest of this book, Buber's article doesn't deal with some mystical spirit world in which we all become one. Rather, he's writing about communication between today's teachers and students, politicians and voters, preachers and parishioners, and between you and me. First, he explains some attitudes and actions that keep people from achieving "genuine dialogue." Then he describes the characteristics of this dialogue, or *I-Thou* relationship. In the outline I've paraphrased each point that he makes.

When you read the essay, you'll probably be able to see where several of the other writers in this book got some of their ideas. For example, compare Carl Rogers's explanation of "congruence" with what Buber says about "being and seeming." Or note Buber's way of talking about the six "persons" in a one-to-one conversation—my me, your you, and so on—which were also identified by Dean Barnlund in Chapter 2 and R. D. Laing in Chapter 6.

Whether or not you note that kind of thing, however, read this article as thoughtfully as you can. It sums up everything in this book. And I know from the experience I have lived that it's worth understanding.

OUTLINE OF MARTIN BUBER'S "ELEMENTS OF THE INTERHUMAN"

  I. Interhuman relationships are not the same as "Social Relationships."
   A. Social relationships can be very close, but no *existential* or person-to-person relation is necessarily involved.
   B. That's because the collective or social suppresses individual persons.
   C. But in the interhuman, person meets person. In other words, "the only thing that matters is that for each of the two men the other happens as the particular other, that each becomes aware of the other and is thus related to him in such a way that he does not regard and

---

*As I noted in Chapter 2, Buber's translators always point out that this "thou" is not the Shakespearian or religious term of formal address. It is a translation of the German *Du,* the familiar form of the pronoun "you." As Walter Kaufmann, one of Buber's translators, explains, "German lovers say *Du* to one another and so do friends. *Du* is spontaneous and unpretentious, remote from formality, pomp, and dignity."

use him as his object, but as his partner in a living event, even if it is no more than a boxing match."

    D. In short, "the sphere of the interhuman is one in which a person is confronted by the other. We [i.e., Buber] call its unfolding the dialogical."

II. There are three problems that get in the way of dialogue.

    A. The first problem is the duality of *being* and *seeming*. Dialogue won't happen if the people involved are only "seeming." They need to "be."

        1. "Seeming" in a relationship involves being concerned with your image or front—with how you wish to appear.

        2. "Being" involves the spontaneous and unreserved presentation of what you really are in your personal dealings with the other.

        3. These two are generally found mixed together. The most we can do is to distinguish between persons in whose essential attitude one or the other (being or seeming) predominates.

        4. When seeming reigns, real interpersonal communication is impossible: "Whatever the meaning of the word 'truth' may be in other realms, in the interhuman realm it means that men communicate themselves to one another as what they are."

        5. The tendency toward seeming, however, is understandable.

           a. We *essentially* need personal confirmation, i.e., we can't live without being confirmed by other people.

           b. Seeming often appears to help us get the confirmation we need.

           c. Consequently, "to yield to seeming is man's essential cowardice, to resist it is his essential courage."

        6. This view indicates that there is no such thing as "bad being," but rather people who are habitually content to "seem" and afraid to "be." "I have never known a young person who seemed to be irretrievably bad."

    B. The second problem involves the way we perceive others.

        1. Many modern fatalists, such as Jean-Paul Sartre, believe that we can ultimately know *only* ourselves, that "man has directly to do only with himself and his own affairs."

        2. But the main prerequisite for dialogue is that you get in direct touch with the other, "that each person should regard his partner as the very one he is."

           a. This means becoming aware of the other person as an essentially unique being. "To be aware of a man . . . means in particular to perceive his wholeness as a person determined by the spirit: it means to perceive the dynamic centre which stamps his every utterance, action, and attitude with the recognizable sign of uniqueness."

           b. But this kind of awareness is impossible so long as I objectify the other.

        3. Perceiving the other in this way is contrary to everything in our world that is analytic or reductive.

           a. This is not to say that the sciences are wrong, only that they are severely limited.

       b. What's dangerous is the extension of the scientific, analytic method to all of life, because it is very difficult for science to remain aware of the essential uniqueness of persons.

    4. This kind of perception is called "personal making present." What enables us to do it is our capacity for "imagining the real" of the other.

       a. Imagining the real "is not a looking at the other but a bold swinging—demanding the most intensive stirring of one's being—into the life of the other."

       b. When I *imagine* what the other person is *really* thinking and feeling, I can make direct contact with him or her.

C. The third problem which impedes the growth of dialogue is the tendency toward imposition instead of unfolding.

    1. One way to affect a person is to impose yourself on him or her.

    2. Another way is to "find and further in the soul of the other the disposition toward" that which you have recognized in yourself as right.

       a. Unfolding is not simply "teaching," but rather *meeting*.

       b. It requires believing in the other person.

       c. It means working as a helper of the growth processes already going on in the other.

    3. The propagandist is the typical "imposer"; the teacher *can* be the correspondingly typical "unfolder."

    4. The ethic implied here is similar to Immanuel Kant's, i.e., persons should never be treated as means to an end, but only as ends in themselves.

       a. The only difference is that Buber stresses that persons exist not in isolation but in the interhuman, and

       b. for the interhuman to occur, there must be:

          (1) as little seeming as possible.

          (2) genuine perceiving ("personal making present") of the other, and

          (3) as little imposing as possible.

III. Summary of the characteristics of genuine dialogue:

A. Each person must turn toward and be open to the other, a "turning of the being."

B. Each must make present the other by imagining the real.

C. Each confirms the other's being; however, confirmation does not necessarily mean approval.

D. Each must be authentically himself or herself.

    1. Each must say whatever she or he "has to say."

    2. Each cannot be ruled by thoughts of his or her own effect or effectiveness as a speaker.

E. Where dialogue becomes genuine, "there is brought into being a memorable common fruitfulness which is to be found nowhere else."

F. Speaking is not always essential; silence can be very important.

G. Finally, all participants must be committed to dialogue; otherwise, it will fail.

Again, Buber's language sometimes can get in the way of understanding him. But if you can listen empathically, I think you will be able to resonate with at least some of what he says.

Elements of the Interhuman
Martin Buber

THE SOCIAL AND THE INTERHUMAN

It is usual to ascribe what takes place between men to the social realm, thereby blurring a basically important line of division between two essentially different areas of human life. I myself, when I began nearly fifty years ago to find my own bearings in the knowledge of society, making use of the then unknown concept of the interhuman, made the same error. From that time it became increasingly clear to me that we have to do here with a separate category of our existence, even a separate dimension, to use a mathematical term, and one with which we are so familiar that its peculiarity has hitherto almost escaped us. Yet insight into its peculiarity is extremely important not only for our thinking but also for our living.

We may speak of social phenomena wherever the life of a number of men, lived with one another, bound up together, brings in its train shared experiences and reactions. But to be thus bound up together means only that each individual existence is enclosed and contained in a group existence. It does not mean that between one member and another of the group there exists any kind of personal relation. They do feel that they belong together in a way that is, so to speak, fundamentally different from every possible belonging together with someone outside the group. And there do arise, especially in the life of smaller groups, contacts which frequently favour the birth of individual relations, but, on the other hand, frequently make it more difficult. In no case, however, does membership in a group necessarily involve an existential relation between one member and another. It is true that there have been groups in history which included highly sensitive and intimate relations between two of their members—as, for instance, in the homosexual relations among the Japanese samurai or among Doric warriors—and these were countenanced for the sake of the stricter cohesion of the group. But in general it must be said that the leading elements in groups, especially in the later course of human history, have rather been inclined to suppress the personal relation in favour of the purely collective element. Where this latter element reigns alone or is predominant, men feel themselves to be carried by the collectivity, which lifts them out of loneliness and fear of the world and lostness. When this happens—and for modern man it is an essential happening—the life between person and person seems to retreat more and more before the advance of the collective. The collective aims at holding in check the inclination to personal life. It is as though those who are bound together in groups should in the main be concerned only with the work of the group and should turn to the personal partners, who are tolerated by the group, only in secondary meetings.

The difference between the two realms became very palpable to me on one occasion when I had joined the procession through a large town of a movement to which I did not belong. I did it out of sympathy for the tragic development which I sensed was at hand in the destiny of a friend who was one of the leaders of the movement. While the procession was forming, I conversed with him and with another, a good-hearted "wild man," who also had the mark of death upon him. At that moment I still felt that the two men really were there, over against me, each of them a man near to me, near even in what was most remote from me; so different from me that my soul continually suffered from this difference, yet by virtue of this very difference confronting me with authentic being. Then the formations started off, and after a short time I was lifted out of all confrontation, drawn into the procession, falling in with its aimless step; and it was obviously the very same for the two with whom I had just exchanged human words. After a while we passed a café where I had been sitting the previous day with a musician whom I knew only slightly. The very moment we passed it the door opened, the musician stood on the threshold, saw me, apparently saw me alone, and waved to me. Straightway it seemed to me as though I were taken out of the procession and of the presence of my marching friends, and set there, confronting the musician. I forgot that I was walking along with the same step; I felt that I was standing over there by the man who had called out to me, and without a word, with a smile of understanding, was answering him. When consciousness of the facts returned to me, the procession, with my companions and myself at its head, had left the café behind.

The realm of the interhuman goes far beyond that of sympathy. Such simple happenings can be part of it as, for instance, when two strangers exchange glances in a crowded streetcar, at once to sink back again into the convenient state of wishing to know nothing about each other. But also every casual encounter between opponents belong to this realm, when it affects the opponent's attitude—that is, when something, however imperceptible, happens between the two, no matter whether it is marked at the time by any feeling or not. The only thing that matters is that for each of the two men the other happens as the particular other, that each becomes aware of the other and is thus related to him in such a way that he does not regard and use him as his object, but as his partner in a living event, even if it is no more than a boxing match. It is well known that some existentialists assert that the basic factor between men is that one is an object for the other. But so far as this is actually the case, the special reality of the interhuman, the fact of the contact, has been largely eliminated. It cannot indeed be entirely eliminated. As a crude example, take two men who are observing one another. The essential thing is not that the one makes the other his object, but the fact that he is not fully able to do so and the reason for his failure. We have in common with all existing things that we can be made objects of observation. But it is my privilege as man that by the hidden activity of my being I can establish an impassable barrier to objectification. Only in partnership can my being be perceived as an existing whole.

The sociologist may object to any separation of the social and the interhuman on the ground that society is actually built upon human relations, and the theory of these relations is therefore to be regarded as the very foundation of sociology. But here an ambiguity in the concept "relation" becomes evident. We speak, for instance, of a comradely relation between two men in their work, and do not merely mean what happens between them as comrades, but also a lasting disposition which is actualized in those happenings and which even includes purely psychological events such as the recollection of the absent comrade. But by the sphere of the interhuman I mean solely actual happenings between men, whether wholly mutual or tending to grow into mutual relations. For the participation of both partners is in principle indispensable. The sphere of the interhuman is one in which a person is confronted by the other. We call its unfolding the dialogical.

In accordance with this, it is basically erroneous to try to understand the interhuman phenomena as psychological. When two men converse together, the psychological is certainly an important part of the situation, as each listens and each prepares to speak. Yet this is only the hidden accompaniment to the conversation itself, the phonetic event fraught with meaning, whose meaning is to be found neither in one of the two partners nor in both together, but only in their dialogue itself, in this "between" which they live together.

BEING AND SEEMING

The essential problem of the sphere of the interhuman is the duality of being and seeming. Although it is a familiar fact that men are often troubled about the impression they make on others, this has been much more discussed in moral philosophy than in anthropology. Yet this is one of the most important subjects for anthropological study.

We may distinguish between two different types of human existence. The one proceeds from what one really is, the other from what one wishes to seem. In general, the two are found mixed together. There have probably been few men who were entirely independent of the impression they made on others, while there has scarcely existed one who was exclusively determined by the impression made by him. We must be content to distinguish between men in whose essential attitude the one or the other predominates.

This distinction is most powerfully at work, as its nature indicates, in the interhuman realm—that is, in men's personal dealings with one another.

Take as the simplest and yet quite clear example the situation in which two persons look at one another—the first belonging to the first type, the second to the second. The one who lives from his being looks at the other just as one looks at someone with whom he has personal dealings. His look is "spontaneous," "without reserve"; of course he is not uninfluenced by the desire to make himself understood by the other, but he is uninfluenced by any thought of the idea of himself which he can or should awaken in the person whom he is looking at. His opposite is different. Since he is concerned with the image which his appearance, and especially his look or glance, produces in the other, he "makes" this look. With the help of the capacity, in greater or lesser degree peculiar to man, to make a definite element of his being appear in his look, he produces a look which is meant to have, and often enough does have, the effect of a spontaneous utterance—not only the utterance of a physical event supposed to be taking place at that very moment, but also, as it were, the reflection of a personal life of such-and-such a kind.

This must, however, be carefully distinguished from another area of seeming whose ontological legitimacy cannot be doubted. I mean the realm of "genuine seeming," where a lad, for instance, imitates his heroic model and while he is doing so is seized by the actuality of heroism, or a man plays the part of a destiny and conjures up authentic destiny. In this situation there is nothing false; the imitation is genuine imitation and the part played is genuine; the mask, too, is a mask and no deceit. But where the semblance originates from the lie and is permeated by it, the interhuman is threatened in its very existence. It is not that someone utters a lie, falsifies some account. The lie I mean does not take place in relation to particular facts, but in relation to existence itself, and it attacks interhuman existence as such. There are times when a man, to satisy some stale conceit, forfeits the great chance of a true happening between I and Thou.

Let us now imagine two men, whose life is dominated by appearance, sitting and talking together. Call them Peter and Paul. Let us list the different configurations which are involved. First, there is Peter as he wishes to appear to Paul, and Paul as he wishes to appear to Peter. Then there is Peter as he really appears to Paul, that is, Paul's image of Peter, which in general does not in the least coincide with what Peter wishes Paul to see; and similarly there is the reverse situation. Further, there is Peter as he appears to himself, and Paul as he appears to himself. Lastly, there are the bodily Peter and the bodily Paul. Two living beings and six ghostly appearances, which mingle in many ways in the conversation between the two. Where is there room for any genuine interhuman life?

Whatever the meaning of the word "truth" may be in other realms, in the interhuman realm it means that men communicate themselves to one another as what they are. It does not depend on one saying to the other everything that occurs to him, but only on his letting no seeming creep in between himself and the other. It does not depend on one letting himself go before another, but on his granting to the man to whom he communicates himself a share in his being. This is a question of the authenticity of the interhuman, and where this is not to be found, neither is the human element itself authentic.

Therefore, as we begin to recognize the crisis of man as the crisis of what is between man and man, we must free the concept of uprightness from the thin moralistic tones which cling to it, and let it take its tone from the concept of bodily uprightness. If a presupposition of human life in primeval times is given in man's walking upright, the fulfillment of human life can only come through the soul's walking upright, through the great uprightness which is not tempted by any seeming because it has conquered all semblance.

But, one may ask, what if a man by his nature makes his life subservient to the images which he produces in others? Can he, in such a case, still become a man living from his being, can he escape from his nature?

The widespread tendency to live from the recurrent impression one makes instead of from the steadiness of one's being is not a "nature." It originates, in fact, on the other side of interhuman life itself, in men's dependence upon one another. It is no light thing to be confirmed in one's being by others, and seeming deceptively offers itself as a help in this. To yield to seeming is man's essential cowardice, to resist it is his essential courage. But this is not an inexorable state of affairs which is as it is and must so remain. One can struggle to come to oneself—that is, to come to confidence in being. One struggles, now more successfully, now less, but never in vain, even when one thinks he is defeated. One must at times pay dearly for life lived from the being; but it is never too dear. Yet is there not bad being, do weeds not grow everywhere? I have never known a young person who seemed to me irretrievably bad. Later indeed it becomes more and more difficult to penetrate the increasingly tough layer which has settled down on a man's being. Thus there arises the false perspective of the seemingly fixed "nature" which cannot be overcome. It is false; the foreground is deceitful; man as man can be redeemed.

Again we see Peter and Paul before us surrounded by the ghosts of the semblances. A ghost can be exorcized. Let us imagine that these two find it more and more repellent to be represented by ghosts. In each of them the will is stirred and strengthened to be confirmed in their being as what they really are and nothing else. We see the forces of real life at work as they drive out the ghosts, till the semblance vanishes and the depths of personal life call to one another.

PERSONAL MAKING PRESENT

By far the greater part of what is today called conversation among men would be more properly and precisely described as speechifying. In general, people do not really speak to one another, but each, although turned to the other, really speaks to a fictitious court of appeal whose life consists of nothing but listening to him. Chekhov has given poetic expression to this state of affairs in *The Cherry Orchard,* where the only use the members of a family make of their being together is to talk past one another. But it is Sartre who has raised to a principle of existence what in Chekhov still appears as the deficiency of a person who is shut up in himself. Sartre regards the walls between the partners in a conversation as simply impassable. For him it is inevitable human destiny that a man has directly to do only with himself and his own affairs. The inner existence of the other is his own concern, not mine; there is no direct relation with the other, nor can there be. This is perhaps the clearest expression of the wretched fatalism of modern man, which regards degeneration as the unchangeable nature of *Homo sapiens* and the misfortune of having run into a blind alley as his primal fate, and which brands every thought of a breakthrough as reactionary romanticism. He who really knows how far our generation has lost the way of true freedom, of free giving between I and Thou, must himself, by virtue of the demand implicit in every great knowledge of this kind, practice directness—even if he were the only man on earth who did it—and not depart from it until scoffers are struck with fear and hear in his voice the voice of their own suppressed longing.

The chief presupposition for the rise of genuine dialogue is that each should regard his partner as the very one he is. I become aware of him, aware that he is different, essentially different from myself, in the definite, unique way which is peculiar to him, and I accept whom I thus see, so that in full earnestness I can direct what I say to him as the person he is. Perhaps from time to time I must offer strict opposition to his view about the subject of our conversation. But I accept this person, the personal bearer of a conviction, in his definite being out of which his conviction has grown—even though I must try to show, bit by bit, the wrongness of this very conviction. I affirm the person I struggle with: I struggle with him as his partner, I confirm him as creature and as creation, I confirm him who is opposed to me as him who is over against me. It is true that it now depends on the other whether genuine dialogue, mutuality in speech arises between us. But if I thus give to the other who confronts me his legitimate standing as a man with whom I am ready to enter into dialogue, then I may trust him and suppose him to be also ready to deal with me as his partner.

But what does it mean to be "aware" of a man in the exact sense in which I use the word? To be aware of a thing or a being means, in quite general terms, to experience it as a whole and yet at the same time without reduction or abstraction, in all its concreteness. But a man, although he exists as a living being among living beings and even as a thing among things, is nevertheless something categorically different from all things and all beings. A man cannot really be grasped except on the basis of the gift of the spirit which belongs to man alone among all things, the spirit as sharing decisively in the personal life of the living man, that is, the spirit which determines the person. To be aware of a man, therefore, means in particular to perceive his wholeness as a person determined by the spirit; it means to perceive the dynamic centre which stamps his every utterance, action, and attitude with the recognizable sign of uniqueness. Such an awareness is impossible, however, if and so long as the other is the separated object of my contemplation or even observation, for this wholeness and its centre do not let themselves be known to contemplation or observation. It is only possible when I step into an elemental relation with the other, that is, when he becomes present to me. Hence I designate awareness in this special sense as "personal making present."

The perception of one's fellow man as a whole, as a unity, and as unique—even if his wholeness, unity, and uniqueness are only partly developed, as is usually the case—is opposed in our time by almost everything that is commonly understood as specifically modern. In our time there predominates an analytical, reductive, and deriving look between man and man. This look is analytical, or rather pseudo analytical, since it treats the whole being as put together and therefore able to be taken apart—not only the so-called unconscious which is accessible to relative objectification, but also the psychic stream itself, which can never, in fact, be grasped as an object. This look is a reductive one because it tries to contract the manifold person, who is nourished by the microcosmic richness of the possible, to some schematically surveyable and recurrent structures. And this look is a deriving one because it supposes it can grasp what a man has become, or even is becoming, in genetic formulae, and it thinks that even the dynamic central principle of the individual in this becoming can be represented by a general concept. An effort is being made today radically to destroy the mystery between man and man. The personal life, the ever-near mystery, once the source of the stillest enthusiasms, is levelled down.

What I have just said is not an attack on the analytical method of the human sciences, a method which is indispensable wherever it furthers knowledge of a phenomenon without impairing the essentially different knowledge of its uniqueness that transcends the valid circle of the method. The science of man that makes use of the analytical method must accordingly always keep in view the boundary of such a contemplation, which stretches like a horizon around it. This duty makes the transportation of the method into life dubious; for it is excessively difficult to see where the boundary is in life.

If we want to do today's work and prepare tomorrow's with clear sight, then we must develop in ourselves and in the next generation a gift which lives in man's inwardness as a Cinderella, one day to be a princess. Some call it intuition, but that is not a wholly unambiguous concept. I prefer the name "imagining the real," for in its essential being this gift is not a looking at the other, but a bold swinging—demanding the most intensive stirring of one's being—into the life of the other. This is the nature of all genuine imagining, only that here the realm of my action is not the all-possible, but the particular real person who confronts me, whom I can attempt to make present to myself just in this way, and not otherwise, in his wholeness, unity, and uniqueness, and with his dynamic centre which realizes all these things ever anew.

Let it be said again that all this can only take place in a living partnership, that is, when I stand in a common situation with the other and expose myself vitally to his share in the situation as really his share. It is true that my basic attitude can remain unanswered, and the dialogue can die in seed. But if mutuality stirs, then the interhuman blossoms into genuine dialogue.

IMPOSITION AND UNFOLDING

I have referred to two things which impede the growth of life between men: the invasion of seeming, and the inadequacy of perception. We are now faced with a third, plainer than the others, and in this critical hour more powerful and more dangerous than ever.

There are two basic ways of affecting men in their views and their attitude to life. In the first a man tries to impose himself, his opinion and his attitude, on the other in such a way that the latter feels the psychical result of the action to be his own insight, which has only been freed by the influence. In the second basic way of affecting others, a man wishes to find and to further in the soul of the other the disposition toward what he has recognized in himself as the right. Because it is the right, it must also be alive in the microcosm of the other, as one possibility. The other need only be opened out in this potentiality of his; moreover, this opening out takes place not essentially by teaching, but by meeting, by existential communication between someone that is in actual being and someone that is in a process of becoming. The first way has been most powerfully developed in the realm of propaganda, the second in that of education.

The propagandist I have in mind, who imposes himself, is not in the least concerned with the person whom he desires to influence, as a person; various individual qualities are of importance only in so far as he can exploit them to win the other and must get to know them for this purpose. In his indifference to everything personal the propagandist goes a substantial distance beyond the party for which he works. For the party, persons in their difference are of significance because each can be used according to his special qualities in a particular function. It is true that the personal is considered only in respect of the specific use to which it can be put, but within these limits it is recognized in practice. To propaganda as such, on the other hand, individual qualities are rather looked on as a burden, for propaganda is concerned simply with *more*—more members, more adherents, an increasing extent of support. Political methods, where they rule in an extreme form, as here, simply mean winning power over the other by depersonalizing him. This kind of propaganda enters upon different relations with force; it supplements it or replaces it, according to the need or the prospects, but it is in the last analysis nothing but sublimated violence, which has become imperceptible as such. It places men's souls under a pressure which allows the illusion of autonomy. Political methods at their height mean the effective abolition of the human factor.

The educator whom I have in mind lives in a world of individuals, a certain number of whom are always at any one time committed to his care. He sees each of these individuals as in a position to become a unique, single person, and thus the bearer of a special task of existence which can be fulfilled through him and through him alone. He sees every personal life as engaged in such a process of actualization, and he knows from his own experience that the forces making for actualization are all the time involved in a microcosmic struggle with counterforces. He has come to see himself as a helper of the actualizing forces. He knows these forces; they have shaped and they still shape him. Now he puts this person shaped by them at their disposal for a new struggle and a new work. He cannot wish to impose himself, for he believes in the effect of the actualizing forces, that is, he believes that in every man what is right is established in a single and uniquely personal way. No other way may be imposed on a man, but another way, that of the educator, may and must unfold what is right, as in this case it struggles for achievement, and help it to develop.

The propagandist, who imposes himself, does not really believe in his own cause, for he does not trust it to attain its effect of its own power without his special methods, whose symbols are the loudspeaker and the television advertisement. The educator who unfolds what is there believes in the primal power which has scattered itself, and still scatters itself, in all human beings in order that it may grow up in each man in the special form of that man. He is confident that this growth needs at each moment only that help which is given in meeting and that he is called to supply that help.

I have illustrated the character of the two basic attitudes and their relation to one another by means of two extremely antithetical examples. But wherever men have dealings with one another, one or the other attitude is to be found to be in more or less degree.

These two principles of imposing oneself on someone and helping someone to unfold should not be confused with concepts such as arrogance and humility. A man can be arrogant without wishing to impose himself on others, and it is not enough to be humble in order to help another unfold. Arrogance and humility are dispositions of the soul, psychological fact with a moral accent, while imposition and helping to unfold are events between men, anthropological facts which point to an ontology, the ontology of the interhuman.

In the moral realm Kant expressed the essential principle that one's fellow man must never be thought of and treated merely as a means, but always at the same time as an independent end. The principle is expressed as an "ought" which is sustained by the idea of human dignity. My point of view, which is near to Kant's in its essential features, has another source and goal. It is concerned with the presuppositions of the interhuman. Man exists anthropologically not in his isolation, but in the completeness of the relation between man and man; what humanity is can be properly grasped only in vital reciprocity. For the proper existence of the interhuman it is necessary, as I have shown, that the semblance does not intervene to spoil the relation of personal being to personal being. It is further necessary, as I have also shown, that each one means and makes present the other in his personal being. That neither should wish to impose himself on the other is the third basic presupposition of the interhuman. These presuppositions do not include the demand that one should influence the other in his unfolding; that is, however, an element that is suited to lead to a higher stage of the interhuman.

That there resides in every man the possibility of attaining authentic human existence in the special way peculiar to him can be grasped in the Aristotelian image of entelechy, innate self-realization; but one must note that it is an entelechy of the work of creation. It would be mistaken to speak here of individuation alone. Individuation is only the indispensable personal stamp of all realization of human existence. The self as such is not ultimately the essential, but the meaning of human existence given in creation again and again fulfills itself as self. The help that men give each other in becoming a self leads the life between men to its height. The dynamic glory of the being of man is first bodily present in the relation between two men each of whom in meaning the other also means the highest to which this person is called, and serves the self-realization of this human life as one true to creation without wishing to impose on the other anything of his own realization.

GENUINE DIALOGUE

We must now summarize and clarify the marks of genuine dialogue.

In genuine dialogue the turning to the partner takes place in all truth, that is, it is a turning of the being. Every speaker "means" the partner of partners to whom he turns as this personal existence. To "mean" someone in this connection is at the same time to exercise that degree of making present which is possible to the speaker at that moment. The experiencing senses and the imagining of the real which completes the findings of the senses work together to make the other present as a whole and as a unique being, as the person that he is. But the speaker does not merely perceive the one who is present to him in this way; he receives him as his partner, and that means that he confirms this other being, so far as it is for him to confirm. The true turning of his person to the other includes this confirmation, this acceptance. Of course, such a confirmation does not mean approval; but no matter in what I am against the other, by accepting him as my partner in genuine dialogue I have affirmed him as a person.

Further, if genuine dialogue is to arise, everyone who takes part in it must bring himself into it. And that also means that he must be willing on each occasion to say what is really in his mind about the subject of the conversation. And that means further that on each occasion he makes the contribution of his spirit without reduction and without shifting his ground. Even men of great integrity are under the illusion that they are not bound to say everything "they have to say." But in the great faithfulness which is the climate of genuine dialogue, what I have to say at any one time already has in me the character of something that wishes to be uttered, and I must not keep it back, keep it in myself. It bears for me the unmistakable sign which indicates that it belongs to the common life of the word. Where the dialogical word genuinely exists, it must be given its right by keeping nothing back. To keep nothing back is the exact opposite of unreserved speech. Everything depends on the legitimacy of "what I have to say." And of course I must also be intent to raise into an inner word and then into a spoken word what I have to say at this moment but do not yet possess as speech. To speak is both nature and work, something that grows and something that is made, and where it appears dialogically, in the climate of great faithfulness, it has to fulfill ever anew the unity of the two.

Associated with this is that overcoming of semblance to which I have referred. In the atmosphere of genuine dialogue, he who is ruled by the thought of his own effect as the speaker of what he has to speak has a destructive effect. If, instead of what has to be said, I try to bring attention to my *I*, I have irrevocably miscarried what I had to say; it enters the dialogue as a failure and the dialogue is a failure. Because genuine dialogue is an ontological sphere which is constituted by the authenticity of being, every invasion of semblance must damage it.

But where the dialogue is fulfilled in its being, between partners who have turned to one another in truth, who express themselves without reserve and are free of the desire for semblance, there is brought into being a memorable common fruitfulness which is to be found nowhere else. At such times, at each such time, the word arises in a substantial way between men who have been seized in their depths and opened out by the dynamic of an elemental togetherness. The interhuman opens out what otherwise remains unopened.

This phenomenon is indeed well known in dialogue between two persons; but I have also sometimes experienced it in a dialogue in which several have taken part.

About Easter of 1914 there met a group consisting of representatives of several European nations for a three-day discussion that was intended to be preliminary to further talks. We wanted to discuss together how the catastrophe, which we all believed was imminent, could be avoided. Without our having agreed beforehand on any sort of modalities for our talk, all the presuppositions of genuine dialogue were fulfilled. From the first hour immediacy reigned between all of us, some of whom had just got to know one another; everyone spoke with an unheard-of unreserve, and clearly not a single one of the participants was in bondage to semblance. In respect of its purpose the meeting must be described as a failure (though even now in my heart it is still not a certainty that it had to be a failure); the irony of the situation was that we arranged the final discussion for the middle of August, and in the course of events the group was soon broken up. Nevertheless, in the time that followed, not one of the participants doubted that he shared in a triumph of the interhuman.

One more point must be noted. Of course it is not necessary for all who are joined in a genuine dialogue actually to speak; those who keep silent can on occasion be especially important. But each must be determined not to withdraw when the course of the conversation makes it proper for him to say what he has to say. No one, of course, can know in advance what it is that he has to say; genuine dialogue cannot be arranged beforehand. It has indeed its basic order in itself from the beginning, but nothing can be determined, the course is of the spirit, and some discover what they have to say only when they catch the call of the spirit.

But it is also a matter of course that all the participants, without exception, must be of such nature that they are capable of satisfying the presuppositions of genuine dialogue and are ready to do so. The genuineness of the dialogue is called in question as soon as even a small number of those present are felt by themselves and by the others as not being expected to take any active part. Such a state of affairs can lead to very serious problems.

I had a friend whom I account one of the most considerable men of our age. He was a master of conversation, and he loved it: his genuineness as a speaker was evident. But once it happened that he was sitting with two friends and with the three wives, and a conversation arose in which by its nature the women were clearly not joining, although their presence in fact had a great influence. The conversation among the men soon developed into a duel between two of them (I was the third). The other "duelist," also a friend of mine, was of a noble nature; he too was a man of true conversation, but given more to objective fairness than to the play of the intellect, and a stranger to any controversy. The friend whom I have called a master of conversation did not speak with his usual composure and strength, but he scintillated, he fought, he triumphed. The dialogue was destroyed.

PROBES

What does it mean to you when Buber says that social contacts don't involve an *existential* relation, but that interhuman contacts do?

How is Buber's discussion of "being" and "seeming" similar to and different from Rogers's discussion of "congruence" (Chapter 14)?

For Buber, does "being" mean total honesty? Is "seeming" lying?

What circumstances make it difficult for you to "be"? How can you best help others to "be" instead of "seem"?

How do Buber's comments about the way we perceive others relate to the discussion of person perception in Chapter 6?

It sounds as if Buber is saying that science *cannot* be used to study human life. Is he saying that? Do you agree with him? Why or why not?

How is Buber's discussion of "imagining the real" related to what Bolton (Chapter 7) and Rogers (Chapter 14) say about empathy? How does it fit what Milt and I say about sculpting mutual meanings (Chapter 7)?

Which teacher that you've had has functioned most as an "imposer"? Which teacher has been most consistently an "unfolder"?

What does "personal making present" mean to you? What do you need to do in order to perceive someone that way?

Have you ever experienced a silent "dialogue" of the kind Buber mentions here? What happened?

*Ideas are clean. They soar in the serene supernal. I can
take them out and look at them, they fit in books, they
lead me down that narrow way. And in the morning
they are there. Ideas are straight—
But the world is round, and a
messy mortal is my friend.
Come walk with me in the mud. . . .*

HUGH PRATHER

Index